"A master salesman in his innovative approach to ministry, famed positive-thinking mega-church founder Robert Schuller was at heart a small-town pastor whose obsessions with church growth grew out of the affinities and tragedies of his youth, and enduring fears that American Christianity (and society) was in sharp decline. In this beautifully crafted, smartly argued biography, esteemed sociologists Mark Mulder and Gerardo Martí explain the complexities of his intentions and thought, as well as the market-driven ambitions that made him a 'how to' model for many of his peers and young pastors nationwide. In the process, they open up a remarkably fresh rendering of late modern American religious culture that should be deemed a must read."

—**Darren Dochuk**
University of Notre Dame

"Mulder and Martí have crafted a masterfully nuanced biography of Robert Schuller. They trace how his spiritual ambition for influence and expansion transformed his beloved Crystal Cathedral empire into a gilded iron cage, ultimately leading to his downfall. This compelling book not only sheds light on a fascinating and complex figure but also serves as a poignant cautionary tale for all clergy."

—**Scott Thumma**
Hartford International University

"These days when negativity prevails in many houses of worship, it is refreshing to recall Robert Schuller's positive 'possibility' messaging. But Mulder and Martí have done much more than that. They challenge us to see in Schuller the origins of a business model through which American faith communities have adapted to the marketization of American culture. Whether readers are wholly convinced or not, they will find much here of value for understanding contemporary faith communities."

—**Robert Wuthnow**
Princeton University

LIBRARY OF RELIGIOUS BIOGRAPHY

Mark A. Noll, Kathryn Gin Lum, and Heath W. Carter, series editors

Long overlooked by historians, religion has emerged in recent years as a key factor in understanding the past. From politics to popular culture, from social struggles to the rhythms of family life, religion shapes every story. Religious biographies open a window to the sometimes surprising influence of religion on the lives of influential people and the worlds they inhabited.

The Library of Religious Biography is a series that brings to life important figures in United States history and beyond. Grounded in careful research, these volumes link the lives of their subjects to the broader cultural contexts and religious issues that surrounded them. The authors are respected historians and recognized authorities in the historical period in which their subject lived and worked.

Marked by careful scholarship yet free of academic jargon, the books in this series are well-written narratives meant to be read and enjoyed as well as studied.

Titles include:

*The Miracle Lady: **Kathryn Kuhlman** and the Transformation of Charismatic Christianity*
by Amy Collier Artman

***Oral Roberts** and the Rise of the Prosperity Gospel*
by Jonathan Root

*One Lost Soul: **Richard Nixon's** Search for Salvation*
by Daniel Silliman

***Howard Thurman** and the Disinherited: A Religious Biography*
by Paul Harvey

***Francis Schaeffer** and the Shaping of Evangelical America*
by Barry Hankins

For a complete list of published volumes, see the back of this volume.

THE CHURCH MUST GROW OR PERISH

Robert H. Schuller and the Business of American Christianity

Mark T. Mulder and Gerardo Martí

WILLIAM B. EERDMANS PUBLISHING COMPANY
GRAND RAPIDS, MICHIGAN

Wm. B. Eerdmans Publishing Co.
2006 44th Street SE, Grand Rapids, MI 49508
www.eerdmans.com

© 2025 Mark T. Mulder and Gerardo Martí
All rights reserved
Published 2025

Book design by Lydia Hall

Printed in the United States of America

31 30 29 28 27 26 25   1 2 3 4 5 6 7

ISBN 978-0-8028-7855-7

Library of Congress Cataloging-in-Publication Data

A catalog record for this book is available from the Library of Congress.

FROM MARK:

For Noelle and Maya

FROM GERARDC:

For my parents, Rafael and Caridad Martí

Where there is growing there is living. The church must either grow or perish.

—Robert H. Schuller,
Your Church Has Real Possibilities!

CONTENTS

	Foreword by Richard J. Mouw	ix
	Preface	xi
1.	Facing Tornadic Winds—Both Natural and Social	1
2.	Restless for More	25
3.	Commitments—Marriage and Ministry	47
4.	Taking the Lessons of Chicago to Orange County	66
5.	Growing Ambition and Magnification	96
6.	Expanding the Ministry's Boundaries	125
7.	Accommodating—and Instigating—Growth	158
8.	Turbulence and Control in the 1980s	182
9.	Good Image and Global Influence in the Glory Days	218
10.	The Ministry Collapses	243
	Epilogue: The Imperative of Church Growth	269
	A Note on Sources	293
	Bibliography	297
	Index	319

FOREWORD

R obert Schuller liked to talk about theology. On occasion he would invite me to have lunch with him in his office and we would talk about John Calvin. As a seminary student he had completed a major project on John Calvin's *Institutes of the Christian Religion*, and he would explain to me that while he still was much influenced by the great Reformer, he saw himself as attempting to find less "dreary" words for getting the message across to our contemporaries.

He did not mind it when I challenged him on specific points. He would argue back, obviously relishing serious theological back-and-forth. I know that he once hosted the Dutch theologian Hendrikus Berkhof and the Canadian Baptist Clark Pinnock for several days of three-way theological exchange.

That kind of experience with Schuller kept me from buying into the all-too-prevalent image in the theological establishment of Schuller as a lightweight celebrity TV preacher with a fondness for slick marketing techniques for spreading his religious message. I never engaged him about his ecclesiology and his ministry practices, but I was aware that he often irritated many leaders in his denomination—which is also the denomination of my own upbringing—for the ways in which he frequently played by his own ecclesiastical rules. I shared some of their concerns, mainly because of Schuller's affinity for the church growth movement. The teachings of that movement had been developed at the seminary where I served as president, and I was not always happy with what was being taught on the subject on our campus.

Reading this fine book, however, has clarified many of the issues for me. While some of my worries about Schuller's strategies for his ministry have been reinforced by what I have read in these pages, I come away also with considerable respect for what he initiated. While he worked closely with the church growth folks, Schuller had his own thoughts about how local churches could be more effective in their ministry. And many of those thoughts were profound. He sensed well before many of us have now come to realize that, for example, the traditional denominational structures are increasingly ineffective for equipping local church ministries.

This is the biography that Robert Schuller deserves. He comes across as a person of integrity, with proper honor given to the gifted Arvella, who played an important role in providing her husband with insightful counsel along the way. The authors allow us to see some flaws, but they obviously are not hiding any seedy gossip. From their portrayal we can see why so many of the talented people who worked closely with him in his ministry admired him greatly. Those who knew him well were also aware of the faults that resulted in the unhappy developments that occurred as his ministry came to a close. But here too the authors tell the story with helpful insights. All of this results in a highly readable account of the life of a man who came from humble origins in cornfields of northwest Iowa to become an important religious leader in twentieth-century America and beyond, with significant accomplishments for the cause of the gospel.

Richard J. Mouw

PREFACE

This book contains new thoughts and new interpretations using previously unreported evidence regarding the life and legacy of Robert H. Schuller. As a religious biography, it is an outgrowth of research that we initiated in 2013 and reported in our previous book, *The Glass Church: Robert H. Schuller, the Crystal Cathedral, and the Strain of Megachurch Ministry*, published in 2020. In that volume, we demonstrated how the accumulated congregational strains, obscured by an optimistic possibility theology, instigated the unanticipated collapse of Schuller's megachurch. We had gathered a wealth of data from a rich mixture of sources, including archival materials, interviews with leaders and members associated with the ministry, and ethnographic observations, which provided an abundance of evidence. We drew from the overflow of these sources to move from an organizational analysis to this biographical exploration.

As such, this book should be seen as a fitting complement to *The Glass Church*. Both books can be read independently. Nevertheless, the reverberations to be found in reading both provide a unique and more comprehensive view not only of Schuller and his church but also of American religion in the latter twentieth century, anticipating the challenges and workings of Christian churches in the twenty-first century.[1] Together,

---

1. The theme of congregational innovation in response to broader social change is found in, for example, Gerardo Martí, *A Mosaic of Believers: Diversity and Innovation in a Multiethnic Church* (Bloomington: Indiana University Press, 2005); Gerardo Martí, *Hollywood Faith: Holiness, Prosperity, and Ambition in a Los Angeles Church*

xii PREFACE

the biographical and organizational lenses reveal a grander picture of the ambitious yet incomplete ecclesial paradigm that Robert H. Schuller earnestly, yet imperfectly, pursued in his ministry.

In producing this writing, both of us bring into our analysis our previous research on American religion in a changing culture. As sociologists, we both participate in and contribute to the scholarship on religious changes, and our focus on congregations has been persistent throughout our careers. In addition, with respect to our subject, we both bring our own distinctive connection to Schuller and his church. Though separated by hundreds of miles and almost half of a century, Schuller and Mulder grew up in similar Dutch Reformed enclaves. In fact, Schuller's Alton, Iowa, and Mulder's Alto, Wisconsin, both derived their name from the same Dutch village, Aalten, Gelderland. Moreover, both communities manifested the same ethnic and religious traditions within rural, agricultural social environments.[2] In both Alto and Alton, the farm and the church functioned as the hubs of economic and social lives, respectively. Raised in Garden Grove, California, Martí could not ignore Schuller's growing church just down the street. Being so close to the ministry, he had frequent occasion to be on-site, to attend, for example, Bible study groups, high school baccalaureate services, massive youth rallies, musical productions, and wedding ceremonies. What was often called "the glass church" maximized use of the campus with a variety of programs and activities every day of the week. And local news, rumors, and assorted happenings that involved Schuller and his church were part of the social environment. Understandably, we both bring *our* biographies in addition to our academic sensibilities in offering this account of Robert H. Schuller's life.

We extend our gratitude to series editor Heath Carter and acquisitions editors David Bratt and Lisa Ann Cockrel at Eerdmans, who received our

---

(New Brunswick, NJ: Rutgers University Press, 2008); Gerardo Martí and Gladys Ganiel, *The Deconstructed Church: Understanding Emerging Christianity* (New York: Oxford University Press, 2014).

2. See Elton J. Bruins, "My Town Alto: The First Dutch Immigrant Community in Wisconsin," in *Diverse Destinies: Dutch Kolonies in Wisconsin and the East*, ed. Nella Kennedy, Mary Risseeuw, and Robert P. Swierenga (Holland, MI: Van Raalte, 2012), 83.

proposal with enthusiasm. Mark Noll offered especially helpful comments on a near-final manuscript. Funding for the research that culminated in this book came from numerous sources.

Our thanks to the Van Raalte Institute (VRI) in Holland, Michigan, where Mulder had the opportunity to access the Hope College Archives and Special Collections as a two-term visiting research fellow. While at the VRI, Mulder enjoyed the hospitality and expertise of folks who knew the Reformed Church in America denomination and Schuller well. In particular, this book benefited from the insights and papers of Dennis Voskuil—who wrote the first Eerdmans book about Schuller in 1983 and allowed us access to all of his relevant papers. Similarly, we are indebted to Ronald Keener and Duane Vander Brug for access to their papers as well. In addition, we offer thanks for funding from the State Historical Society of Iowa Research Grant for Authors. At Calvin University, this biography received generous support from the Calvin Center for Christian Scholarship, the Department of Sociology and Social Work's Deur Award, the McGregor Fellowship, the Civitas Lab, and the Writing Co-op. Mulder extends a special gratefulness to Emily Steen and Jenna Allman, Calvin University sociology majors and student research assistants who provided invaluable support to this project over the course of two years. We also benefited from almost forty interviews with Schuller family members, staff, congregants, musicians, copastors, friends, and attendees at Schuller's Leadership Institute sessions. Martí is grateful for conversations with family and friends who offered informal reflections on their experience with Schuller and his church. The archives of the Garden Grove Public Library provided key insights, including a membership directory with pictures that captured the ministry at a crucial time in the mid-1970s. Surprisingly, antique malls and thrift stores often yielded various editions of Schuller's and Arvella's books in addition to a variety of ministerial and church-growth books that either included information about or featured Schuller, or were endorsed by him. At times, specially themed donation envelopes, letters, and other material related to the ministry that accompanied these vintage items offered additional glimpses of contemporaneous, cultivated images and tangible marketing efforts. (Once, what appeared to be a handwritten note was found with Schuller's signature, saying, "God Loves You, and So Do I!" Later, it was

xiv   PREFACE

discovered that thousands of these machine-written notes were placed in every copy of his autobiography, feigning an intimacy for donors who received the book.) For travel and assorted purchases that resourced the research, this work received Faculty Study and Research funding as well as funding provided through the endowment of the William R. Kenan Jr. professorship at Davidson College.

1

FACING TORNADIC WINDS—BOTH
NATURAL AND SOCIAL

While Robert H. Schuller was home on break from college during the summer of 1944, a dark funnel cloud formed near the family farmstead. As it drew closer, his father, Anthony, shouted for Robert, his mother, and sister Margaret to get into the Chevy—quickly!—and together they careened down the road a mile west, then veering on a side road south two miles farther, ultimately up and away to safety. Stopping on a hillside, they watched as the tornado rumbled a brutal path through their farm. Though the family remained unharmed, the powerful winds destroyed all nine buildings. It took only ten minutes to flatten everything to the foundations.[1]

The spate of tornadoes (estimated to be three or four different funnels that may have merged at one point) damaged seventy farms in northwest Iowa that day.[2] A local reporter found Anthony Schuller and his son sitting on a fallen tree in the midst of the "kindling wood" that had been their farm: "Not a stick of their farm buildings had been left standing."[3] Anthony revealed that they had fled the storm in his son's car because Robert remembered that he did not have insurance on his vehicle while

---

1. Robert H. Schuller, *My Journey: From an Iowa Farm to a Cathedral of Dreams* (San Francisco: HarperOne, 2001), 101–7.

2. "Seventy Farms Are Hit—Guards Police Ruins," *Alton (IA) Democrat*, June 22, 1944, https://tinyurl.com/6d63b5bn.

3. "Huge Twisters Devastate Three Different Areas," *Alton (IA) Democrat*, June 22, 1944, https://tinyurl.com/6d63b5bn. See pages 1 and 8 for Schuller family details.

2 CHAPTER 1

his parents had coverage on theirs. It turned out to be a wise decision—the tornado left the family car an "unrecognizable heap of junk." The father and son detailed for the reporter that their flight away from the tornado had been especially stressful since the dead-end road required the family to first drive west *toward* the funnel cloud before driving south and around the storm. The family eventually circled back to assess the damage. Anthony Schuller recounted the animal inventory for the *Alton Democrat*: all horses and over one thousand chickens lost; twelve milking cows, though, still grazed on the premises. They had discovered one of their horses, Mabel, dead in a ditch along the driveway, impaled by a two-by-four.[4]

Schuller's father, sixty-six years old at the time, resolved to restore the farm. Even as they drove away from the wreckage, father and son devised a plan to buy and dismantle a four-story vacant house in nearby Orange City and rebuild—board by board, shingle by shingle, nail by nail—their beloved home. After the tornado, the Schullers moved in with their daughter and son-in-law while they rebuilt their house. In addition, Henry, Schuller's older brother, received a short leave from the army to help reconstruct the destroyed farm.[5] With $50 and three weeks of intense toil, the Schullers secured all the materials they needed to do the job.

In reassembling the house, the family salvaged and reused every bit of the old structure. It took long days laboring to load piles of assorted lumber and buckets of straightened nails for the short wagon ride back to the farm and begin the reassembly. Schuller would eventually write with pride that of the nine families whose farms were destroyed around Alton that day, "My father was the only one to rebuild."[6]

Throughout his career, Schuller often drew on this vivid story as a message of resilience. His father and mother's fortitude that summer offered the evidence that he personally knew tragedy and possessed the

4. Schuller, *My Journey*, 107.

5. "10 Years Ago (1944)," *Alton (IA) Democrat*, July 1, 1954, https://tinyurl.com/2kh esuyn.

6. Robert H. Schuller, *Tough Times Never Last, but Tough People Do!* (New York: Bantam Books, 1984), 29; Michael Nason and Donna Nason, *Robert Schuller: The Inside Story* (Waco, TX: Word, 1983), 32. See also Sheila Schuller Coleman, *Robert Schuller: My Father and My Friend* (Milwaukee: Ideals Publishing Corp., 1980), 24–26.

ability to overcome it. However, in his autobiography, Schuller failed to note that his father relented on his original intention to rebuild the farm beyond the house. Instead, he set about leasing the land to another farmer as part of his plan to "discontinue farming."[7] Within a couple of weeks, the local paper reported that the family intended to sell their remaining cows. A complete rebuilding, though, made for a better narrative.

The emphasis on unheralded devastation and painstaking rebuilding provoked an even grander significance to his life and ministry. Viewed through the lens of his astonishing pastoral ministry, the story of the tornado and its aftermath revealed the core motivation for Schuller. In our telling, the tornado faced by Schuller represented not merely a precursor to tragedy but a metaphor for the forceful winds of social change. Robert H. Schuller staked his reputation on the belief that modern Christianity faced its own tornado of history, with disastrous cultural currents tearing apart the familiar church he loved.

Similar to his father's dedication to rebuilding the family home, Schuller committed to fortifying the modern church. Rather than witnessing the church utterly destroyed amid unforeseen developments within an exhausting and accelerating pace of social change, Schuller initiated a decades-long project of assessing new ecclesial structures toward reassembling his cherished spiritual home. He resolved to never sit back and merely watch secularizing elements weaken and blow away houses of faith. Schuller asserted that if Christianity had a future, then church leaders would need to acknowledge the devastating path carved by the forces of a rapidly changing culture and then dedicate themselves to deploying innovative methods. After his stature had grown, he wrote, "I call upon the church to make a commitment to remodel itself."[8] He promoted innovative techniques to reconstruct newly resistant congregations, made from a durable, yet pliable, theology.[9]

---

7. "A. Schuller Will Sell Dairy Herd," *Alton (IA) Democrat*, June 29, 1944, https://tinyurl.com/4dzcv3zz.

8. Robert H. Schuller, *Self-Esteem: The New Reformation* (Waco, TX: Word, 1982), 21.

9. For insight into our social scientific approach to analyzing theology, see Gerardo Martí, "Found Theologies versus Imposed Theologies: Remarks on Theology and Ethnography from a Sociological Perspective," *Ecclesial Practices* 3, no. 2 (2016):

4   CHAPTER 1

Rather than pander to a wistful nostalgia that harkened to a comfortable past, the minister urged pastors to hone new tools crafted for fresh challenges to build soundly structured churches that ensured their existence for tomorrow and beyond. Rightly done, new churches with innovative methodologies would be engines of numerical growth—with steadily increasing finances and reliably increasing membership. Not only would churches *survive*, he claimed that these new churches would *grow*. This was possible because, in Schuller's estimation, the historic elements from previously vibrant generations could be reused and retrofitted to build newly strengthened houses of faith. The only requirement for the task: the will to accomplish it.

When he died in April 2015, Schuller had significantly influenced American Christianity. Some of the most prominent names in ministry—Rick Warren of Saddleback Church and Bill Hybels of Willow Creek Church—"explicitly drew from Schuller's model to start churches that would attract the spiritually curious by feeling less like churches and more like theaters, malls, and community centers all in one."[10] Even though Schuller clearly had a vision for his role in maintaining the vitality of the late twentieth-century church, his background would have never predicted his part. How did a mainline Protestant, preaching in his vestments, discern the keys to megachurch ministry? Who would have anticipated that a staunch Calvinist would nurture a brand of Christianity that became a template for worship by appearing every Sunday morning on the *Hour of Power*? What was it that allowed a self-admitted underachieving academic to open an institute to train fellow pastors in his proven techniques? Why would someone drilled on Reformed catechisms craft the self-actualization theologies of possibility thinking and self-esteem? Where did a farm boy find the inspiration to commission

---

157–72; Gerardo Martí, "Ethnographic Theology: Integrating the Social Sciences and Theological Reflection," *Cuestiones Teológicas* 49, no. 111 (2022): 1–18; Gerardo Martí, "Ethnography as a Tool for Genuine Surprise: Found Theologies versus Imposed Theologies," in *The Wiley Blackwell Companion to Theology and Qualitative Research*, ed. Pete Ward and Knut Tveitereid (Hoboken, NJ: Wiley Blackwell, 2023), 471–82.

10. Katelyn Beaty, *Celebrities for Jesus: How Personas, Platforms, and Profits Are Hurting the Church* (Grand Rapids: Brazos, 2022), 45.

one of the world's most aggressive religious structures, the all-glass Crystal Cathedral?

While providing touchstones for flourishing congregations, ultimately, Schuller's biography also includes a tragic arc that lays bare the issues confronting the leaders of declining mainline Protestant churches— a waning influence that defined both the reaction of nondenominational evangelical churches and the attempt to attract new members from the rising ranks of the religiously "unchurched." More than that, Schuller's life also reveals the vital matters of churches as financially hungry institutions and perpetually precarious structures in need of continual infusions of resources to maintain even the appearance of capable ministry.

Legacy amid Criticism

Born on September 16, 1926, Robert Harold Schuller characterized his farm in northwest Iowa as "nowhere." Such a framing suggested rural origins while also accentuating the God-inspired *ex nihilo* (out of nowhere) character of his life story. By the time of his death in 2015, Schuller's unexpected biography encompassed a dramatic era of church life in the United States, especially in the developments of a maturing baby boom alongside the expansion of American megachurches, both of which coincided with his entry into pastoral ministry. As a pastor, he consistently adopted as common sense the notion that healthy churches should *always* grow, both in the number and quality of people and buildings. Already in his first advice manual for pastors, Schuller insisted, "One thing is certain: *a church must never stop growing.* When it ceases to grow, it will start to die."[11] At the same time, for the minister, congregational growth did not occur in an unplanned way through demographic osmosis, meaning that Schuller also accepted that conscious decision making and strategic planning remained necessary to harness any potential for a church's development.

Even though he regarded it as nowhere, Schuller often indicated that his experiences growing up on a rural farm in Iowa made him a "possi-

---

11. Robert H. Schuller, *Your Church Has Real Possibilities!* (Glendale, CA: G/L Publications, 1974), 34.

6 CHAPTER 1

bility thinker." In 1975, with plans to expand his Southern California church with yet another bold building project, the minister remarked, "Take the empty ground I saw there in Iowa. In it we planted seeds out of which many more came. This is true of life anywhere. When I came to Garden Grove, there was only empty ground before me. There was no church. Nothing. But seeds were planted. Today we have a membership of 7,000."[12] By 1985, the publicized number swelled to 10,000.[13] Schuller's stance toward church innovation provides a vivid representation of both the paradigm and the archetype of the early megachurch, televangelism, evangelical entrepreneurship, and the suburbanization of white Christianity. His role in rationalizing the Sunday morning worship experience had profound influence throughout the United States, and his legacy reverberates in high-profile sites that include not only Saddleback and Willow Creek but also Mark Driscoll's now-closed Mars Hill and Joel Osteen's Lakewood.

Robert H. Schuller accomplished much as a pastor. With decades of growing membership, an innovative inside/outside hybrid building designed by Richard Neutra in Southern California, the *Hour of Power* broadcast (perhaps) inspired by Billy Graham and reaching a global audience of millions, a stream of best-selling books, and the historic and award-winning all-glass Crystal Cathedral designed by Philip Johnson, Schuller's ministry featured many tangible measures of a successful religious organization. Yet, the minister presented an easy target for criticism; his message and his methods received constant scrutiny. Recently, when mention was made of Schuller's ministry and the spectacular collapse of his iconic megachurch into bankruptcy, a prominent theologian derisively remarked (off the record): "The chickens come home to roost."

Schuller advocated for a different approach to congregational ministry, and thousands of pastors agreed and followed his lead, eagerly reading his writings and flocking to his eponymously named Robert H. Schuller Institute for Successful Church Leadership. The minister con-

12. Jan Franzen, "The Possibility Thinker Says: You Can Have a Happy Family," *Christian Life*, April 1975, 20-21, 54-55, Dennis Voskuil Papers, Holland, MI (hereafter cited as DVP).

13. For example, see the descriptive blurb touting a "10,000 member congregation" on the back cover of Schuller's 1985 paperback edition of *Self-Esteem: The New Reformation* published by Jove Books.

cluded that the American church had entered an era of decline. Old models had exhausted their use. Societal change had swept aside the relevance of usual practices. If churches hoped not only to survive but to thrive in fulfilling their mission to serve an increasingly destabilized, insecure, and migrating population, then clergy would need imaginative structures of ministry. They would have to do things no one had anticipated, relying less on the tested models from the past and more on newly ascendant methods for a possible future.

In reaching for an alternative paradigm for ministry, Schuller tacitly acknowledged a distinctly changed societal system in which his congregants and audience lived. Although Schuller never directly named this new era, the transformation he discerned has come to be known as market society: a global economic and political system placing market processes at the center of all our lives.[14] The birthing of market society uprooted traditions, dislodged familiar practices, featured new technology, instigated planned obsolescence, and presented unforeseen challenges. All institutions became market-centered and required all human activity to become market-oriented. Schuller surely followed precedent in reconciling his style of ministry to market mechanisms. He recognized that churches, whether desired or not, were carried into evolving market processes. Yet most other church leaders seemed to refuse to accept that these changes required an intentionally different approach to pastoral ministry. Even as religious bodies increasingly reclustered in suburban spaces, denominational traditions prevailed and clergy assumed they could continue to sustain their churches by appealing to families already loyal to their tradition.[15] Schuller sidestepped these considerations, ultimately by necessity.

---

14. See Karl Polanyi, *The Great Transformation: The Political and Economic Origins of Our Time* (New York: Farrar & Rinehart, 1944); Grahame Thompson et al., eds., *Markets, Hierarchies, and Networks: The Coordination of Social Life* (London: Sage, 1991); Richard Swedberg, "Markets as Social Structures," in *Handbook of Economic Sociology*, ed. Neil Smelser and Richard Swedberg (New York and Princeton: Russell Sage Foundation and Princeton University Press, 1994), 255–82; Don Slater and Fran Tonkiss, *Market Society: Markets and Modern Social Theory* (Cambridge: Polity Press/ Blackwell, 2001); Benjamin Spies-Butcher, Damien Cahill, and Joy Paton, *Market Society: History, Theory, Practice* (Cambridge: Cambridge University Press, 2012).

15. For instance, see Mark T. Mulder, *Shades of White Flight: Evangelical Congregations and Urban Departure* (New Brunswick, NJ: Rutgers University Press, 2015).

8 CHAPTER 1

Schuller crafted a style of ministry that assumed the challenges and worries of people, as well as their dreams and opportunities, as catalyzed by the disruptions and uncertainties of market society. The minister notably accommodated the discomforts and displacements of market forces that affected the church and its members. Consciously operating as a therapist in the pulpit, the minister's "theology of self-esteem" synergized a familiar old-time religion with contemporary cultural sensibilities. According to Robert P. Jones, it is this distinctive combination "that transformed Schuller into one of the most influential Christian pastors of the late twentieth century."[16]

Even more, Schuller believed that changing market dynamics required the structures of church ministry to conform to them. With its dominating familiarity, the market offered a reality to be faced, not feared; its possibilities to be leveraged, not avoided. Therefore, for the church to survive and succeed in its mission, Schuller concluded that ministry leaders needed to proactively bring their preaching and their churches into the market. In acting on this imperative, Schuller was crafty, paying attention to his environment, eager to implement new tools, savvy in communication style, and clever in obtaining financial credit to access funding.

He never lost faith in the church, yet in seeking a more assured future, he sought to master the mechanisms of the market, with special attention to the changing workings of finance by prioritizing land purchase and building use and stretching his capacity to secure committed donors to raise substantial capital. His eventual—and strategic—alignment with the leaders of the church growth movement indicated that Schuller assumed that his market-focused techniques answered many of the questions posed by the clergy of the seeker churches. But for nearly the entirety of Schuller's ministry, he would outpace both allies and competitors, centering his efforts less on gimmicks of growth and more on adapting the persistent strengths of church life in unanticipated ways, leading his congregation through an active and shifting market.

Schuller knew the risks of untried strategies, and he lived with a fear of failure. The full extent of his ministry may not have survived, but the

---

16. Robert P. Jones, *The End of White Christian America* (New York: Simon & Schuster, 2017).

church he built persevered (even if in a diminished form). More significantly, his explicit market orientation both anticipated and further institutionalized the importance of church management style. Despite the many disparagements the minister endured during his life, the market-driven ministry curated by Robert H. Schuller continues to dominate a large segment of American public religion, a dominance that his life and influence do much to explain.

Ministry and Market Logic

Once Schuller graduated from seminary, he committed himself to pastoring people in relation to their lived experiences. Most importantly, moving from his rural origins surrounded by family farms to Greater Chicago and then to Southern California, the minister began to understand that his potential parishioners had become forced participants in a relentless and often degrading marketplace. And it was these disconnected economic persons—especially men working to establish and build their young families, men like him who moved hundreds of miles away from their families of origin in an attempt to build a new life—that Schuller sought to recruit into his church. An expanding cohort of upwardly mobile men sought to become economically self-sustaining, which during the mid-twentieth century folded into a broad sense of what it meant to be a patriotic, God-fearing American (versus being an antiestablishment, atheistic Communist). Schuller's ministry participated in modernization by shifting its messages and programming toward the perceived needs of wealth-builders in a competitive market society. He also acknowledged that women also participated, although he thought they did so while presumably starting families, raising children, and forging new marital partnerships with their husbands.

The manner in which he aggressively leaned into market logic made Schuller's pastoral ministry distinctive. In 1983, with his wife Arvella's editorial help, Schuller published a book of 366 daily devotions titled *Tough-Minded Faith for Tender-Hearted People*.[17] Every page began with

---

17. Robert H. Schuller, *Tough-Minded Faith for Tender-Hearted People* (Nashville: Nelson, 1983).

10 CHAPTER 1

"FAITH IS . . ." and then defined an aspect of the Christian faith life the minister sought to encourage in the life of his readers. Many of the devotions oriented "faith in action" to market dynamics. For example, day 43 indicated that "FAITH IS . . . Entering the contest," and provided a prayer: "Almighty God, there is a race I should run, a contest I should enter, a competition I should be involved in." Day 137 insisted that "FAITH IS . . . Positioning yourself in the marketplace," by selling a service that "will solve someone's problem." He wrote, "Even churches sell something—spiritual and emotional services—to people whose problems can only be solved by a personal relationship with God and Jesus Christ!" And day 148 reported that "FAITH IS . . . Creating new products and services," and that "Faith finally adds up to this: We have to keep creating new products and services to meet the changing needs in a shifting society. . . . For unless we keep creating new products or service lines, we will be out of business before we know it." For Schuller, a vibrant faith manifested through diligent participation in a changing marketplace—even churches.

Schuller's embrace of market logic went further than a reworking of his sermons. As a minister, he applied and translated the mechanisms of market society to a radical reconsideration of how churches should operate, with particular attention on how the American church would need to change if it was to endure. In fact, in 1980, Schuller adamantly argued that journalists should not call the Crystal Cathedral a "church." He told the *Chicago Tribune*, "Electronic church is not a valid term; we are more a corporate colony of caring persons. . . . What you see on television is not a church. Call it emotional therapy, or ministry or ecclesiastical activity, but don't call it a church."[18] While churches, being adaptable, embodied structures, had already been integrating the dominant ethos of market society, Schuller articulated the imperative and principles of a market-fitting church in a distilled, clear, even charismatic manner.

Although other pastors had felt the undeniable effects of a pervasive market, Schuller intentionally embraced market logic and made it explicit in the management of his ministry. The intentional adaptability of ministry required in a changing social environment manifested in

---

18. Ronald Yates, "From Outdoor Theater to 'Cathedral'—a Religious Success Story," *Chicago Tribune Magazine*, July 27, 1980 (DVP).

the minister's bold actions. Schuller moved from his roots in the Midwest, leaving a successful pastorate in Illinois to launch himself to the religious frontier of the West Coast, establishing his "mission church" by necessity at a drive-in theater in 1955, preaching from the top of a snack bar in Orange County, California. Twenty-five years after arriving in Southern California, a more mature Schuller stood at the top of a custom-built marble pulpit to celebrate the opening of a commissioned and architecturally innovative glass-sheathed building he named "the Crystal Cathedral," a design marvel and a pinnacle of achievement that both affirmed his philosophy of ministry and expanded his platform for proclaiming it to other leaders. At each step, he refurbished familiar spiritual materials that he thought would shelter and sustain hosts of vibrant and self-fulfilled congregants well into the distant future.

The constant compulsion for growth, though, forced the minister to explore innovations that broke with assumed orthodoxy. In those apparent departures from traditional Christianity, Schuller always presented his rearrangements as instances of continuity through a repackaging of core materials for the modern era. His urgency for reconstructing the church is illustrated when Schuller lobbied directly to his denomination, the Reformed Church in America (RCA), in 1968: "We must constantly offer new challenges in the form of new programs or projects: a building program, an addition to the staff, an additional missionary project. But every year we should add something new, something that will challenge, inspire, and highly motivate people spiritually." In short, Schuller sought to find *resonance* in his ministry through the strategy of growth.[19]

Indeed, the minister himself never saw these as radical departures but as a truer form of traditionalism. In sermons, workshops, books, articles, or interviews, his reading of the Scripture and his interpretation of historic theologians like John Calvin produced steady insights and rationale for all of his stances. Moreover, he believed his approach to innovation was not dictated by a whim of novelty for its own sake but was required by a faithful pastoral response to the circumstances of culture. Although journalists have recently reported fresh trends of

---

19. Robert H. Schuller, "Make Them Want to Give," *Church Herald*, November 22, 1968, 11 (DVP).

12   CHAPTER 1

American irreligion and secularization, Schuller himself would not be shocked at the decline in church attendance, nor would he be surprised at the rise of religious "nones" either.[20] He anticipated such developments. His pastoral ministry—not just his messages to his members but, more importantly, his response to legions of clergy asking for advice from his experience—was his attempt to intervene in Christianity's gloaming. In the vein of a self-styled psychologist, he proposed an intervention to arrest the decline of the church before it eclipsed into nothing at all.

Pastoral messages aimed at the public eventually won him a broad audience. At his peak, few ministers could match Robert H. Schuller's stature in American cultural and religious life. On broadcast television every Sunday morning for over four decades beginning in 1970, he was recognized by generations of Americans as the friendly pastor who never yelled at them or made them fear for their ultimate salvation. With a gracious smile and a soothing tone, prominently positioned alongside a recognizable pulpit, he counseled young and old that almost any circumstance could be overcome—as long as one adopted the proper attitude. Schuller spoke and wrote extensively, producing thousands of cassettes and videos, his plain message featured in *New York Times* best-selling books, yet his actual theology remained difficult to pin down. He sounded right enough—and certainly confident enough—that millions of viewers tuned in to watch the Orange County–based worship service before—or in lieu of—going to their own local church. None of his televised ministerial peers could match Schuller's profile (forty years on *Hour of Power*) or his artifacts (the iconic, glass-clad Crystal Cathedral). The *Orange County Register* described their local minister as a "superstar" in the universe of 1980s religious television, "on par with Bill Cosby or Michael J. Fox."[21]

Because of his leadership and management of Christian congregational life, Schuller became a dominant presence in the religious ecology of late twentieth-century America. The *Los Angeles Times*, though, also described the Orange County minister as presiding over "perhaps

---

20. For more, see Ryan P. Burge, *The Nones: Where They Came From, Who They Are, and Where They Are Going* (Minneapolis: Fortress, 2021).

21. Ronald Campbell, "TV Superstar: 'Hour of Power' is No. 1 or 2 Religious Show," *Orange County Register*, August 9, 1987, M3 (DVP).

the most controversial church in America."[22] In a moment that attested to Schuller's fame, boxer Muhammad Ali once asked the minister for his autograph—at an event where the two men found themselves in the select, invitation-only company of the Queen of England. Schuller also claimed to have *literally* written University of Alabama football coach Bear Bryant's "ticket to heaven."[23] Another time, a journalist recalled traveling with Schuller and found the minister constantly besieged by fans—one pilot even came out of the cockpit to shake the hand of his famous passenger.[24] Even during the best of times, though, theologians, journalists, and fellow pastors—at times members of his own church staff—never tired of criticizing his messages or his methods. Through it all, Schuller maintained a stature that, even with the specter of critique and condescension in some corners, demanded attention and fealty.

Church Growth Movement and Mastering the Market

Schuller recognized that the church teetered on the precipice of decline. Indeed, the post–World War II boom of church attendance and construction reached in the 1950s would be followed by a precipitous waning that continued well into the second decade of the twenty-first century. Yet he insisted that pastors should not accept this deterioration as inevitable, that growth should be their explicit goal, and that leaders should pursue deliberate strategies using every means available to achieve expansive growth as quickly as possible—even if such methods seemed at first to be atypical for church leaders. His explicit rationalization and routinization of church-growth techniques spoke to the uncertainty and worry of church leaders about their own continued relevance as clergy. Schuller promoted mechanisms that sought to stimulate church growth that accentuated the sentiment that ministers could control their own fate, modeling on a therapeutic approach to preaching unmoored from

22. Bella Stumbo, "The Time Muhammad Ali Asked for Robert Schuller's Autograph," *Los Angeles Times*, May 29, 1983, https://tinyurl.com/29rprty5.

23. Greg Garrison, "Did Bear Bryant Go to Heaven? Evangelist Robert Schuller Gave Him a 'Ticket,'" *AL.com*, April 2, 2015, https://tinyurl.com/yc33567y.

24. Stumbo, "The Time Muhammad Ali Asked for Robert Schuller's Autograph."

14 CHAPTER 1

the dead-weight drag of denominationalism—all while promoting aggressive plans for site expansion. The minister synced both the message and methods to the perceived successes of entrepreneurial businessmen flourishing within the new possibilities of capitalist development and strategic management.

Schuller's elaboration and promotion of a strategic approach to church growth functioned as the fulcrum of his pastoral creativity. In tracing his life, we repeatedly find an assertive diligence in perfecting and replicating a distinctive religious strategy, a modernized ecclesiology sensitive to the need for financial capital and architectural intentionality, consciously intended to secure the long-term legacy of the Christian church. In performing his cultivated practices for church leadership, Schuller attracted millions of admirers and inspired thousands of pastoral imitators. For his audience, Schuller crafted a theology that sidestepped the thornier issues of orthodox Christianity that might snag a person's capacity for immersive trust and intentionally avoided the tedium of abstruse doctrine or rote liturgy. For his pastoral colleagues and lay leaders, he produced seminars and "how to" guides to inspire and pass along accumulated lessons from experience, energizing the efforts of increasingly uncertain clergy yearning for wisdom not provided by their backgrounds or seminary training. While doing so, Schuller continued to accumulate evidence of the soundness of his church management principles.

At a time of profound congregational shifts—decline in historic churches, rise of new charismatic congregations, population movement away from rural to urban and suburban areas, larger migration flows from Rust Belt and Midwest toward Sunbelt, rapid expansion of suburban housing, financial anxiety for working- and middle-class households, transformation in means of communication and technology—Schuller built his reputation as an expert on church-growth techniques and played a pivotal role in catalyzing the evolution of the church growth movement (CGM) into strategies that helped assure a church's success in a changing marketplace. Prominent voices of what became the CGM affirmed his stature as a key innovator. For example, C. Peter Wagner, a chief proponent of church growth at Fuller Theological Seminary, provided a laudatory foreword for Schuller's best-selling *Your Church Has a Fantastic Future!*, writing, "As a professor of church growth, I am personally indebted to Robert Schuller for much of what I know and teach."[25] As CGM leaders began to think of white, middle-class suburbanites as an anthropologically cohesive "tribe," Schuller's seemingly traditional worship style, message of optimism, desire to bless socioeconomic striving, and advantageous location all converged to allow him to seize the moment to become a formative leader in the field.[26]

After seeing a gaggle of celebrated gurus drawing their own followers, Schuller staked his own claim of expertise, having built a ministry in sync with major societal changes, eventually labeling himself "the founder of the church growth movement."[27] In the late 1980s and early 1990s, Schuller's Crystal Cathedral in sunny Southern California held the highest profile of *any* congregation in the country. Consequently, Schuller and the other leaders within the CGM tended to see their relationship as mutually beneficial—even though the case could be made that, despite their close proximity in Southern California, they initially had been working more parallel than in concert. In fact, at one point, Donald McGavran (a colleague of Wagner's at Fuller) marveled that Schuller had *intuited* the principles of church growth before anyone had published on the topic.[28] For his part, McGavran asserted that he himself had proven the methodology on foreign mission fields. Schuller may have stumbled onto the "principles" of church growth, but McGavran and others believed they had secured the definitive analysis that proved the techniques were sound. And Schuller's large success-oriented ministry offered the best evidence that his methods worked and represented the future of Christianity.

Schuller's ministry in California presumed church-growth techniques on the path to establishing the template for the future of church

---

25. Schuller, *Your Church Has Real Possibilities!*, 16. This sentence from Wagner's foreword is featured on the dustcover of the hardbound edition.

26. See Jesse Curtis, "White Evangelicals as a 'People': The Church Growth Movement from India to the United States," *Journal of Religion and American Culture* 30, no. 1 (2020): 108–46.

27. Robert H. Schuller, *Your Church Has a Fantastic Future! A Possibility Thinker's Guide to a Successful Church* (Ventura, CA: Regal Books, 1986), and John Curran Hardin, "Retailing Religion: Business Promotionalism in American Christian Churches in the Twentieth Century" (PhD diss., University of Maryland, 2011), 292.

28. Hardin, "Retailing Religion," 292.

16   CHAPTER 1

ministry. By asserting methods that could guide every church in the country, Schuller manifested a profoundly *modern* desire to employ established *techniques* for accomplishing a clear end. Both he and CGM leaders agreed that if the church was to grow, then new means were required. In distilling his methods for church leaders, Schuller had already concluded that the principles of sound business practices offered superior outcomes when compared to the worn-out approaches of denominational structures. Business firms utilized organizational principles that proved better and would last longer in new cultural and economic circumstances. No longer would reconsideration of the design of services to provide a more meaningful liturgical experience or cultivation of a more meditative presence in church spaces be sufficient, as if they ever were. For the church not only to survive but to thrive, pastoral leaders would need to adopt managerial processes and principles that resulted in measurable patterns of growth and vitality as seen among American corporations.

In that effort to nurture church growth, historian Molly Worthen described Schuller as "the grandfather of seeker-sensitive megachurches."[29] Schuller upended the tried and true revivalist tactic of scolding sinners into repentance and salvation. Instead, the minister synthesized an affirmational theology with pop psychology in a methodology that attempted to mitigate the obstacles to church attendance. And, in fact, church attendance and growth became the most sought-after markers of faithful Christian leadership. If Schuller honed the pattern of growth-focused, strategically planned, and financially-savvy mega-ministry, his progeny (as mentioned previously) included both Rick Warren of Saddleback Church and Bill Hybels of Willow Creek Community Church. Both ministers attended trainings conducted by Schuller for ministry leaders. Hybels, in particular, seemed quite taken with what he learned in Garden Grove and attempted perhaps the most systemic application of Schuller's methods in suburban Chicago. Hybels surveyed local suburbanites to identify the key reasons that kept them from church—and found out that "guilt-inducing sermons" and worship that failed to "meet

---

29. Molly Worthen, *Apostles of Reason: The Crisis of Authority in American Evangelicalism* (New York: Oxford University Press, 2014), 155.

FACING TORNADIC WINDS—BOTH NATURAL AND SOCIAL   **17**

my needs" represented two of the key reasons. Hybels created a worship that addressed both concerns—a Midwest version of Schuller's key principles. Worthen explained that Schuller's form of church management grew tentacles that transcended geographic boundaries and became a national phenomenon.[30]

In fact, Hybels attended Schuller's leadership institute in 1975 and, having been soundly impressed by what he learned, returned the next year with roughly twenty-five leaders from Willow Creek. In 1977, Schuller spoke at a development event at Willow Creek. Soon Schuller and Hybels started meeting regularly. The relationship grew so close that one pastor of a nondenominational church in California described Hybels's approach as an "updated version of Schuller."[31] Another Pennsylvania pastor evaluated Willow Creek as a "mainstreaming of the Schuller concept."[32] In his book on seeker churches, sociologist Kimon Howland Sargeant assessed that Willow Creek played a pivotal role in establishing seeker-sensitive worship as the dominant form of white evangelical worship. Following Schuller's method of gathering ministry leaders to share techniques, Hybels created the Willow Creek Association—a network of similar-minded congregations that functioned in ways that almost mimicked a denomination, a notion that Schuller himself at least contemplated. And Hybels went on to create his own church leader conference, advocating for his own stylized methods, packaged for accessibility, and readily adopted by thousands of church leaders. Similarly, Rick Warren of Saddleback Community Church did the same, eventually publishing his approach in his own best-selling book *The Purpose Driven Church*.

Sargeant also identified the practices most associated with these congregations. In most ways, Schuller marked the path that so many pastors followed. Sargeant noted that seeker churches tended to downplay denominational identity or affiliation. That decision frequently rested on the notion that some denominations carried negative connotations among the seekers. Schuller not only went this route, he often advo-

---

30. Worthen, *Apostles of Reason*, 156.

31. Kimon Howland Sargeant, *Seeker Churches: Promoting Traditional Religion in a Nontraditional Way* (New Brunswick, NJ: Rutgers University Press, 2000), 196.

32. Sargeant, *Seeker Churches*, 196.

cated for dropping denominational identity markers entirely—while still maintaining affiliation. Although in his early years in Garden Grove Schuller remained fixated on more traditional church structures, the completion of the Crystal Cathedral demonstrated how a nontraditional religious building design could offer a dramatic, yet familiar, venue to entice potential congregants. Sargeant suggested that seeker churches sought to create and maintain "a safe environment for seekers, an environment that is not unlike other places in the secular world."[33] The Cathedral arguably became the highest-profile instance of how a nontraditional church structure could be utilized to lure the curious and the hesitant. Sargeant also reported that seeker churches demonstrated low regard for traditions. For Schuller, this manifested in distancing himself from some of the hallmarks of Reformed worship: reading catechisms, time for confession and assurance, and the centrality of Scripture as a basis for sermons. The minister saw all of the above as alienating for the expanding market of the "unchurched." As the CGM evolved, its practitioners maintained aspects of Schuller's template—especially the de-emphasis on confession and creeds and catechisms. Seeker churches also departed from traditional hymns. While Schuller maintained the use of hymns, he did change the lyrics in an effort to update the language to be more relatable and less offensive. Seeker churches invested in multimedia to enhance the worship experience—the Crystal Cathedral functioned as a large television production venue. Sargeant also noted that seeker churches offered worship where attenders could dress informally. Schuller's loyalty to the drive-in experience allowed congregants the ultimate privacy in clothing—they could remain in their pajamas in their car if they wanted.

Some critics watching the spread of seeker-sensitive and adjacent models of ecclesial practices expressed concern that the CGM borrowed too heavily from business and marketing, becoming overly dependent on clever financing and the spectacle of showmanship. Schuller suffered no such qualms. Instead, he forcefully advocated that church growth *should* look like and borrow from the best practices of business, including the entertainment industry. Indeed, he insisted the future of the Christian

---

33. Sargeant, *Seeker Churches*, 61.

church required these adaptations. Such persistently bold claims made the minister vulnerable to broadsides from skeptics.

Paul D. Simmons, professor of Christian ethics at Southern Baptist Theological Seminary, focused on Schuller in particular as he critiqued the CGM. For Simmons, *Hour of Power* represented the worst of the movement in that the show included "all the sweet smells of success but no hint of the scandal of the cross. It seems pure Hollywood rather than the simple but demanding Gospel." Indeed, no less than celebrity talk show host Phil Donahue offered *Hour of Power* a show business blessing when he deemed it "a truly beautiful program."[34] For Simmons, though, Schuller demonstrated "style but little substance, preaching comfortable Christianity and substituting middle-class morality for disciplined service."[35] Moreover, historian Jesse Curtis argued that in Schuller, the CGM reached its apex (or nadir) in exploiting "sleek marketing and business practices to sell the gospel." As Schuller refined his approach, church growth "looked like nothing so much as an in-your-face invitation to treat religion as another consumer good in the modern capitalist economy."[36] Because of Schuller's bold approach, Curtis also noted that the CGM "tended to describe Schuller as a man who made them look good, a successful religious entrepreneur who had 'intuitively' understood their principles before they were widely known."[37]

For his part, Schuller seemed only too glad to be welcomed into the fold of the CGM—he expressed gratitude for their appreciation of his marketing and business acumen in selling the gospel. The CGM embrace of the minister contrasted with the minister's relationship with his own denomination—in the RCA, he acutely felt undervalued. To be esteemed by fellow church growth entrepreneurs felt both flattering and beguiling.

Schuller's audience for his message and his methods remained large because of his established media presence. Due to his outsized profile on

34. "Dr. Robert Schuller Interviewed on the Donahue Show," 1976, transcript, folder "Crystal Cathedral Robert H. Schuller—Interviews, 1976," box 26, Robert H. Schuller Collection, H93-1188, Hope College Archives and Special Collections, Holland, MI, 37.

35. Quoted by Curtis, "White Evangelicals as a 'People,'" 130.

36. Curtis, "White Evangelicals as a 'People,'" 128.

37. Curtis, "White Evangelicals as a 'People,'" 127.

Hour of Power, the Orange County minister had a platform unmatched by his contemporaries in the CGM. Thus, when Schuller translated church growth into a market-oriented Christianity, it resonated beyond evangelicalism. In fact, when the conservative Christian magazine *Eternity* lampooned CGM in 1976, the editors seemed to target Schuller in particular. The article described a visit by "Pilgrim and his family" to the "Chapel of the Winns," also known as the "First Church of the American Dream"—where automobile parking became such an important preoccupation that the staff included a pastor dedicated to the lot (a former used car salesman). The fictitious founding pastor, Wyatt T. Winn, preached on television and traveled the globe so much that he rarely made an appearance in his own sanctuary. What surely represented a parody of Schuller's leadership institute, the fictional Reverend Winn had formed the "Consortium of Church Management." To ensure that they become members, the Vigilance Units processed information cards from all members—and the "Minister of Statistics" used the cards to project "future growth trends for the chapel." And, in what had to be another poke at Schuller's plans for the eventual Crystal Cathedral, Pastor Winn promoted his plan for a new 144,000-seat chapel. The attention to detail in the parody of Schuller's ministry indicated the significance of its profile within American Christianity.

Schuller as a Barometer of American Religious Life

Decades into the twenty-first century, we continue to witness Schuller's influence—even in unexpected corners of Christianity. In their discussion of "Independent Network Charismatic (INC) Christianity," sociologists Brad Christerson and Richard Flory argued that Schuller plausibly functioned as a prototype for the new "independent apostles" who have exerted leadership over a significant swath of American Christianity in recent years. Indeed, Schuller's *Hour of Power* offered a "religious product" that replicated a church worship service—but operated largely independently of denominational oversight. In that way, Schuller's innovative revision of a familiar religion without supervision or guidelines became a template for wielding religious authority while expanding congregation size and global audience share. By discarding the constraints of denominational authority, autonomous pastorpreneurs could experiment with unprecedented freedom under the deregulation of an explicitly market-driven Christianity.[38]

Christerson and Flory described INC Christianity as independent collections of dynamic individual leaders who exert influence not through institutions or organizations but "through media, conferences, and their relationships with other individual leaders in religious and secular professions."[39] Moreover, the two sociologists gauged that INC Christianity had become the "fastest-growing edge of Protestantism."[40] They also argued that these loose networks also offer three advantages: (1) They allow the freedom to experiment with constraints from hierarchical authorities; (2) they offer an opportunity for charismatic leaders to extend their influence beyond the local congregation; and (3) they afford more avenues to access revenue sources beyond the local church.[41] In all three instances, Schuller offers the most high-profile and successful exemplar.

What is surprising to many who consider Schuller's innovative posture, though, is how he kept so many traditional elements. Within the embrace of the modern, why keep so many vestiges of the past? For example, every Sunday morning for four decades, Schuller continued to faithfully don his clerical robes. Why did he cling to this visual residue of mainline Protestantism—a declining religious tradition from which the minister did all he could to distance himself and his church? Why keep these ceremonial vestments? As with everything for one of America's first megachurch pastors, the rationale morphed to fit the context. A Schuller family member explained that the vestments represented the office of minister—a method to remove the distraction of the person delivering the word of God to their congregation. A laudably humble explanation.

Yet, another family member cautioned that the reason for the robes likely had less lofty origins: Schuller struggled with his weight and related body image issues—the robes comfortably covered that anxiety.

---

38. Brad Christerson and Richard Flory, *The Rise of Network Christianity: How Independent Leaders Are Changing the Religious Landscape* (New York: Oxford University Press, 2017), 122–23.

39. Christerson and Flory, *Rise of Network Christianity*, 11.

40. Christerson and Flory, *Rise of Network Christianity*, 14.

41. Christerson and Flory, *Rise of Network Christianity*, 65.

Moreover, the minister liked a snack here and there on Sunday mornings, and a spill of ketchup or mustard on the tie between services could be an unnecessary distraction for viewers of the *Hour of Power*. Both rationales likely included truth and encapsulated a burgeoning type of religious tradition that synthesized image and pragmatics, elegant architecture and evangelism, the hopeful confidence of possibility thinking and the cold calculations of business management. We also suggest a further reason for keeping the vestments—signaling continuity with tradition.

The centrality of a church building, with the primacy of the pulpit, offers another instance of the profound traditionalism within Schuller's pursuit of innovation. For Schuller, the church as a building represented the center of the spiritual universe; to recruit, protect, and expand the sanctuary to hold more people functioned as the essence of Christian ministry. As the charismatic center of the church, the pastor sought to inspire the faithful while leaving room to reach out to those who remained not yet fully connected. Schuller insisted on new construction to allow for the seats that he *anticipated* as necessary for the new members who had not yet arrived. The expansion of buildings would lead to greater massing of bodies, always leaving room for the stranger. Therefore, the size of a church's main sanctuary gestured to the expected growing size of population, the coordinated growth indicating the forward progression of the church.

Schuller's unique position as someone who straddled mainline Protestantism and evangelicalism allowed him unparalleled opportunity to test the principles of church growth. Within his modern accommodation, a rather orthodox ecclesiology persisted. As typified by the billowing robes within the grandeur of an all-glass church, the constant negotiation between the traditional and the innovative, the sacred familiar and the secular improvised for the spiritual, manifested the unexpected versatility of the Dutch farm boy from rural Iowa. His ministry philosophy engaged how messages should be crafted, how public media attention must be sought, the kinds of buildings that would best showcase the importance of the church, how to craft a relevant and contemporary identity as a person of faith, and how to best interact with the economic and political structures of the day.

Schuller did not promote a style of ministry geared toward growth simply because he saw it as a "good idea" or just an alternative to conventional models; he crafted this approach to ministry because he believed it to be absolutely necessary to cultivate a living and sustaining presence for the church. Schuller believed that, at this point in history, it was the place of the church of Jesus to reorient its operations and retrain for new priorities—but the content remained, in his mind, essentially unchanging. His lifelong reassembling of old materials within new structures made manifest his convictions on reinvention, displaying the constant negotiations of what could be remade amid what should be kept in perpetuity.

Today, Schuller's achievements, challenges, and failures, while important to post-WWII history and relevant for understanding the orientation of congregational Christianity, remain poorly understood. Some critics emphasize their perception of a shallow, proto-prosperity theology in Schuller. The minister himself admitted, "I'm willing to compromise my own position and be prepared to pay the price of being probably criticized or laughed at because I'm corny or shallow and all of these things. I'm willing to pay that price if that's the price I have to pay to help a human being."[42] Others focus on a cash-hungry enterprise in a seemingly egoistic ministry, building a glass church that only served to reflect Schuller back to himself. After all, the minister once proclaimed, "I'm not just a trend. I'm not just a fashion," then adding, "I intend to be around for a long time. I intend to become an American classic."[43] Yet neither perspective offers sufficient explanation. A giant of late twentieth-century American Christianity, Schuller adopted a theology, a persona, a set of priorities, and a set of practices that he believed were necessary to keep the faith vibrant into the long-term future.

He had witnessed the devastation visited by a tornado on his family's farm as a young man. As a minister on the West Coast, Schuller worried that the storm of secularization would now similarly destroy the church. Rather than rebuilding after the cataclysm, the minister sought

42. Quoted from personal interview on February 24, 1983. See Thomas Robert Ahlersmeyer, "The Rhetoric of Reformation: A Fantasy Theme Analysis of the Rhetorical Vision of Robert Harold Schuller" (PhD diss., Bowling Green State University, 1989), 2.

43. Alan Cartnal, "Gimme That Prime-Time Religion," *New West Magazine*, April 24, 1978, 33–38, here 38.

to gird his ministry by recruiting as wide of a market as possible to prevail through the growling winds of contemporary skepticism and the desire for self-actualization. His formula emphasized resilience and longevity through growth.

By placing himself in the suburban Sunbelt of Southern California, Schuller aligned his ministry with the personal and political objectives of his members, embracing the logics of business planning and capital investment, and widely spreading principles of church management that he trusted would serve any pastor in any context. Therefore, for him, congregational ministry should aim to address the anxiety of the modern self, speaking to the desires of people seeking upward mobility in pursuit of a self-willed economic security amid the uncertainty of the labor market and injecting a spirituality to those managing their increasing wealth.

For Schuller, congregational ministry should also be ambitious and image-conscious, smartly devising approaches to raising funding, and expanding as rapidly as possible to enable the luring and catching of people before a rapidly secularizing culture left them irretrievably lost. The minister famously quipped, "I'd rather attempt to do something great and fail than to attempt to do nothing and succeed."[44] Attempt he did. Along the way, Schuller built a religious empire with increasing vulnerabilities—a charismatic structure of apparent strength that would eventually, and unexpectedly, collapse.

44. Schuller, *Tough Times*, 98.

2

RESTLESS FOR MORE

Robert H. Schuller vividly remembered his uncle Henry Beltman's first words to him. A missionary with the Reformed Church in America (RCA) to China, Henry visited the farm of his sister, Jennie, when Schuller was five years old. Being a man of considerable spiritual stature in this Dutch immigrant enclave in northwest Iowa, Uncle Henry received a hero's welcome. On meeting his nephew, this great man of the faith looked at young Schuller and predicted, "You will be a preacher when you grow up!"

The moment served as an inflection point. Schuller later claimed: "My initial encounter with Uncle Henry, and his proclamation that I would be a preacher, would be the single most defining moment of my earthly life."[1] As both an anointing and an affirmation, the call to become a preacher provided a lifelong sense of identity, and it drove Schuller to prepare for the role as he grew older. He understood that in the Dutch Reformed tradition, the sermon represented the pinnacle of the worship service—the *dominee* (Dutch for "pastor," from the Latin *dominus*, which means "master" or "lord") needed to *deliver* the word of God. With that in mind, the young Schuller boy often practiced preaching to the cows cooling themselves from the summer heat in the creek that crossed the family farm.[2] Such clear objectives in a young child set Schuller apart

1. Robert H. Schuller, *My Journey: From an Iowa Farm to a Cathedral of Dreams* (San Francisco: HarperOne, 2001), 47.

2. Michael Nason and Donna Nason, *Robert Schuller: The Inside Story* (Waco, TX: Word, 1983), 24. This story is in dispute. While writing their book on Schuller's life,

26 CHAPTER 2

from his peers: "Never mind that I was the only child in all the school with such grand aspirations. I now had a confidence that no one could take from me."[3] Though he did not name it as such, it seemed that as an adult he cast his younger self as set apart from his community distinctly because of his nascent possibility thinking, consciously willing himself into the position decreed by his beloved uncle Henry.

Schuller often narrated his own life story, including writing a full autobiography, and consistently framed his call to ministry as destiny.[4] Part of Schuller's self-asserted myth revolved around the idea that he had been preordained (as any good Calvinist would assume) to be a minister. Even before his birth, the story went, Schuller's father had kneeled between the furrows of his freshly plowed Iowa field to pray for a son who would not be content to be a farmer, a son who would be a dreamer, a son who would eventually feel the call to be a minister.[5] According to Schuller's daughter Sheila, family lore indicated that the earnest prayer included these words of petition: "O Lord, I know my Jennie is past her childbearing years. But please plant one more seed—in my Jennie. And let it grow and bear a son—a son who will be a minister—who will in turn plant seeds, Your seeds of love in many hearts."[6] Indeed, Schuller's sense of

---

Michael (the minister's longtime aide) and Donna Nason included the story about the minister preaching to a herd of his dad's dairy cows in northwest Iowa. However, when Bella Stumbo of the *Los Angeles Times* asked Schuller about the tale, a clearly embarrassed Schuller responded "stiffly" and "without humor" that he had no recollection of ever preaching to cows. Frowning and shrugging, the minister categorized the story as "bull" and indicated that he had no idea how the Nasons would have ever created such a fabrication. When the reporter asked Nason about the inconsistency, the aide smiled and ruminated, "Well, Bob's such a busy man, he has so much on his mind all the time, he probably just forgot about it." For more, see Bella Stumbo, "The Time Muhammad Ali Asked for Robert Schuller's Autograph," *Los Angeles Times*, May 29, 1983, https://tinyurl.com/29rprty5. It should also be noted that Schuller's daughter, Sheila Schuller Coleman, retold the same story in her own book about her father. See page 34.

3. Schuller, *My Journey*, 49.

4. Schuller, *My Journey*. Unsurprisingly, Schuller's autobiography was also printed in a gold clothbound "Crystal Cathedral" edition with gold-embossed text on the cover as a fund-raiser.

5. Nason and Nason, *Robert Schuller*, 18.

6. Sheila Schuller Coleman, *Robert Schuller: My Father and My Friend* (Milwaukee: Ideals Publishing, 1980), 24.

call profoundly bonded the young Schuller with his father. In his autobiography, he reminisced how tears welled up in his father's eyes when he announced his plans to go into ministry and that the two shared a "deep *knowing*" with each other at the kitchen table.

Despite belief in his own destiny, Schuller always asserted that any success he ever achieved depended on his own strategic initiative. In a 1983 theological examination of Schuller, Hope College (Schuller's undergraduate alma mater) professor Dennis Voskuil noted a persistent pattern in the minister's story about himself: "Again Schuller draws upon his life's story, testifying that every obstacle has been turned into an opportunity, every pain into gain, and every trial into triumph."[7] In many respects, his life sounds like an updated version of the once-popular "rags-to-riches" stories of Horatio Alger: poor farm boy from northwest Iowa becomes pastor of one of the greatest churches in America through prayer, persistence, and possibility thinking.[8] (And, in fact, Schuller would receive the Horatio Alger Award in 1989. The minister described the honor as "unsurpassed" among all his achievements.)[9] To be sure, Schuller displayed a libertarian bent as he discussed work ethic and social safety nets: "Here is a major signpost on God's way to good living: The unhappy man is the one who is not working. The unemployed, the forcibly retired, the physically handicapped have a constant battle against boredom, monotony and that feeling of uselessness. . . . Are you unhappy? How long has it been since you have done a good day's work?"[10] Schuller surely believed in grit.

Hardscrabble beginnings lent to a more dramatic narrative of determined ascension to success—becoming an internationally famous celebrity minister who wrote books so profound that they should probably be read, as the author told one journalist, "two or three times to understand what I'm really trying to say."[11] Ministry was destiny, but ministerial

---

7. Dennis Voskuil, *Mountains into Goldmines: Robert Schuller and the Gospel of Success* (Grand Rapids: Eerdmans, 1983).

8. Nason and Nason, *Robert Schuller*, 264.

9. For more details, see the announcement at the Horatio Alger Association of Distinguished Americans website, https://horatioalger.org/members/member-detail/robert-h-schuller.

10. Robert H. Schuller, *God's Way to the Good Life* (New Canaan, CT: Keats, 1974), 103.

11. Stumbo, "The Time Muhammad Ali Asked for Robert Schuller's Autograph."

28   CHAPTER 2

success was achieved. Therefore, those seeking to mimic the growth of Schuller's churches should learn to decode the life of the minister who had made it possible, the details of his life making successful church management accessible to any ordinary person.

The complete accuracy of these tales remains difficult to discern; nevertheless, Schuller's personal narrative mattered, of course, because his life story offered the most robust evidence of the efficacy of his methods. Here we find an intriguing paradox: while Schuller believed God set him apart for ministry, the success of his ministry was not guaranteed. Who would have imagined that a Dutch boy in dusty overalls, having neither privilege nor prestige, from a rural hinterland in northwest Iowa—an unspectacular corner of a state that has come to exemplify Midwestern American averageness—would mature into one of the most famous Christian ministers in the world?

The Man from Nowhere

In his autobiography, Schuller highlighted the state of Iowa in the book title. The place meant much to him. The fact that he rose from a small, backwater location to become one of the most famous religious leaders in the world contributed to his status. The journey from the rural Midwest farm to the cosmopolitan West Coast megalopolis demonstrated the efficacy of both his grit and his theology of possibility thinking. The first sentences of his autobiography indicated an arc of accomplishment, of traveling from the boondocks to the hub: "You can go anywhere from nowhere. My life is witness to that. I was born at the end of a dead-end dirt road that had no name and no number—in a flood."[12] On that dusty farm, Robert Schuller (pronounced "Skuller" in Iowa) discovered, perhaps counterintuitively for a staunch Calvinist, the "formidable power of [his] own free will to create [his] own destiny."[13]

As he cherished noting, Schuller grew up on a farm on a dead-end road. Remote and secluded, the family farm received little to no traffic. The area had been largely settled by Dutch Calvinist immigrants in the

12. Schuller, *My Journey*, 3.
13. Schuller, *My Journey*, 15

late nineteenth century. These immigrants had been part of a wave from the Netherlands who settled mostly in proximity to the southern shores of Lake Michigan, but also included some farther-flung communities in Iowa and Minnesota. The settlers had sought more religious freedom and economic opportunity. Members of the RCA (the oldest denomination in North America, dating to 1628), still largely Dutch in their ethnicity, provided valuable aid and networking for the transatlantic journeys. With warm relationships in place, many of the new Dutch immigrants established congregations that affiliated with the RCA—including Schuller's.[14] Hope College historian Voskuil surmised that the Dutch "Midwestern immigrants took comfort in the fact that the old American denomination held steadfastly to the familiar confessions of the Dutch Reformation—the Heidelberg Catechism, the Belgic Confession, and the Canons of the Synod of Dort."[15] For many years, the older RCA congregations on the East Coast held sway in the denomination—they maintained the most influence and produced most of the denominational leaders. By the 1920s, though, the midwestern churches grew in numbers while the eastern churches lost members and contributed less to denominational coffers. With that in mind, "some members in the Midwest began to wonder why they were still treated as the church's poor and powerless younger sibling."[16] Indeed, though the RCA remained mainline Protestant, some outside observers witnessed its manifestation in rural Iowa and labeled it a "Calvinist sect, as stark and strict as an Iowa winter."[17]

Schuller reported that his father's parents emigrated from the Netherlands, taking "all that they had—mostly poverty—to America."[18] Born in a sod house, young Tony Schuller saw his nascent dream of becoming a preacher end when both of his parents died young, forcing him to drop out of school in the sixth grade to become a farmer. He purchased his

14. Lynn Japinga, *Loyalty and Loss: The Reformed Church in America, 1945–1994* (Grand Rapids: Eerdmans, 2013), 8–10.

15. Voskuil, *Mountains into Goldmines*, 5.

16. Japinga, *Loyalty and Loss*, 12.

17. See the cable network A&E's treatment of Schuller on *Biography*. Originally broadcast in 1998. The description of the religious life for the Dutch Reformed in Alton can be found at 3:56: https://www.youtube.com/watch?v=U4nYEf8F-9g.

18. Nason and Nason, *Robert Schuller*, 6.

30   CHAPTER 2

farm during a time of inflationary prices in the 1920s and almost lost it all in the Great Depression. At one point, Tony sold a cow worth fifty dollars for ten dollars, only to discover that the bank holding the notes had gone under, making the animal worthless.[19]

The threat of impoverishment seemed to preoccupy Schuller's father throughout his life, despite his strong faith. During the Dust Bowl, while other farmers sold out, Tony persevered on his 120 acres—and offered his son a lesson in possibility thinking.[20] The Schullers typically harvested one hundred wagons full of corn. But the lack of rain that year had reduced the entirety of the crop to half a wagon load. Rather than despair, Schuller recalled how his father, Tony, offered a prayer of thanks to God that the wagon had the exact amount of seed he would need to plan for the next spring. Michael Nason, the minister's longtime assistant in Garden Grove, California, reported that this childhood experience of hearing his father's prayer of gratitude led Schuller to create a favorite aphorism: "Never look at what you have lost; look at what you have left."[21] The family survived those lean years and even ended the decade with the installation of electricity on the farm. In 1928, the *Alton Democrat* described Anthony Schuller as "a successful breeder of Ayrshire cattle, a breed rather rare" in northwest Iowa.[22] Indeed, Schuller's father carried a modicum of respect in the Alton area.

Yet, according to Schuller's son-in-law, James Penner, the fear of failure that haunted Schuller's father also preoccupied the minister. In a biography of his father-in-law, Penner suggested that the specter of imminent failure plagued the younger Schuller throughout his life and represented a personal "Goliath."[23] Even in the midst of apparent success, Schuller often referred to his family as being poor. Although it lent more credibility to his dramatic arc of overcoming obstacles to emerge as a successful possibility thinker, it also indicated the emotional difficulty

19. Schuller, *My Journey*, 59.

20. "Farmers Directory of Floyd Township," *Atlas of Sioux County*, January 1, 1908, https://tinyurl.com/bdct9vnh.

21. Nason and Nason, *Robert Schuller*, 23–24.

22. "Alton Items," *Alton (IA) Democrat*, May 11, 1928, https://tinyurl.com/38dyudvj.

23. James Penner, *Goliath: The Life of Robert Schuller* (Anaheim, CA: New Hope Publishing, 1992), 439.

of strained finances and his fear of bringing himself and his family back to a place of economic insecurity.

Schuller's mother, Jennie Beltman, descended from a Dutch baron, and her family carried esteem in the Newkirk, Iowa, area.[24] In fact, Jennie's father, "a wealthy and imposing man," often filled the venerated role of substitute preacher when sickness or travel kept the *dominee* away on Sundays. With their mismatched socioeconomic positions, Schuller described his parents as the "princess" and the "pauper."[25] Because of her father's standing, locals assumed Jennie to be special, a "social elite" coming from "good blood."[26] She clung to the family's noble lineage and even claimed to see traits of the Dutch baron in her young Harold—she constantly challenged him to offer excellence because she planned for him to take on an even more prestigious position in the community, specifically by becoming a medical doctor.[27]

Schuller's parents married at 11:30 a.m. on a January Friday in 1913. The local paper reported that after a ceremony that included an "appropriate solo," the newly married couple celebrated with guests at an "elaborate three course wedding dinner." The article described Jennie Beltman in details that connoted high social standing in the area: "A well-known and popular woman in this vicinity who by her lovable and pleasant qualities has won hosts of friends among her many acquaintances. She is prominent in the Reformed church circles of our city and has always been a willing helper in all kinds of church work." Jennie's groom, though, seemed more of a postscript in the press. After noting that both of Anthony's parents had died, the newspaper account suggested that the groom stood out as "one of our prosperous young men who has been farming for himself and has made good and has the qualities necessary for a successful life."[28]

Though certainly not wealthy, the Schuller family held a position of respect in the northwest Iowa Dutch Reformed community.[29] Schuller's

24. Coleman, *Robert Schuller*, 23.

25. Schuller, *My Journey*, 7–8.

26. Schuller, *My Journey*, 17.

27. Nason and Nason, *Robert Schuller*, 20.

28. "Wedding Bells," *Alton (IA) Democrat*, January 11, 1913, https://tinyurl.com/3z25p28y.

29. Nason and Nason, *Robert Schuller*, 6.

parents, Tony and Jennie, worshiped at Newkirk Reformed Church (later renamed First Reformed Church of Orange City). Scattered on surrounding farms, the eighty families that composed the congregation averaged six children per household. Every family had their own pew and showed up for both Sunday services, fifty-two weeks a year, without question. While faithfully attending twice every Sunday, a young Schuller "listened to sermons which stressed human depravity and divine judgements, repeated the Ten Commandments, and memorized questions and answers from the Heidelberg Catechism."[30] Even more, children participated in midweek classes studying the Heidelberg Catechism. Schuller described the church as his entire world: "its views were my precincts and my boundaries—never to be challenged or questioned."[31]

Within the modesty-preoccupied circles of the Dutch Calvinists, the Protestant clergyman serving as *dominee* enjoyed a privileged status in the community. No other occupation offered the same high level of prestige and admiration. The *dominee* functioned as the "unquestioned core of [the] community." In a story that clearly molded a young Schuller, he recounted how the *dominee* once came for a pastoral visit and insinuated that the family's low socioeconomic standing offered evidence of his father's lack of piety. Rather than argue with the pastor, Schuller related that his disheartened father silently absorbed the "absurd" and "shattering" opinion of the minister and thanked him for coming—because "no one confronts the Dominee."[32]

In addition to the minister, the Ten Commandments held an exalted position in ordering society in this northwest corner of Iowa. Profanity, dancing, alcohol, Sabbath violations (shopping, fishing, using certain tools), premarital sex, and watching movies all represented significant and embarrassing sin. Tobacco? Just fine—for men, as "a good preacher always smoked. The elders and deacons smoked and most of the men in [the Schuller] family smoked."[33] Schuller himself, though, indicated that a smoking woman risked being labeled a "harlot."[34]

30. Schuller, *My Journey*, 37.
31. Schuller, *My Journey*, 19.
32. Schuller, *My Journey*, 17–20.
33. Nason and Nason, *Robert Schuller*, 27–28.
34. Schuller, *My Journey*, 18.

The many stories of Schuller's family and church reinforce that the Schuller family's primary—perhaps sole—social and economic commitments revolved around their ethnically Dutch and theologically conservative RCA congregation.[35] Indeed, one of Schuller's daughters once described neighbors in the area as "separated by miles of farmland but connected by party lines and church activities."[36] Most in his community likely assumed that young Harold (he would move to "Robert" in college after he had a good distance from his mom, who had preferred and insisted on "Harold") would follow his father's occupational trajectory. Everything seemed geared toward his eventually assuming control of the family farm—even though his mother dreamed of a career in medicine for young Harold.

But this young boy took note of the influence of people like his missionary uncle, Henry, and the *dominee* of the family church and dreamed of becoming a minister. Yes, a career as a rural minister with a small flock seemed plausible for the young Schuller. But none would have predicted that a child from tiny Alton, Iowa, would have the wherewithal to intuit a new form of Christianity, an approach advantageously crafted and contoured for the latter half of the twentieth century in America. Questions remain, though, as to the path of Schuller's ascendancy from a Dutch Reformed region of Iowa to become the epitome of the new, dominant form of Christianity in the United States.

Glimpse of Future Promise

Schuller grew up in a Sears Roebuck house ordered from a catalogue (which also proved useful for practical items like toilet paper) and assembled by his father on the farmstead. With three bedrooms and no bathroom, the house barely contained the family. Water had to be carried in from outside. According to Schuller, the surrounding farmland, a "vast, flat, nothingness," included only acres of corn, oats, and pasture. Town,

---

35. For more on the tendency toward social insularity in Dutch Reformed communities, see Mark T. Mulder, *Shades of White Flight: Evangelical Congregations and Urban Departure* (New Brunswick, NJ: Rutgers University Press, 2015), and James D. Bratt, *Dutch Calvinism in Modern America: A History of a Conservative Subculture* (Grand Rapids: Eerdmans, 1984).

36. Coleman, *Robert Schuller*, 36.

34 CHAPTER 2

so to speak, was an intersection. The four corners included a general store, a church, a school, and a cornfield.[37] The area included only one paved road; all others remained gravel.

As a boy, Schuller felt that he spent an inordinate amount of time collecting corncobs that could be used for heating the small house. Unlike his older brother, Henry (named after his uncle), Schuller had trouble rousing himself in the morning for chores and proved not to be a natural at farm tasks. He reminisced about his lack of skill on the farm: "I didn't *mean* to hate the smell of the barn or the squish of a cow pie in the pasture. I didn't *choose* to be an out-of-place farmer's son. I just was."[38] He eventually earned a reputation for regularly returning the cows late from pasture for evening milking—he had been too busy daydreaming and preaching to the herd.[39] The boy realized farm life likely would not make him happy.

Schuller reported that he learned to be emotionally self-sufficient. He described growing up in a loving—if not overly affectionate—household. Spankings with a flat board occurred near the outhouse, but Schuller reported that he "never once saw or heard a sign of verbal or physical assault from one parent to the other or toward any of us kids."[40] His accounts depicted his father as a quiet, gentle man, while his mother presented as the more dominant personality of the two.[41] Schuller's sister, Violet, attested to her brother's depiction—describing her father as "humble" and "very kind" while remarking that their mother required you "to toe the mark."[42] In fact, Tony often "volunteered himself to be the quiet subject of [Jennie's] verbal admonitions."[43] Schuller opined that though he would always be his mother's "baby boy," he still desired more concrete manifestations of her affection: "Never would I hear the words I wanted more than anything to hear: 'I'm proud of you, Bob.' I'm sure that

---

37. Coleman, *Robert Schuller*, 34-35.

38. Schuller, *My Journey*, 36.

39. Coleman, *Robert Schuller*, 22.

40. Schuller, *My Journey*, 34.

41. And his daughter, Sheila, affirmed that description in her biography of her father; see Coleman, *Robert Schuller*, 23-27.

42. See *Biography: Robert Schuller*, A&E, 1998, at 3:20.

43. Schuller, *My Journey*, 34.

she *was* proud of her one child who would become a Dominee. After all, for her this meant returning the family to its honorable roots. But affirmation and affection were emotions that she seldom expressed. After all, pride was a sin. Even as a small child, I can't recall ever hearing from her lips the words 'I love you.'"[44] This self-revealing story demonstrated the young Schuller's desire for esteem rooted in a mother's affection.

The reported lack of outright affection and implied independence further exhibited how Schuller consistently framed his story as one of personal grit and determination leading to success. The emotional obstacles faced at home would be mirrored in the lack of esteem he faced away from home as well. He described himself as a boy in Iowa as "overweight, academically mediocre, and socially unpopular. Girls only giggled at his shy overtures and the boys groaned when they ended up with him, always the last chosen, on their after-school sandlot baseball team."[45] Consistently chosen last for sports teams on the school playground, young Harold learned to cope and find his place.

Lacking physical ability to the point that recess became "hell," Schuller developed into the "talker" and the "clown." With a quick wit and gift for words, he would eventually become the captain of the high school debate team.[46] As he made his way through Newkirk High School, the United States entered World War II. The moment proved pivotal in Schuller's memory: "Sioux County was suddenly not its own little isolated colony—a world apart from the rest. We had been initiated into the larger body of the United States of America, and all of us now were aware of a great world across the oceans! My first global consciousness. Protestants fought alongside Catholics, town and city boys alongside country farmboys."[47] Schuller's provincial world expanded, even if he was not yet sure of the place he would find in it for himself.

Finally, as a young teenager, a glimpse of future promise became evident. A teacher noticed Schuller's performance abilities and asked him, though only a junior, to join the senior play. Schuller jumped at the

44. Schuller, *My Journey*, 35.
45. Stumbo, "The Time Muhammad Ali Asked for Robert Schuller's Autograph."
46. Schuller, *My Journey*, 51–52, and Nason and Nason, *Robert Schuller*, 27.
47. Schuller, *My Journey*, 71.

36 CHAPTER 2

chance. Cast as a female character, fake bosoms and all, he improvised and reported that the crowd "clap[ped] with joy."[48] He began to understand the allure of costumes and personas. Swept away by the reaction, Schuller found it delightful to perform for an audience: "During those years of World War II, laughter was gravely needed to compensate for all the heavy hearts the war had created. In a funny way I began to see such uplift as a form of ministry. . . . Subconsciously, this would motivate me in later years to become a preacher who entertained people *and* honored God as well!"[49] The basis for an appealing Christianity was forming in the young Schuller—and, counterintuitively, dressed as a woman in the context of a somewhat dour Calvinism in some of the deepest reaches of rural America.

Building Blocks of a Career in Ministry

Stories from his childhood reveal that Robert Schuller would never have been content as a farmer on the plains of Iowa. He believed that God had elected him for something far more grand. He had felt the intoxicating effervescence of being on stage in front of a crowd. Within the Dutch Reformed enclave, though, there existed only one clear path to becoming a public performer: a local *dominee*. And Schuller found contentment in that path—after all, none other than Uncle Henry had predicted that young Harold would be a pastor.

Certainly, the role of pastor fit well in the imagination of any ambitious young man in this highly religious Dutch enclave. The church had been the central institution in the Schuller family's life. Dutch American philosopher Nicholas Wolterstorff's recounting of his Sunday experience (forty miles north of Schuller in Bigelow, Minnesota, but largely concurrent in the 1930s) offers a glimpse of what a young Schuller experienced while participating twice every Sunday growing up:

> We "dressed up" on the Lord's Day, dressed up *for* the Lord's Day, and entered church well in advance of the beginning of the service to col-

48. Schuller, *My Journey*, 74.
49. Schuller, *My Journey*, 74.

lect ourselves in silence, silence so intense it could be touched. . . . We faced forward, looking at the Communion table front center, and behind that the raised pulpit. Before I understood a word of what was said, I was inducted by [the church's] architecture into the tradition. Every service included psalms, always sung, often to the Genevan tunes. There was no fear of repetition. The view that only the fresh and innovative is meaningful had not invaded this transplant of the Dutch Reformed tradition in Bigelow, Minnesota. Through repetition, elements of the liturgy and of Scripture sank their roots so deep into consciousness that nothing thereafter, short of senility, could remove them. During the liturgy as a whole but especially in the sermon and most of all in the Lord's Supper, I was confronted by the speech and actions of an awesome, majestic God.[50]

Note the reverence and normative nature of church on Sundays. The performer in Schuller was attracted to the opportunity to lead the central event of his community life. Also note, though, the negative commentary on "fresh and innovative" worship practices. Wolterstorff's description of the congregation's devotion to repetition and reliance on liturgy makes it difficult to understand how Schuller—out of the same ethnoreligious milieu—would come to design and epitomize a new form of Christianity that sought to distance itself from anything associated with dourness or rigidity.

The evolution of his approach to ministry would catalyze when Schuller departed Iowa. To begin his journey toward becoming a pastor, Schuller would travel for undergraduate and seminary training three states to the east to Holland, Michigan—the site of another Dutch Reformed enclave that looked, in many ways, not much different from the one in northwest Iowa. Located on the eastern shore of Lake Michigan, Holland—and the bigger city of Grand Rapids, just thirty-five miles to the northeast—functioned as an intellectual center of Dutch Reformed

---

50. Nicholas Wolterstorff, "The Grace That Shaped My Life," in *Finding God at Harvard*, ed. Kelly K. Monroe (Grand Rapids: Zondervan, 1996), 150–51, quoted by Kimon Howland Sargeant, *Seeker Churches: Promoting Traditional Religion in a Nontraditional Way* (New Brunswick, NJ: Rutgers University Press, 2000), 3.

38   CHAPTER 2

culture in North America. Traversing to Michigan represented a necessary step toward leadership, and the city of Holland seemed positively
cosmopolitan compared to Alton. It opened his world.[51]

Hope College—Expanding the Tradition

When Schuller's parents balked at the financial implications of college tuition, his older sister Margaret stepped in with the offer to pay it
with funds drawn from her teacher's salary.[52] The subsidy from Margaret allowed a sixteen-year-old Schuller to leave Iowa in 1943 and begin
his studies at Hope College. Schuller reported his thoughts as he drove
away from the farm, recalling that he clearly relished the opportunity
to escape rural Iowa: "I smiled as we sped past the endless rows of corn.
I would never again live at the end of a dead-end road."[53]

Just the drive to Holland, however, challenged his provincialism.
As he neared Chicago, Schuller was scandalized by the many Lutheran,
Methodist, Episcopal, Pentecostal, and Catholic churches he saw. He had
been taught that anything outside the Reformed tradition would likely
be best categorized as a "cult." How could it be, then, that so many people
could be so deluded? After all, many of the cult churches dwarfed those
scattered around Sioux County, Iowa. He had caught his first glimpse of
the vastness of the competition that existed within the church marketplace. Schuller began to realize that perhaps the demands for evangelism
remained more pressing than he could have imagined.

After a quick stop in Chicago for a burger at a coffee shop (located
tantalizingly close to a movie theater that seemed to beckon—but had
he indicated any desire to enter the establishment, it likely would have
been a moral breach), Schuller arrived on campus in Holland in the
late afternoon. Presenting himself to an administrative assistant who
asked his name, "Harold," for the first time, indicated that he preferred
"Robert"—a symbolic departure from his Iowa farm roots being "Mama's

51. Nason and Nason, *Robert Schuller*, 26.
52. Schuller, *My Journey*, 81.
53. Schuller, *My Journey*, 86.

boy" (the change from "Skuller" to "Shooler" would come later).[54] Schuller had taken a significant step in crafting a new identity.

Soon after arrival at Hope, Schuller learned that his brother, Henry, had been drafted into the wartime military. Concerned about having two sons involved in the war effort, his mother urged Schuller to explore a clerical deferment—likely a stretch, but she thought that as an undergraduate student *interested* in ministry, her younger son could avoid military service. For his part, Schuller explained that as fellow male students disappeared around campus as part of the war effort, he felt like he might be the only man in the United States not getting ready to wear a uniform. While convalescing from a burn suffered from boiling water while filling coffee pots in Hope's cafeteria (his student-work job), Schuller wondered whether he should abandon his ministerial goals and just join the military. But he knew his mother would object.

Eventually acquiescing to his mom and settling on applying for deferment, Schuller still needed the president of Hope, Willard Wichers, to sign off on the paperwork. Having not earned any special attention from his professors, the rural Iowan had failed to register as an extraordinary student for whom the president typically reserved deferments. Despite his misgivings, Wichers signed the papers, and Schuller found himself freed to focus on his studies. His continued struggles in math and science failed to offer evidence of any singlemindedness.[55] On the other hand, Schuller thrived in classes related to speech, history, and psychology. He remembered one professor exclaiming, "Beginning is half done!"[56] The phrase would figure into Schuller's possibility-tinged ministry in the decades to come.

It was during this period of curricular intensity that Schuller gained a lifelong interest in psychology. He was transfixed by the way psychology would explain human behavior in ways unapproached by the historical theology in which Schuller had been bred. Questions about the ability of

54. Schuller, *My Journey*, 89.

55. In fact, Schuller himself reported that he only passed his first math class because the professor offered to change an F to an incomplete with a special arrangement that allowed him take a private test after six weeks of tutoring. Schuller eventually received his "hard-won D." Schuller, *My Journey*, 95.

56. Schuller, *My Journey*, 98.

40   CHAPTER 2

systematic Calvinist theology to explain *everything* began to percolate in the college student. His desire to integrate the insights from psychology and theology would emerge in convictions centered on helping others achieve their greatest human potential as loved children of God.

Perhaps most significantly, as Schuller finished his first year at Hope, he became convinced that his tribe of Dutch Reformed Calvinists had misinterpreted John Calvin. Rather than emphasizing the dismal depravity of human beings, Calvin's theology, in Schuller's interpretation, offered hope and joy: "Liberating humanity from a shaming, blaming, cowering Christianity, with its railing against the 'sin' of pride, and replacing that view with a God-inspired drive for self-worth."[57] He reported that though he failed to fully understand the scope, the seeds of a liberating notion of personal value and esteem that would become his life's work had been planted.

Schuller found himself reflecting on these themes while he worked to support himself. His parents could not offer much financial support to their college student, so he worked hard to earn money while at Hope—first on campus in the cafeteria, then in an elite women's club, and eventually at an exclusive summer resort near Lake Michigan. A good worker, he rose to busboy and, eventually, waiter. He also started to become more aware of his own socioeconomic status. Schuller struggled to eat well while maintaining his two-pack-a-day smoking habit (as already mentioned, smoking tobacco functioned as an acceptable custom among the Dutch Reformed at that time rather than as a stigmatized habit). A desperate Schuller would occasionally smoke leftover butts he found in hallway trash cans.[58] The juxtaposition of his debasement with the "stupendous" details club patrons demanded he follow through on never left Schuller. His eventual ministry would not overlook the minutiae.[59]

The financial vulnerability of the Schuller family became vivid when the tornado struck the farmstead while Robert visited over his summer break from college.[60] Within minutes, fierce winds removed every

---

57. Schuller, *My Journey*, 99.

58. Nason and Nason, *Robert Schuller*, 27–28, and Penner, *Goliath*, 55.

59. Nason and Nason, *Robert Schuller*, 27.

60. "Fierce Tornado Strikes Sioux County," *Alton (IA) Democrat*, June 22, 1944, https://tinyurl.com/6d63b5bn.

building right up from its foundation. Over two hundred trees were completely uprooted and taken into the sky. Farm animals were killed, and the whole of that summer's crop was wiped out.[61] The same storm system destroyed eight other local farms that day, and Schuller claimed that his would be the only family to rebuild.[62] His father's commitment to reconstruct the family home after this disaster became an anchor in the shaping of Schuller's own identity.[63]

After the rebuild, Schuller returned to his studies in the late summer. And when the war ended in 1945, fellow male students flooded back to Holland and Hope's campus. Schuller found himself buoyed by the new camaraderie and took initiative to found the Arcadian Four, Hope's "unofficial" male quartet.[64] Always a performer, Schuller had again been invigorated by the reception when he sang two songs at his sister Margaret's wedding during the summer of 1946: "Oh, Promise Me" and "I Love You Truly."[65] Deciding that he wanted to expand the audience from churches in Michigan and Iowa, Schuller secured permission from the college president for the Arcadia Four to commence a musical tour from the Midwest to the Pacific during the summer. Driving from Wisconsin to Iowa to Nebraska to Colorado to California, the quartet received warm welcomes in every Dutch Reformed congregation they could stop at along the way. In fact, the visit from the Arcadian Four found mention in the *Alton Democrat*, Schuller's hometown newspaper.[66]

A trip of a lifetime, seeing different churches while traveling hundreds of miles, the drive expanded Schuller's horizons further. Consistent with the general theme of his life story, Schuller's musical quartet experienced several difficulties on the long drive across the country. Yet these challenges served as yet another prelude to significance. When they all finally arrived in California, after numerous car calamities, Schuller

61. Penner, *Goliath*, 63, and Coleman, *Robert Schuller*, 24–26.

62. Nason and Nason, *Robert Schuller*, 32.

63. See the beginning of chapter 1.

64. Schuller, *My Journey*, 114.

65. "A. L. Reekers Weds Margaret Schuller," *Alton (IA) Democrat*, June 6, 1946, https://tinyurl.com/3pway89a.

66. "Orange City," *Alton (IA) Democrat*, December 4, 1947, https://tinyurl.com/36zcpkzp.

42 CHAPTER 2

reported that he felt a call. The Golden State felt like home, and Schuller claimed in his autobiography that he vowed to himself that one day he would return for good. He remembered saying, "Not now, but someday this is where I'll spend my life as a preacher."[67]

Western Theological Seminary—Refining the Ministry Tool Kit

A twenty-one-year-old Schuller graduated from Hope College in 1947. Remaining in Holland, he crossed the street to Western Theological Seminary (WTS), one of two RCA seminaries in the United States. At the time, WTS remained "extremely orthodox, very conservative, ultra-Dutch, and small."[68] Dissatisfied with receiving "only" a professional certificate for his academic work, Schuller chose to write a thesis to upgrade his certification to a bachelor of divinity degree. He chose Calvin's four-volume *Institutes of the Christian Religion* as his subject matter. Schuller produced what he described as the "first topical and scriptural index of Calvin's magnum opus"—about which he would later claim that he received book contract offers.[69] The three-year project caused Schuller to grapple with "theological negativism versus theological positivism."[70] As a seminarian, he had begun wrestling with the theological tenets of Calvinism, and in accomplishing this work, he insisted that he had "found the gaps in Calvin's theology."[71] While Schuller took pride in the fact that the tradition starkly influenced so much of the modern economic world, he also began to lament the *perceived* dour nature of the religious tradition.[72] Schuller claimed that his careful work corrected deep misunderstandings in Calvinism, leading him to assert for the rest of his life that his pastoral views were not only theologically sound but also profoundly orthodox, more so than the views of the legion of pastors who failed to contend with the actual works of John Calvin.

67. Schuller, *My Journey*, 125, and Coleman, *Robert Schuller*, 37–38.
68. Nason and Nason, *Robert Schuller*, 33.
69. Interview, Robert Schuller and Dennis Voskuil, March 3, 1983, Dennis Voskuil Papers, Holland, MI.
70. Schuller, *My Journey*, 126.
71. Nason and Nason, *Robert Schuller*, 40.
72. Schuller and Voskuil interview.

As a seminarian, Schuller continued to forge his own unique theology. He became convinced that "negative extremists" from the Reformed tradition had misconstrued Calvin's suggestion of total depravity—fetishizing humiliation and conviction. As he reflected on the *dominees* he had heard throughout his childhood, Schuller began to see the promotion of condemnation as a problematic contest among preachers: "Any sermon that made every person feel guilty as hell was a great sermon." He decided his theology, instead, would be consequential not for the negative assertions but for messages of uplift and agency. In January 1948, Schuller visited his hometown and delivered a series of sermons over a week on the subject of prayer. The titles offered a sense of the seminarian's thinking at that point already: "Prayer Changes Things," "Things Wrought by Prayer," and "The Power of Prayer."[73] The early shoots of possibility thinking germinated.

Schuller summarized the core of his theological turn: "I would come to define sin as primarily a *condition* rather than an *action* (though that condition is often revealed in action); an inborn *absence of faith* more than a *turning from faith*." Schuller then deduced that he should use his eventual preaching to generate hope rather than guilt. With this, the seminarian decided he would focus on nurturing "positive thinkers" within his denomination—a middle ground that spurned what Schuller described as the "fundamentalists" who adored the law above all else and the "liberals" who expressed "shallow interpretations" of sin.[74]

As Schuller formulated his positive inflection of Calvin, he also gained exposure to charismatic figures outside the Reformed tradition. For example, he was assigned to conduct research on George Truett for a homiletics class. Not knowing about Truett or his place in American Christianity, Schuller felt inspired to learn more about the young Baptist minister who had grown a small congregation in Dallas, Texas, into one of the largest churches in the world. Still somewhat shackled by Calvinist guilt, Schuller wrestled with the pride that might be associated with his dream to be a charismatic pastor at a "trophy church" (his term) like

73. "Orange City," *Alton (IA) Democrat*, January 15, 1948, https://tinyurl.com/2s3nt657.

74. Schuller, *My Journey*, 126–28.

CHAPTER 2

Truett's. He later described himself as a seminarian "with a lot of ambi-tion." He went on, "That is, I had a lot of drive. Which meant I wanted to do something great in my lifetime," a desire that could be "potentially dangerous."[75] Schuller grew concerned that such a heavy charge would lead him into a poisonous career marked with the vices of jealousy and opportunism.[76]

Indeed, midway through his divinity training, Schuller got caught up in the cutthroat world—so it seemed to him—of seminarian competi-tion. In the coffee shops around Holland, he overheard "new ministers competing against each other" in their conversations and began to sense "professional jealousy."[77] Though wary, Schuller felt compelled to join the competition. As a sign of his preaching bona fides, during the sum-mer of 1949, Schuller secured a position as "student preacher" at an RCA church up the road from WTS in Spring Lake, Michigan.[78] He seemed to have separated himself from the pack. Further confirmation arrived when Schuller received the 1950 George Nathan Makely sermon delivery first prize at WTS.[79] Yet, the campus roiled with covetousness as other competent young men sought calls to high-profile, affluent congrega-tions. Though appalled by the crass careerism he saw, Schuller admitted that ambition and clear signs of personal achievement had been strong motivators for him. The realization cut against his desire for humble and noble animation—and "scared the hell out of him."[80] Schuller forged a compromise that he had witnessed in Truett: he would "look for a small church in a big city—a venue where there'd be lots of folk who needed divine forgiveness and assistance in dealing with 'life's realities' in a posi-tive thinking way."[81] Though not clearly expressed, Schuller's calculation seemed obvious: a small church had nowhere to go but toward growth,

---

75. "Tom Snyder Interview," 1976, transcript, folder "Crystal Cathedral Robert H. Schuller—Interviews, 1976," box 26, Robert H. Schuller Collection, H93-1188, Hope College Archives and Special Collections.

76. Schuller, *My Journey*, 130.

77. "Tom Snyder Interview."

78. "Orange City," *Alton (IA) Democrat*, July 21, 1949, https://tinyurl.com/2kkskjx4.

79. "Orange City," *Alton (IA) Democrat*, June 1, 1950, https://tinyurl.com/2w2tbtty.

80. Nason and Nason, *Robert Schuller*, 34.

81. Schuller, *My Journey*, 131.

and the population density of an urban or suburban location allowed for more potential congregants in close proximity.

Navigating his own ambition, he unexpectedly encountered the preaching of Norman Vincent Peale. During his last year in seminary, Schuller was assigned to a field trip to Marble Collegiate Church in New York City—the oldest congregation in the RCA and pastored by the prominent Dr. Peale. The seminary professors, though, sent their students not to emulate Peale, the highest-profile minister in the denomination. Instead, they suggested that the pastor be assessed as a case study in how to *not* deliver a Reformed sermon. After all, Peale's sermons with titles like "Formula for Efficiency" and "Science of a Satisfying Life" had little resonance with the Dutch Reformed in the Great Lakes area.[82] Within and outside the RCA, Christian leaders worried about the notorious Peale's "cult of reassurance" and "syrupy" sermons.[83] Indeed, "the purists in the Reformed Church did not approve of Peale's low-demand approach and regularly criticized the shallow state of American religion" that it nurtured.[84] To that end, around the WTS, the knowing quip suggested that while "Paul was appealing, Peale was appalling."[85] Peale, of course, had never attended a Reformed seminary and, thus, proved a sizable and easy target. (His Methodist background notwithstanding, Marble Collegiate had been attracted to Peale's profile as host of the radio program *The Art of Living*.)

With only a class obligation to complete an assignment motivating him, Schuller and a handful of seminarians piled in a car for the trip east to experience Peale's preaching for themselves. In an auditorium with a crowd of three thousand, sure enough, Schuller found himself underwhelmed by Peale's presentation. The seminarian described it as "melodramatic," lacking "intellectual rigor," and bereft of "theological profundity."[86] As disillusioned as he was, Schuller noted that the audience seemed to love it—laughing, crying, and listening intently. Confused by

82. Christopher Lane, *Surge of Piety: Norman Vincent Peale and the Remaking of American Religious Life* (New Haven: Yale University Press, 2016), 81.

83. Lane, *Surge of Piety*, 91.

84. Japinga, *Loyalty and Loss*, 59.

85. Schuller, *My Journey*, 141.

86. Schuller, *My Journey*, 141.

the warm reception, the seminarian returned to Holland mocking Peale by stalking the dormitory halls, wildly swinging his arms and modulating his voice with enthusiastic exaggeration.

While still in seminary, Schuller had not yet embraced the church as participating in a broader marketplace. Peale's success appeared to be due to idiosyncrasies in performance that appeared unnecessary, even silly. But once Schuller saw Peale's church as one of many competing institutions and began to assess how this New York pastor had successfully attracted a steady stream of members who were, themselves, pulled by various pressures to and fro in their busy lives, then the young minister started to consciously calculate how he might forge his own pastoral path. In his autobiography, Schuller confessed that he had no idea at the time that Peale represented his future.[87]

87. Schuller, *My Journey*, 142.

3

COMMITMENTS—MARRIAGE AND MINISTRY

Unsurprisingly, Schuller met his future wife in church. During summer break after his first year at WTS, Schuller received an invitation to preach at Sunday afternoon service at Newkirk Reformed Church. The regional paper indicated that a "large audience" had turned out for the local boy—including one Arvella DeHaan.[1] Though Arvella was the younger sister of one of his longtime friends, Schuller noted her in a new way when she served as the organist for the service. The seminarian admitted to being distracted by the attractive organist while leading worship. She, on the other hand, initially found nothing remarkable about Schuller.[2] Nevertheless, and quite transfixed, Schuller followed Arvella into Newkirk the next day and asked if she would be his guest the following Sunday when he preached at another church in the area.[3] When Arvella consented, the couple had their first date—although she did offer a critique of his preaching that second Sunday, telling him, "Now that's one sermon out of left field. I don't think you'll want to preach it again."[4] Not overly offended by her assessment, Schuller asked Arvella on a more conventional date to a movie (perhaps a sign that college life

---

1. "Newkirk," *Alton (IA) Democrat*, May 27, 1948, https://tinyurl.com/upav3ywv.

2. James Penner, *Goliath: The Life of Robert Schuller* (Anaheim, CA: New Hope Publishing, 1992), 75, and Sheila Schuller Coleman, *Robert Schuller: My Father and My Friend* (Milwaukee: Ideals Publishing Corp., 1980), 33-35.

3. Robert H. Schuller, *My Journey: From an Iowa Farm to a Cathedral of Dreams* (San Francisco: HarperOne, 2001), 134-38.

4. Robert H. Schuller, *My Journey*, 139.

48   CHAPTER 3

had allowed him to reconsider the sinfulness of the cinema?) the next night, and after that, he wrote his best friend from Hope College that he felt sure he had met his wife.[5]

After Arvella permitted the seminarian to write her, Schuller initiated a steady stream of romantic missives from West Michigan to northwest Iowa. The letters from Schuller came with such frequency that Arvella's mother once wondered aloud, "Don't they have girls in Holland, Michigan?"[6] He even took the precaution of writing his letters in Dutch so that her brothers and sisters would not be able to read them.[7] Whenever back in Iowa, Schuller made sure to spend as much time as possible with Arvella—but he spent most of the year hundreds of miles away in Michigan.[8] After a number of months, a smitten Schuller could no longer endure their separation. Unable to resist, he made plans to steal away from the seminary while the president was away traveling to ask Arvella to marry him. Upon his surprise arrival, Schuller found Arvella at the church practicing the organ. He invited her for a walk to the banks of the Floyd River—the same water that crossed through his family farm. Arvella accepted his proposal for marriage.

Schuller's elation at being engaged was soon tempered by the president of the seminary when he discovered that one of his students had left campus without permission—a serious breach of student conduct in the late 1940s. The delinquency left Schuller confined to his dorm room and initiated a review by the board of trustees. Twice over a two-week period, the seminary president convened student body assemblies to scold Schuller (and the friend who had driven him to Iowa) for "ditching class." Finally, three weeks into this punishment, Schuller saw an opportunity and scheduled himself to lead chapel. He offered a rhetorical prayer: "Today, we pray for Your blessings upon this chapel service, and ask Your forgiveness of our transgressions, as we forgive those who fail us. When we bury the hatchet, Lord, may we not keep the handle above

---

5. Michael Nason and Donna Nason, *Robert Schuller: The Inside Story* (Waco, TX: Word, 1983), 39, and Penner, *Goliath*, 76.

6. Penner, *Goliath*, 81.

7. Penner, *Goliath*, 38.

8. "Birthday Reunion at Rexwinkel's," *Alton (IA) Democrat*, June 2, 1949, https://tinyurl.com/72te2rdh.

COMMITMENTS—MARRIAGE AND MINISTRY   **49**

the ground." The prayer worked, and Schuller found himself forgiven by the president and permitted to complete his seminary studies.[9]

June a year later included a number of celebratory events—seminary commencement, a classical examination that allowed him to be officially called to a church, and multiple weddings. Shortly before their marriage, Arvella and Schuller celebrated with a bridal shower at her parents' home that included over fifty guests.[10] A week before the wedding, Schuller attended the nuptials of a seminary friend in South Dakota. During the ceremony, Schuller confessed to panicking about his decision to marry Arvella. As a soloist sang "I Surrender All," he described himself as "gripped with anxiety" as he realized that he could be on the cusp of a commitment to "surrender *all* [his] freedom and personhood for the rest of [his] life." Schuller spun into a mild depression. He confessed his misgivings to his mother after she noticed his dark mood. She convinced her son that big decisions almost always instigated cold feet—he should just move forward with faith. Buoyed by his mother's encouragement, Schuller overcame his last-minute reservations. Schuller and Arvella married near family and friends in Iowa.

He and Arvella began a sixty-four-year marriage in the church where both had been baptized as infants (Schuller's family had transferred local RCA congregations when he was a boy).[11] At this point, many of Schuller's milestones were compressed within a few days. His marriage to Arvella occurred one week after seminary graduation and one week before his ordination and installation as pastor of Ivanhoe RCA in suburban Chicago. The whirlwind month of June 1950 exhilarated Schuller: he graduated with the seminary's highest award for preaching and accepted a call to "a tiny, thirty-five member church," always remembering the lesson of Truett that it is much easier to grow a large church than to maintain one.[12]

Arvella would prove to be crucial for Schuller's ministry. She was not just the expected pastor's wife who lent him emotional support and

9. Penner, *Goliath*, 81–90.

10. "Orange City News," *Sioux Center (IA) News*, June 29, 1950, https://tinyurl.com/p3c69zyn.

11. Robert H. Schuller, *My Journey*, 146–50.

12. Robert H. Schuller, *My Journey*, 144–48; Penner, *Goliath*, 91–92; and Coleman, *Robert Schuller*, 36–41.

50 CHAPTER 3

mothered his children. As his most constant partner and intimate companion, she began by coleading the church's liturgy. She later developed the production mechanics of the television ministry and supervised much of expanding video and fund-raising activities. Michael Nason, Schuller's longtime assistant and confidant, remarked, "Arvella, she was the program director, and she's the one with tremendous skills in the music area, and a great sense of message."[13]

Crucially, she often reminded Schuller of his own convictions. More than offering moral support to her husband, Arvella reflected back to him his own "possibility thinking" in times when he felt deflated and dismayed, distressed and depressed, when the burdens of his projects were strained to the brink. Indeed, traced amid his own writings, Schuller revealed that his public image did not always conform to his private feelings. His wife often saw his tears first and lent quick assurance, saying things like, "Have a little faith, Bob."[14] A testimony of their togetherness through adversities is found at the start of Schuller's biography *Goliath*: "This is a love story. It is the true story of a man and a woman who overcame great obstacles and personal tragedy to realize their hopes and dreams."[15] It was Arvella who was most likely to encourage him, restoring the minister to his possibility thinking at key moments, thereby rescuing the ministry itself.

Ivanhoe RCA in Riverdale, Illinois

After a traditional Dutch Reformed wedding ceremony (eight o'clock on a Thursday evening) and reception—chicken sandwiches, punch, coffee, cake, and no dancing or alcohol in the church basement—the couple left for a short honeymoon in Minnesota before they ended the week by moving into their parsonage in the Chicago suburb of Riverdale.[16] A contingent, including Schuller's father and sister and brother-in-law, traveled from northwest Iowa to Chicago for the young minister's in-

---

13. Interview with Mulder, January 22, 2018.

14. Penner, *Goliath*, 125.

15. Penner, *Goliath*, 15.

16. Josie Harmelink, "Orange City News," *Sioux Center (IA) News*, June 22, 1950, https://tinyurl.com/m93fsxkw.

stallation at Ivanhoe.[17] Becoming an RCA *dominee* was an accomplishment to be proud of, and the unprecedented bus ride was worth it for the Schuller family.[18]

On the day of his installation at Ivanhoe Reformed Church, Schuller, alone in meditation and prayer, recalled Isaiah 58:12: "You shall be called the repairer of the breach and the restorer of paths to dwell in" (KJV). The young minister tingled and felt that God had given him his "biblical north star"—a verse that would shape his ministry. Later that morning, his former seminary professor looked at Schuller directly while delivering the sermon and challenged the new minister: "Robert Schuller! Go— and build a great church!"[19] The combination of verse and exhortation gave Schuller an optimism that he would have a significant ministry.

Overall, Schuller would have been hard pressed to find a better decade in which to become a pastor.[20] From 1945 to 1955, church membership in the United States rose from 70 million to 100 million—"Americans started going to church in record numbers."[21] That trend continued throughout the rest of the 1950s: while the US population grew at about 19 percent during the decade, the percentage of persons attending a church or synagogue increased by over 30 percent.[22] And they invested in their houses of worship. The amount of money spent on church construction rose from

17. "Orange City," *Alton (IA) Democrat*, June 29, 1950, https://tinyurl.com/y2v u377s. See also Josie Harmelink, "Orange City News," *Sioux Center (IA) News*, July 6, 1950, https://tinyurl.com/yjkpcccp.

18. Sheila Schuller Coleman intimated that it had been a hugely symbolic endeavor for Schuller's father to make the bus and cab trip to suburban Chicago: Grandpa "had never left Alton." See Coleman, *Robert Schuller*, 27-28.

19. Robert H. Schuller, *My Journey*, 155.

20. However, in the decades previous, the RCA had been a stagnant outlier when compared to other religious traditions. From 1927 to 1947, the RCA grew by 10 percent while Lutherans grew by 30 percent, Southern Baptists by 60 percent, and Assemblies of God by 374 percent. See Lynn Japinga, *Loyalty and Loss: The Reformed Church in America, 1945-1994* (Grand Rapids: Eerdmans, 2013), 24.

21. Frances FitzGerald, *The Evangelicals: The Struggle to Shape America* (New York: Simon & Schuster, 2017), 145.

22. James Hudnut-Beumler, *Looking for God in the Suburbs: The Religion of the American Dream and Its Critics, 1945-1965* (New Brunswick, NJ: Rutgers University Press, 1994), 33.

$400 million in 1950 to more than $1 billion in 1960. In short, "the 1950s witnessed the greatest church-building boom in American history."[23]

According to historian Frances FitzGerald, the increase in church growth had little to do with new methods or techniques: "This upsurge in churchgoing took place without the creativity, the enthusiasms, and chaos of previous periods of national revival. If it was a revival at all, it was a sedate, orderly, and respectable affair."[24] Fortuitously, Schuller entered into ministry at a time when the country seemed primed for a restrained and traditional model of church growth. Despite the manner in which his own denomination seemed to have plateaued in its growth (the RCA had not experienced growth like Lutherans or Baptists), the larger conditions fueled Schuller's optimism, even though these historically optimal circumstances would not persist, eventually necessitating new tactics.

The pastorate at Ivanhoe marked the beginning of what Schuller described as "the wonder years." However, in his first week at the church, he learned that bitter divisions wracked the little congregation. In fact, the congregation had recently been larger—the antipathy between members had caused it to dwindle in numbers. The vice chairman of the council reported that the rancor basically amounted to seventeen versus seventeen—he himself had remained neutral as number thirty-five, so that half of the church would not just up and leave. He counseled Schuller not to take sides and allow the congregation time to heal. The young minister settled on a strategy that would serve him well: recruit new members unencumbered by the congregation's history. Eventually, new members would outnumber the old members and bring fresh vitality.

In striving for new members, Schuller began to recruit in earnest, walking the surrounding neighborhoods, knocking on doors, and inviting families to worship at Ivanhoe. Success, though, proved difficult to measure, and he began to think in terms that would morph into a core conviction: "For the first time in many years I was living without the security of expert help from professors. I didn't have a grade or a test score to tell me where I was succeeding and where I was failing. For this feedback

23. Hudnut-Beumler, *Looking for God*, 37.
24. FitzGerald, *The Evangelicals*, 146.

I had to rely on the audience. If the congregation grew, I was succeeding. If it didn't grow—or, God forbid, if it went down in numbers—then I was failing."[25] Growth offered not only a goal; for Schuller, numerical growth became the dominant, sometimes the only, metric for measuring his success as a pastor. A market orientation was taking root.

Fear of Failure

Schuller began his professional ministry in 1950 in suburban Chicago in the midst of an American church attendance boom. Nevertheless, the early days of his first pastorate evoked fears of failure. And not because of lack of effort. Schuller practiced his sermon delivery to the minute every Saturday evening. He loaded the narrative with orthodox Calvinism. Despite meeting the apparent demands of weekly preaching, nothing seemed to register within the thinly attended sanctuary. Back in Iowa, the *dominee* received respect simply for his title and role—no matter how poor of a preacher or pastor he was, his credentials legitimated his authority and gravitas. Suburban Chicago failed to award young ministers the same fealty, and Schuller could not understand the consistent futility of his theological bona fides. Finally, over morning coffee, Arvella asked him who he sought to impress with his sermons: the congregation sitting there or the seminary professors back in Holland, Michigan?[26]

Arvella's question prompted the minister to realize that while he had won WTS's prize for preaching, the seminary had failed to teach him how to connect with his congregation. Schuller felt he had been offered few resources or strategies to win both the respect and the affection of his parishioners. He became disillusioned with his seminary education and questioned whether it had fully prepared him to pastor a congregation successfully. The theological arguments of the classroom seemed useless, leaving young ministers with barren tool kits for communicating with and relating to their congregants in a manner that caused them to truly *listen*.

While wrestling with these shortcomings, Schuller had somehow been added to Norman Vincent Peale's mailing list. Peale, the pastor of

25. Robert H. Schuller, *My Journey*, 159–63.
26. Robert H. Schuller, *My Journey*, 164.

54   CHAPTER 3

Marble Collegiate Church, a historic RCA congregation in Manhattan, famously promoted a psychology-infused Christianity. His 1952 book, *The Power of Positive Thinking*, remained on the nonfiction best-seller list for 186 weeks and, excepting the Bible, outsold every fiction and nonfiction book in the United States from 1953 to 1954.[27] Though Schuller had mocked Peale while in seminary, the innovative and newly employed young pastor took notice of the renowned clergyman from his own denomination.

Desperate to overcome his initial disdain for Peale, Schuller bought a copy of *The Power of Positive Thinking*—after all, he remembered how the New York City minister had really *connected* with his audience when he had visited Marble Collegiate as a seminarian. The young minister found himself disabused of his previous critiques of Peale, characterizing the effect of Peale's theories on his own theology and methodology of church work as nothing less than amazing: "What a contrast between the professors and Peale! Peale's words were therapy; professorial words were arguments. Peale's style, spirit, and substance were humble and helpful; classroom lectures were full of facts and theories, but they weren't inspirational or motivational. No wonder I was losing my audience!"[28]

Schuller began to take Peale's sermonic practices seriously—up to a point: "I certainly wasn't willing to become like Peale—flailing my arms and the like; I needed to retain at least some element of dignity."[29] But he did stop with the "heavy sermons" and started to "preach positive." He remembered his acting days from high school and began to develop a "dramatic persona" for the pulpit. In addition, in October 1950, Schuller began his foray into mass media when he accepted a position as announcer for *Temple Time*—an RCA radio broadcast that produced fifteen-minute "sacred programs" heard by listeners in Illinois and Iowa.[30]

One Sunday morning, off the cuff, Schuller exhorted his congregation to "find a need and fill it!" After the words left his mouth, the min-

---

27. Christopher Lane, *Surge of Piety: Norman Vincent Peale and the Remaking of American Religious Life* (New Haven: Yale University Press, 2016), 11.

28. Robert H. Schuller, *My Journey*, 170.

29. Robert H. Schuller, *My Journey*, 171.

30. "Name Rev. Schuller as Radio Announcer," *Alton (IA) Democrat*, October 12, 1950, https://tinyurl.com/35hea82c.

COMMITMENTS—MARRIAGE AND MINISTRY   **55**

ister realized that, yes, this sentiment represented his understanding of the secret to success. The words combined a market orientation with a moral compass, inspiring people for practical action in their everyday world. In the days that followed, Schuller decided to no longer preach to teach or convert people. Instead, he would encourage them as their "therapist" in the pulpit.[31]

Schuller's pastoral shift toward therapy occurred at the inception of the "psychological decade" of the twentieth century. World War II had given millions of Americans new exposure to the benefits of psychology and psychiatrists—and, after the war, demand for their services from the business sector soared. During the 1950s, Hollywood took notice and released dozens of films that featured psychology. Historian James Hudnut-Beumler noted that "As the postwar years went on, the public's fascination with psychology led to an increased interest in personal counseling and therapeutic psychology for the individual"—and that "How can I be happy?" became a much more pressing concern than "What must I do to be saved?"[32] Schuller would eventually seek Peale out as mentor and craft a West Coast blend of therapeutic Christianity that borrowed from positive thinking and morphed into the concepts of possibility thinking and the theology of self-esteem.

In addition to crafting a pulpit persona, the minister decided he needed to engage the community surrounding Ivanhoe with vigor.[33] Beyond Peale, Schuller had also been reading Dale Carnegie's *How to Win Friends and Influence People*. In another abrupt departure from his seminary stance, where Carnegie had been disdained by both professors and students, Schuller was distressed enough to take a fresh look at the popular volume. Intended for aspirational and public-facing businessmen, the book was part of a breed of advice manuals for those competing for success in the marketplace—and included elements of New Thought. And after reading the volume, the minister was convinced to shirk his tendency to want to argue with people about his Christian convictions. Instead, he focused on being polite and humble—and found that it sig-

31. Robert H. Schuller, *My Journey*, 171–72.
32. Hudnut-Beumler, *Looking for God*, 10.
33. Nason and Nason, *Robert Schuller*, 43.

56 CHAPTER 3

nificantly improved his "interactions with unchurched people."[34] He embraced the new posture with a "contagious" enthusiasm.

Advocates of New Thought, or "mentalism," insisted in their confidence that the correct—or positive—mental posture could change personal circumstances for the better. Like the deliberate synthesis of Christianity and capitalism, New Thought in the United States gained momentum in the post-Civil War era. Though not all practitioners identified as Christians, they all tended to assert that their belief could master misery and deliver bliss.[35] Mary Baker Eddy, founder of the Church of Christ, Scientist, became a well-known advocate. Eddy invented a "quasi-Christian pseudoscientific belief system" that advocated that pain and evil only existed in the mind—and these illusions could be overcome with a proper mentality. Eddy gained a following of more than one thousand churches within thirty years.[36]

After World War II, though, Peale's attractive repackaging of New Thought as "positive thinking" allowed it to saturate society to an unprecedented level. For example, multilevel marketing company Amway instructed its marketers to read one "positive thinking" book per month.[37] Whereas Peale made New Thought palatable to progressive mainline Protestants, Schuller's contribution resided in a theological authority that allowed him to promote the same synthesis to more conservative evangelical Christians. Schuller insisted that the gravitas of Calvinistic, Reformed theology "never washed out" in possibility thinking.[38] The assessment of a Congregational pastor from Berkeley, California, reflected the balance Schuller managed to capture in his amalgamation of Reformed Christianity and New Thought that eluded Peale: "I have never known Peale to grapple with atonement, grace, and justification."[39] Schuller, though, had completed a three-hundred-page index of Calvin's

---

34. Robert H. Schuller, *My Journey*, 170.

35. Kurt Andersen, *Fantasyland: How America Went Haywire; A 500-Year History* (New York: Random House, 2017), 79.

36. Andersen, *Fantasyland*, 79.

37. Stephen Butterfield, *Amway: The Cult of Free Enterprise* (Boston: South End, 1985), 100.

38. Interview with Dennis Voskuil, April 2017.

39. Browne Barr, "Finding the Good at Garden Grove," *Christian Century*, May 4, 1977, 426-27, https://www.religion-online.org/article/finding-the-good-at-garden -grove/.

Institutes of the Christian Religion, and therefore was deemed as "scarcely ignorant of the issues in Reformed theology."[40] Schuller himself did not quibble, noting that he had indeed learned from Peale but "taken it a step further" by developing a "systematic theology of self-esteem."[41]

With savvy mentalist-Christian leaders like Schuller, historian Kate Bowler argued that the exact scale of New Thought's social influence remains elusive for measurement because of its overwhelming pervasiveness.[42] The informal, grassroots nature of the movement allowed it to soak into society largely undetected. Indeed, there continues to exist an entire industry of "motivation" that relies on mentalism and positive attitudes.[43] Moreover, even United States presidents ranging from Ronald Reagan to Donald Trump have boldly articulated assumptions of New Thought.[44] In fact, both Schuller and Trump (who grew up in Manhattan's Marble Collegiate Church) shared Peale as mentor.

Christian mentalism, of course, became most potent when blended with the postwar blessing of the marketplace. Social theorist Christopher Lasch identified Peale as a key figure in indicating that positive thinking necessarily approved of the desire for wealth: "Success itself retained moral and social overtones, by virtue of its contribution to the sum of human comfort and progress."[45]

40. Barr, "Finding the Good," 426–27.

41. Marti Ayres, "Minister Rejects Idea of 'Electronic Church,'" *Holland (MI) Sentinel*, March 5, 1982, 3.

42. Kate Bowler, *Blessed: A History of the American Prosperity Gospel* (New York: Oxford University Press, 2013), 36.

43. Barbara Ehrenreich, *Bright-Sided: How Positive Thinking Is Undermining America* (New York: Picador, 2009), 97–122.

44. Donald Meyer, *The Positive Thinkers: Popular Religious Psychology from Mary Baker Eddy to Norman Vincent Peale and Ronald Reagan* (Middletown, CT: Wesleyan University Press, 1988). See also Mark T. Mulder and Gerardo Martí, "The President, the Pandemic, and the Limits of Positive Thinking," Religion News Service, March 30, 2020, https://tinyurl.com/342ac2uy. Regarding Reagan, sociologist Philip Gorski described the former president as anti-Augustinian in his denial of original sin and in his belief in the inherent goodness of humans. See *American Covenant: A History of Civil Religion from the Puritans to the Present* (Princeton: Princeton University Press, 2017), 177–78.

45. Christopher Lasch, *The Culture of Narcissism: American Life in an Age of Diminishing Expectations* (New York: Norton, 1979), 58.

58   CHAPTER 3

In addition to borrowing from Peale, Schuller also became more disciplined and organized in recruiting neighbors to Ivanhoe Reformed. He continued to go door to door and took a new approach to building a mailing list that reflected the probability of those he visited coming to his church. Adopting a rough measure of the likelihood of attendance, the ranking ranged from "A" (really good prospect, they said they would come to church) to "D" (not good, but keep them on the mailing list anyway). This small shift and strategic use of Carnegie's interactive advice, while adopting a new set of benchmarks that were better suited to his goals, fueled his optimism about new church visitors.

Schuller also demonstrated a knack for getting free newspaper publicity for his little church. When the trim on the parsonage needed painting, the minister arranged for two shifts of twenty men from the congregation to show up on Saturday to complete the task in one fell swoop. He also notified the local newspaper photographer to snap pictures at noon—the changing of shifts—when the full complement of forty painters would be on hand, so that Ivanhoe Reformed would be portrayed as a large, committed church (Schuller would use a similar strategy a few years later with cars and the parking lot of his drive-in church in Orange County, California).[46] Appearance mattered, and he employed strategic opportunities to broadcast a positive image of the church to potential visitors.

Only three years into his ministry in suburban Chicago, Schuller continued to demonstrate an intuition for marketing and mass media. In March 1953, his parents planned to visit. The young minister arranged for them to be interviewed on a Chicago-based radio program, *Welcome Travelers*. The Schullers retold the story of the 1944 tornado and the destruction of their farm. In compensation for their account, the couple received "silver service, an 8 ft. deep freezer, lounge chairs, and several other valuable gifts."[47] Schuller realized that the story offered him dra-

---

46. Nason and Nason, *Robert Schuller*, 43.

47. "Mr. and Mrs. Anthony Schuller on Radio Program Tell of 1944 Tornado," *Alton (IA) Democrat*, March 5, 1953, https://tinyurl.com/uj5t9xt8. *Welcome Travelers* eventually morphed into a television show. For more, see https://www.imdb.com/title/tt1753104/.

matic gravitas—and the radio program not only compensated his parents, it also offered him free advertising.

With Schuller's newfound approach to preaching and outreach, one that acknowledged that the church participated in a broader market of potential churchgoers, Ivanhoe began to outgrow its 150-seat sanctuary within two years of his arrival (during his four years, the congregation would grow to an eventual four hundred congregants).[48] One of his former seminary professors suggested Schuller contact Benjamin Franklin Olson, a renowned architect who happened to be located in Chicago. The minister made arrangements to meet the architect, though he confessed that he had no plan for raising the funds for what would likely be an elaborate and expensive design. Olson impressed upon the minister that architecture should never be limited by financial resources, giving Schuller a broader vision for how to expand his ministry. If the congregation could not raise the money from within, Schuller should broaden his financial base. How?

As Ivanhoe's pastor, he turned to a professional development office with a growing reputation among church leaders run by H. P. Demand (known as "High Power" Demand by local church pastors for his effectiveness).[49] Demand most certainly sophisticated the young minister in the means and messages for accessing considerable capital. After Demand demonstrated a deft touch in raising all the necessary funds for the church expansion, he also left Schuller a book written by J. Wallace Hamilton, a Methodist minister from Florida who wrote sermons "that turned a negative emotion into a positive energy force."[50] Moreover, the pastor surely took note that Hamilton preached at a drive-in church (something Schuller and Arvella had already experienced while visiting Spirit Lake on their honeymoon—a Lutheran pastor had delivered his sermon from the snack bar roof while his congregants sat in a dozen or so cars). Schuller admired Hamilton's multifaceted ingenuity.

The combination of Olson's encouragement and Demand's fundraising success allowed the minister to double the size of Ivanhoe's sanc-

---

48. Nason and Nason, *Robert Schuller*, 43.

49. C. James Strand, "Mt. Zion Lutheran Church: A History of Her First Fifty Years: 1946–1996" (unpublished manuscript, April 30, 1997), 14.

50. Robert H. Schuller, *My Journey*, 180.

60 CHAPTER 3

tuary, build a pretty brick parsonage across the street, *and* add the coup de grace: a proper steeple topped by a wooden cross. His modern church would feature the central symbol of a traditional building. Moreover, the dedication of the new edifice would be an *event* in the community.[51] Intuiting the value of free advertising, Schuller cast himself in the role of finish carpenter: he would attach the cross atop the steeple. In front of a gaggle of reporters—surely invited by the young minister himself—clicking their cameras, Schuller waved the cross "dramatically" as he rode up the crane to finally secure it, completing the successful construction project with a flourish.[52]

The practical demands of pastoral ministry, combined with Schuller's conviction that growth was a key measure of success, prodded the minister to continue his learning. Whatever successful urban pastoral ministry would be, he concluded that it could not be attained by the doctrinal correctness of his sermons or rote visits with parishioners or random encounters in the community. As he continued his ad hoc postseminary education, Schuller focused on the actual responses of people in his church. What messages would people come to hear? And what ministry projects inspired people to commit to giving? In short, what motivated people to regularly attend church and to generously give from their wealth? With continual support from Arvella, the informal tutelage of Schuller continued to open his eyes to the possibilities of new forms of church growth and management, with attention to expanding potential sources of capital.

A Growing Family . . .

While at Ivanhoe RCA, Arvella gave birth to two children: first Sheila and then Robert Jr. Arvella described her husband as initially "completely baffled by fatherhood."[53] The night that they came home from the hos-

---

51. *Alton (IA) Democrat*, January 14, 1954, https://tinyurl.com/eyvy2zwv.

52. Nason and Nason, *Robert Schuller*, 43.

53. Arvella Schuller, *The Positive Family: Possibility Thinking in the Christian Home* (Garden City, NY: Doubleday, 1982), 72. Hereafter, page references from this work will be given in parentheses in the text.

pital with Sheila, their firstborn, also served as the first opportunity for Schuller to fix dinner. It did not go well. He badly burned a hamburger and beans combination. Just as he muttered to himself, "this is enough to make a preacher cuss," the doorbell rang. There stood two RCA representatives stopping in for a meal and overnight lodging (a fairly typical occurrence in that era for Dutch Reformed travelers). Sensing (maybe smelling) the drama of a young couple adjusting to parenthood, the two visitors thought better of the bed and breakfast and excused themselves in under thirty minutes (72-73). Not every day represented a storybook for the young couple in Riverdale. In fact, Arvella remembered her husband having some "unfavorite" casseroles that she occasionally served for dinner. When that happened, Schuller typically asked his wife to ask the blessing—a positive strategy to make the "dinner hour into a happy time instead of a pouting, complaining hour" (18).

Amid the start of his pastorate and the growth of his family, change remained constant for the minister and his wife. It would be hard to illustrate the scope of the Schullers' lifestyle transformations better than when Arvella marveled that her family's first car had been a Model T Ford and yet in 1976 she had traveled at Mach 2 on the Concorde during a flight from Paris to Washington, DC (22-23). As the pace of societal change sped up, the shadow of Iowa agricultural life always loomed for the Schullers. Arvella's experience growing up on an Iowa farm had resembled aspects of *Little House on the Prairie*—the family cooked meals on a wood-burning stove, had no electricity until her teenage years, and used an outhouse for the toilet (22). Although changes would continue, Arvella sought to keep their home life consistent and to maintain a marriage that kept them together.

Arvella reminisced that acquaintances and friends often commented that the Schullers seemed to have a "super marriage." And while the couple embraced the notion (they freely shared methods and tips for successful marriages), they also argued that their "shared work" offered an extra dimension to their relationship that allowed it to flourish. Schuller, throughout his career, earnestly disclosed his love for and fidelity to his wife.[54] Even as Arvella discussed the nature of their marriage, she har-

---

54. See, for example, Robert H. Schuller, *God s Way to the Good Life* (Grand Rapids: Eerdmans, 1963), 71-79, and Coleman, *Robert Schuller*, 105-18.

62 CHAPTER 3

kened back to her early days in Iowa, noting a cooperative pattern of marital relationship that was characteristic of her own parents: "I first learned of team marriages as I watched my mother team up with Dad in the struggle to succeed on the farm in northwest Iowa. Year after year, season after season, crisis after crisis, they pulled together to make ends meet from the harvest of the crops. Together they milked the cows; together they planted the fields; together they struggled through freezing blizzards to keep their livestock alive; together they saved their pennies to buy the farm, to send their seven children to school."[55] Even the family rules outlined by Arvella traced back to the rural Midwest: "For instance, we have never given the children automatic allowances. Because my husband and I grew up in a farming community in Iowa, we were conditioned in the 'no work, no eat' philosophy which we both feel is a healthy, highly motivating attitude."[56] Their shared background on these family farms seems to have given them both a ready consensus on expectations for their family responsibilities.

Indeed, the image of the family farm became fundamental. Although household chores did not revolve around a barnyard, Arvella readily accepted that she had work to do beyond parenting responsibilities. She would accommodate herself to roles within what became in their lives the new family farm, which was their church. The careful and long-term cultivation of people, programs, and building projects would consume them both. In accomplishing this congregational work together, Arvella consistently gave evidence of her "team marriage" with her husband. She would come to say that the couple's career goals had "melted together."[57] The scope of ministerial activity generated and managed between the two of them was considerable. With so much overlap in their respective work, they had "so much to talk about" that they were "seldom bored with each other." Beyond that, the enmeshment of careers ensured that neither would "brood and wonder about the secret details of the other's eight-to-five world."[58] The partnership would last all their lives together.

---

55. Arvella Schuller, *The Positive Family*, 68.
56. Arvella Schuller, *The Positive Family*, 79.
57. Arvella Schuller, *The Positive Family*, 67.
58. Arvella Schuller, *The Positive Family*, 67.

. . . And a Growing Restlessness

The couple's shared vision would prove pivotal as both began to feel disillusioned by the congregational life and financial constraints at Ivanhoe Reformed. After more than four years in suburban Chicago, Schuller had a daughter, a son, a new addition on the church, and a congregation of over four hundred members.[59] And the ministry had gained attention: in 1955, Schuller appeared on *Church of the Air* (a nondenominational radio broadcast) on CBS.[60] Both the family and the ministry had grown significantly. And yet the minister continued to draw only his original $200-a-month salary. When he told a trusted elder that the family occasionally had money for milk only because Schuller's mother still included $5 bills in her letters, the elder assuaged his minister by assuring him that he would recommend a "good raise" in the next year's budget. True to his word, the elder did recommend—and it passed unanimously—an increase in pay for Schuller. However, the $20 per month represented much less than the minister had expected. A disappointed Schuller began to feel pangs of disquiet—perhaps he would not remain at Ivanhoe Reformed and retire from the church in his old age.

In his autobiography, Schuller opined that the inadequate raise played a key role in his being receptive to a new ministerial call elsewhere. He felt that the growth of the church over his four and a half years there and the successful fund-raising for the new addition had earned a much more significant raise. Moreover, the scant increase should not have occurred only after a reluctant revealing of financial insufficiency in conversation with a lay leader. The motion for the raise passed unanimously—but only because Schuller did not have voting rights during that meeting. Were he able to vote, the minister would have registered a no to the salary increase in order to protest the miserliness of the church. The vote that evening represented a watershed disruption of his affinity for Ivanhoe:

59. Letter from Robert H. Schuller to Members and Friends of Ivanhoe Reformed Church, n.d., Robert H. Schuller Correspondence, Robert H. Schuller/Crystal Cathedral, box 30, Hope College Archives and Special Collections, Holland, MI (hereafter cited as HCASC).

60. "Orange City Oracle," *Alton (IA) Democrat*, September 1, 1955, https://tinyurl.com/ycku5fce.

64   CHAPTER 3

"The deep bond that I felt for this parish, the bond that had connected me with passion and enthusiasm to this church, suddenly and completely unraveled. I left the building that night completely disappointed."[61]

The minister's disillusionment with his congregation manifested in a public scolding. In a Sunday morning sermon, the minister told his Ivanhoe congregation that they would "get out of the church what they put into it." The minister seemed to indicate that investment in church could be understood as a calculated exchange. In his message, Schuller elaborated that "the people who get a lot out of the church are the folks who put a lot of their time, talent, tithe, interest, attention, concern into the church."[62] On the surface, Schuller's comments appeared to be an encouragement for congregants to live up to the church's vision. Although Schuller found the stinginess of the congregation affecting his own welfare, surely he read into their lack of commitment to him a lack of commitment to the broader possibilities of the church's future. In short, despite the undeniable growth and expansion of the church, their failure to support his efforts made visible their lack of will to invest even more fully in his leadership to achieve an even more ambitious future for their church. The minister had clearly grown perturbed by the limitations of growing the Ivanhoe church in Riverdale.

Schuller's disquiet in suburban Chicago set the stage for receiving a phone call from a representative of Classis California (the denominational organization comprised of RCA congregations in the state) asking the minister whether he would consider moving to Orange County to start a church. The denomination saw potential in the growing area and noted that "a guy by the name of Walt Disney is building a theme park just a few miles away."[63] Schuller initially balked—he had two young children, and a move to the West Coast could be unmooring: it would take the kids, he wrote, "away from our solid midwestern family roots to an area of the country that had a reputation for glitz and glamour rather than the solid moral, ethical, and spiritual values into which Arvella and I had been born, by which we had lived, and to which we were com-

---

61. Robert H. Schuller, *My Journey*, 184.
62. Robert H. Schuller, "Profitable Living," Ivanhoe RCA sermon text, n.d , CC-Correspondence, Robert H. Schuller/Crystal Cathedral.
63. Robert H. Schuller, *My Journey*, 185.

mitted."[64] The minister also seemed concerned about the moral values of Californians compared to his own.

He skeptically accepted a train ticket from one of his Ivanhoe congregants to at least visit Garden Grove. In the middle of January, the warmth and color of California enticed Schuller. Upon realizing that the area seemed ripe for the development of one of "the greatest churches in the world," Schuller arrived back in suburban Chicago with a changed outlook. Arvella, though she had reservations about the move, could tell from the look in her husband's eyes that they would be accepting the call.[65] Already in late January 1955, Schuller told his parents he would be accepting the call to Garden Grove—and they, in turn, ensured that the local paper in Iowa also made the announcement.[66] At the same time, the Schullers informed the congregation and began to plan for the move.

Although Schuller never intimated that he felt constrained by the social expectations of ministry at Ivanhoe, a church located near the center of gravity for the Dutch Reformed communities in the United States, one eventual copastor at the Crystal Cathedral remarked that "Bob was too progressive for the Midwest." In retrospect, Schuller's ability to remain in good standing with his congregation in Riverdale, Illinois, likely had limited shelf life. Moreover, the call from Classis California represented an undeniably good opportunity to experiment with his evolving ecclesiology.

With the benefit of hindsight, the decision to move to California represented yet another pivotal point in Schuller's ministry. Most calls for an RCA pastor have a stable congregation waiting. Not so in Orange County. The minister would have to grow his own church. Schuller himself reported, "I won't have a group of people to welcome me there."[67] How do you build a Dutch Reformed church when there are no Dutch Reformed people in the area? How do you create a need for a market that does not yet exist? Answering these questions would prompt the ecclesial philosophy that would come to characterize Robert H. Schuller for the rest of his life.

---

64. Robert H. Schuller, *My Journey*, 185.

65. Robert H. Schuller, *My Journey*, 186, and Coleman, *Robert Schuller*, 41.

66. "About Town," *Alton (IA) Democrat*, January 27, 1955, https://tinyurl.com/35ha3b87.

67. Robert H. Schuller, *My Journey*, 191.

4

TAKING THE LESSONS OF CHICAGO
TO ORANGE COUNTY

Robert Schuller claimed that his desire to build as much as he did drew inspiration from a conversation with his father. As Schuller, Arvella, and the two young kids drove to their new ministry assignment in Southern California, they stopped in Iowa for two weeks to visit family.[1] Surveying the acreage as he strolled with his father on the family farm, the minister noted a new grove of apple trees. They walked the lane together, and Schuller wondered out loud to his father why he had bothered to plant such small trees—after all, he probably would not live long enough to really enjoy the fruit. The elder Schuller responded, "We don't plant trees just for ourselves, but for those who come after us."[2]

Although the minister had an instinct to increase the size of his first congregation at Ivanhoe, he had been unable to articulate to himself why he found the task so compelling. Now it was suddenly obvious: What kind of church failed to plan to build and grow? With those apple saplings in mind, the minister reflected that he would follow his father's example. The goal to grow would revolve around those who come after us. He "would build a church, erect structures . . . creating a place of enduring beauty for future generations to enjoy."[3]

---

1. "About Town," *Alton (IA) Democrat*, February 24, 1955, https://tinyurl.com/2sy8rmtz.

2. Robert H. Schuller, *My Journey: From an Iowa Farm to a Cathedral of Dreams* (New York: HarperOne, 2001), 195.

3. Schuller, *My Journey*, 195.

By cultivating a vision centered on the future, the younger Schuller began to conceive of a legitimate rationale for why all churches *should* be about numerical growth. It was not merely for the pastor's ego or a collective awe of a spectacle; he would secure the enthusiasm of his members by directing their focus past pressing needs to a larger ambition of building their church's legacy. He would channel their efforts to erect durable structures of ministry characterized by a time-defying strength to draw and serve legions of families who were not yet there—because they simply had not yet arrived. Schuller understood this as a path for Christianity to endure the fickle winds of contemporary American society.

Crafting the Orange County Recipe

Even as Schuller worried that the tornado of fast-paced and unrelenting change would eventually leave pews empty, he became more expressive and confident in his conviction that churches must grow or they would inevitably perish. The minister intuited what, decades later, social theorist Hartmut Rosa would describe as "acceleration": an attribute of late modernity where the unrelenting pace of social change would result in more rapid cycles of obsolescence not only for individual organizations but also for whole institutions.[4] In a preemptive strike, the minister decided that church growth would provide a bulwark against acceleration.

As Schuller prepared a few days earlier to leave suburban Chicago for Orange County, he reflected on what he had learned during his five years at Ivanhoe. He found himself composing a list of individuals he should thank. Those he was grateful for included Dale Carnegie (for insights on winning the respect of the nonreligious), Norman Vincent Peale (for insights on delivering "messages that would witness, not preach"), and H. P. Demand (for insights on "how to raise money to achieve the highest level of artistic excellence without compromising for the sake of the bottom line").[5] The list of his influencers demonstrates how Schuller—already in suburban Chicago—had begun to deviate from the typical

---

4. See Hartmut Rosa, *Social Acceleration: A Theory of Modernity* (New York: Columbia University Press, 2013); Hartmut Rosa, *Resonance: A Sociology of Our Relationship to the World* (New York: Polity, 2019).

5. Schuller, *My Journey*, 188.

68 CHAPTER 4

patterns of ministers from his denomination. He would not be content to be the *dominee* of a small, stable RCA congregation within the denominational strongholds of the Midwest states. He would grow as large as he could and use the best methods available to achieve that growth.

Schuller's famous embrace of corporate techniques of strategic management and finance offered a key to his success. His acumen resided not in mere performance. Behind the easy smile of comfort and public presence of assurance, Schuller assiduously schemed, eventually organizing his congregation as a business firm, working financial, marketing, and other managerial angles to expand the infrastructure of his ministry. Long before he achieved nationwide stature—and the same month that he arrived in Garden Grove—Schuller reflected on his growth intuition and subsequent methodology, publishing an article in his denomination's magazine, the *Church Herald*. In this article, the minister foreshadowed his concerns that church growth rested on the ability to read a local context, asserting, "If you want to be successful you must have a proper understanding of your environment. An honest evaluation of the school, the community, and the country will reveal points of strength and areas of weakness."[6] He pursued expansion as a means to stability, and the Orange County ministry's unrelenting focus on growth would eventually outstrip the contextual concerns for which the younger version of the minister offered caution. Although he initially suggested the crucial significance of careful empirical assessment of local social patterns, over the years, Schuller pivoted to delivering a continual series of sure-fire techniques and insisted that his strategies had applicability *anywhere*.

Sensing what was coming and perhaps anxious that other clergy failed to understand the stakes, the minister lamented that some churches simply had no desire to grow. Indeed, a primary obstacle to church growth was what Schuller labeled "entrenched lay leadership." The minister would eventually become convinced that certain lay leaders feared losing their positions of power within the congregation if the congregation would "win the dynamic leaders in their community."[7] These lay leaders

6. Robert H. Schuller, "What's Wrong with the World?" *Church Herald*, February 11, 1955, 16, 23.

7. Robert H. Schuller, *Your Church Has a Fantastic Future! A Possibility Thinker's Guide to a Successful Church* (Ventura, CA: Regal Books, 1986), 165.

relished their positions of power—being big fish in a small pond. In his advice to fellow pastors, Schuller seemed preoccupied with lay leaders who threatened the vibrancy of a congregation with their selfish motivations to retain a modicum of influence.

In his first published guide to pastors, the minister offered an anecdote as a caution against making congregational ministry dependent on lay leadership:

> I think of one particular congregation represented in our files of hundreds of churches whose pastors have come through our Institute for Successful Church Leadership. Let's call this the Case of Church 127. Located in the suburb of a great midwestern city, this church organized with 43 charter members. A church board was formed with 12 officers—elders, deacons, and trustees. Not a single one of these 12 men had ever been a member of a decision-making, policy-setting board of directors before. Not a single one among this group demonstrated anything higher than a notch above failure in private life.
>
> Now suddenly, the power of this church was in the hands of 12 men who felt strangely and powerfully important. But they lacked the vision, imagination, courage, and determination that makes for qualified and dynamic leadership. Because they were both inexperienced and insecure, they were natural obstructionists to their young pastor. He enthusiastically won the interest of unchurched people who then attended his worship services, only to receive a cold shoulder from the entrenched charter church board members.[8]

Note that excepting a few minor details, the vignette clearly rehearsed Schuller's personal history at Ivanhoe Reformed in Riverdale: the young minister served as the protagonist, hounded by an underwhelming, nonprofessional church board. As Schuller reflected on this and similar experiences, he became convinced that churches should not shy away from preferring professionalism over and above volunteerism. The minister saw potential attenders as savvy customers: "If I'm shopping for a shirt, I want to know that the store where I stop has the shirt I want—right

---

8. Schuller, *Your Church Has a Fantastic Future!*, 165–66.

70 CHAPTER 4

neck size, sleeve length and color."[9] Moreover, the church should aim to attract lay leaders with civic and other professional leadership experience who could effectively compete for influence over others, demonstrating their skill and sophistication at successfully participating in the power dynamics of the broader marketplace.

Despite the clarity of conviction conveyed in the coming years, as Schuller drove out to California in 1955, he offered little evidence that he had a plan to become a disruptive pastor who would affect the contours of much of American Christianity. Yes, he knew he wanted to build a grand, thriving church with a lot of members. But he also stopped at home in Iowa along the way and bought the most traditional of church instruments: an organ, purchased with a down payment of $400 (almost the entirety of a cash gift from Ivanhoe RCA) and a mortgage of $1,300.[10] The minister had an inkling that he had some creative ideas for church growth, but he still found himself desiring to implement more traditional markers of Christianity in the United States. He was still assessing the tools best suited to compete in a dense Christian market.

Arriving in a Religious Hothouse

Quite fortuitously, the Orange County that awaited Schuller presented a ripe context for his eventual amalgamation of old and new religious forms. The municipalities of Santa Ana, Garden Grove, and Anaheim merged indiscernibly—the county functioned as a centerless suburban landscape, with city after city immediately adjacent to one another. The newly constructed highways delivered a booming population of upwardly mobile professionals—businessmen, professors, doctors, and dentists—to all corners of the county within a twenty-minute drive. Federal spending drove much of the growth in Orange County—sharp increases in military expenditures catalyzed the regional "economy into frenetic state of ex-

---

9. George R. Plaegenz, "'Church with Big Parking Lot' Called a Necessity," *Memphis Press-Scimitar*, April 19, 1978, CC-News Clippings, Robert H. Schuller/Crystal Cathedral (hereafter cited as RHS/CC), box 29, Hope College Archives and Special Collections, Holland, MI (hereafter cited as HCASC).

10. Schuller, *My Journey*, 196–97.

pansion."[11] Historian Darren Dochuk described Orange County as a "cold war production center" that had the military-industrial complex "imprinted on its soul."[12] With all the spending and need for labor, Southern California represented a most desirable location to attempt to participate in the American Dream. And these mostly young, white, and upwardly mobile families ensured that they had churches to sanctify their newfound economic security. Coming from highly churched communities in the South and Midwest, these successful migrants "set about making sure that their churches' fortunes grew in sync with the advancements that had redefined their personal lives."[13]

Thus, the newly arrived Reverend Schuller had company: many ministers registered that Southern California represented a "new promised land" for any religious leader with a bit of entrepreneurial spirit. In fact, the raw population growth assured that new churches would be needed. In 1940, only 130,760 people lived in Orange County, but by 1960 that had surged to around 700,000 (a 385 percent increase).[14] The accumulating population mostly included white middle-class families with comfortable incomes. Historian Lisa McGirr indicated that churches offered a significant cultural contribution in the county—as grounding institutions, a congregation provided a sense of community, and incoming citizens gravitated toward them because of their own culturally conservative and religious upbringing. Every major denomination seemed to benefit from the influx of migrants. Between 1950 and 1960, six Episcopal churches increased to thirteen, Lutheran churches "more than quadrupled to thirty-five," Baptist churches grew from six to fifty-seven, and Assembly of God congregations went from two to thirteen.[15] Though he was slow to comprehend its rich fertility, Schuller would be entering a religious hothouse.

Where would he begin his own new congregation? As the Schuller family traveled the interstate highways toward California, the minister

11. Darren Dochuk, *From Bible Belt to Sunbelt: Plain-Folk Religion, Grassroots Politics, and the Rise of Evangelical Conservatism* (New York: Norton, 2011), 170.

12. Dochuk, *From Bible Belt to Sunbelt*, 170 and 171.

13. Dochuk, *From Bible Belt to Sunbelt*, 173–74.

14. Lisa McGirr, *Suburban Warriors: The Origins of the New American Right* (Princeton: Princeton University Press, 2001), 22, 43–48.

15. McGirr, *Suburban Warriors*, 48–49.

72   CHAPTER 4

passed the miles by ruminating over the fact that the RCA representatives had reported that it would be difficult, if not impossible, to find a suitable worship location in the Garden Grove area. Available spaces were already scooped up. Stopping at a diner in Albuquerque, New Mexico, Schuller crafted a list of ten possible venues on his napkin:

1. Rent a school building
2. Rent a masonic hall
3. Rent an empty warehouse
4. Rent a mortuary chapel
5. Rent an Elk's Lodge hall
6. Rent a theater
7. Rent the Seventh Day Adventist church (they'd be closed on Sundays)
8. Rent a Jewish synagogue (they'd be empty on Sundays too)
9. Rent a drive-in theater (shades of the Sunday morning church service on our honeymoon)
10. Rent an empty piece of ground—put up a tent like Oral Roberts does.[16]

Upon arrival, Schuller discovered California to be a good fit for his family. Though both he and Arvella found their tract house to be drab and underwhelming, they loved the weather. And even though the minister bit into his first avocado—assuming it was a pear—they soon learned to navigate the geography and culture of Orange County.

Local pastors, one Methodist and the other Presbyterian, met with Schuller and encouraged him that the region had proven to be generative for both of their churches: each had recently grown by about 150 members. An impressed Schuller soon realized, though, that the new members did not necessarily represent "church growth." Both pastors acknowledged that almost all their newcomers had already been members in their respective denominations. More than "church growth," the Methodist and Presbyterian records seemed to indicate more a "church reshuffling."

A bemused Schuller realized that the RCA simply did not have the membership numbers in California for him to duplicate what these two

16. Schuller, *My Journey*, 199–200.

TAKING THE LESSONS OF CHICAGO TO ORANGE COUNTY **73**

pastors had accomplished. He then had a revelation, which he described as the precursor to "a revolution in new-church development": he said to himself, "Bob, this town doesn't need a Reformed Church. What it needs is a positive-thinking mission that will meet the needs of the people here who don't go to any church!"[17] The minister was beginning to trace the outlines of an entirely new church market.

Even while Schuller discerned his target congregation of the un-churched, he still had no location to hold worship services. The minister would need some speedy legwork in Orange County to find a place for worship. The RCA representatives had been correct—Garden Grove had no suitable venues. Schuller found that in California, school buildings could not be rented for religious services. No Masonic or Elk Lodge halls were located in Garden Grove. No synagogues, either. And no movie theater. The Baptists beat him to the mortuary chapel, while the Pres-byterians had claimed the Seventh-day Adventist church. Competition was fierce, and he would have to become creative in establishing his own mission post.

An Unanticipated Innovation

If not for Arvella, the experiment at the drive-in might never have been attempted. In their kitchen, Schuller worked through his list of church-site possibilities and crossed off "drive-in theater" while chuckling to himself. Arvella asked her husband what was so funny. The despondent minister responded, "Nobody's going to come and listen to me preach in a drive-in." Unconvinced, Arvella challenged her husband: "What's wrong with a drive-in? We passed a big theater on the way to the house yesterday." She then flipped open the paper to show Schuller all the good movies being shown. The minister paused and reconsidered, "Well, I guess anything's worth a try."[18] Arvella then reminded her husband of their honeymoon outdoor worship experience and reminisced about farm life in Iowa: "There was something very special about worshipping

---

17. Schuller, *My Journey*, 205.

18. James Penner, *Goliath: The Life of Robert Schuller* (Anaheim, CA: New Hope Publishing, 1992), 104.

74   CHAPTER 4

God outdoors. I always felt nearest to God when I was bringing lunch to Dad out on the tractor or helping with the chores. The weather is so great here, and summer isn't too far away. I think it's a great idea!"[19]

Three miles away in Orange, California, Schuller stumbled upon his future church site. Encouraged by Arvella, Schuller approached the manager of the drive-in theater, Norman Miner, with his proposal for a Sunday morning worship service. After a week of consideration, Miner telephoned. "It's yours for ten dollars a Sunday," he said. "That's what I have to pay the union sound technician."[20] Though ad hoc drive-in churches had existed previously, historian Lisa McGirr declared that Schuller's Garden Grove Community Church represented the first permanent drive-in church in the world.[21] With a site secured, Schuller began his marketing campaign by using what became a reliable technique: posting an advertisement in the local paper: "On Sunday morning, March 27, 1955, Orange County's newest and most inspiring Protestant church will hold its first service at 11:00 A.M. in the Orange Drive-in Theater." The minister also plastered the area with posters inviting families to "attend Southern California's beautiful drive-in church. Held in the Orange Drive-in Theatre, Santa Ana Freeway (Highway 101) and Chapman Avenue." Perhaps most importantly, the ad promised a casual atmosphere: "worship as you are . . . in the family car."[22]

Before he held his first service at the drive-in theater, Schuller received what he described as "backlash." Indeed, even though "it was the height of the drive-in craze, worshipping at a windshield theater was a radical, potential heretical departure from sacred architectural norms."[23] An unnamed fellow RCA pastor dropped in and "lambasted" Schuller for having the temerity to hold a church service in a "passion pit."[24] "Devastated" by the critique, Schuller began to wonder whether he should re-

19. Schuller, *My Journey*, 206.
20. Schuller, *My Journey*, 206.
21. McGirr, *Suburban Warriors*, 105–6.
22. "The Story of a Dream, 1955–1979," n.d., Shepherd's Grove Church Archive, Irvine, CA (hereafter cited as SGCA).
23. Erica Robles-Anderson, "The Crystal Cathedral: Architecture for Mediated Congregation," *Public Culture* 24 no. 3 (2012): 580.
24. Schuller, *My Journey*, 208.

TAKING THE LESSONS OF CHICAGO TO ORANGE COUNTY **75**

consider. He likely still had time to back out. He even worried to Arvella, "I'm just not sure anybody's going to come. I don't know if people in Garden Grove are ready for a Dutch preacher from Iowa. In many ways, it's like a different country out here."[25] Indeed, an eventual copastor at the Crystal Cathedral who grew up in Orange County reminisced about being both intrigued and scandalized as a teenager when he heard about the drive-in church and decided to be adventurous and visit one Sunday morning. He recalled his cognitive dissonance: "I'd take girls over [to the drive-in] to date. You know, and you sit there with a little [speaker] on while you don't watch the movie, you kind of mess with your girl—and then to sit there on Sunday morning and have a worship service? I, I . . . let me put it this way: I struggled with it."[26] Even for younger folks, worshiping in a theater proved a disruptive notion.

While considering how to move forward, the minister and Arvella drove over an hour north to visit Hollywood Presbyterian Church and hear the preaching of Raymond Lindquist. Schuller found the morning to be providential. He received Lindquist's sermon, "God's Formula for Your Self-Confidence," like a "bolt from heaven."[27] Schuller interpreted the sermon as a communication from God to move forward with the radical plan for the drive-in. Buoyed by his newfound confidence, the minister went straight to the lumber yard the next Monday morning to purchase materials to build an altar and cross. He built a simple scaffold structure and placed it on top of the snack bar as background for his preaching. Although not a steeple, this minimal setup would serve to legitimate the site as a "real" church.

The Experiment Begins

Sociologists of religion understand congregational cultures as including accounts (the stories they tell and retell, the language they employ), activities (how they spend their time and energy), and artifacts (the

25. Penner, *Goliath*, 106.

26. As told to Mulder in an interview. For more on anonymous quotes, see "A Note on Sources."

27. Schuller, *My Journey*, 208.

76 CHAPTER 4

physical residue of their time together, the places they build, the props they use).[28] When Schuller acquiesced to holding his church services in a drive-in theater, the decision demanded a move away from traditional Christian congregational culture in the United States. Consider, first, accounts. Traditional RCA sermons focused on biblical exegesis and the catechisms. Not so for Schuller. Knowing that his audience no longer included Dutch farmers who had been through years of catechism classes, he would have to change the substance of the Christian story he told to fit the people he wanted to attract. The minister's first sermon at the drive-in, "Power for Successful Living," presciently pointed to the new direction Schuller would pursue in the next half century. Rather than scripturally based homilies, Schuller would offer macro-doses of spiritual therapy or counseling, fit for migrants facing a competitive and stressful marketplace.

In terms of activities, Schuller "borrowed" a choir for the first service from a local RCA congregation and specifically requested that each member arrive in a separate car—an attempt to make the theater lot appear full (nearly half of the hundred or so people in attendance were members of the guest choir). The minister also offered pointed directions in the bulletin for his audience/congregants (he obviously assumed that they would be unfamiliar with worship rituals in an atypical space): "Welcome to the first service of worship in the Orange Drive-in Theater. Remove the speaker and place it in your car, adjusting the volume as needed. Pray that God may bless the hour you spend here. Participate in your car. During prayer, bow your head; during the singing of hymns, join in the singing; during the sermon, listen and apply the vital truths to your own life. Return next week with friends and relatives. Thank you kindly."[29]

Arvella described that first worship service as risky and disruptive: "There was no stained-glass window, no gold cross, no props. Just a microphone and Bob standing alone on a sticky tarpaper roof. He had to dip into his own imagination and become an entertainer, an inspirer.

---

28. See Nancy T. Ammerman, "Culture and Identity in the Congregation," in *Studying Congregations: A New Handbook*, ed. Nancy T. Ammerman et al. (Nashville: Abingdon, 1998), 78–104.

29. Schuller, *My Journey*, 212–13.

Call it theatrical presence, and you won't be far wrong."[30] And at the end of the service, Schuller included in his benediction a practical warning: "Caution! Be sure that the speaker is returned to the rack before you drive away from the park stand." That first Sunday of worship, the corded speakers became a significant artifact in Schuller's new church. The disruption of accounts, activities, and artifacts portended the substantial shift that Schuller would contribute in his fledgling ministry in Orange County. Cultural historian Erica Robles-Anderson described how Schuller's ministry allowed both a sense of community and a connection while permitting private space: "Viewers were separated into subregions and yet connected through technologies that generated an overarching, albeit mediated, event in view. Every windshield framed the common scene. Speaker boxes, suspended from car doors, penetrated these semiprivate spaces with the broadcast of a soundtrack. The effect is simultaneous privatization and co-orientation."[31] Southern Californians could worship in community—but with a measure of privacy and anonymity.

Schuller's main concern for that first service, though, revolved around numbers. He had spent $110 on lumber and another $75 on a microphone compatible with the theater's sound system.[32] When the RCA pastor who had warned Schuller against using the "passion pit" called to confirm that the service had gone terribly wrong, he found, instead, a defiant colleague. Schuller challenged the contentious pastor: "How many more people did you have in church yesterday compared to the week before?" When the minister acknowledged a slight dip in attendance, Schuller struck: "I had a one hundred percent increase."[33] In truth, the drive-in service attracted a total of fifty cars, although twenty were driven by members of the borrowed choir. Still, the new church managed to collect $83.75 in the offering plates passed from car to car.

Schuller saw his drive-in church as a rationalization of worship in a car culture: "The same families in the drive-in church tend to park in the

30. Michael Nason and Donna Nason, *Robert Schuller: The Inside Story* (Waco, TX: Word, 1983), 51–52.
31. Robles-Anderson, "The Crystal Cathedral," 583.
32. Nason and Nason, *Robert Schuller*, 48.
33. Schuller, *My Journey*, 213.

78 CHAPTER 4

same spots every week. Windows are rolled down, heads nod greetings, and there is as much fellowship in worship at the drive-in as there is in the sanctuary—which is not very much!"[34] He also admitted that the drive-in nature of worship likely hindered intimacy and that he knew many congregants better by the make, model, and color of their car than by their faces.[35] Nevertheless, he confidently reported that much of what happened in a typical walk-in worship service could be replicated—with ingenuity—at a drive-in. Schuller would find ways to adapt the core experience of a church service to new circumstances. Every week Schuller attempted to reinterpret the theater infrastructure "to make the space legible as a church."[36] For instance, communion elements would be passed car to car. In the process of communicating expected churchly things, he also encouraged visitors and new members to reconsider church practices anew. This new church might not be able to compete with other, more established and more predictably routinized services, yet no other church could ever match the ability of members to personalize their own space, accommodate their desire for privacy, and individualize their participation.

An accident born out of scarcity of space became a design attuned to circumstance. Expectations of a traditional church would never be fully realized at the drive-in theater, yet new capacities and new opportunities for church engagement presented themselves. Schuller entered a dynamic religious market and forged a product characterized by its own distinctive merits.[37] More and more residents of Orange County became convinced, and on September 27, 1955, Schuller submitted papers to the California State Charter for Garden Grove Community Church (GGCC) to become formally organized. By that point, GGCC boasted 154 members.[38]

---

34. Robert H. Schuller, "The Drive-In Church—a Modern Technique of Outreach," *Reformed Review* 23, no. 22 (1969): 47.

35. Schuller, *My Journey*, 221.

36. Robles-Anderson, "The Crystal Cathedral," 580.

37. And Schuller acknowledged that he had always had an "intense interest" in "publicity and promotion" for the church. See Schuller to George Douma, February 27, 1959, "Crystal Cathedral Correspondence, 1956–1959," RHS/CC, box 4 (HCASC).

38. Schuller, *My Journey*, 216.

Schuller could not have found a more symbolically appropriate place to convene a worship service in 1955 America: a drive-in theater in the suburbs of Southern California. Postwar white American families saw the new developments on the outskirts of the core cities as idylls: they could reside in an ostensibly safer, more pastoral setting while having the amenities of the core city in reach—and soon enough, many of those resources and conveniences would also be relocated to the suburbs.[39] In short, they became "havens" for families who marked certain demographic boxes.[40] By the 1980s, more than 40 percent of the US population lived in suburbs like Garden Grove. In fact, the suburbs became such a dominant mode of American residential life that historian Kenneth Jackson described suburbia as "the quintessential physical achievement of the United States."[41] And as the built physicality of suburbia centered on the automobile, "a drive-in society" had manifested.[42]

It should be noted, though, that the suburban boom was not simply the result of personal preference or choice for middle-class white families—in fact, the impetus resided in policy and design. Local, state, and federal policies ushered certain families out of core cities and into suburbs.[43] For instance, the Interstate Highway Act of 1956 prioritized truck and private car transportation, thus making far-flung suburbs more accessible. Previous to that, the establishment of the Home Owners Loan Corporation by the federal government in 1933, an effort to protect homeownership, ultimately worked to fuel suburban relocation by undervaluing dense, demographically mixed (thin code for the presence of racial minorities), and aging neighborhoods through its rating system (often referred to as "redlining") that pushed and pulled white

39. Mark T. Mulder, *Shades of White Flight: Evangelical Congregations and Urban Departure* (New Brunswick, NJ: Rutgers University Press, 2015).

40. Kenneth T. Jackson, *Crabgrass Frontier: The Suburbanization of the United States* (New York: Oxford University Press, 1985), 3.

41. Jackson, *Crabgrass Frontier*, 4.

42. Jackson, *Crabgrass Frontier*, 263.

43. See Jessica Trounstine, *Segregated by Design: Local Politics and Inequality in American Cities* (New York: Cambridge University Press, 2018), and Richard Rothstein, *The Color of Law: A Forgotten History of How Our Government Segregated America* (New York: Norton, 2018).

80 CHAPTER 4

middle-class homeowners out of cities. Finally, the Federal Housing Administration (FHA) efforts to guarantee home loan mortgages effectively made it cheaper to own a home than to rent. Moreover, the FHA's 1939 *Underwriting Manual* cautioned against insuring projects in crowded neighborhoods with older properties. Again, in racially coded language, appraisers received warnings to be wary of "inferior and non-productive characteristics of the areas surrounding the site."[44] In short, if you had the means and the right demographic background, it made sense in postwar America to move to the suburbs—the government subsidized it.[45]

Though suburbanization occurred across the nation, Southern California "led the way in developing automobile suburbs."[46] The sunny suburbs of Orange County offered a stark contrast to the polluted, crowded city centers of the Rust Belt in the Midwest and on the East Coast. For families who could afford it, suburbia eventually became the normative option. Moreover, the nurturing of the nuclear family functioned as the fulcrum of suburban life: with growing anonymity, "families found that they had to turn inward to maintain their sense of community. They did this by purchasing single-family dwellings on large suburban lots in homogeneous neighborhoods. By doing so, middle-class white natives could avoid what they believed were the undesirable foreign ethnic groups that had begun immigrating to the United States in large numbers."[47] In other words, the suburban home became the "spatial center" and "cultural refuge."[48] Schuller's innovation that allowed the nuclear family to worship in the relative privacy of their car (an extension of the home) suited these folks very well.

A Plan for Growth

Even as Schuller challenged the conventional practices of congregational culture, he still felt compelled to pursue the markers of traditional church

44. Quoted by Jackson, *Crabgrass Frontier*, 207.

45. Jackson, *Crabgrass Frontier*, 190–218.

46. Scott L. Bottles, *Los Angeles and the Automobile: The Making of the Modern City* (Berkeley: University of California Press, 1987), 190.

47. Bottles, *Los Angeles and the Automobile*, 178–79.

48. Justin G. Wilford, *Sacred Subdivisions: The Postsuburban Transformation of American Evangelicalism* (New York: New York University Press, 2012), 166.

life. The novelty of the drive-in proved wearing on a week-to-week basis. Though the Schullers enjoyed the California weather compared to the extremes of Iowa, outdoor worship services remained susceptible to heat, rain, winds, and smoke from wildfires. The minister desired a more stable, robust edifice for his young church. About three miles west of the drive-in location, the RCA had purchased two acres of land for Schuller to build a traditional church. Classis California suggested to the minister that he consult with a local dairy farmer who had experience designing and constructing barns to create the architectural renderings. An appalled Schuller refused to entertain the possibility. He had learned in the Chicago suburbs to never compromise on design. He would not grow a successful West Coast church in the banality of a cattle shed.

Finding an architect who agreed to design the church on a payment plan, GGCC moved forward with construction. As the building rose from the ground, Schuller described the early days of personally seeking out new members who lived in the area:

> In my first year in California, I personally rang more than thirty-five hundred doorbells! I went door-to-door not only in Garden Grove, but also in the adjacent communities of Orange, Anaheim, and Santa Ana. When a person first greeted me, I always asked, "Are you an active member of a local church?" If the answer was yes, I encouraged him or her to stay with that church, expressed my thanks and left. I didn't want to take people away from their churches. Proselytizing of that sort was against my ethics as a member of the ministerial association. My goal was to reach people who had no church relationship.
>
> If the answer to my question was no, I asked, "What will you be looking for in any church you might decide to attend?" Depending on the person's response, I typically went on to ask two more questions to refine my understanding: "What would attract you to a church?" and "What might your spouse, your children, and other members of your family want to find in a church?"

As Schuller canvassed Orange County neighborhoods, the notions guiding seeker-sensitive, church-growth, and market-centered Christianity began to take form. Rather than suggesting to the residents that

82   CHAPTER 4

Christianity could transform their lives, Schuller instead cast a template in which his church could palatably fit into their established lifestyles: "I carried a yellow legal pad with me and wrote down every response. It was this information that guided me in developing programs as I ministered to our new and growing congregation."[49] Like a market researcher, Schuller framed a service to suit his desired clients.

Schuller grew convinced that quotes from the Bible would leave many of the people he met cold. What could he do? Schuller's training at WTS centered on Scripture and, thus, left him ill-prepared to grow a church for the people he encountered in Orange County. The minister came to believe that theological rigor would only hinder his ability to connect with potential congregants. Facing pressures from newly suburbanizing circumstances and exhaustion from their work, "They just wanted relief from their pain; they just needed inspiration to make it through the week."[50]

It did not take long for the drive-in congregation to find its financial footing, and Schuller eagerly asked the RCA's Board of Domestic Missions to remove GGCC from their list of "salary aided churches." The minister had no interest in the stigma of needing financial support from the denomination; his ministry claimed financial independence as soon as possible.[51] In a letter to the congregation, the minister described the newfound self-sufficiency as "[getting] off the relief rolls of the church."[52] Indeed, within just eighteen months of arriving in Garden Grove, Schuller celebrated dedication of the chapel, on September 23, 1956.[53] Though he received $4,000 from the denomination to buy the land, the minister took a risk and established credit by securing a bank loan of $70,000 to build a three-hundred-seat sanctuary.[54] Eager to preach to as many as possible, the minister would conduct services every Sunday morning—

49. Schuller, *My Journey*, 220.

50. Schuller, *My Journey*, 225.

51. Schuller to Richard Vanden Berg, August 8, 1956, CC-Correspondence, 1956–1959, RHS/CC, box 30 (HCASC).

52. Schuller to Garden Grove Community Church, October 4, 1956, CC-Correspondence, 1956–1959, RHS/CC, box 30 (HCASC).

53. Schuller, *My Journey*, 224.

54. Penner, *Goliath*, 119.

both at the drive-in and at the chapel. After just over two years in Orange County, Schuller's fledgling church had sufficient attendance to schedule three worship services per Sunday.[55] Moreover, the minister seemed to have a limitless imagination when considering the scale of automobile-oriented worship. At one point, he suggested "a ten-acre facility under domed glass at a major freeway interchange outside of Chicago, Illinois." The minister had considered the details: "Under this giant astrodome, in a climatized situation, people would worship in pew arrangements, but also in the privacy of their cars. The same would be true just outside of New York City."[56]

Schuller certainly enjoyed the accolades of being a *dominee* in exotic California. When he visited Iowa during the summer of 1958, a local paper noted that guests gathered at the Anthony Schuller house as "a courtesy" to the minister's family from out of state. Curiously, the article described Schuller as an RCA Church Extension board representative who "does double duty on Sunday in California, serving both his church at Garden Grove and preaching at a Drive-In center, six miles distant."[57] The vague, somewhat inaccurate description of Schuller's role in California betrayed that some in the family—Schuller himself? his father? his mother?—likely preferred that the faithful Dutch Reformed of northwest Iowa not know that Robert Schuller's congregation in California actually formed in the passion pit of a drive-in movie theater and obliquely mentioned the "Drive-In center" only in passing.

The Influence of Norman Vincent Peale

Marks of success arrived quickly in Schuller's new location. The minister planned for growth soon after his arrival in Southern California, and just two years into his drive-in ministry, he contacted the owner of Pacific Drive-In Theatres about planting another church at one of their

---

55. Schuller to Norman Vincent Peale, September 26, 1957, CC-Correspondence, RHS/CC, box 30 (HCASC).

56. Schuller, "The Drive-In Church," 50.

57. "Orange City News," *Sioux Center (IA) News*, May 8, 1958, https://tinyurl.com/37xykt54.

84 CHAPTER 4

other drive-ins.[58] A few months later, the minister estimated that four thousand individuals had attended GGCC's Easter Sunday service. That same year, Schuller accepted an invitation to preach at Norman Vincent Peale's Marble Collegiate Church in Manhattan.[59]

Though perhaps not entirely accurate, Schuller understood his young church as reaching non-Christians—or, as he described them, the "un-churched." In a 1957 letter to Peale's secretary, the younger minister described his congregation as coming "from every level of society. There will be young parents with their little babies, old people too feeble to walk into a traditional church, parents with children afflicted with crippling sickness, paraplegics with their wheelchairs in the back seat, besides hundreds who attend because they prefer the privacy of their cars. A large majority of the audience will be people who have never yet discovered the dynamic life that is possible through faith in Jesus Christ."[60] Even as he conceived of his audience as broadly as possible, Schuller clearly relished an opportunity to be affirmed by the fellow RCA pastor whom he now saw as a mentor.

The relationship between Peale and Schuller solidified when the famous New York minister flew to Orange County to guest-preach at the drive-in. As Schuller made the decision to move away from the Bible in his preaching, he realized that Peale had already pioneered a path that had "[blurred] the boundary between the religious and the secular."[61] Though Schuller surely saw Peale as a mentor, that deference did not stop him from strong-arming the Manhattan minister when he tried to back out of a commitment to preach at the drive-in during the summer of 1957. Word reached Schuller while on vacation in Alton, Iowa, in June, that Peale had expressed some reservations about making the cross-country trip. Schuller quickly wrote to Peale's secretary that the "senior advisors" at GGCC indicated their "unanimous opinion" that they attempt to carry

58. Schuller to William R. Forman, February 5, 1957, CC-Correspondence, RHS/CC, box 30 (HCASC).

59. Schuller to Doris Phillips, May 8, 1957, CC-Correspondence, RHS/CC, box 30 (HCASC).

60. Schuller to Phillips, June 3, 1957, CC-Correspondence, 1956–1959, RHS/CC, box 30 (HCASC).

61. Schuller, *My Journey*, 226.

out their published plans. "The community has already been excited by the first news release that Dr. Peale will be preaching." Maintaining the confident posture that Peale would keep the commitment, Schuller then asked that he forward the title for his sermon that Sunday morning.[62] Peale, indeed, relented and kept the commitment.

On June 30, 1957, Schuller received an inspirational glimpse of how celebrity could fill pews (or drive-in lots). Schuller made sure to let people know Peale would be speaking, and, following a pattern of intentional marketing, he took out an ad in the local newspaper. His appeal worked. Thirty minutes prior to the worship service, cars had already filled the drive-in lot. With families still streaming in, how would all have access to the speakers necessary for hearing the service? Schuller spoke over the sound system to ask any who had space in their vehicles to turn on their lights so that latecomers might join them, climbing inside their cars, to hear the service. In the end, the minister estimated that four thousand people showed up on that Sunday to hear Peale—in fact, the marquee advertised an intriguing sequence with its billing of two very different events at the drive-in: "To Hell and Back with Audie Murphy and Norman Vincent Peale in Person."[63]

Schuller expressed gratitude for the "dignity" the Manhattan pastor brought to the "open-air church" and characterized the day as the catalyst for a further metamorphosis.[64] He recalled that the New York City minister challenged the parking lot congregation to "change their thinking and believe that any human being can be anything he wants to be through the power of Jesus Christ."[65] Peale closed his sermon by asserting that Jesus had never called anyone a sinner. A dubious Schuller found himself later that day scouring his red-letter edition of the Bible to confirm that Peale had been incorrect. When he actually found verification, the minister claimed that he decided at that moment he needed to start preaching more like Jesus and less like Saint Paul. As Schuller recounted,

62. Schuller to Phillips, June 14, 1957, CC-Correspondence, RHS/CC, box 30 (HCASC).

63. Schuller, *My Journey*, 228.

64. Schuller to Peale, July 3, 1957, CC-Correspondence, RHS/CC, box 30 (HCASC).

65. Nason and Nason, *Robert Schuller*, 63.

86 CHAPTER 4

"I discovered that [Jesus] focused not on people's weaknesses, but on their strengths, not on their shortcomings but on their possibilities, not on their failures but on their successes."[66]

Schuller wrote to Peale in December 1957 (addressing him as "Norman" rather than "Dr. Peale" for the first time):

> And I cannot allow this fast flying year to pass without expressing my personal thanks to you for making this year the most exciting one of my life. I thank God that He has permitted our paths to cross so closely. Your most recent letter was a real encouragement. I am so honored to hear that you took the time to listen to a recording of my sermon. Your comments and compliments are a tremendous encouragement to me. For I felt my morning sermon was decidedly below par. I was overwhelmed by the importance of the assignment, but what a thrill it was to stand where you stand each Sunday and join in worship with such a historic congregation! And I had the wonderful feeling that I was in the midst of old friends. I shall be forever grateful to you for extending to me the privilege of preaching in the Marble Church. If, as you suggest, I have a great future, it will be due to the immeasurable inspiration I have received from contacts with you. May I ask for an autographed photo of yourself which I could hang in my office?[67]

The minister felt that Peale had invigorated a belief system that had been dormant within him for years—a sense that Christianity for the twentieth century could not focus on criticism if it wanted to convince new believers.[68] With that in mind, Schuller set to the task of nurturing a preaching style that would be "inclusive and inviting."[69] More than that, he decided to jettison the "reserved" style of RCA ministers in exchange for Peale's exaggerated gesticulating and dramatic body language—he had

---

66. Schuller, *My Journey*, 230.

67. Schuller to Peale, December 13, 1957, CC-Correspondence, RHS/CC, box 30 (HCASC).

68. Schuller, *My Journey*, 231.

69. Schuller, *My Journey*, 232.

come full circle from his mocking of Peale throughout the dormitory in Holland, Michigan. Even more, by 1957, Schuller had garnered enough stature to be invited to guest-preach in Peale's own pulpit at Marble Collegiate in Manhattan.[70] Moreover, the sermons must have been well received, as the minister found himself invited back the next two summers as well.[71]

The influence of Peale on Schuller demonstrated the minister's willingness to experiment and even change his methods—as long as he concluded that they were biblically consistent and theologically sound.[72] Over the years, the means he selected to achieve particular ends, like greater attendance in church services, would always be filtered through his own assessment of religious orthodoxy. Schuller was willing to switch tactics, but not for the sake of growth alone. His ministry would feature a thoughtful enactment of appropriately sensitive approaches that accommodated ecclesial structures to contemporary pastoral needs. The more confidently he articulated his approach to himself, the more bold he became in proclaiming his practices as a mandate to other pastors.

Bumps in the Road

Within months of Peale's visit, Schuller estimated that he typically preached to a combined 450 congregants between the drive-in and the recently completed chapel. But the minister also lamented the toll of driving (trailered organ and all) between the two venues every Sunday. Even the choir would chase themselves between the two locations, robes billowing out the car windows. And though the weather of Southern California typically cooperated, the minister also had Sundays where

70. Schuller to Phillips, April 30, 1959, CC-Correspondence, RHS/CC, box 30 (HCASC).

71. Schuller to Richard Kruizenga, May 7, 1958, and Schuller to Phillips, April 30, 1959, CC-Correspondence, RHS/CC, box 30 (HCASC). See also "Rev. Robert Schuller Will Preach at Marble Collegiate," *Alton (IA) Democrat*, July 16, 1959, https://tinyurl.com/bdhx5evy.

72. In fact, Schuller suggested that Peale should broadcast the Marble Collegiate worship services already in the late 1960s. See Schuller to Peale, January 26, 1968, CC-Correspondence, 1968–1973, box 32 (HCASC).

he preached in a raincoat under an umbrella.[73] The rushing about and vagaries of the weather wore on him. Schuller felt he had limited bandwidth and would not be able to continue serving both venues for much longer. To abandon one for the other, though, struck him as untenable. The minister felt restless.[74]

To mull over the next steps, the Schuller family retreated to Yosemite National Park on a camping trip. While the Schullers vacationed (though the details remain vague since accounts vary as to how much the minister knew about the search process),[75] an elder at GGCC, somehow, hired a recent seminary graduate as an associate pastor. Upon the family's return, a bewildered and chagrined Schuller met his new colleague. The situation worsened when he learned that the young pastor (who remained unnamed in Schuller's autobiography) described himself as a "fundamentalist"—a known epithet among the Dutch Reformed.

Soon, Schuller found himself in the midst of an attempted usurping of his position. His copastor suggested that Schuller limit himself to the drive-in while he would gladly lead services at the chapel: "People want the Bible, Schuller, not Possibility Thinking. . . . Go back to your drive-in church! Leave the Chapel to me."[76] Schuller demurred and informed his copastor that he had founded both and that in RCA polity he functioned as "the president of the corporation and the chairman of the board."[77] Undaunted by the assertion of authority, the copastor instigated secret meetings with congregational allies and pressed charges against Schuller to the RCA—asserting a failure to preach the gospel.

The minister suffered the humiliation of examination by RCA colleagues within Classis California. Though he passed the "trial," Schuller found himself quite depressed and wondered whether he might be in the midst of a psychological and spiritual breakdown.[78] The burdens seemed

---

73. "Tom Snyder Interview," 1976, transcript, folder "Crystal Cathedral Robert H. Schuller—Interviews, 1976," box 26, Robert H. Schuller Collection, H93-1188 (HCASC), 37.

74. Nason and Nason, *Robert Schuller*, 65.

75. Nason and Nason, *Robert Schuller*, 66.

76. Penner, *Goliath*, 119.

77. Schuller, *My Journey*, 236.

78. Schuller, *My Journey*, 236, and Nason and Nason, *Robert Schuller*, 67–68.

to be piling up. He reported night terrors and awakening to find his bed soaked with his sweat. One night, Arvella asked her husband what was wrong, and he replied, "I'm afraid of failing. I've always been afraid of failing. Ever since I can remember, I've been afraid of failing."[79] He was inconsolable. As she sought to assure him, saying, "It's going to be all right, Bob," he responded with a sigh: "I wish I could believe that."[80]

During this time, the minister's nose, because of his rhinophyma (a physical condition that made his nose red and bulbous), had become more inflamed. Occasionally, his nose would begin to bleed spontaneously during worship or wedding or funeral services. Schuller reported being horribly embarrassed by the condition and that it threatened to "to take away what was left of [his] self-esteem."[81] He eventually turned to surgery that provided relief but also left behind scarring around the minister's nose.

The aftermath of surgery, combined with the pace of the ministry, left Schuller utterly miserable. He recounted, "One night, shortly after the procedure, I sat in front of my bathroom mirror and went into an unrealistic, exaggerated, negative-thinking tailspin. I imagined that the people I had loved and served hated me. I was absolutely *convinced* of it. The colleagues whose approval of my theological skills I so desperately wanted were examining my basic worthiness for the ministry. Now even my wife and children, I was convinced, would see me as ugly."[82]

In later years, Schuller revealed to his longtime assistant Michael Nason that in those days he "was haunted by terrifying specters" and that his hair had "turned prematurely gray practically overnight." Schuller wondered what would happen if he "flipped out and killed his wife and children." The minister thought, "My God. [I am] going crazy."[83] He once wondered to his wife, "Where is my God now, Arvella?"[84]

Crippled with anxiety to the point of wishing for death ("for a fatal heart attack"),[85] Schuller finally prayed a prayer of last resort: "Jesus, if You're

---

79. Penner, *Goliath*, 121.
80. Penner, *Goliath*, 122.
81. Schuller, *My Journey*, 236.
82. Schuller, *My Journey*, 236–37.
83. Nason and Nason, *Robert Schuller*, 69.
84. Penner, *Goliath*, 122.
85. Schuller, *Your Church Has a Fantastic Future!*, 20.

90 CHAPTER 4

really alive, heal me before it's too late. Remove this obsession. Deliver me from negative thinking. Amen."[86] In his autobiography, the minister recounted that a sudden thought came to him from heaven: "Schuller—turn your scars into stars!"[87] The minister described the moment as transcendent, an epoch experience where he felt the literal touch of God: "At that instant, an amazing thing happened—something that had never happened before and hadn't happened since. I felt, out of nowhere, the genuine, physical sensation of a finger pressing through my skull and into my brain. I could feel the bones and flesh yield as that finger pushed deeper. It went in as far as it could. Then it began to pull out, to move back in the direction from which it had come, and it dragged something with it. It was gone, suddenly, and so were the anxiety, the fear, the depression, the darkness!"[88]

In a rush of relief, Schuller found new confidence in proposing his favored solution to the drive-in-versus-chapel dilemma: a hybrid church that synthesized the walk-in and drive-in worship atmospheres. Opposition, though, proved robust. When Schuller suggested the new hybrid church at a congregational meeting, the mood became "tempestuous" over financial concerns related to securing a loan.[89] The vote—55-48 in favor—demonstrated the division in the room. Even with just a slim majority, Schuller felt vindicated and moved forward with construction plans after Classis California also approved the proposal by a vote of 23-9 in favor.[90] Making matters even sweeter, his antagonistic copastor accepted a call to a new church.

After one tantalizing real estate opportunity fell through at the last moment, Schuller found a ten-acre orange grove three miles from the chapel and one mile from the drive-in, at the corner of Chapman Avenue and Lewis Street. At the time, the real estate agent offered a caveat: "It's out in the sticks."[91] Of course, that prediction would prove to be limited

86. Schuller, *My Journey*, 237.

87. Schuller, *My Journey*, 237.

88. Schuller, *My Journey*, 237.

89. Schuller to Russell Bedeker, February 5, 1959, CC-Correspondence, 1959–1962, RHS/CC, box 30 (HCASC).

90. Schuller to Henry Beltman, February 5, 1959, CC-Correspondence, 1959–1962, RHS/CC, box 30 (HCASC).

91. Schuller to Louis Benes (editor of the *Church Herald*), April 6, 1959,

by time. Eventually, the campus would be as close to a downtown as existed in Orange County.

The pace of Schuller's ministry was rapidly increasing. From the drive-in to the chapel to the new campus featuring an innovative architectural design, the minister sensed that timely decisions needed to be made to capture the growth occurring in his ministry. The three-hundred-seat chapel was not necessarily small, yet it was clearly inadequate to handle the steady rise in attendance. Before the possibilities of further growth were stymied, new land and a bigger building were required. Schuller was ready to act swiftly. Many of his leaders were not.

Indeed, many of Schuller's key constituents did not share in his aggressive desire to build such an audacious church structure. The day after the real estate deal was approved, the minister found letters of resignation at his office door from the vice president of the congregation, the clerk, the treasurer, and his personal secretary. Soon thereafter, another three dozen or so members left the congregation. A concern over Schuller's motives fueled the mass exodus—the minister seemed to constantly be striving for more and more growth. New developments in a quickly changing Orange County would vindicate the minister's instincts to expand quickly.

Shortly after the deal for the land had been signed for $66,000, Schuller learned that the newly planned Santa Ana Freeway would be sited just to the east of the church's new property.[92] The congregation would be well served in the future as that freeway was joined by two others to become an interchange of three freeways known as the "Orange Crush." At the time, however, speculation caused land prices to instantly double in the area. In the meantime, GGCC had yet to close on the purchase. The owner of the acreage, in fact, hoped that the church would fail to close because he now had an opportunity to relist at a much higher price. Knowing that there would be no grace in this transaction, Schuller and Arvella scrambled to find the $18,000 still needed for the down payment. Demonstrating their commitment to the church structure, they cashed in insurance policies

---

CC-Correspondence, 1959-1962, RHS/CC, box 30 (HCASC), and Schuller, *My Journey*, 242.

92. Nason and Nason, *Robert Schuller*, 75.

92 CHAPTER 4

and made last-minute phone calls to potential donors and managed to meet the obligation with just an hour to spare.[93]

The Architecture—and Theology—of Biorealism

With the hurdle of buying land negotiated, Schuller set himself to hiring an architect worthy of the formidable task of designing the world's first hybrid church—for the minister, the scale and spectacle of the architecture served as "silent advertising."[94] In this effort, everyone was operating outside of any customary sense of typical design. The minister landed on the renowned architect Richard Neutra and his concept of biorealism: an integration of the indoor and outdoor, built and natural environment—an effort that theoretically relaxed human beings in a context that allowed for better communication. Beginning with Neutra, Schuller initiated a habit of nurturing relationships with his architects in tackling boundary-pushing projects. The minister found himself fascinated with how imaginative design could have theological implications.

One architectural critic described the synergy that Schuller and Neutra found in each other: "For both preacher and architect, the fundamental problem was that humans were divorced from their natural origins."[95] For Neutra, humans longed to be connected to the tranquility of the natural world. For Schuller, humans longed to be connected to the created goodness of themselves that the natural world represented. At one point, Schuller reminisced that his thinking had been "straightened out" by the "sound theology and psychology" of Neutra and described the architect's influence on him as "profound."[96] Schuller intuited that his potential "unchurched" congregation desired a feeling of transcendence that Neutra's design could provide. Had the sociologist Hartmut Rosa ever spoken to Schuller, he would affirm that the minister was on to something. Rosa

93. Schuller, *My Journey*, 244–46.

94. Dan L. Thrapp, "Size of Church Vital to Success, Pastor Says," *Los Angeles Times*, February 21, 1970, Dennis Voskuil Papers, Holland, MI.

95. Robles-Anderson, "The Crystal Cathedral," 586–87.

96. Robert H. Schuller and James Coleman, *A Place of Beauty, a Joy Forever: The Glorious Gardens and Grounds of the Crystal Cathedral in Garden Grove, California* (Garden Grove, CA: Crystal Cathedral Creative Services, 2005), 74.

indicated that in the current societal context of acceleration, human beings in our fast-paced society yearn for "resonance"—a feeling of transcendent connection. Rosa specifically mentioned sports and music as pathways, but Schuller strategized that magnificent architecture would satiate his congregation's desire for resonance.[97]

In June 1959, Schuller wrote to Neutra with the good news that he had received permission to commission the architect. At that point, Schuller reported the council authorized an expenditure of $150,000 for the sanctuary. Ever ambitious, though, in the next sentence the minister indicated that he thought that the church could actually spend up to $350,000. Even as Schuller contracted with a world-class architect, his Midwestern thrift managed to escape his facade. The minister wondered to Neutra whether he could minimize construction costs by using volunteer labor from within the congregation.[58] Later, the minister demonstrated concern regarding the details. Schuller wrote to Neutra regarding the sanctuary: "I feel we need a pulpit. . . . It should be at least 3 to 4 feet wide and should be a dramatic point of attention to the people in the pews as well as the people in the cars. Perhaps you might want to call me to talk about this is in greater detail."[99] Schuller also maintained his consistent and fixed focus on growth. Before Neutra had completed his renderings for the hybrid church, the minister suggested that the plans include an eventual extension of fifty feet to the south—to accommodate the new attenders who would undoubtedly be arriving.[100] At the same time, Schuller promoted the church by submitting an article about GG-CC's new construction to *Protestant Church Buildings*—a magazine that focused on sacred architecture.[101]

97. Schuller assumed that hybrid churches would become a national phenomenon. See Schuller, "The Drive-In Church," 50.

98. Schuller to Neutra, June 25, 1959, CC-Correspondence, 1959–1962, RHS/CC, box 30 (HCASC).

99. Schuller to Neutra, January 20, 1961, CC-Correspondence, 1959–1962, RHS/CC, box 30 (HCASC).

100. Schuller to Neutra, November 27, 1959, CC-Correspondence, 1959–1962, RHS/CC, box 30 (HCASC).

101. Schuller to Neutra, September 9, 1959, CC-Correspondence, 1959–1962, RHS/CC, box 30 (HCASC).

94 CHAPTER 4

In May 1959 Schuller confided to a friend from seminary that he had no intentions to ever leave Orange County.[102] As he anticipated the hybrid church, Schuller began to consider how the new structure could become a county-wide destination for worship. In September 1959, the minister intimated to the congregation that he really thought that the new structure should not be limited by the geographic constraints connoted by "Garden Grove Community Church." After all, the ministry's "interest [extended] to all of Orange County." Though he waited for a couple of decades to actually change the name officially, his thinking at the time revealed a sense that "Community Church" likely connoted a too-parochial brand. The minister desired a grander, more expansive name for his church. How might the broader market of potential churchgoers respond? In the monthly newsletter, Schuller suggested three names: the Cathedral Park Church, Pacific Park Church, and Christ Memorial Church.[103]

Anticipating new growth, Schuller also augmented his early church management practices, even more directly melding prevalent business measurement processes into his own organization. As the minister geared up for the opening of the hybrid church, he announced that the church's Sunday school had contracted with Christian Institutional Associates of Costa Mesa for an attendance system that utilized a system designed by IBM: weekly reports would indicate those present, those absent, visitors, and the total number in attendance. The use of state-of-the-art quantitative benchmarks would become increasingly important in the ministry as a tool for strategic planning.

In September 1959, GGCC broke ground for their new Neutra-designed church and held its first service in the new building on November 6, 1961.[104] Schuller marveled at the innovative, disruptive design: "There was no stained glass—lines were clean, sharp, and vertical."[105] The sanctuary measured 132 feet by 64 feet and stood 30 feet high. Sticking with tradition, Schuller invited Peale to preach the first sermon in the

102. Schuller to Kruizenga, May 7, 1958, CC-Correspondence, RHS/CC, box 30 (HCASC).

103. "Community Church News," September 1959, CC-GGCC Community Church News, March 1958–October 1965, RHS/CC, box 29 (HCASC).

104. Schuller, *My Journey*, 250-52, 264.

105. Schuller and Coleman, *A Place of Beauty, a Joy Forever*, 19.

new sanctuary—quite generously, the New York City minister delivered the sermon at both the 9:30 and 11:00 a.m. services.[106]

As the service began, Schuller pushed one button on the pulpit: two sections of the glass wall alongside the pulpit began to silently slide, creating an opening 24 feet wide and 20 feet tall to allow the drive-in worshipers parked just outside to participate in the service.[107] When he preached, those in the parking lot heard the minister's voice resounding through the 104 high fidelity speakers.[108] Every detail had been considered. Schuller reported that he finally felt he had a legitimate church in Orange County, that he had finally arrived, and that he planned to never leave.[109]

106. "Community Church News," November 1961, CC-GGCC Community Church News, March 1958–October 1965, RHS/CC, box 29 (HCASC).

107. Schuller, *My Journey*, 265.

108. "Peale to Dedicate Walk-in, Drive-in Church," *Register*, November 2, 1961 (DVP).

109. Schuller, *My Journey*, 266.

5

GROWING AMBITION AND MAGNIFICATION

In 1965, in celebration of the tenth anniversary of its founding, Garden Grove Community Church gifted Schuller and Arvella with an overseas trip. The leg home included time in Italy, where Schuller became infatuated with the cypress trees surrounding Lake Como. He made plans to have a perimeter of these trees surrounding the hybrid church, bordering and decorating an otherwise bland landscape. But the church's leadership council assessed the plan as impractical—the drive-in portion necessitated asphalt.

Schuller committed himself to getting those cypress trees planted. He began to consider how to authorize his plan without violating the rules of governance for his congregation. "I couldn't forget my dream of a glorious, lofty green curtain encircling the drive-in church," he wrote. "I just *knew* that someday it would become a reality. So I bided my time." Schuller recounted his long-game plan to eventually get his way, a calculation that demonstrated his patience and foresight:

> In reviewing the minutes of the board meeting I discovered that each elder and deacon's term of office was for a certain number of years. I realized that in four years a slim majority would all see their terms expire at the same time. One week later they would be replaced in a general election. There would be a period of six days without a quorum on the board. In that time, I—as president and chairman—would have the power to act! I began to plan for that six-day window of opportunity four years hence. I would have bulldozers waiting to rip out

GROWING AMBITION AND MAGNIFICATION **97**

the asphalt covering. Then trucks could deliver my order of three-foot-tall Italian cypress. By the week's close, all could be planted![1]

For Schuller, much of congregational leadership involved the initiation and execution of projects. Yet his projects tended to be outside of what was generally accepted as feasible or even reasonable. Therefore, his leadership involved the conscious working of the politics of his church. He refused to operate in a starkly autocratic manner. Nevertheless, Schuller's active management of congregational life and growth demanded more than just stating goals; it also involved scheming about ways to achieve them. In this case, the minister determined to the day when he could exert his unopposed authority to get his border of trees around the church grounds.

Even more, the political maneuvering required to plant the cypress trees revealed a stark contrast the minister faced in terms of timing, specifically, how long it would take to work congregational initiatives through lay leaders versus how long it could take if decisions were left to Schuller alone. Once a plan was assessed and actionable items presented, it seemed right to enact them. The minister always preferred to act quickly before crucial circumstances changed. Yet the staff and lay leaders around him rarely seemed to be on a similar time line. Schuller would therefore constantly exercise his executive leadership by toggling between the vision he saw and the processes required to actualize a project. His leadership would develop between the opportunities he sought to seize and the mobilization of constituents and capital necessary to complete any particular project.

Soon, he would apply his maturing leadership skills toward bigger initiatives, leveraging bigger budgets for bigger buildings and expanding the property of church grounds across larger swaths of local city blocks.

Migrants—and Seekers

Orange County proved to be the ideal locale for establishing an innovative ministry in the post–World War II era. Schuller certainly had com-

---

1. Robert H. Schuller, *My Journey: From an Iowa Farm to a Cathedral of Dreams* (New York: HarperCollins, 2001), 279.

petitors, but his unique ability to synthesize a Midwestern reserve with mainline Protestant familiarity—invigorated by West Coast newness and innovation—allowed the minister to uniquely distinguish himself and his ministry. Government funding poured into the county—establishing a hub for defense contractors. The robust job market attracted millions of migrants from out of state. Service industries rose swiftly alongside. Developers struggled to maintain pace with the booming population. And these new residents needed churches.

Coming from the South and Midwest, many of these families attended church regularly. Religious leaders and denominational offices seeking to capture these population flows "rushed to minister to the influx of transplants that sought community."[2] The minister achieved a foothold in this emerging market as he struggled to build a ministry in the midst of a dynamic mix of Christian churches with overlapping sensibilities and a stream of new residents establishing themselves in their new homes, schools, and workplaces.[3] With Schuller's church, the migrants to California found comfort in a familiar liturgy at Garden Grove, since it had elements that reminded them of the church back home. And yet, his conspicuous reinterpretation of religious places and rituals appealed to the desires for change that brought these migrants to the West Coast in the first place.

A core cultural phenomenon included the strain of conservatism that pervaded the growing region. Contrary to its twenty-first-century reputation as a progressive stronghold, California in the middle of the twentieth century functioned as a bastion of probusiness conservative thought.[4] Schuller fit the mold. Historian Kathryn Olmstead noted that California actually cleared new paths already in the 1930s and 1940s

2. David Clary, *Soul Winners: The Ascent of America's Evangelical Entrepreneurs* (Guilford, CT: Prometheus Books, 2022), 101.

3. Elsie Dearborn, "Rock Valley Roundup," *Sioux Center (IA) News*, April 16, 1959, https://tinyurl.com/3jt46t9p. Schuller's stature as a pastor of a church on the frontier of California afforded him gravitas in his home state. In 1959 he accepted an invitation to speak at the Spring Brotherhood Rally.

4. Mark T. Mulder and Gerardo Martí, *The Glass Church: Robert H. Schuller, the Crystal Cathedral, and the Strain of Megachurch Ministry* (New Brunswick, NJ: Rutgers University Press, 2020).

when political operatives there marketed conservatism in religious terms: "These Western conservatives did not stress their defense of private property; instead, they promised to protect the family, the church, and the white race from radical leftists."[5]

By the late 1950s and early 1960s, Schuller took that Western conservative prototype and enhanced it with the gloss of modern innovation. Historian Todd Kerstetter assessed that Schuller's initial template for reaching the post–World War II consumer culture had no worthy rivals. In short, "no one did it better" than Schuller. Until he started training fellow pastors who would grow megachurches using his principles, the Orange County pastor stood alone in figuring out how to draw a massive crowd of relative strangers to a religious service.[6] While appealing to conservative sensibilities, Schuller stretched the range of who might be attracted to the young church.

Though the language did not yet exist, Schuller—in his first decade in California—had begun puzzling a new form of Christian worship designed to draw in a broad and religiously diverse public: "seeker-sensitive." Sociologist Kimon Howland Sargeant defined "seeker churches" as those who sought to attract people who did not currently attend church—what Schuller labeled as the "unchurched." Though Schuller occasionally and strategically affirmed his affiliation in the RCA, much of the template he created in Garden Grove served as a repudiation of what he experienced growing up in northwest Iowa's Newkirk Reformed Church. His church would not revolve around the religiously committed but would be more geared toward the religiously indifferent.

In fact, Schuller would have to exchange much of the mainline residue of the RCA for signals and codes of a more generic evangelicalism. A new liturgical sensibility was taking root. In her book on evangelicals in America, historian Frances FitzGerald described Schuller as a pioneer who developed techniques for "attracting nonchurchgoers."[7] She

5. Kathryn S. Olmstead, *Right Out of California: The 1930s and the Big Business Roots of Modern Conservatism* (New York: New Press, 2016), 148.

6. Todd M. Kerstetter, *Inspiration and Innovation: Religion in the American West* (Oxford: Wiley Blackwell, 2015), 215.

7. Frances FitzGerald, *The Evangelicals: The Struggle to Shape America* (New York: Simon & Schuster, 2017), 545.

100 CHAPTER 5

credited the minister with redefining the church market by identifying the "felt needs" that would attract families to "seeker-sensitive" services.[8] FitzGerald significantly also identified Schuller as having tremendous influence on the next generation of market-centered Christianity—and cited both Bill Hybels of Willow Creek Church in suburban Chicago and Rick Warren of Saddleback Valley Community Church as heirs of the Orange County minister. These two pastors—themselves beholden to Schuller's ecclesial approach—would become known for creating fresh and dynamic versions of seeker-sensitive congregational life.

Of course, innovation in religious practice to appeal to a changing religious market had long functioned as an integral aspect of Christianity in America. For instance, already in the 1700s George Whitefield, in many ways, marked the path followed by Schuller. In his innovations for Anglican worship, Whitefield disregarded denominational norms and practices. In addition, as a preacher, Whitefield's style synthesized a more dramatic and theatrical element. And, borrowing from Whitefield's tool kit, Schuller added to his own gravitas with his background in drama: "Schuller cut an impressive figure as a preacher, even from the roof of a refreshment stand. The taunts he endured in childhood for being fat were well in the past. He filled into a strapping young man who moved gracefully in his heavy clerical garments. His confidence shone through in his arresting preaching style in which his voice suddenly rose to a crescendo when emphasizing a point and then just as quickly fell almost to a whisper, forcing listeners to lean forward in their seats to hear."[9] Sargeant noted, however, that Whitefield's expressive preaching style *never* utilized the "soft sell"—an emphasis on "personal satisfaction through Jesus Christ."[10] The "soft sell" operated as the rhetorical opposite of fire and brimstone. Judgment had been expunged from the message. Some seeker pastors who engaged in the "soft sell" preferred to label the strategy the "back door": an introduction to a Christian message that included a theology within the "friendly guise of an egalitarian, fulfillment-enhancing, fun religious encounter with God."[11] Schuller once described his wor-

8. FitzGerald, *The Evangelicals*, 546.

9. Clary, *Soul Winners*, 102.

10. Kimon Howland Sargeant, *Seeker Churches: Promoting Traditional Religion in a Nontraditional Way* (New Brunswick, NJ: Rutgers University Press, 2000), 98.

11. Sargeant, *Seeker Churches*, 99.

ship philosophy: "If you started a church and nobody but non-Christians showed up, what would you do on Sunday morning? You couldn't offer the confession of sins. You can't blame them for not playing by the rules of the game, they haven't even decided to play the game."[12]

In Sargeant's analysis, Schuller functioned as a pioneer in the "task of translating Christian theology into a language that makes sense to seekers."[13] In other words, Schuller refined a version of the "soft sell." Sargeant also criticized Schuller, though, for "subjectivizing" Christian theology by "explicitly shifting its focus from God to the human craving for self-worth."[14] Moreover, Sargeant indicated that "Schuller's 'new reformation'" offered a case study in "how catering messages to the needs of seekers has the potential to transform the theology undergirding the message."[15] Among critics, then, Schuller's theological orientation came to lack much connection with the Reformed tradition at all and distanced him from the priorities and practices of his own denomination, the RCA.

Schuller certainly acknowledged that he actively sought to buck the harness of the RCA's denominational authority. He indicated that if a local church wanted to achieve growth, they should stop acceding to the narrow and often distant notions of denominational and seminary leaders. He asserted that the folks entrenched in those institutions had little to no native knowledge, and they failed to have any contextual understanding required to connect with a church's local community. As he himself advised, "The local pastor who looks to a national executive officer for leadership is seldom the dynamo that a local church needs for exciting forward movement," and, even more troublesome, "the theological professor is prone to be lost in his own mental world of academics and tends to be detached from the heartbeat and the soul throb of the people who live within the radius of the local church."[16]

---

12. Interview, Robert Schuller and Dennis Voskuil, March 3, 1983, Dennis Voskuil Papers, Holland, MI (hereafter cited as DVP).

13. Sargeant, *Seeker Churches*, 101.

14. Sargeant, *Seeker Churches*, 102.

15. Sargeant, *Seeker Churches*, 103–4.

16. Robert H. Schuller, *Your Church Has a Fantastic Future! A Possibility Thinker's Guide to a Successful Church* (Ventura, CA: Regal Books, 1986), 133–34. For more on Schuller's thoughts on denominationalism, see the transcript of *The World of Religion*, January 3, 1975, included as an attachment in a letter from John Stapert

CHAPTER 5

And though Schuller remained a bit more circumspect about the role of voluntary councils or consistories, he lobbied for a governing structure in churches that resembled that of a corporate board of directors. The board, then, served in an advisory capacity and functioned similar to consultants: "Leadership does not rest with the board of directors. Leadership rests in the hands of full-time executives who are hired by the board to think ahead, plan ahead, and envision great possibilities, as well as ways in which these possibilities can be profitably exploited and ways in which potential problems can be solved. Leadership then rests in the hands of full-time, salaried people."[17] Leaders should be given the authority to act decisively. Schuller clarified further how churches should mimic business: "If I were a capitalist financing an enterprise, I would insist that the unchallenged leadership be placed in the hands of full-time thinkers and planners." Personalizing this imperative, he unequivocally stated, "As a pastor heading up a church, I insist on the same."[18]

Schuller steadily enacted his claim that churches should be led by clergy who serve as organizational professionals. He posited that the professionalization of congregations run by strategically minded executive pastors would offer a key to their growth. Only a dedicated pastoral professional could dedicate the attention needed to keep the congregation on track of strength and vitality. In contrast, he estimated that for deacons and elders, the church, at best, represented a third-level priority in their lives (after family and work). How could they possibly be trusted, even with good intentions and high-level commitment, to guide what for them would be a tertiary organization? Schuller became direct: "Pastor? Do you hear me? You should be the spark plug. You should be the inspiring commander leading the troops up the hill!"[19]

Similarly, denominations also lacked the intentional focus required by pastors in contemporary society to draw in those outside of their typical constituencies. In particular, the minister felt that denominations had

---

to Schuller, May 29, 1975, CC-Correspondence, 1975, Robert H. Schuller/Crystal Cathedral (hereafter cited as RHS/CC), box 4, Hope College Archives and Special Collections, Holland, MI (hereafter cited as HCASC); and letter from Schuller to Stapert (never sent), June 3, 1975, CC-Correspondence, 1975, RHS/CC, box 4 (HCASC).

17. Robert H. Schuller, *Your Church Has a Fantastic Future!*, 136.

18. Robert H. Schuller, *Your Church Has a Fantastic Future!*, 136.

19. Robert H. Schuller, *Your Church Has a Fantastic Future!*, 136–37.

little imagination for pursuing the unchurched. He fixated on that demographic. As Schuller toured his church grounds at one point with Richard Neutra, the architect sought to understand the minister's desires for the campus. Neutra asked Schuller: "Who is it you really want to impress?" Schuller struggled to find an answer. Prodding the minister to really consider the question, Neutra clarified his concern: "I'm Jewish, but I don't practice the Jewish faith. And when I go into a place with stained glass windows, I feel threatened. I feel like people are shouting sermons at me." Schuller confirmed to him that he had little interest in impressing "religious people." Instead, he told Neutra he wanted a church grounds "comfortable for people of all faiths or no faith to come to a church service!"[20] Schuller's conception of potential members busted open any usual denominational considerations of church membership.

In fact, rather than being beholden to denominational structures, Schuller preferred to cast GGCC as "affiliated" with Peale's Marble Collegiate Church in Manhattan—even though no such form of relationship existed within the RCA. A 1964 article in Schuller's hometown paper, the *Alton Democrat*, noted that the Southern California minister had returned to Iowa for his family vacation. After an interview with Schuller, the journalist reported to readers about the "unique and beautiful features of the walk-in, drive-in sanctuary," and that the ministry planned to build an "18-story Tower of Hope." Mostly, Schuller wanted readers in Iowa to know that he found himself blessed to shepherd a congregation of folks "who look for 'the possibilities' rather than see the obstacles" as an "affiliate of Dr. Norman Vincent Peale's Marble Collegiate Church in New York City."[21] The Orange County minister sought the reflected glow of his high-status colleague.

A Tower of Hope on a Growing Campus

Having completed the hybrid church in 1961 and looking to the remaining open acres on current church grounds, Schuller initiated his foray into crafting a sacred version of the suburban corporate campus or estate.

20. James Penner, *Goliath: The Life of Robert Schuller* (Anaheim, CA: New Hope Publishing, 1992), 154.

21. "Pastor Drive-In, Walk-In California Church Now Vacationing in Alton with Family," *Alton (IA) Democrat*, August 20, 1964, https://tinyurl.com/4zweadjk.

104 CHAPTER 5

Though he had felt satisfaction in the completion of the new Neutra-designed hybrid sanctuary, Schuller felt compelled to keep building on the campus for an array of ministries and services. Intent on emphasizing an image whose appeal would reach beyond the typical churchgoer, the template for a secular version of the campus/estate would present a "tidy and prosperous face to the public," which included water features and sculpture gardens.[22] As he considered the overall design of the church grounds, Schuller continued to emphasize the balance with nature as restorative. Though it looked like a corporate campus, the "church grounds" (Schuller's preferred term) would serve the ministry by locating its activities in a pastoral setting. In his planning, the minister exuded an incessant *need* for projects around his ministry. Schuller struggled with depression and anxiety, and developing the church grounds alleviated a continual desire.

As he pondered his next project for the campus, Schuller's father died unexpectedly after a weeklong bout with pneumonia in May 1964 at age eighty-one. The local obituary recalled that he had been "the only farmer who completely rebuilt his farm by hand" after the devastation of the 1944 tornado.[23] Moreover, locals remembered him as "an excellent farmer, a good neighbor, and a devoted husband and father." His death likely caused Schuller to become more convinced of the necessity to grow and leave a legacy—plant those trees for later generations to enjoy. Even after outstanding triumphs, his restlessness would get the best of him. Once, after returning from a vacation, he slumped in his office chair and admitted to deep depression as he realized he had no imminent challenges or goals. Sure, Schuller had built a landmark sanctuary and landscaped the church grounds to perfection, but he worried that his life work had been completed. In an effort to shake the doldrums, the minister decided he needed to cast a new vision for his ministry. He needed to build something—again.

22. Susan Power Bratton, *Churchscape: Megachurches and the Iconography of Environment* (Waco, TX: Baylor University Press, 2016), 118.

23. Beverly Green, "Anthony Schuller Succumbs at Age 81," *Sioux County (IA) Capital*, May 7, 1964, https://tinyurl.com/2s3z5zb3. See also "Anthony Schuller, Lifelong Resident Passes Beyond; Funeral Monday," *Alton (IA) Democrat*, May 7, 1964, https://tinyurl.com/87jzdycu.

Schuller consistently acted on the belief that a completed building served as an expression of ecclesial hope. And the more ambitious the building, the greater its capacity to fulfill the promise of that hope. It could be argued that Schuller's unyielding need to build manifested his inherent sense that the broader society continued to evolve with new cultural currents always forming, and that the church should actively join in those currents. In the attempt to grapple with social change, the minister engaged in projects that would participate in the inescapable torrent of change, and, if possible, intervene in the flow of history to ensure that the Christian church took its place within it. If there was a hope of participating in that change and finding opportunity for engaging the church in the future, then building projects that planted enduring structures were among the most tangible actions that could stake their claim for that future. Otherwise, if the church did nothing, hoping the inertia of custom would carry Christianity forward, then the currents of change would soon overtake it.

Given the rapid pace at which Schuller wanted to implement his projects, it is no surprise that he chafed against traditional funding of church buildings. At one point, Schuller asserted that his sophisticated fundraising techniques kept him above the fray: "We have never had to stoop to beg for money from the pulpit, or cheapen our church by selling tickets, selling suppers, or selling bingo games."[24] To that end, he broached a creative funding model with the board of pensions at the RCA, inquiring whether that body would consider letting pastors borrow against their pensions to fund construction projects at their respective churches. To make the proposition more palatable, the minister suggested that the borrowed funds be limited to those that had been directly paid in by the pastor—so the risk would really be all his.[25] For all his scheming for growth, Schuller willingly put in his own money—including risking his own retirement funding—and consistently demonstrated enough confidence to risk his limited wealth to see plans though to fruition as fast as possible.

24. GGCC-CC "Community Church News, October 27, 1965, RHS/CC, box 5 (HCASC).
25. Robert H. Schuller to Gerard Gnade, April 23, 1959 (DVP).

106 CHAPTER 5

Whatever his next project would be, limited available land adjacent to the campus inhibited any grand designs. Acreage remained tight. Yet the constraint fueled inspiration. Verticality became the remedy. A structure with a small footprint, a tall expansion, fit the bill. Schuller convinced himself that the campus needed a tower to complete the symmetry with the hybrid sanctuary, so he "began to envision a two-hundred-fifty-foot tower silhouetted against the skyline of Orange County."[26] To sell the vision to his board, though, the minister needed to press the case for the tower as an instrument rather than a monument. Schuller realized that he had paid a price for the construction of the hybrid sanctuary—seeing council members resign in protest—and that he would need to gird himself with a vivid depiction of the ministry's need for a tower. Schuller initially contracted with Southern California architect Albert C. Martin. The minister, though, decided to return to Neutra when Martin unveiled a model of a "pedestrian black box" that had no ability to inspire fundraising because "it was a boring structure."[27]

True to form, Schuller pitched his dream building to Neutra in 1964: a twenty-five-story high-rise capped by a 12-foot cross. Of course, Neutra and Schuller also quickly learned that California building codes around earthquake damage mitigation disallowed structures that tall. They settled on a twelve-floor building capped by a chapel at the top—160 feet.[28] To start the new building fund, Schuller donated the entire advance ($6,000) from his newly signed book contract (which would become 1967's *Move Ahead with Possibility Thinking*) (276).

He had a project—now Schuller had to prove the need. The minister began to brainstorm for potential uses for a tower to his board:

> We could put a chapel on the top floor. What an inspiration it would be to worship high above the sights and sounds of the world. We need more space for classrooms. And offices; you know our office space is

26. Michael Nason and Donna Nason, *Robert Schuller: The Inside Story* (Waco, TX: Word, 1983), 101.

27. Interview, Robert Schuller and Dennis Voskuil, March 3, 1983.

28. Robert H. Schuller, *My Journey*, 276-77. Hereafter, page references from this work will be given in parentheses in the text.

limited now. We could put a board room in it. Our vision wouldn't be restricted like it is now. When we meet, we will be forced to look out on all those hundreds of thousands of cars, all those homes and offices. We'll be forced to see far, think big, aim high, reach wide. We could even put in a psychological clinic, a Christian counseling center. (276)

After the minister had packaged the proposal as a practical—yet inspirational—response to a ministerial need, the board approved the plan for a tower on the church grounds. Nason, Schuller's assistant for decades, recalled that the minister could often be aloof and distant when business meetings bored him. When he wanted approval for a project, though, his charismatic gifts came through, and the minister exuded friendliness and charm "from every pore" (103).

The next Sunday, Schuller unveiled the approved project to his congregation in a sermon entitled "How to Make Your Dreams Come True." The minister detailed the high-speed elevator, the floors dedicated to classrooms and counseling, and a twenty-four-hour suicide prevention hotline—and, of course, "a little chapel at the top of the tower that would be a twinkling diamond of hope in the night sky at the freeway hub of this great county" (104). In a pattern he often repeated, he appealed to constituents with a grand vision in the pursuit of a known need for capital.

Later that year, GGCC held a tenth-anniversary celebration that functioned as a fund-raiser for the new construction project. By that time, the church staff included Schuller as senior minister, Harold Leestma as minister of evangelism, Kenneth Van Wyk as minister of education, and Henry Poppen as minister of visitation. In the anniversary booklet for the evening, GGCC described itself as "broad enough to accept anyone, yet narrow enough to maintain the distinctiveness of the Christian faith." In those growing, exciting days of a booming California and an expanding Orange County, the scale of what the ministry planned to build seemed fitting.

In promoting the Tower of Hope, Schuller wrote in grandiose terms:

Towering nearly a city block into the sky, this great edifice will hum with activity seven days a week! Every Sunday 500 young people will be educated in the Christian life here! From Monday through Satur-

108 CHAPTER 5

day, ministers, Christian psychologists, will talk with, pray with, listen to, and give Hope to thousands of Southern Californians who come seeking God's love and understanding!

It's a tremendous thrill to know that we are picked by God to build this inspiring structure that should stand for more than 1000 years! The pyramids are 5000 years old! The Pisa Tower is 500 years old! The London Tower is 1000 years old! And these are Towers of Pride, Vanity, and Greed!

Now we will build God's Tower! A Tower of Hope![29]

Not content to just sway attendees with a fanciful vision, Schuller also delivered management details ensuring that the tower could lure donations. At the "pace-setting" level, Schuller suggested a gift of $5,200. However, rather than asking for the rather staggering sum up front, the brochure suggested weekly $10.00 gifts for 520 weeks. If that proved too much, the brochure suggested that the tower would need 350 benefactors to give $3.50 per week for 520 weeks ($1,800).[30] Such pledges for future giving would not only establish anticipated revenue but also unlock the lines of credit from local banks to allow construction to begin.

In promotional materials for the anniversary event, the minister made a bold prediction, indicating that he anticipated the event would raise $385,000 within ten minutes. In his entire career, he had never "stooped to beg for money from the pulpit"—and yet, here he stood on church grounds now estimated to be worth $1,600,000. He knew how to raise money for ministerial growth projects and opined that "perhaps that's the reason ministers and financial leaders from denominations from all over America write and visit Garden Grove Community Church almost weekly to discover the secret of this Church's almost unbelievable financial success!"[31] (It seemed that already in 1965, Schuller started to see himself as a ministry management consultant to his fellow pastors

29. Tenth Birthday Dinner Party, November 15 and 16, 1965, CC Anniversary Celebration, Tenth, 1965, RHS/CC, box 5 (HCASC).

30. Tenth Birthday Dinner Party.

31. "Community Church News," October 27, 1965, CC Anniversary Celebration, Tenth, 1965, RHS/CC, box 5 (HCASC).

across the nation.) Ultimately, to build the Tower of Hope, the congregation paid 6 percent interest on all notes borrowed for construction. Schuller suggested that if members knew "anyone who wants to earn top interest on his savings and know that his savings are underwritten by the largest congregation in the oldest Protestant denomination in America, let him write us a letter and we will be very grateful."[32] GGCC eventually secured all the necessary funding.

For the tower dedication service in September 1969, Schuller once again brought in Peale to deliver a sermon. Schuller claimed that he began the day assuming that the tower represented the end of construction on the campus. As he spied the parking lot from his twelfth floor office, though, he noticed cars circling and circling—with no spaces left. He recalled being sickened by the lack of parking—"That was like inviting someone to a dinner party and not providing him or her with a place setting."[33] His restlessness stirred again.

It would be difficult to overestimate the role of the automobile in the success of Schuller's ministerial career. Schuller's assistant Michael Nason estimated that the location of the campus in car-centric Southern California proved crucial to the ministry's growth: "We do not have a good mass transit system in Southern California, so everybody's in a car, and very used to getting in a car to go places. The location where we were, being only a mile from Disneyland, and him being in a drive-in, all of that combined [reinforced that] this was the location for growth. Of course the amount of growth in California was huge in the 50s, the 60s, and the 70s."[34] Indeed, an advertisement for GGCC in 1966 described the church as "located at the freeway hub of Orange County."[35]

And, for a time, the tower stood as the tallest building in Orange County, and its lighted cross made it readily visible to residents and commuters for miles. Decades later, architectural critic Deyan Sudjic asserted that the ability to glimpse the campus (especially the eventual

32. Robert H. Schuller to Friends of GGCC, April 4, 1966, Shepherd's Grove Church Archives, Irvine, CA (hereafter cited as SGCA).
33. Robert H. Schuller, *My Journey*, 285.
34. Interview with Mulder, January 22, 2018.
35. See advertisement in the *Register*, April 9, 1966, 7.

110   CHAPTER 5

Cathedral and Tower of Hope) from the freeway played a critical role in attracting an audience. Driving through Orange County, past Disneyland and Angel Stadium, "on the right, the Crystal Cathedral comes into view. Slightly detached from the main building, world-renowned architect Philip Johnson's chrome-plated paraphrase of a campanile marks out the presence of the complex on the Orange County flatlands, just like the turrets of Disneyland a mile away. There is no danger of actually hearing the bells from the freeway, but Schuller wanted the tower anyway. It's both a signpost and a billboard. The diffuse scale of Los Angeles makes the bell tower an essential response to its context, providing an updated version of the very traditional element on the urban skyline."[36]

Knowing that limited parking could inhibit growth, the minister began to plan to buy another ten acres the very morning of the tower dedication. After scrambling for funding (including borrowing $150,000 from another church), GGCC signed a contract for ten adjacent acres. Schuller acknowledged that he had no actionable vision for the land beyond parking, but he felt invigorated by the possibilities.

A School for Church Growth

The minister claimed that his success in purchasing adjacent land for his ministry, without even knowing its eventual utility, caused him to realize that a crucial type of business acumen failed to be included in any seminary training: "I had received the best education that a minister could have, but I'd never been taught how to be a successful *leader*—let alone how to challenge impossibilities. Leadership principles simply weren't part of the ministerial curriculum."[37] Schuller recognized that he likely knew as much about church management as anyone, but that he also had no platform from which to share. With that in mind, he decided to start his own "school." In 1969, the minister established the Robert H. Schuller Institute for Successful Church Leadership. Schuller described the initial lectures as challenging some of the accepted dogma of prominent religious

---

36. Deyan Sudjic, *The Edifice Complex: How the Rich and Powerful Shape the World* (New York: Penguin Press, 2005), 307.

37. Sudjic, *The Edifice Complex*, 290.

GROWING AMBITION AND MAGNIFICATION   **111**

leaders. His cumulative experiences at GGCC revealed to him how he had violated some of the basic ground rules of congregational life—much to his success. His anecdotes soon translated into formulaic principles.

For example, Schuller made the dubious claim that high-profile Christian leaders of that day believed that churches should be planted in suburbs, but that they remain small (fewer than five hundred members) and tucked on no more than two acres. Having established that straw man, the minister went to work offering his counterstrategy: "A small church is great if your mission is to serve only the indoctrinated members of your sectarian denomination—Lutheran, Dutch Reformed, Presbyterian, Episcopal, or whatever. But if you want to win unchurched people, drop the label from your name. Call it a community church. And program your services and your sermons and your activities to appeal to the spiritual needs of the unchurched."[38] Assuming that typical pastors oriented themselves around a highly local and parochial style of ministry, he urged otherwise. Church leaders should be ambitious and plan accordingly, deliberately looking beyond their denominational labels and initiating programs targeting those disconnected from any church. For many clergy, the advice was not only counterintuitive, it was revolutionary.

In 1968, Schuller offered a clear glimpse into his philosophy of church success. He received a request to write a note about GGCC for the RCA's denominational magazine, the *Church Herald*. Rather than discussing discipleship programs, the minister explained that the church plant had been a solid monetary investment for the RCA. He recounted that within thirteen years, an initial investment of $2,000 in 1955 would be realized as more than $500,000 in 1968 (GGCC's projected general offering receipts for the year). Moreover, Schuller estimated that the congregation had contributed another $500,000 to denominational and benevolent causes since its founding.[39]

Reflecting on the early days of his ministry, Schuller averred that he had "launched what came to be called the 'mega-church movement.'"[40]

---

38. Sudjic, *The Edifice Complex*, 291.

39. Robert H. Schuller to James W. Barr, September 20, 1968, CC-Correspondence, RHS/CC, box 34 (HCASC).

40. Sudjic, *The Edifice Complex*, 292.

112 CHAPTER 5

A central component of that included an eye on design that focused on the *comfort* of the congregant while maintaining some of the familiar hallmarks of traditional Christianity. Indeed, architecture critic Sudjic insisted on the central role of design for Schuller—that the minister attempted to find a balance between the old and the new, a refreshingly new version of Christianity that still retained the essentials of the faith tradition. Historically, religious buildings functioned to "tie worshippers together over long periods of history and across huge distances."[41] But for Schuller, this alone was insufficient. As Sudjic explained: "When he set up in Garden Grove, Schuller was creating a new version of Christianity and, like so many clergymen before him, part of his strategy was to attract attention with the architecture of the church. That is to say that he wanted to retain enough of the traditional signals to reflect that this still was a Christian church—bell tower, cross, altar, and so on—but to put them together in a different configuration that would make his organization look impressive and, at the same time, modern and forward-looking."[42] Schuller, then, advocated for a bold "architectural language" on the campus to signal a revised form of Christianity. Simply said, the design needed to communicate a theology compelling enough to make the congregation (or audience) identify with it—that they had a sense of belonging to something much larger, an experiential sense of resonance.

Signifiers of Schuller's correctness started to accumulate. In 1968, GGCC received the "Church of the Year" award from *Guideposts* magazine. Schuller saw the recognition as an opportunity to promote his recent book, *Move Ahead with Possibility Thinking*. To that end, he suggested to an editor at Doubleday that perhaps they should print a brochure that would capitalize on the award and use it to promote Schuller's book. The minister insisted in the letter that the "principles of success" that had been experimented at GGCC could be "applied in almost any Protestant church." According to Schuller, any minister who read his book would compel members of his church board to read it, who, in turn, would "order it for members of their own business and industry."[43]

41. Sudjic, *The Edifice Complex*, 297.
42. Sudjic, *The Edifice Complex*, 296.
43. Robert H. Schuller to Ferris Mack, January 26, 1968, CC-Correspondence, RHS/CC, box 32 (HCASC).

As Schuller moved forward with the expansion of his church, he dedicated himself to bringing other ministers along on the journey. Through his Institute, Schuller committed to sharing his own experience—although his message to ministers would be abstracted from messy details and distilled to serve pastors regardless of their specific context. Schuller crafted positive, encouraging messages that he geared to church leaders working on the ground; he answered questions and addressed curiosities from eager pastors begging for his attention. By hosting meetings on the campus—an immersive display of the results of his approach to ministry— and creating tapes, workbooks, and other instruction materials, Schuller endeavored to routinize the process of growth, thereby expanding the capacity of ministry not only in his own church but also in churches across the nation, and perhaps even the world. Schuller was now dedicated to producing the mavericks of a market-oriented Christianity, with himself as the primary exemplar.

Managing a Church, Managing a Family

As the minister nurtured his ministry and national profile, he and Arvella also managed their young family. In terms of parental dynamics, Nason described Schuller as the "powerhouse," while Arvella provided tempering and balance.[44] As their platform grew, Arvella publicly promoted fostering positive family environments: "The persons in that comfortable environment become creative, beautiful people full of respect for each other. They have open minds to new ideas, especially in times of stress and tension."[45] And, it should be noted, she accomplished this in her own home. The Schullers, contrary to other televangelists, remained untainted by sexual scandal. In fact, the marriage demonstrated a consistent tenderness. After a breast cancer diagnosis, Arvella underwent a mastectomy two weeks before her fiftieth birthday. She reported that Schuller took on a role as her comforter and encourager with no reservations—even purchasing Arvella three different bathing

---

44. Nason and Nason, *Robert Schuller*, 83.

45. Arvella Schuller, *The Positive Family: Possibility Thinking in the Christian Home* (Garden City, NY: Doubleday, 1982), 19–20. Hereafter, page references from this work will be given in parentheses in the text.

114   CHAPTER 5

suits specifically designed for women who had had mastectomies for a vacation to Hawaii, knowing that his wife had concerns about how she would look (27–28).

Schuller and Arvella also reported a fairly egalitarian marriage for the 1960s and 1970s. The minister once joked: "We have a happy marriage, frankly, because I rule the roost. But she rules the rooster. See?"[46] And after describing her ability to repair an electrical cord and her husband's knack for cleaning up the kitchen messes or tossing a salad, Arvella noted, "We do not see these physical tasks or skills as being 'male' or 'female.' We all pitch in to get the work done" (22). Schuller even wrote and copyrighted a song about their marriage that include the following lyric: "I am the captivated husband of a liberated wife" (36). In another sign of relative progressiveness in family life, Arvella recounted how she and her husband once discovered "a popular magazine about sex tucked between the mattress and spring of [their] son's bed." Arvella described Schuller's response as "immediately positive: 'Well, at least we know he is a healthy, normal, growing boy!'" (42–43). Early in his publishing career, Schuller freely wrote about the importance of sex to a healthy and vital marriage.[47] And Arvella went on to indicate that couples should not fear shifts in their respective roles in the family: "Along with a positive look at changing roles, we must emphasize that there are certain roles that remain unchanged through the years" (Arvella Schuller, *The Positive Family*, 25).

Although Arvella emphasized their marriage as a partnership, she maintained the importance of gender differences in their marriage, describing how she shifted her marital priorities after a conversation with Norman Vincent Peale's wife, Ruth, to a more traditional arrangement. When Arvella had asked Ruth about her latest projects, she responded that she had "only *one* project" and "*He* [was her] *Husband*," Norman (24). Arvella, from that point on, reported her rearranged priorities: "Hus-

---

46. "Dr. Robert Schuller Interviewed on the Donahue Show," 1976, transcript, folder "Crystal Cathedral Robert H. Schuller—Interviews, 1976," box 26, Robert H. Schuller Collection, H93-1188 (HCASC), 37.

47. See, for instance, Robert H. Schuller, *God's Way to the Good Life* (Grand Rapids: Eerdmans, 1963), 71–79.

band first; children second; career third; music fourth; volunteer organizations fifth" (24). With Ruth's advice in mind, Arvella's responsibilities included hanging out appropriate suits and ties for Schuller—based on her conversations with his secretary regarding the minister's daily calendar: she noted that Schuller resisted "the mundane decision about what to wear at the start of a new day" (27).

The Schullers, of course, had a busy household with their eventual five children. And the many demands caused the minister to become quite sedentary. He struggled with his weight. At one point, he estimated being about forty pounds overweight as he balanced church and family management in the mid and late 1960s. He ultimately began running daily around 1970 and claimed to eventually cover eight miles a day. (In 1980, he suggested he was in the best shape of his life.)[48] Exercise and yard work became the minister's distractions when he sought to avoid or reduce "negative emotions."[49]

Indeed, Schuller and Arvella expressed a great deal of confidence in their positive family culture. The minister at one point claimed that "women libbers may want to criticize our philosophy, but before they do, they better come up with a better system of rearing children. Ours works. And our five children prove it." Moreover, he elaborated that "all five are Spirit-filled and don't know what rebellion is."[50] Schuller indicated that he considered his family to constitute a "mini-nation." In other words, the husband served as king, wife as queen, and "children are taught that they are ambassadors-at-large for their family." Moreover, the Schuller parents, though they strove to protect their children's self-esteem and dignity through a "right to liberty within the system," also perceived their family rules as "very firm." Schuller also reported that he and his wife inculcated their children with possibility thinking: "We don't allow our children to have down moods. We believe anyone can control his moods."[51]

48. Robert H. Schuller, *The Peak to Peek Principle: How Possibility Thinkers Succeed* (Garden City, NY: Doubleday, 1980), 136–37.

49. Nason and Nason, *Robert Schuller*, 262.

50. Jan Franzen, "The Possibility Thinker Says: You Can Have a Happy Family," *Christian Life*, April 1975, 20–21, 54–55 (DVP).

51. Franzen, "The Possibility Thinker Says," 54.

116   CHAPTER 5

Not surprisingly, the Schullers extolled the disciplined administration of family. Schuller himself described their parenting as "exercising 'management by objectives' for the family."[52] For the difficult teen years, they suggested that the children maintain an involvement in music and sports. Moreover, Arvella reported that her experience parenting teenagers taught her that goal setting functioned to distract "them from the puzzling physical changes taking place in their bodies."[53] As with congregational life, even families with teenagers could be successful following the Schuller method: "What does a goal do for a teen? The dedication of young energy and bright wisdom gives *direction* for a fantastic future and forms *discipline* for a creative life-style free from ruinous habits" (91).

As part of family management, the Schullers labeled New Year's resolutions a "must": "We make quite a production of sharing our New Year's goals with each other, for we have found that we have a stronger commitment to those goals and dreams that we dare to share aloud than to those we lack the courage to express" (29). They also gathered for breakfast together every weekday. In the evening, they would often gather and Schuller would announce an "evening schedule."[54] Arvella framed commitment to family meals as one that would help the family *succeed*: "I can't begin to measure the success of our family without paying tribute to the great times we regularly experienced around the table" (Arvella Schuller, *The Positive Family*, 44). Always well managed, the Schuller table included a designated "runner" to answer the phone and retrieve forgotten items from the kitchen, cloth napkins, and devotions at both breakfast and dinner (44–45).

Arvella put a distinctively domestic twist in applying market logic to the faithful administration of a Christian home. She indicated that by attending conferences and seminars on executive and business management, she deepened her understanding about how to run a family: "Time after time I have noted that the different categories they enumerate coincide perfectly with the problem areas of home management: budgets,

---

52. Franzen, "The Possibility Thinker Says," 20–21, 54–55.

53. Arvella Schuller, *The Positive Family*, 89–90. Hereafter, page references from this work will be given in parentheses in the text.

54. Penner, *Goliath*, 226–27.

personnel, motivation, and productivity" (69). The priorities of market society were evident in their own household. In fact, Arvella encouraged "homemakers" to recast themselves as "home-executives" and suggested that young parents attend management or business seminars together. There, the family could learn the details of "management by objective." Arvella even listed the necessary steps for young parents to manage their families:

1. Clarify our values.
2. Establish priorities.
3. Set goals.
4. Make decisions.
5. Calculate the resources needed to reach the goals and carry out the decisions.
6. Review and adjust our resources (time, money, energy) to accommodate our carefully selected objectives.
7. Establish a calendar, setting time limits on decisions to make sure we don't procrastinate.
8. Set aside "meeting times" where "the team" reviews progress made toward realizing our determined objectives. (70)

Overall, Arvella ran a goal-oriented family. At the beginning of every month, she established a new list for herself. The list became such an orienting aspect of her life, she admitted to becoming "unglued" if she misplaced it. As Arvella mentored young mothers during seminars, she instructed them to always have a "to-do" list—"a practice of writing down what [they] wanted to accomplish" so that it "became an act of commitment, a most important actualization of [their] positive mental activity" (135–36). Obviously, Schuller and Arvella translated the management strategies used in their church into the family sphere—and shared those practices so as to be emulated by others.

The Allure of the Free Market

Even while the Schullers seemed to maintain a disciplined orderliness for their growing family, the social tumult and ongoing acceleration of the

118 CHAPTER 5

1960s did not escape the minister's attention. He revealed his concerns when he discussed the Psalms: "The Psalmist did not have to worry about cancer, or Communism, or thermonuclear war, or airplane crashes, or highway accidents, or labor-management conflicts."[55] While a late-career Schuller would attempt to stay above the political fray, in the 1960s he saw promotion of the free market and anticommunism as a viable route to church maintenance and growth.

The focus on the free market may have been pragmatic since Schuller frequently worried about losing control of his church property—and it eventually became clear that he saw the ministry as a family legacy. In the early 1960s he fretted in the pages of the RCA's *Church Herald* that the government could begin to start taxing churches. He wrote forcefully in opposition, suggesting that the impetus for such a terrible notion obviously originated with the Communist Party in America. Moreover, the minister explained that tax exemptions saved GGCC $22,000 per year, and he estimated that without them, the congregation would likely lose the title to the property within twenty-five years.[56]

Schuller's concern about the fate of the physical structures he had built continued throughout his career. In 1968 the minister intimated this distress to Peale. At the time, the RCA considered a "Union Plan" with the Southern Presbyterian Church. While Schuller supported mergers with denominations that maintained presbyterian forms of polity, he worried that the RCA would eventually merge with mainline Protestant denominations that maintained more hierarchical forms of church government where bishops held strong authority. Fretting over ceding control of his property, Schuller confided to Peale that GGCC would withdraw and become an independent congregation.[57] (Again in 1975, he voiced concern that his church property, appraised at $7,000,000, "for all practical purposes, belong[ed] to the Reformed Church in America"—even though "the denomination [had] not contributed to the purchase of the property and the building of this base of operation." Indeed, Schuller fretted

55. Robert H. Schuller, *Your Future Is Your Friend: An Inspirational Pilgrimage through the Twenty-Third Psalm* (Grand Rapids: Eerdmans, 1964), 78.

56. Robert H. Schuller, "Tax Church Properties?!" *Church Herald*, March 13, 1964, 12 (DVP).

57. Robert H. Schuller to Peale, July 5, 1968, CC-Correspondence, RHS/CC, box 32 (HCASC).

GROWING AMBITION AND MAGNIFICATION   **119**

that he really had no ability to leave the denomination—except with the approval of that very denomination. Schuller suggested that he had no intention to leave the RCA but would be much more comfortable if he had assurances that he "could split it off or my descendants in power could split it off and form an independent congregation.")[58]

Second, Schuller also realized that outspoken anticommunism offered a path to a public profile in the 1960s. Already early in the decade, the minister articulated a noted concern regarding communism. The minister recounted attending a meeting at the United Nations with "hard-core international Communists" in the early 1960s. While dining in the delegates room, Schuller attempted to reconcile how men wearing "gray flannel suit, neat white shirt, Windsor tie, and placid, disarming smiles" would "not stop at murder if they felt it would be a quicker and more successful way to win the world struggle."[59]

Intrigued by an advertisement that offered to reveal the "psychology behind communism," Schuller went to a three-day seminar (underwritten by a congregant) given by Australian psychiatrist Fred Schwarz. Schuller left provoked and confused—Schwarz claimed that communism had ensnared both religious and corporate leaders in America. According to Schwarz, many capitalists only posed as such. Underneath, Schwarz asserted, communist infiltration poisoned them into being dupes. Schuller's radar went on high alert, and he even suggested that pamphlets from the National Council of Churches had included communist talking points.[60] And after reading FBI director J. Edgar Hoover's *The Masters of Deceit: The Story of Communism in America and How to Fight It*, Schuller became further convinced that "the majority of ministers, churches, and even missionaries in foreign fields do not understand what communism really is and are being subtly brain-washed through publications that come from the radical liberal wing of the world religious movements."[61]

Deeply concerned about the fate of free enterprise, Schuller started preaching sermons that railed against communism. And criticism from

58. Robert H. Schuller to Henry DeRooy, October 30, 1975, CC-Correspondence, RHS/CC, box 35 (HCASC).

59. Robert H. Schuller, *Your Future*, 45.

60. Robert H. Schuller, *My Journey*, 256–57.

61. Robert H. Schuller to Henry Bast, November 23, 1960, CC-Correspondence, 1959–1962, RHS/CC, box 30 (HCASC).

120   CHAPTER 5

the RCA and the National Council of Churches served to deepen the minister's commitment. He felt isolated on the issue both in the denomination and among mainline Protestant pastors in Orange County.[62] Schuller seemed to become somewhat radicalized as he lamented that so many previously assumed kindred spirits in the ministry expressed more concern about the John Birch Society than they did about communism. In fact, he almost committed his whole career to anticommunism—the minister considered leaving the pulpit to dedicate himself full time. Only the counsel of Arvella dissuaded him: "Step aside from your anticommunism, Bob. Stay out of politics and focus on Jesus Christ and positive thinking."[63] With Arvella's encouragement, Schuller made a clear break from the anticommunist dogma. He realized that being a one-issue public intellectual would alienate many of the people he sought to persuade. The minister decided to forge what he understood as a lasting political neutrality while allowing other clergy to embrace a political and religious fusion that swirled in a "dangerous and macabre dance."[64] Eventually, Schuller even described his anticommunist foray as a "naïve excursion into politics."[65]

Given his previous shifts away from "hellfire" sermons and toward more positively oriented messages, as well as the minister's willingness to engage in nontraditional tactics for his church ministry, Schuller was in some danger of being seen as not conservative enough, not reliably orthodox. However, during the years in which he spoke strongly against communism and decidedly for free-market capitalism, the talk of politics provided an anchor of trust for church leaders who may have had some reservations. While confronting criticism for his pastoral decisions, Schuller's politics during this time protected him from suspicions of his

---

62. For more, see Robert H. Schuller to GGCC members, November 16, 1960, CC-Membership Mailings and Press release, "Will Communism Conquer America?" November 9, 1960, GGCC-News Releases, 1956–1965, RHS/CC, box 6 (HCASC).

63. Robert H. Schuller, *My Journey*, 259.

64. Robert H. Schuller, *My Journey*, 260.

65. Robert H. Schuller, *My Journey*, 254. However, at the time, Schuller also used his strident anticommunism as a defense when he sometimes interacted with controversial guests; see Hollis Green to Robert H. Schuller, November 5, 1976, CC-Correspondence, and Robert H. Schuller to Green, November 12, 1976, CC-Correspondence, 1976, RHS/CC, box 4 (HCASC).

general orthodoxy. As the minister moved away from explicit political statements, he did so on a reliable platform built on steady themes consistent with the general tenor of mainstream American conservatism, a stance that served him well in attracting corporate leaders to his board as well as when raising funds from megadonors beyond the local church.

As Schuller expanded his influence by becoming a popular theologian, in 1964 he published his ruminations on Psalm 23 in *Your Future Is Your Friend: An Inspirational Pilgrimage through the Twenty-Third Psalm*. In a rather short book of less than one hundred pages, the young minister explained to his readers the life lessons that they could absorb from this particular psalm. He registered acute concerns, revealing his political leanings, in particular, regarding communism throughout the narrative. At one point, Schuller indicated that "collectivism" and "the declining emphasis upon the individual" eroded human dignity.[66]

Ever in favor of free markets, Schuller once recounted an occasion where he returned to northwest Iowa and witnessed the decline of a farm that he remembered as a child as "stately, dignified, beautiful, with tall rows of green corn and golden acres of waving grain." Driving past during his visit, the minister described the farm as devolving into "weeds, bent and dry and dead." The cause? Government intervention, according to Schuller—the farm had become part of the soil bank, and the family received payments to allow the land to remain idle.[67] The importance of effort on the individual's part always lurked within Schuller's theology. As he discussed Psalm 23 in 1964, the minister suggested Christians could experience the presence of God when they "sharpen [their] spiritual capacity or sensitivity."[68] Moreover, if a person wants faith, the person should "choose it!"[69s]

The broader social concerns of the 1960s had, at first, seemed a distant unease for Schuller and his ministry. Discussing the civil rights movement, he commented that it "seemed far away" from "white Anglo Saxon Protestant Garden Grove, California."[70] The boundary of a conservative-

66. Robert H. Schuller, *Your Future*, 15.
67. Robert H. Schuller, *Your Future*, 16.
68. Robert H. Schuller, *Your Future*, 67.
69. Robert H. Schuller, *Your Future*, 87.
70. Robert H. Schuller, *My Journey*, 266.

122   CHAPTER 5

leaning, white suburbia created a buffer that obscured Schuller's vision from appreciating the depth of the issues involved. In fact, the minister expressed condescension for mainline Protestant pastors who had spent so much of their time and energy marching in the streets and fighting social injustice. Although he expressed sympathy for the interests of clergy concerned about social injustices, he felt that the "mental, emotional, and spiritual hurts of the average person were being totally ignored."[71]

His foray through anticommunism served to root his faith in the free market. Nevertheless, he acknowledged that those who competed in the free market faced significant challenges. As a result, his pastoral focus continually remained on the economic anxieties of career-minded men and women—car-centric and daily commuting to school and work—struggling with family and finances in a suburbanizing middle-class community. So while many of his ministerial colleagues joined protests, Schuller attended psychiatry conferences in Europe: "I returned home and launched both an alternative message and alternative strategy for turning a declining American church around." Turning away from larger structural problems, he focused his attention squarely on spiritually serving the fragile psyche of aspirational yet anomic people striving for upward mobility. "I had survived politics. I had survived the lures of ambition. My message was now ringing clear inside of me: I was called to be a preacher, and I was called to preach hope. Nothing more and nothing less."[72]

Yet, Schuller's eventual emphasis on possibility thinking explicitly assumed that opportunity abounded for everyone in the United States—regardless of their identity or status:

> At the bottom of every ladder, there is a crowd of talented, trained people with academic degrees and credentials who can drop names and claim connections, but they aren't going anywhere. Really, success is not a matter of talent, training, territory as much as it is the skillful and prayerful management of divinely-inspired ideas. The difference between the people at the top of the ladder and those at the middle and the bottom is so basic. The people at the top have learned

71. Robert H. Schuller, *My Journey*, 281–82.
72. Robert H. Schuller, *My Journey*, 282.

GROWING AMBITION AND MAGNIFICATION **123**

how to handle good ideas, but those who stay in the middle or at the bottom of the ladder have never learned to hatch, harbor, and handle creative thoughts.[73]

From Schuller's perspective, individuals must creatively work to fit themselves into the needs of market society. In contrast, social structures and systems can overwhelm individual initiative, often exploiting a "person's natural inclination to remain an invalid all of his life."[74] By that, the minister explained that political, social, and religious organizations tended to offer too much security in their programs—to the point that they inhibited individuals from learning to trust and develop their own independence.

Schuller's 1983 devotional, *Tough-Minded Faith for Tender-Hearted People*, frequently defined "faith in action" as active participation in the competitive free market.[75] At the outset, Schuller wrote in the introduction: "Now, my friend, let me be your guide to super-successful living. My promise? You can climb to the top!" Day 7 mentioned "the enormous decision-making powers" of "the chief executive officer." Day 22 and 23 described setting goals leading to upward mobility and taking responsibility for your own success: "You must develop a strategy and a scheme that will allow you to succeed." Day 29 introduced "a successful black multimillionaire and entrepreneur." Day 43 included a prayer when entering competition. Day 54 featured success with a job interview. Day 72 highlighted the president of a major corporation. Day 86 asked, "Are you starting a new business? Are you unemployed? Did you get laid off?" Days 100 through 110 all focused on timing, scheduling, life planning, and fear of the unknown. A sampling of future days revealed a consistent thrust on attaining an opportunity mind-set for employment and business success. Day 137 suggested, "Faith in action is positioning yourself in the marketplace." Day 149 stated, "Possibility thinkers thrive on competition." Day 195 encouraged investment risks as "gambling God's

---

73. Robert H. Schuller, *Self-Esteem: The New Reformation* (Waco, TX: Word, 1982), 85.

74. Robert H. Schuller, *Self-Esteem*, 88.

75. Robert H. Schuller, *Tough-Minded Faith for Tender-Hearted People* (Nashville: Nelson, 1983).

124 CHAPTER 5

way." In essence, enthusiasm, goal setting, strategic planning, and sheer grit represented the quality of Schuller's faith-filled person—with an eye toward anticipating executive leadership responsibilities of delegation, fiscal planning, hiring decisions, negotiation, and living under pressure. (Later devotions emphasized living for success despite ongoing disappointment and frequently reminded readers to pledge financial support to their church and tithe their income.)

Schuller endorsed the assumption that everyone in America had economic opportunity—if they had the right disposition and work ethic. He once noted that "one out of every 435 persons in the U.S.A. today is a millionaire. Almost all started small: a paycheck, some little money saved."[76] And the minister especially liked the story of two fellow Reformed Dutch Americans who would become famous for their business model: "When I was starting our church, in 1955, two men, Rich DeVos and Jay Van Andel, were starting a new sales organization with a clever marketing program in Ada, Michigan. (You can go anywhere from where you are!) All they had was a desk—and an idea! Today their business—Amway Corporation—has created dozens of millionaires out of policemen, teachers, and janitors! And Rich and Jay are reportedly worth many millions each! More important, they're using their success to build people, families, and stronger communities and churches, and doing more to relieve unemployment than anyone else I know!"[77] DeVos and Van Andel of Amway functioned as exemplars for Schuller. He shared with them an ethnic identity and religious tradition. Based on the quote above, the minister also saw Ada, Michigan, as similar in its "nowhere-ness" to northwest Iowa. And the two men found a creative method for becoming successful.

As Schuller departed from the political sphere and embraced the potential of psychology for meeting the modern demands of self-esteem and economic freedom, he turned his attention to the possibility of television—and more expansively marketing his techniques of church growth to pastors.

---

76. Robert H. Schuller, *The Peak to Peek Principle*, 136–37.
77. Robert H. Schuller, *Self-Esteem*, 137.

6

EXPANDING THE MINISTRY'S BOUNDARIES

Though Schuller promoted an open, more easygoing brand of Christianity, he remained beholden to certain levels of decorum during worship—"dignity" always remained a marker of congregational life at GGCC. In late 1968, the minister became suspicious that the nascent Jesus Movement would attempt to infiltrate his sanctuary. All head ushers received a memorandum from Schuller in November:

Be alert! If any barefooted, or guitar carrying, or other "hippie" people arrive, be prepared to *prohibit* their entrance into the sanctuary.

1. Advise them that their attire is improper. We have the right to establish these rules. If they don't like it—too bad.
2. *Do not let them get into the sanctuary.* Block their bodies with yours. Join hands to form a line if need be.
3. If they become physically difficult, call one of the policemen.
4. No musical instruments are permitted in the sanctuary.

Pray and hope that we have no difficulty.[1]

---

1. Memorandum, Robert Schuller to Head Ushers in the Sanctuary, November 27, 1968, CC-Correspondence, Robert H. Schuller/Crystal Cathedral (hereafter cited as RHS/CC), box 34, Hope College Archives and Special Collections, Holland, MI (hereafter cited as HCASC).

126 CHAPTER 6

Whether prescient or forewarned, Schuller's anticipated disruption came to pass. The GGCC ushers, indeed, forced some perceived interlopers from Sunday worship. The minister worried that the move could be interpreted as a form of "rudeness" or as "unchristian." However, Schuller defended the expulsion when a local military officer blanched at the unseemliness of attendees being forced out of a worship service and wrote a letter of complaint: "The reason this group was asked to leave was because they were in violation of an ordinance that prohibits people from sitting on the floor in the Chancel area or in the aisles that could block the exits. . . . I don't care if they were dressed in tuxedos!" He elaborated that a "General in the Army" in full dress would have also been escorted out if he chose to "squat" in the sanctuary. Schuller viewed it as a freedom of religion issue: "They are welcome to return any Sunday, providing 1) they are willing to sit on the pews or the chairs provided, 2) provided they will respect our form of worship. This is what you are fighting for—the freedom of churches to worship in their own way. Freedom for people to worship as they see fit—without interruption or disturbance."[2]

His insistence on decorum functioned as a key aspect of proper management of the church, and Schuller sought to perfect the administration of congregational life. Already within a decade of arriving in California, Schuller's ministry garnered attention from religious leaders intending to rationalize congregational organization. In 1962, and again in 1967, the Orange County minister was featured on the cover of *Church Management* magazine.[3] Sound administrative organization would become a primary method for strengthening churches. By 1969, Schuller had convinced himself that he had a foolproof formula for training congregational leaders and established the Robert H. Schuller Institute for Church Leadership (hereafter cited as the Institute). The minister hired Wilbert Eichenberger to direct the Institute and instructed him to "sell" the curriculum with a "money back guarantee."[4]

2. Schuller to Curt Roberts, December 4, 1968, CC-Correspondence, RHS/CC, box 34 (HCASC).

3. John Curran Hardin, "Retailing Religion: Business Promotionalism in American Christian Churches in the Twentieth Century" (PhD diss., University of Maryland, 2011), 289.

4. Schuller to Eichenberger, February 9, 1970, CC-Correspondence, 1968–1973, RHS/CC, box 4 (HCASC).

EXPANDING THE MINISTRY'S BOUNDARIES   **127**

Schuller bounded with confidence in the newly established Institute. Proving that he did not fear the financial risks in the endeavor, Schuller found himself $2,000 in the red after the first Institute event—sixty congregational leaders attended, but only forty had paid. Assessing it as a marketing problem, Schuller reckoned that he only needed seventy paying attendees to break even and proceeded to secure endorsements from Billy Graham ("I highly recommend the Robert Schuller Institute") and Donald McGavran ("Interested in Church Growth? Attend the Schuller Institute").[5] His marketing stratagem worked. Registrations soared.[6]

Schuller diversified his source of revenue for the Institute by lobbying for funding from sympathetic business corporations to subsidize the pastors and elders—and their spouses—to fly to Garden Grove to participate. The minister discovered that he could stabilize the funding for the Institute by convincing sympathetic corporations to pay for significant numbers of religious leaders and, at the same time, simplify the accounting with one simple check. For example, the minister prevailed upon Jay Van Andel, one of the founders of Amway, to underwrite the costs of delegates from his denomination, the Christian Reformed Church in North America (CRC). In correspondence with Van Andel, Schuller imagined the church and the business as allies in the growth of Christianity. In a note that indicated the significance of his singular persona, the minister wrote to Van Andel that it "thrilled" him "that between Amway and Schuller, we've been able to make a difference." He then expressed his belief that more could be accomplished if they tightened their alliance with a $145,000 gift to fully fund the experience for CRC leaders: "We could make a final impact that would produce positive results 100 years from now!"[7] His targeted outreach proved to be yet another savvy move. Van Andel wrote the check.

Even skeptical pastors found a fully funded trip to Southern California difficult to resist. One related to us that he held Schuller mostly in contempt—as a fellow minister in the Dutch Reformed tradition, he found *Hour of Power* embarrassing in its shallowness. When initially

5. Schuller to Eichenberger, February 9, 1970.

6. "The Robert Schuller Institute Continues to Grow," *Cathedral Chronicle*, September 3, 1981, Dennis Voskuil Papers, Holland, MI (hereafter cited as DVP).

7. Schuller to Van Andel, February 9, 1989, personal papers of Duane Vander Brug, Grand Rapids, MI.

128 CHAPTER 6

invited to the Institute, he declined. However, when his wife heard about the expenses-paid trip to Garden Grove, he gave in to her wishes and went. And then he felt chastened by the significant ways in which the experience shaped the rest of his ministry career. He was even able to talk to Schuller in person. Because the minister considered them brethren in ethnic and religious tradition, Schuller hosted the CRC contingent privately in his office on the twelfth floor of the Tower of Hope. The Michigan pastor recalled the meeting:

> We could ask [Schuller] questions, and I don't remember what questions we asked, but you know, one of the questions that troubled us [was] that he never mentioned sin, and his answer was—he says, "Listen, when the gardener works in my yard, and he comes to the door, and he has muddy boots, and I open the door to him, and I say, 'You can come in,' I don't have to tell him he's got to take his boots off when he sees that white clean carpet. He does that automatically. You don't have to hammer away at sin."[8]

In roughly its first decade of existence, the Institute claimed to have trained over twelve thousand pastors and lay leaders. Ever the entrepreneur, Schuller expanded the curriculum to a "Film Workshop" series, a nifty and portable package that allowed for local screenings in churches and homes around the country.[9] Within the first three years of launching the medium, the ministry estimated that over sixteen thousand individuals had been exposed to Schuller's Leadership Institute lectures.

Not Just a Movement—Church Growth Christianity

The church growth movement (CGM) rested on a conviction that the church had lost something, that it had begun a decline. Just as the twenty-first-century Christian church in the United States wrings its

8. This quote and those following were told to Mulder in interviews. For more on anonymous quotes, see "A Note on Sources."

9. Herman J. Ridder, "How We Did It: The Schuller Film Workshop," *Church Herald*, January 23, 1981, 14–15; "Film Workshop Workbook," Robert H. Schuller Institute for Successful Church Leadership, 1975-1980, RHS/CC, box 26 (HCASC); and "Schuller Institute Goes on the Road," *Cathedral Chronicle*, September 1981, 4 (DVP).

collective hands about the increasing number of self-identified religious "nones" and "dones," religious leaders in the late twentieth century registered the same concerns decades earlier. The post–World War II religious boom ebbed, and religious leaders became troubled. By 1981, a Baptist minister reported "every mainline denomination is faced with the same agonies of declining membership."[10]

Counterintuitively, Schuller, positioned within the oldest denomination in the United States, became a key personality driving the mainstreaming of the CGM. The Orange County minister even declared himself "the founder of the church growth movement."[11] With his Tower of Hope built, Schuller gained the attention of most drivers on the highway near Garden Grove and Anaheim. Vacationers to Disney would wonder at the tall office building topped with a cross. Yet, to make his influence on Christianity fully realized, the Orange County minister would have to pivot to less immediately tangible markers of success and leadership during the early 1970s.

In addition, as Schuller's profile grew during the decade, so did the critiques. With new attention coming from broadcasting the church's worship service, *Hour of Power*, and the expanding attendance for the Leadership Institute, the scrutiny arrived in force. Some criticized the seemingly vapid version of Christianity that Schuller preached. Others criticized him for sanctifying the pursuit of wealth and translating business practices into a system of church management.

Despite the scrutiny, Schuller found himself in the right place at the right time. *Newsweek* in 1971 assessed that much of GGCC's success resided in geography: "Borne on the tides of technicians attracted by Orange County's booming electronics and aerospace industries in the 1960s, Schuller's ministry flourished spectacularly."[12] The social and political conservatism of California nurtured a fusion of religion and business. Historian Darren Dochuk argued that Southern California became the locus for the "gospel of wealth." Through notions of stewardship and responsibility preached from the pulpit, Christians living in the economically booming region discovered they had license to throw themselves

10. Ralph Elliot, "Dangers of the Church Growth Movement," *Christian Century*, August 12–19, 1981, 799–801.

11. Robert H. Schuller, *Your Church Has a Fantastic Future! A Possibility Thinker's Guide to a Successful Church* (Ventura, CA: Regal Books, 1986), 292.

12. "Divine Property?" *Newsweek*, July 5, 1971, 51.

130   CHAPTER 6

into the profit-driven market and "enjoy the excess fruits of their labor."[13] Schuller found himself perfectly located in Orange County in particular, where "free enterprise economics grew into a pastime for the entire family to enjoy."[14] Touring families could experience an integrated vacation in which all the stops celebrated a promising future through economic freedom—including the GGCC campus, which played a key role in sacralizing the drive for family financial security.

As religious leaders unabashedly baptized the benefits of the market economy, they openly borrowed strategies from business management. A bit to the north of Garden Grove, in Pasadena at Fuller Theological Seminary, the CGM began to take shape throughout the 1960s. In many ways, the CGM translated rational business management practices into techniques for expanding church ministries. Applied within the United States, CGM tactics also took on racialized overtones. Historian Jesse Curtis demonstrated that within the growing influence of the CGM, white, middle-class suburbanite evangelicals effectively became a "people group." That is, they came to be seen as "a distinct cultural group with a strong sense of ethnic identity and loyalty," as equally distinct as any nation or tribal group to be diligently reached through missionary efforts across the globe.[15] The missionary underpinnings of the CGM allowed white evangelicals to justify not only their movement to the suburbs but also the maintenance of racial segregation in their work, residential, and faith communities. Keeping cultural boundaries was necessary to efficiently reach a distinct and culturally specific population—faithful evangelism (and sustained church growth) demanded it.

As certain white people felt threatened by the advance of civil rights in the 1960s, the principles of the CGM represented a safe refuge. Specifically, Curtis noted that the CGM "openly described racial integration as a threat to the health of American churches."[16] The mixing of racial

---

13. Darren Dochuk, *From Bible Belt to Sunbelt: Plain-Folk Religion, Grassroots Politics, and the Rise of Evangelical Conservatism* (New York: Norton, 2011), 184.

14. Dochuk, *From Bible Belt to Sunbelt*, 187.

15. Jesse Curtis, "White Evangelicals as a 'People': The Church Growth Movement from India to the United States," *Journal of Religion and American Culture* 30, no. 1 (March 20, 2020): 109.

16. Curtis, "White Evangelicals," 129.

groups hindered church growth by instigating unnecessary friction on the path to expanding membership. Amid justifying racial segregation, the assumed and uninterrogated benefits of church growth became widespread. Christian publishers leveraged the attention by expanding their publishing initiatives: "Eerdmans, the major evangelical publishing house, launched a church growth book series" in the 1960s.[17]

The early leaders of the CGM, Donald A. McGavran and C. Peter Wagner, taught at Fuller Theological Seminary. Though their work only paralleled Schuller's for many years, the CGM would claim Schuller as one of their own in the early 1970s.[18] In 1974 the CGM held its first national conference: the American Convocation for Church Growth—hosted by Schuller at GGCC. Over four hundred individuals gathered to learn from the leading names in the CGM: Schuller, Win Arn, W. A. Criswell, D. James Kennedy, McGavran, and Wagner. Schuller extolled the breadth of the attendees and asserted that they represented "the broadest spectrum of Protestantism—from the extreme fundamentalists to the extreme Liberals."[19] In his opening remarks at the event, cosponsored by Schuller's Leadership Institute and Fuller Seminary's Institute for Church Growth, Schuller declared it the greatest gathering of church growth authorities in history. He tantalized the audience by promising that the speakers would reveal the "secrets of successful church growth." Schuller concluded by insisting on the universality of the strategies, that they could "be applied by a church in an inner-city section of America, in slum sections of international cities abroad, and in suburban churches of affluent people." Schuller's growing stature (broadcasting *Hour of Power*) and enhanced legitimacy (establishing the Institute) made him a religious figure with whom to be associated. And the Orange County minister obliged the CGM—he also enjoyed their affirmation of his "tested" strategies.

However, Schuller's association with the CGM brought costs. Contemporary critics viewed church growth advocates as offering something

17. Curtis, "White Evangelicals," 119.

18. Jesse Curtis, *The Myth of Colorblind Christians: Evangelicals and White Supremacy in the Civil Rights Era* (New York: New York University Press, 2021), 101.

19. "Dr. Schuller Addresses Ministers on Final Day of Convocation," GGCC Press Release, February 22, 1975, CC-GGCC Press Releases, February 1975–June 1975, RHS/CC, box 29 (HCASC).

132 CHAPTER 6

different from traditional Christianity. Ralph Elliot, pastor of a prominent Baptist church in Chicago, warned in an article in *Christian Century*
that "the dangers inherent in the church growth movement are many,
and the crucial issue in assessing those dangers is whether we are talking
about becoming Christians or about building institutional membership."
Elliot asserted that the CGM offered a "pseudo gospel," and that, given
the promise "to assuage the guilt with the minimum of pain and connecting that promise with marketing techniques, there will be success. The
question is whether the result will bear any similarity to the church."[20]
Elliot identified Schuller, by name, as one of the most prominent pro-
ponents of the CGM and warned that too often the movement depended
on a pastor who could catalyze the entire congregation into the effort of
growing the ministry. Such a central role for one individual reeked of a
personality cult—the pastor became the "commander-in-chief" and dis-
solved "a plurality of committees that may dilute the power."[21]

In another critique, an assistant professor at Western Theological Seminary (WTS), Robert Nykamp, sent a delegation of students to the Leadership Institute—perhaps to critique their alum, Schuller, much in the way
he had scrutinized Norman Vincent Peale as a seminarian. Indeed, much
as a younger Schuller had mocked Peale, these ministry students had appeared to Schuller to be overly critical. When Schuller learned why they
were so critical, he became angry: they had been assigned to read "an article which was negative, inflammatory, judgmental, and prejudicial about
[Schuller's] ministry." The minister registered his disgust that these "young
minds" would be "pre-programmed"; he considered it "one of the most irresponsible acts from a pedagogical standpoint." Because of that experience,
Schuller became ambivalent about financially supporting WTS in the
future: "I am not about to finance, subsidize, and pay the salaries of people
who are going to use their influence to undermine our ministry."[22]

Despite those stewing concerns and critiques from within his own
tradition, historian Curtis saw the alliance of Schuller and the Fuller
Seminary line of the CGM as a watershed moment: "The CGM's posi-

20. Elliot, "Dangers of the Church Growth Movement," 801.
21. Elliot, "Dangers of the Church Growth Movement," 800.
22. Schuller to Nykamp, February 6, 1975, CC-Correspondence, 1975, RHS/CC,
box 34 (HCASC).

tive appraisal of Schuller is a striking indication of its comfort with the use of sleek marketing and business practices to sell the gospel. In these moments the CGM looked like nothing so much as an invitation to treat religion as another consumer good in the modern capitalist economy. American consumers had high standards and many options on Sunday morning. Churches needed to sell themselves or they would lose market share."[23] Curtis's assessment supports that Schuller had indeed cultivated a Christianity attentive to market dynamics, one that contained a suite of techniques that resonated with the goals of CGM. And with Schuller's platform on television and the Leadership Institute, the CGM elevated itself to another echelon in stature.

While the CGM advocates worked on growing the size of congregations, other churches focused on socioeconomic issues. In 1975, the National Council of Churches released a statement that condemned capitalism as "basically unjust" in that it exploited "the many for the few."[24] Shortly thereafter, the RCA's Classis California—during a meeting at GGCC— offered a public riposte that appeared to have been written largely by Schuller:

> A call not for the abolition of, but the Christianizing of the capitalist economic system, that faulty though it is, is unsurpassed in historical record of lifting people through the self-dignity-producing private enterprise system to a higher level of human welfare—with greater personal freedom—than any other economic system ever devised. We do not believe that the forced equal distribution of all economic wealth worldwide would eliminate the poverty problem. It would in fact eliminate the entire base of economic wealth. We believe that what is necessary is to produce more wealth with a spirit of Christ's loving, sharing attitude seeing the world as one organismic unity.[25]

In other words, then, the classis (and Schuller) affirmed capitalism as a system with which churches needed to partner—especially since CGM and capitalism both fixated on expansion.

---

23. Curtis, *Myth of Colorblind Christians*, 102.

24. "Capitalism 'Basically Unjust,' Ecumenical Consultation States," September 27, 1975, Shepherds Grove Church Archive, Irvine, CA (hereafter SGCA).

25. Resolution of the Classis of California, September 30, 1975 (SGCA).

134 CHAPTER 6

Schuller's alignment with CGM continued to sustain the path he had established for building and perfecting a market-driven Christianity. Interviewing the minister in 1976 on the *Tomorrow* show, Tom Snyder noted a concern: "Religion is a big business, really, and I wonder if it should be." Schuller scoffed: "You think it shouldn't be? The point is, we have to hire people, we have to pay postage, we have to pay taxes, we have to pay salaries, and we have to buy property."[26] More than just embracing free-enterprise capitalism and a business-friendly Christianity,[27] Schuller firmly believed that contemporary church leaders needed to embrace the same techniques used by successful corporations: designing products fitted to the felt needs of the masses, securing the financial means to start and viably sustain new ventures, and marketing aggressively through multiple channels to intentionally advertise offered services and confidently legitimate the entire enterprise. As he himself wrote, "I began to observe marketing principles that were operating in American business and then tried to apply them to our work in the church and to our ministry through television . . . we applied old principles to new situations."[28]

Thus, Schuller's aligning with the CGM in the 1970s was symptomatic of a larger turn occurring among American clergy, namely, a growing conviction that in order to succeed, church leaders must enter the now-dominant reality of market society by leveraging the mechanisms of the market to both sustain and grow their ministries in the coming century.

The Gospel of Free Enterprise and Wealth

Schuller's amalgamation of religious faith and capitalism represented a further sophistication of probusiness sentiments within American

---

26. "Tom Snyder Interview," 1976, transcript, folder "Crystal Cathedral Robert H. Schuller–Interviews, 1976," box 26, Robert H. Schuller Collection, H93-1188 (HCASC), 37.

27. Mark T. Mulder and Gerardo Martí, *The Glass Church: Robert H. Schuller, the Crystal Cathedral, and the Strain of Megachurch Ministry* (New Brunswick, NJ: Rutgers University Press, 2020); see also Gerardo Martí, *American Blindspot: Race, Class, Religion, and the Trump Presidency* (Lanham, MD: Rowman & Littlefield, 2020).

28. Schuller, *Tough-Minded Faith*, 164.

Christianity. Of course, Protestantism and capitalism have always had a synergistic relationship—beginning in post-Reformation Europe.[29] In the United States, though, the relationship took on a new fervor. In the colonial period, intentionally religious businesses affected the development of American capitalism, although its future direction remained ambiguous.[30] Between the Civil War and World War I, though, "corporate evangelicals" deliberately sought to synthesize Christianity and modern consumer capitalism. Historian Timothy Gloege documented how business leaders in places like Chicago allied with evangelist Dwight Moody (founder of Moody Bible Institute [MBI]) to recalibrate Christianity as a procapitalism faith tradition in order to quell unrest among workers and unions in the city. Religion, in other words, could be manipulated to maintain the moral order that benefited elites.[31] Conservative Christian leaders saw unions as one step away from communism.[32] Instead, they wanted the United States to lean into its ethos of the market that rewarded rugged individualism.

In fact, places like Chicago's MBI became significant sites for Christian fundamentalists to learn and disseminate a "commercial conception of Christianity" schema.[33] MBI's longtime board of trustees president, Henry Parsons Crowell, saw the institution as a strategic place to normalize "corporate strategies in the religious world."[34] Crowell had had experience in creating strategies adaptable to many similar others—as the founder of the Quaker Oats Company, his tools for promoting consumer goods proved so effective that they became widely seen as assumed

---

29. Max Weber, *The Protestant Ethic and the Spirit of Capitalism* (London: Routledge, 1905).

30. Joseph P. Slaughter, *Faith in Markets: Christian Capitalism in the Early American Republic* (New York: Columbia University Press, 2023).

31. Timothy E. W. Gloege, *Guaranteed Pure: The Moody Bible Institute, Business, and the Making of Modern Evangelicalism* (Chapel Hill: University of North Carolina Press, 2015), 44.

32. Matthew Avery Sutton, *American Apocalypse: A History of Modern Evangelicalism* (Cambridge, MA: Belknap Press of Harvard University Press, 2014), 247.

33. For more on the manufactured linkages between conservative evangelicalism and modern consumer capitalism, see Gloege, *Guaranteed Pure*.

34. Gloege, *Guaranteed Pure*, 137.

136 CHAPTER 6

"techniques of modern consumer capitalism."[35] Gloege argued that "in the ideological overlap between modern consumer capitalism and religion, evangelicals at MBI forged a consuming faith."[36] Historian Darren Dochuk echoed that fundamentalist leaders like Crowell "wanted their youth trained for evangelism overseas, but also equipped with technical managerial skills for the manufacturing sector at home."[37] To that end, ministers and other religious leaders morphed into "religious 'retailers'" while the laity became the "consumer."[38] Similarly, in southern Illinois, Robert LeTournea, owner of a company that designed and built land-excavating equipment, sought to synthesize evangelical outreach and business technique. In the late 1930s he founded the LeTournea Technical Institute in East Texas (away from labor unions and government regulations) to begin "training youth to advance a new Christian, capitalist order."[39]

In sum, these evangelical leaders found a "vibrant relationship between Christian education and corporate populism."[40] And this new gospel spread quickly. Eventually, according to historian Darren Grem, conservative evangelicalism, in particular, "became grounded private sector modes of thought and action."[41] In other words, evangelicals became ever more adept at implementing the tools of the marketplace; though technically not an evangelical, Schuller would become proficient at melding faith and business and become a champion of using development and management methodologies.

In part, the gospel of free enterprise became more appealing to Christians because it offered a countermove against the growth of government instigated by President Franklin Roosevelt's New Deal. Already in 1936, as the Roosevelt administration geared up for the president's reelection campaign, they found that the most robust opposition to the New Deal

35. Gloege, *Guaranteed Pure*, 137.
36. Gloege, *Guaranteed Pure*, 139.
37. Dochuk, *From Bible Belt to Sunbelt*, 54.
38. Gloege, *Guaranteed Pure*, 177.
39. Dochuk, *From Bible Belt to Sunbelt*, 55.
40. Dochuk, *From Bible Belt to Sunbelt*, 57.
41. Darren E. Grem, *The Blessings of Business: How Corporations Shaped Conservative Christianity* (New York: Oxford University Press, 2016), 236.

EXPANDING THE MINISTRY'S BOUNDARIES **137**

and the FDR administration arose not from the "economic reactionaries" but from the "religious reactionaries": "The opposition of what one can call the evangelical churches is growing steadily more bitter and open."[42] These evangelicals saw the New Deal undermining "traditional American capitalist values."[43] No less than the president of evangelical Wheaton College decried the advent of Social Security in 1935 as "contrary to the spirit and the detailed teachings of the Word of God."[44] In fact, many fundamentalist and conservative Christians began to see the encroaching power of the federal government as a manifestation of "the Antichrist, and his minions."[45] As noted earlier, Schuller himself eventually considered leaving congregational ministry to establish an anticommunism movement. The fear for these Christian and corporate leaders: a slide toward citizens expecting too much from the government, being seduced into dependence by life on the dole, and, ultimately, being made vulnerable to communism. What could offer the most significant bulwark against this evil?

As many conservative Christians expressed their concern that FDR's policies would lead the nation into godless communism, they became convinced that the most effective remedy, then, would be unfettered business, the free market, and the sanctity of private property. Historian Dochuk explained that in postwar America, "Evangelical preachers and entrepreneurs took this moment to trumpet a new gospel of wealth that identified threats to pristine capitalism in big government."[46] And historian James Hudnut-Beumler argued that conservative Christianity found itself so enthralled with business practices that "after World War II, the majority of the books about church finances concerned technique rather theology."[47] Theological rationale was assumed or obscured in favor of prescribing *habits* of giving (especially among the youth) and attitudes of steward-

42. Sutton, *American Apocalypse*, 232.
43. Sutton, *American Apocalypse*, 240.
44. Sutton, *American Apocalypse*, 244.
45. Sutton, *American Apocalypse*, 258.
46. Dochuk, *From Bible Belt to Sunbelt*, 169.
47. James Hudnut-Beumler, *In Pursuit of the Almighty's Dollar: A History of Money and American Protestantism* (Chapel Hill: University of North Carolina Press, 2007), 155.

138 CHAPTER 6

ship—"people who canvassed for the pledge [a financial commitment to a church] were guided in the classic salesman fashion to deflect objections."[48] Sales, capitalism, and Christianity became difficult to disentangle.

Coming into pastoral ministry in the 1950s, Schuller found himself surrounded by a Christianity that had been melded with procapitalist sentiments. By this time, mainstream Christian commitment came to include a blessing of wealth—namely, that Christians *should* attempt to be wealthy as part of their faithfulness. Such a theology proved attractive to newly middle-class families in the booming economy of Schuller's new church home in Orange County. And the repository of their generosity would be the church.

Finding the Money

As Schuller increasingly accommodated the church to contemporary business practices, money management would function as a key marker of integrity for the GGCC ministry. Good accounting was crucial. Even as Schuller kept planning for growth, he remained primed to remind anyone who would listen that the ministry had always been frugal. In a 1972 memorandum to the staff business administration committee, the minister enumerated the lengths the church had undertaken to limit costs in previous years: "Persons should be reminded that we waited three years to upholster the pews and that long to replace the carpeting in the sanctuary, and we have waited seven years to put in the sound system that we needed seven years ago!! And we have waited twelve years with the fence, gatehouse, and our drive in worship sound system."[49]

In the same memo, Schuller estimated that the ministry would grow by 600 members every year and that he would eventually need a sanctuary to handle 4,000 congregants. Demonstrating his optimistic trajectory of growth, Schuller anticipated an astonishing membership figure of 18,000 by 1992. In considering future attendance, the minister was attentive to capital. He wondered to his staff what kind of income would

48. Hudnut-Beumler, *In Pursuit of the Almighty's Dollar*, 155 and 168–69.
49. Memorandum, June 16, 1972, Schuller to Staff Business Administration Committee, CC-Correspondence, 1968–1973, RHS/CC, box 4 (HCASC).

Ivanhoe Reformed Church, site of Schuller's first pastorate

Reverend and Mrs. Schuller posing with the mortgaged organ

Cars filling the parking lot for a worship service at the Orange Drive-In

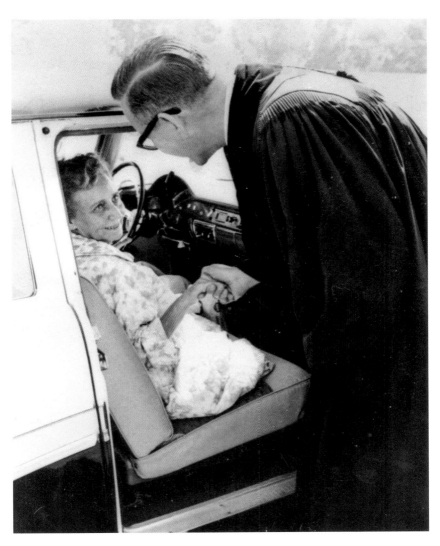

Schuller greeting a worshiper in her car at the drive-in

Cars gathered in the Garden Grove Community Church parking lot for drive-in worship

Schuller in his office lounge

The Schuller family

Schuller and architect Richard Neutra

Norman Vincent Peale and Schuller at the groundbreaking ceremony for the Tower of Hope

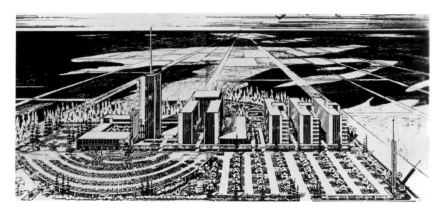

We urgently need the land..
1. To enlarge the drive-in by 300 cars.
2. Provide parking space for 500 cars.
3. Building space for our youth.
4. Three acres will be sold for a Christian Retirement Center.

A brochure cover from Garden Grove Community Church requesting donations to purchase more land by offering a glimpse of the future church grounds

Reverend and Mrs. Schuller on the Garden Grove Community Church grounds

Reverend and Mrs. Schuller pose in front of Christ the Good Shepherd statue

The Garden Grove Community Church sign as seen from the street

The Crystal Cathedral under construction

The interior of the Crystal Cathedral

Schuller with boxes of bumper stickers with his trademark phrase

An interior shot of Schuller preaching at the Crystal Cathedral

The Crystal Cathedral and Tower of Hope

The Crystal Cathdedral at twilight

EXPANDING THE MINISTRY'S BOUNDARIES   **139**

the ministry produce if 50 to 100 percent of the members actually tithed. With these financial estimates in mind, Schuller instructed the committee: "Review *constructive critical attitude* and *be prepared to improve* the program that educates people in stewardship when they join this church."[50] In other words, Schuller wanted to ensure that new members of GGCC knew that the ministry expected tithing. While casting grand visions, he remained quite preoccupied with the details of funding. The memo indicated that Schuller would be leaving for vacation. Seemingly concerned about how financial issues might spiral in his absence, the minister allowed his missive to balloon to six single-spaced pages. Schuller even instructed the committee about when to meet (Tuesday morning at nine), where (his office), and how long (up to "three hours or more!").

As Schuller framed church-growth advice while being attentive to business models, he utilized suburban shopping centers as the ultimate template. The metaphor of the modern mall was apt. First, it offered accessibility—located at the intersections of major highways or arterial streets. Churches should do the same and avoid placement in "the heart of a community."[51] Second, successful retailing demands not just "ample" parking but "surplus" parking. In fact, Americans had "become spoiled by easy parking" and now expected it everywhere, including at their churches: an American's "behavior pattern, shaped by parking as he knows it in the business world, is not going to change radically on Sunday when he comes shopping for church—unless he is deeply committed."[52] (In fact, Schuller had long *advertised* parking as a feature of his church—a 1962 advertisement boasted "parking for 700 cars.")[53] Third, shopping centers offered plenty of inventory. The expectation of a wide-ranging inventory, according to Schuller, caused significant problems for small churches since they simply could not offer the vast array of programs and services that modern consumers had grown to expect. Fourth,

---

50. Memorandum, June 16, 1972.

51. Schuller, *Your Church Has a Fantastic Future!*, 246.

52. Schuller, *Your Church Has a Fantastic Future!*, 247.

53. See advertisement for "Garden Grove Community Drive-in Church," *Register*, June 30, 1962, 7.

140 CHAPTER 6

successful shopping centers offered good customer service. Churches thus needed a stable team of well-trained laypeople who could offer welcome and hospitality. Fifth, businesses drew customers through effective advertising. Thus, churches should raise their visibility by devoting a significant portion of their budget to marketing. Sixth, possibility thinking. For this point Schuller offered no analogy to the shopping mall. Instead, the minister extolled the virtues of a value system grounded in possibility thinking. At his church, that system translated into the fact that great ideas never get derailed by the question, "What will it cost?" Which also led to the seventh and final principle: good cash flow. Schuller implored churches to never be afraid of debt. They should, however, only take out loans for exciting and dynamic projects that members of the congregation and potential attenders would find interesting.

Some of the minister's most well-formed concepts centered on the role of debt. Using a story from early in his ministry at Ivanhoe Reformed in suburban Chicago, Schuller warned that churches "should never borrow money for coal." He explained that as a first-time homeowner, he didn't have enough cash to buy coal to heat his home for the winter in October of 1950. A congregant had estimated that Schuller would need about five tons of coal for the entire winter—at $15 per ton, for a total of $75. The family did not have that much money on hand, and Schuller asked the coal yard to charge him for it. The yard refused and suggested trying to borrow from the bank. Looking into that strategy, the minister quickly learned that banks also tended to not lend money for nonappreciable items—especially items like coal that literally went up in smoke. While the banker took pity on him and loaned the funds for the coal, he also offered some insight, relating that the bank would finance cars and houses because those items appreciated in value or at least retained equity, so the bank could also be assured of some value if the borrower defaulted. Schuller explained: "Now that's a fundamental principle. We borrow money for this church, but we don't borrow money for coal! We borrow money for everything that has collateral, nondepreciable value. But we don't borrow money for our television ministry, for interest on capital debt, for salaries or for utilities. That's coal money."[54]

---

54. Schuller, *Your Church Has a Fantastic Future!*, 255.

Appreciating the immense power of credit, the minister had a policy within his ministry to borrow as much as possible, as fast as possible.[55] And the ministry used debt as a motivator for giving: "The truth is, financial debt frequently is a spur to church growth. Members of the church know that their support is needed there, and people need to be needed. As a result, they do not resist maximum contributions."[56] Borrowing demonstrated need, which spurred more giving. At the same time, the fact that the church had the ability to borrow significant funds signaled to financially astute members that the congregation was fundamentally sound, that the future was deemed secure.

Even as he offered counsel on the willingness to take on debt, Schuller also advised that fund-raising could be an enjoyable endeavor. In fact, the minister reveled in this aspect of his duties, remarking that "fundraising can be fun."[57] Such a suggestion, though, seemed to be aspirational as Schuller, at times, found development work quite overwhelming—especially when being critiqued.[58] To do it well, then, Schuller also revealed some specific principles that he followed. First, churches should promote themselves as financially solvent, good investments for potential benefactors: "Remember that you can spoil the whole 'money tree' if you give the impression that you are having money problems! Nobody likes to invest in a shaky business. Plead and beg and you will only reveal your weakness. And a weak institution does not inspire generous contributions."[59] More than that, fund-raising should focus on dramatic projects and avoid "small pickings" like suppers, sales, or second offerings.[60] To that end, Schuller suggested that "every year you must offer some new challenge in the form of a new program, a new project, a new building,

---

55. Schuller, *Your Church Has a Fantastic Future!*, 263.

56. Draft mailer from GGCC to note holders, November 1974, GGCC Stewardship Materials, RHS/CC, box 6 (HCASC), and Schuller, *Your Church Has a Fantastic Future!*, 264.

57. Schuller, *Your Church Has a Fantastic Future!*, 303.

58. Michael Nason and Donna Nason, *Robert Schuller: The Inside Story* (Waco, TX: Word, 1983), 242–43.

59. Schuller, *Your Church Has a Fantastic Future!*, 304.

60. Schuller, *Your Church Has a Fantastic Future!*, 305.

142 CHAPTER 6

a new addition to the staff or a new missionary project."[61] If churches did not, fickle congregants would assume that the organization had started to decline. Moreover, building programs should be framed for church boards or councils as "once-in-a-lifetime" opportunities—and to miss out would risk the future of the ministry.[62] To the pastors who allowed themselves to be duped or intimidated into stagnation, Schuller warned, "*You* are making this growth-retarding decision based on *your negative assumption* that God has no other possible sources of financial aid to meet your increased budget!"[63]

And while some pastors expressed a hesitancy to harangue their congregations about tithing, Schuller offered more advice. He suggested a "once-a-year message" on giving that focused on how tithing functioned as "the most fantastic key to financial security."[64] In other words, by giving to the church, members would receive even more financial blessing from God. More than that, Schuller advised that pastors employ their heaviest advertising "when people are in a buying mood."[65] Just as an appliance store knows to market air conditioners in July and not in December, pastors should consider pushing hard for giving around peak holy days on the church calendar—especially Easter. Schuller recalled that his discovery of the efficiencies of direct mailing led him to send invitations to the 130,000 homes within a ten-mile radius of the church grounds. In considering the imaging on the promotional material, Schuller insisted that pastors refrain from trying to "impress Christians or religious people."[66] The appeal should be directed toward the unchurched—the minister suggested using sermon titles that could appear on articles in secular magazines (Schuller's example: "How to Make Marriage Succeed in Today's World"). The pastor gravitated toward "topical and relational messages about overcoming fears, worries, and anxieties." In fact, he

61. Schuller, *Your Church Has a Fantastic Future!*, 306.
62. Nason and Nason, *Robert Schuller*, 109.
63. Schuller, *Your Church Has a Fantastic Future!*, 307.
64. Schuller, *Your Church Has a Fantastic Future!*, 309, and Robert H. Schuller, "Make Them Want to Give," *Church Herald*, November 22, 1968, 11 (DVP).
65. Schuller, *Your Church Has a Fantastic Future!*, 329.
66. Schuller, *Your Church Has a Fantastic Future!*, 330.

acknowledged having given up on scriptural exposition quite early in his tenure in Orange County.[67]

Schuller recognized the repeated hounding of his ministry by detractors, but he triumphantly reported that his "church program has continued to grow by leaps and bounds while those who have criticized have declined astonishingly."[68] By 1975, the ministry proudly claimed all the following:

"America's first drive-in church!"
A 262-foot lighted cross that could be seen across the highways of Orange County.
A twenty-four-hour telephone counseling service.
The county's largest Sunday school (5,000 enrolled).
A lay ministry training center (1,100 enrolled).
Five different singles ministry programs—and sponsorship of National Positive Christian Singles Conference.
A "Keenagers" ministry for retirees and senior citizens.
The Orange County Christian Youth Center—a 25,000-square-foot facility for junior high, senior high, and college students.
"California's largest literacy training center!"
The Inspiration Foundation, a trust for "inheritive monies which will continue to underwrite the dynamic GGCC missions for decades and centuries to come!"
The "Mother of new churches!"—GGCC claimed lineage over the more than fifty drive-in churches that had started in the previous twenty years.
The *Hour of Power*—the "first mainline Protestant church service to be televised regularly in the United States."
The Leadership Institute: over 4,000 graduates in the first six years of existence.[69]

67. Schuller, *Your Church Has a Fantastic Future!*, 334.
68. Schuller, *Your Church Has a Fantastic Future!*, 257.
69. "Come Celebrate with Us!" Promotional flyer for Tenth Anniversary Celebration, 1980 (DVP). CC Anniversary Celebration, Twentieth, 1975, RHS/CC, box 5 (HCASC).

144 CHAPTER 6

GGCC and its related ministries proved to be a Southern California religious juggernaut.

For a minister fixated on church growth, even Schuller had limits as to whom he wanted in his pews. He did not want "impossibility thinkers." These obstructionists would only hamper dynamic growth. The minister advised to not preach the kinds of sermons that would attract these types of congregants. These included "anti" sermons. That is, sermons that criticized a political system (curious since Schuller had made a name for himself as an anticommunist during his early days in Orange County) or another religious tradition. If that strategy failed, Schuller offered methods for chasing off these "neurotic negativists." He suggested avoiding preaching negative sermons. He also reported that *Robert's Rules of Order and Parliamentary Procedure* allowed him as the president and chairman to "keep impossibility thinkers from disrupting a meeting or taking the reins."[70]

In a lecture at the Leadership Institute in 1975, Schuller indicated that he saw Sunday worship not as a transformative experience but, rather, as an affirming one: "I think when God made the human being, He made us with an inspirational gas tank that has only a seven day supply, and after that starts sputtering whether we know it or not."[71] His audience-oriented methodology worked. However the ministry was assessed, both the praises and the criticisms recognized that Schuller explicitly mobilized a variety of market-oriented mechanisms—from targeted marketing to bureaucratic administration to financial management—to lead his church.

And the quantifiable results were undeniable. In 1976, the *Wall Street Journal* highlighted Schuller and GGCC as defying the trends of decay within mainline Protestantism. While most denominations recorded declines, including the RCA, Schuller reported that his church had grown from 2,100 members in 1965 to 8,000 ten years later. The arti-

---

70. Schuller, *Your Church Has a Fantastic Future!*, 280–81.

71. Barry Willbanks to Schuller, April 3, 1975, CC-Correspondence, RHS/CC, box 34 (HCASC). Willbanks actually appended to the letter a doctorate of ministry paper he had written about Schuller's theology after attending the Leadership Institute in February 1974: "Robert H. Schuller's Gospel of Self Esteem." This quote can be found on page 4 of the paper and derived from a recorded lesson of Schuller's.

cle highlighted that the minister saw his church as a business within the service industry—and that local pastors in Orange County sensitive to their competition estimated that Schuller derived numerical growth through "sheep stealing" (simply luring members away from other congregations). Without documentation, Schuller, though, averred that two-thirds of GGCC's membership had been unchurched prior to their arrival—an assertion that was, itself, a marketing move.[72]

Hour of Power—*Broadcasting Evidence*

Schuller was remarkably successful according to the standard measure of pastoral excellence: the expansion of church buildings and grounds. Moreover, the ability to attract members, raise significant funding, gain more land, and build bigger in order to attract even more members was the *sine qua non* of clerical achievement. Yet the ambitious Schuller always sought to expand the ministry in new ways. The next stage of growth would necessitate finding a means to broaden his charismatic influence beyond the building. Enter Schuller's foray into a televised broadcast ministry.

Although signals would suggest that Schuller had been mulling a broadcast ministry for years, he preferred to tell the story wherein evangelist Billy Graham, in town for a crusade at Angel Stadium, broached the idea for the first time. Graham, in Schuller's narrative, had been impressed by the infrastructure support the Orange County minister had mustered for his crusade. And according to the local newspaper, the ministry had been approached by a television production entity, the Walter J. Bennet Company, who wanted to broadcast GGCC's services "in color."[73] Either way, Schuller reported that he initially resisted the concept and decided that he would only do it if his congregation agreed to underwrite the annual costs.

In truth, though, it seemed that the minister both sought and instigated the opportunity to broadcast the worship services. Schuller's comments at

---

72. William Abrams, "'Possibility Thinking' and Shrewd Marketing Pay Off for a Preacher," *Wall Street Journal*, August 26, 1976, 1, 9–10.

73. Bertha Barron, "G.G. Community Church Moves Ahead," *Register*, November 15, 1969, 13.

146   CHAPTER 6

the time could be interpreted as an ultimatum to his congregation. At one point he intimated that he likely would not remain at GGCC if the church failed to support the broadcast: "If God wants me to remain here in this church, I know that the $200,000 to finance the broadcast in 1970 will be forthcoming."[74] After donation pledges passed the $200,000 threshold within just eight days, the ministry began to pursue broadcasting Sunday morning services on a Gene Autry-owned local station, KTLA-TV (Channel 5).[75] Schuller saw symmetry in the idea—he had arrived in California fifteen years earlier and preached to people who remained in the privacy and safe spaces of their cars. With the broadcast, he would advance that effort by preaching to them in the privacy and safe spaces of their living rooms.

Schuller, at times, reframed *Hour of Power* as a strategic attempt to solve the church's capacity problem. In other words, the minister suggested that he had hoped that the broadcast could satiate all the people who wanted to worship at GGCC but couldn't because of space. He told one interviewer that, in 1970, when the church began to go on television, "I hoped that would conclude the necessity of enlarging the structure." The minister based that logic on hearing that local sports teams typically lost gate revenue when their games appeared on television. Schuller eventually claimed *Hour of Power* catalyzed the opposite effect: inducing higher attendance for worship. When the situation was framed in that way, the minister felt he had no choice but to eventually build the Crystal Cathedral, critics be damned: "My critics have been shooting at me, they don't have to solve my problem, and they've never come up with any suggestions, they have never walked my walk, they have never been in my moccasins, and they probably themselves more often than not walked away, and I swear to God most of them would've walked away what I would not walk away from because I never walked away from doing the chores. You have to milk the cows come hell or high water—the cows get milked [pounding on desk]. And I have integrity."[76] The farm metaphors always seemed to offer resonance for Schuller's explanations for ministry decisions.

74. Barron, "G.G. Community Church Moves Ahead."
75. Schuller, *My Journey*, 293-94.
76. Interview, Robert Schuller and Dennis Voskuil, March 3, 1983 (DVP).

Of course, though, as with every Schuller-led endeavor, there seemed to be a moment of panic and insurmountable failure. As the ministry planned to broadcast the first service in early 1970, they suddenly realized that the lighting demands would necessitate the installation of a new transformer at a cost of $10,000. At that moment, the ministry had only a stack of index cards with pledges of financial support—it had no cash on hand, and no money in the bank. Schuller insisted that he felt mostly relief, since he had little appetite for opening himself to more critiques that would surely follow the broadcasting of his sermons. He decided to let the situation sort itself out, as he would not pursue any miracles or benefactors to find an emergency donation of $10,000. Yet, that very afternoon, a young couple appeared on his appointment schedule. Schuller assumed that they had scheduled time with him to discuss their marriage. When they arrived, though, they revealed that they had started a business the previous year that had yielded them a net profit of $100,000, and they wanted to make GGCC their congregation. The couple presented Schuller with their first tithe: $10,000. The minister reported that he looked at them and said, "You have just launched a television ministry!"[77]

The move to television began in earnest. The minister delegated content control to Arvella, likely because she had always been integral to orchestrating the liturgy of the worship services. In an interview with *Creation* magazine, she said part of their broadcast strategy for *Hour of Power* included a careful curation of songs. Prerequisites for inclusion included "singability," nonsexist wording, and modern language. Her first task involved replacing any sexist language in hymns and removing archaic "thees" and "thous" from Scripture passages.[78] It seemed that nothing escaped her watchful eye.

In fact, anyone with access to the inner workings of *Hour of Power* gave absolutely "full credit" for its success to Arvella. They noted that the show ascended to become the most-professional religious program on Sunday mornings because of Arvella's "critical, creative, and artistic side" and her refusal to tolerate even minor sloppiness in the produc-

---

77. Schuller, *My Journey*, 306.
78. "Arvella Schuller Interview," *Creator*, January 1980, 17 (DVP).

148 CHAPTER 6

tion.[79] Historian Kate Bowler reported that Arvella gained a reputation as a "stickler for the details" and that she "relished her role as the silent orchestrator of the television program that made her husband a star and her church into an icon of Christian entertainment." In fact, "her staff jokingly called her position 'The Man Upstairs' for her omnipresent perch in the Cathedral broadcast center."[80] If the camera happened to film an unhappy or surly face, Arvella had it edited out. If Schuller himself made a mistake, his wife made arrangements for a later retake to be seamlessly edited into the service.

The forty-three-year-old minister became acquainted with the mechanics and makeup expectations of television production, and soon he was booming every Sunday what would become his signature opening line: "This is the day the Lord has made! Let us rejoice and be glad in it!"[81] Schuller liked to think that he would be reaching a new audience of the unchurched. He described them as "nonsectarian, secular people"—the same people who had shown up at the drive-in in 1955.[82] And the minister began to see himself as delivering a therapeutic good news.[83]

By February 1971, just a year after the first broadcast, Hour of Power proved a solid investment. Through congregational pledges, major donors, and checks that arrived through the mail from viewers, the show even achieved a small surplus. Eventually, the revenue derived from donors to the broadcast would far outpace the revenue from member offerings to the church itself, leading to its own complications given the dependence of Hour of Power to the person at the center of the broadcast.[84] By June 1978, Hour of Power's national prominence garnered enough interest to merit a profile on CBS's popular 60 Minutes program.[85]

---

79. Bella Stumbo, "The Time Muhammad Ali Asked for Robert Schuller's Autograph," Los Angeles Times, May 29, 1983, https://tinyurl.com/29rprty5.

80. Kate Bowler, The Preacher's Wife: The Precarious Power of Evangelical Women Celebrities (Princeton: Princeton University Press, 2019), 120.

81. Schuller, My Journey, 309–10.

82. Schuller, My Journey, 311.

83. Schuller, My Journey, 312.

84. Mulder and Martí, The Glass Church, 2020.

85. Hour of Power was the lead segment on CBS's 60 Minutes on June 25, 1978, https://www.imdb.com/title/tt10957786/?ref_=ttep_ep42.

Schuller's personality worked well on television. His longtime assistant, Michael Nason, described the minister's rhetoric as "unabashedly corny."[86] And that Schuller "was rank with puns and other forms of corny humor, making a joke out of everything."[87] As might be guessed with someone who understood himself as a religious innovator, Nason described Schuller as better at speaking than listening.[88] Other copastors would learn that meetings with Schuller functioned as listening sessions more than discussions. The minister excelled with monologues—and turned up the charisma with the cameras on.

The minister also had his hand forced by the growth of the "Jesus people" on the Christian scene. Schuller felt he needed to respond to the charismatic movement when it arrived in Southern California in the late 1960s. After all, both the Anaheim Vineyard Christian Fellowship and Calvary Chapel Costa Mesa, charismatic churches founded just a few miles away from GGCC, were expanding while simultaneously spinning out similarly named church plants in surrounding communities. Was this an unexpected movement of the Spirit? As a means of discernment, Schuller spent a day in prayer with another RCA pastor, Harold Bredeson, who had been considered a proponent of the charismatic movement as it existed within the Reformed tradition. After many hours, the two pastors concluded that Schuller likely would never have the gift of speaking in tongues. However, Bredeson assured Schuller that the Holy Spirit was indeed active in his life—a newly important qualification for valid ministry—and that he would always have the "gift of sayings, that he would always be able to speak English in a way with which people could identify and understand."[89] As he refined his identity, Schuller was assured that he was in step with the Spirit, operating from his unique spiritual gifting, knowing that his soft-sell version of Christianity resonated well on television.

Schuller also took pains to assure people of his orthodoxy. After meeting Jesse Jackson in 1975, the minister tried to nurture the relationship

---

86. Nason and Nason, *Robert Schuller*, 146.
87. Nason and Nason, *Robert Schuller*, 188.
88. Nason and Nason, *Robert Schuller*, 144.
89. Nason and Nason, *Robert Schuller*, 145.

150 CHAPTER 6

with a follow-up letter—he really wanted Jackson to appear on *Hour of Power*. In an effort to convince Jackson, Schuller offered a testimony: "1. I am a believer in Jesus Christ, and have accepted Him as my personal Lord and Savior. In that sense, I am of the Evangelical theological tradition. 2. I believe in Positive Thinking. It is almost as important as the resurrection of Jesus Christ! A negative-thinking Christian isn't much good to God or to his fellowmen."[90] Schuller concluded the letter by noting that he would be sending Jackson copies of his books and that he really felt that they could be "mutually helpful."

To broaden the appeal of Christianity and to avoid offense, Schuller eschewed much of the traditional church calendar and liturgy. Though the minister remained elusive on controversial and obscure doctrinal matters, Nason described Schuller as "committed to an orthodox, evangelical, historical Christian theology. He believes in the Apostles' Creed, the virgin birth of Christ, the physical resurrection of Jesus, the second coming of Christ." Beyond that, though: "Anything he doesn't comprehend himself, he doesn't deal with, either in print or from the pulpit."[91]

For Schuller, the modest success of the broadcast meant expanding the reach of *Hour of Power*, and New York City represented a symbolic challenge. As he explored strategies for the market, he consulted an unnamed pastor in the city who tried to dissuade Schuller: "If you've got $4,000 a week to throw away, fine, buy your time. But if you expect listeners in New York City to support your TV program, forget it. New York is made up of stubborn Jews, narrow-minded Catholics, and lukewarm Protestants! And to be honest, Bob, you and your showy church services are much too 'California' for East Coast taste."[92] It seems Peale could have been the "friend" in ministry who offered the sobering assessment. Nevertheless, in spite of the advice to stay away, Schuller plowed ahead and noticed a much cooler Peale the next time the two met in California. Schuller wondered whether his mentor felt threatened by his incursion into the New York market—and even offered to hand the broadcast rights

90. Schuller to Jackson, June 13, 1975, CC-Correspondence, 1975, RHS/CC, box 34 (HCASC).

91. Nason and Nason, *Robert Schuller*, 145–46.

92. Schuller, *My Journey*, 316.

to Marble Collegiate. A "guarded and remote" Peale demurred. Schuller, though, felt that moment marked "the beginning of a rift that would last for years."[93]

To that point, *Los Angeles Times* journalist Bella Stumbo noted in 1983 that "despite several invitations," Peale had not returned to Schuller's church in over a decade. Stumbo reported that Schuller looked "saddened" when discussing Peale. When Stumbo wondered if Peale was jealous, Schuller seemed to acquiesce: "It's unfortunate, but, well, I think maybe he *has* had some trouble dealing with it; but it would be presumptuous of me, of course, to speak for him."[94] Schuller would later protest when an observer suggested that Peale had bequeathed him his status: "Not true. The mantle may have fallen, but Peale didn't choose it."[95] Schuller eventually indicated that he had outstripped his mentor: "I learned a great deal from Peale, but I went a step further than he ever has—I developed a systematic theology of self-esteem."[96]

To lose that friendship was a blow. Schuller had reveled in leveraging his proximity to and association with Peale—even to the point of embellishing the Manhattan pastor's relationship to GGCC. In 1968, when attempting to purchase ten acres adjacent to the church grounds, he ghostwrote a letter to the property owner from Peale: "Suggested Letter from Norman Vincent Peale to Edgar Kaiser." He enclosed his proposed letter to the property owner in another missive to Peale and suggested it could be copied or rejected "in its entirety." Schuller, in Peale's name, lobbied Kaiser: "That 10 acre parcel is contiguous to a great church I have been building on the west coast, with the help of Robert Schuller who is my hand-picked pastor. I've been working hard with Rev. Schuller to develop what I believe is going to be the greatest church on the Pacific Coast. In fact, it is that, in my judgement, today. Now we have completed in our church development a 15 story Tower of Hope where I am housing my West Coast Branch of the American Foundation of Religion and Psychi-

93. Schuller, *My Journey*, 317.

94. See Stumbo, "The Time Muhammad Ali Asked for Robert Schuller's Autograph."

95. Interview, Schuller and Voskuil, March 3, 1983.

96. Marti Ayres, "Minister Rejects Idea of 'Electronic Church,'" *Holland (MI) Sentinel*, March 5, 1982, 3 (DVP).

152 CHAPTER 6

atry."[97] The letter demonstrated that, for many years, Schuller preferred to be associated with Peale over the RCA.

However, even as his friendship with Peale waned, Schuller entered a new orbit of celebrities who enjoyed watching the minister on Sunday mornings. His own growing celebrity status as a broadcasted presence in the homes of millions, just a channel or two away from the most prominent movie and television stars in the world, brought him into a privileged circle of luminaries in the Hollywood entertainment industry. As *Hour of Power* became a national fixture, his very first fan letter from a celebrity arrived from Doris Day. Soon, Schuller found himself in conversations with Glenn Ford, John Wayne, and Lucille Ball. At one point, after many dinners and private seats at Las Vegas shows, Schuller claimed that he had convinced Frank Sinatra to appear on *Hour of Power* to sing his trademark song, "I Did It My Way." The minister, though, requested a slight revision: "Then we'll dissolve to the empty cross, and you'll change the last words to 'He did it—His way'!" Schuller recounted that Sinatra had "loved the idea!" but "then some personal troubles erupted in his life, and the song never happened."[98]

Even with all these connections to high-profile, successful personalities, Schuller still felt like a "lonely dreamer." The minister rued the fact that "No letter ever came from my [RCA] denominational leaders in New York." Even more, despite his many achievements, "No letter during that entire decade from the one man who had done more for me than anyone else, the one man who had remained my friend through all the other times of separation from peers and colleagues: Dr. Norman Vincent Peale."[99] Schuller seemed especially haunted by the antipathy from Peale.

Despite the loss of Peale's collegiality, Schuller remained buoyed by the relative success of the Leadership Institute (established in 1969) and the weekly broadcast of *Hour of Power* (1970). The minister assumed his methods had a transcendent resonance that would reverberate well beyond Orange County, and he possessed years of anecdotal evidence from

---

97. Schuller to Peale, November 27, 1968, CC-Correspondence, RHS/CC, box 34 (HCASC).

98. Schuller, *My Journey*, 320.

99. Schuller, *My Journey*, 321.

his many ministerial "students" to prove it. The principles suggested in his books stimulated only more attention, and his Leadership Institute welcomed thousands of pastors to learn his methods firsthand. In *Your Church Has Real Possibilities!* (published in 1974), Schuller stated, "God has revealed certain techniques for success in our ministry," and the minister chose to share them "as a stewardship of responsibility." He added, "I absolutely guarantee that if you follow the prescriptions laid down in this book, your church will grow."[100] It appeared that Schuller kept no secrets—he promoted church growth as accessible to all who heeded his advice.

Greater visibility provided more opportunities for critique, and as his prestige soared, criticism erupted from distant corners of Christianity—but also much closer. Less-than-friendly fire also erupted within the larger Dutch Reformed tradition. In 1976, a theology student at Princeton, Neal Plantinga (who would one day be president of Calvin Theological Seminary in Grand Rapids, Michigan), wondered about Schuller's methodology: "Suppose people, in this age of unbelief, want not sermons but snappy little pep talks; not creeds but jingles; not appearances by missionaries but ones by celebrities; not repentance and sacrifice, but gimmicks and giveaways."[101] Plantinga then questioned the replicability of Schuller's template:

> Leaving to the side the question whether other ministers in the Reformed tradition *may* achieve growth through the same methods, *can* they? Schuller is himself one of the important, magnetic personalities with which he likes to attract unbelievers. But what if a minister is only average looking? What if he is not a dynamo bursting with fire-'em up razzle dazzle and get-up-and-go, but is rather an ordinary and subdued person? Suppose he lacks flash and charisma and is no entrepreneur. What if he only wants, humbly and prayerfully, to preach the gospel? This may be a recipe for failure by American suc-

100. Robert H. Schuller, *Your Church Has Real Possibilities!* (Glendale, CA: G/L Publications, 1974), xiii.

101. Neal Plantinga, "Schullerism and Church Growth," *Banner*, March 19, 1976, 4–5, 5 (DVP).

154 CHAPTER 6

cess standards. But do we have to succeed by *those* standards? Is it not conceivable that even when some of God's servants are being good and faithful their churches might still dwindle?[102]

Even close by, within his own congregation, some felt ambivalent about the broadcast of the worship service and Schuller's seemingly "Christianity-lite" preaching. One member shrugged, recalling that "we were consciously aware at the time that Schuller's approach was to try to get people to the church. As a rebuttal to the criticism that he didn't preach fire and brimstone, he didn't consider that his role. He tried to get people there, and if he could get them there then all these other functions could teach."[103] There existed a palpable sense that discipleship from the pulpit would be sacrificed for evangelism.

Schuller's celebrity also inevitably affected connections with the members of his own church. One longtime member reminisced: "There was a struggle for many, many years of the congregation versus the *Hour of Power*. Which is more important? Who's running the show? Where's the money going? Who's paying for all this? And at some points it was proclaimed they were all along, other times they would proclaim they're two separate things. And there was a time when they were definitely two separate things, two separate boards, one for the church and one for the ministry—I mean the TV." Another couple who had been members for years echoed some of the discomfort. The husband remarked, "Looking back on it, I realize at church I did feel like part of the audience." And his wife echoed, "Mm, like a spectator."

Despite the misgivings of some members of the local congregation, the *Hour of Power* broadcast granted Schuller an almost-unparalleled stature in American religion. And the minister reveled in the attention. Schuller closely tracked his standing in the world of broadcast ministry—and how he might expand *Hour of Power*'s footprint. A 1975 analysis, for instance, revealed that women accounted for 70 percent of Schuller's audience while competitor Oral Roberts attracted more men.[104] Such

102. Plantinga, "Schullerism and Church Growth."

103. This quote and those following were told to Mulder in interviews. For more on anonymous quotes, see "A Note on Sources."

104. Edward Shaw to Charles Eckman, April 23, 1975, CC-Correspondence, 1975, RHS/CC, box 34 (HCASC).

a discrepancy represented a problem to be solved, and the minister assigned his marketing folks to figure out the gender disparity; the broadcast could not contain any masked flaws because it now offered the ministry's most public face.

As a singular and consistent Sunday morning presence, Schuller's profile continued to grow. His grandson Bobby Schuller (who would eventually take over the broadcast in the early twenty-first century) ascribed almost all of his grandfather's success to the *Hour of Power*:

> It's just TV, it's just simple, it's just TV. When my grandpa was doing TV in the 70s, back then you actually had to turn a dial, and most people had 7 stations—actually lots of people had 3 stations. So, on Sunday morning, you'd wake up, and you've got 3 choices, and one of them is Dr. Schuller [chuckles]. And the TV became the fire that people gathered around, like in the caveman days. It's where people gathered to tell stories and hear about what's happening. That's where you get your news. He was just so far ahead of the curve, I mean, he was nationwide in the 70s and stayed that way, and people appreciated it.[105]

Wesley Granberg-Michaelson, who served as general secretary of the RCA and developed a good relationship with Schuller, echoed Bobby's analysis:

> It became internationally successful, in part, [because of Schuller's] ability to have a televised ministry at a time when broadcasting technology was making the whole world far more accessible to broadcast television [through the] development of cable . . . your upper classes (and sometimes more than that) in countries around the world, they could turn on their TVs and see an American preacher. I can't tell you how often I travel around the world, and people will tell me they watch Bob Schuller every Sunday, and were blessed by him, and blah, blah. You had a confluence of technological development, what folks call the forces of globalization in a communications world, that picked up his particular gifts.[106]

105. Interview with Mulder, May 16, 2017.
106. Interview with Mulder, October 17, 2016.

156 CHAPTER 6

Granberg-Michaelson recollected about *Hour of Power*: "People don't realize he was watched by many, many more people around the world than he was in the United States. His broadcast ministry internationally is not recognized for what it was."

As Granberg-Michaelson noted, already by 1972 the success of *Hour of Power* had pushed Schuller's national profile into global proportions. For Schuller, the weekly program was becoming a world-historical force in service of the global church. In an espionage-soaked atmosphere portrayed in his autobiography, he told of a stranger who appeared at the family door and insisted that the minister "must forget" his name because he had been "working with underground churches in Russia." He went on, flattering Schuller:

> Your world-famed skyscraper—the Tower of Hope—has made news in Moscow. All architects in the USSR respect Richard Neutra as the greatest architect of the day. They cannot believe that in this scientific age such a revered man would build a huge church tower. Dr. Schuller, they are very upset with what the communists describe as a "structure that robs the poor." They're aghast at this "monument to superstition." However, a number of English-speaking Christians in the underground Russian church have been reading books and articles by you and have begged me to ask you to come and visit them. They need possibility thinking, Dr. Schuller. I would be honored to line up visits for you with one of these underground churches.[107]

Of course, visiting an underground church in the USSR proved difficult. Later that year, though, Schuller had the opportunity to teach as a visiting instructor on Chapman University's semester at sea. The university credentials allowed the minister legitimate cover to visit the country as a scholar. In fact, when questioned at customs, Schuller told the officers, "I'm with Chapman University. I study religion and wanted to visit your famous Museum of Atheism in Leningrad."[108] The explanation seemed plausible, and Schuller gained entry—with an assigned

107. Schuller, *My Journey*, 324.
108. Schuller, *My Journey*, 330.

"guide" whom Schuller assumed to be KGB. During his tour of the museum, Schuller discovered his own portrait in a display that included the pope, Martin Luther King Jr., and Billy Graham. Unfortunately, the "guide" also recognized the "professor" in the exhibit as well. The minister's ruse had been discovered. He would no longer be able to visit the underground churches without potentially revealing them to the KGB. Both disappointed and relieved, Schuller headed back to Garden Grove, hoping never to return to the USSR.[109]

His stature as the leading figure within a market-centered Christianity meant the farmer's son from Iowa had arrived on the international stage. Even so, at that point the minister seemed to have no idea that his global profile would continue to grow.

109. Schuller, *My Journey*, 334.

7

ACCOMMODATING—AND INSTIGATING—GROWTH

Robert Schuller liked to build. Or at least he seemed to like the *idea* of building. Schuller gained deep satisfaction from the enduring testaments to his ministry—and he also advocated that big, visionary, aggressive projects served to energize congregations and audiences. That is, he believed that the psychology of humans predisposed them to a desire to attach themselves to projects that captured their imaginations and created resonance. But the actual process of building tended to reveal deep anxiety and insecurity.

Though he spent a ministerial career in which a hammer seemed always to be striking a nail in the background, he also betrayed a tendency toward anxiety and dread while in the midst of every project. Raising the funding required for his projects catalyzed that anxiety. Schuller understood himself as one of the most accomplished fund-raisers of the past century, yet he confided to family and friends that he often wallowed in the fear of failing to complete high-profile projects.[1] Even more, although he had forged new territory in hiring professional development officers ever since his first pastorate in suburban Chicago, his assistant Michael Nason claimed that Schuller *hated* asking potential benefactors for money.[2]

---

1. For more on Schuller's continual management of flows of capital, see Gerardo Martí and Mark T. Mulder, "Capital and the Cathedral: Robert H. Schuller's Continual Fundraising for Church Growth," *Religion and American Culture: A Journal of Interpretation* 30, no. 1 (Winter 2020): 63–107.

2. Michael Nason and Donna Nason, *Robert Schuller: The Inside Story* (Waco, TX: Word, 1983), 221.

In spite of trepidations, the minister did ask, finding techniques to make the ask in a manner that was not only more natural to him but also cleverly accommodating of the enormous amounts required to fulfill his vision. Among the most important realizations was understanding that his own congregation was never large enough to finance the size of his ambitions. He learned to reach out to wealthy people outside the congregation, seeking benefactors who were not even members of his church yet who could be drawn into a vision that resonated with the extent of their wealth.

Creating a Need to Build

The growth of GGCC led to problems of capacity. According to Nason, only a year or so after the opening of the hybrid church, the minister complained that the existing sanctuary limited growth—it "chafed" Schuller and "gnawed at his very soul."[3] Within only a few years, the sanctuary had to be extended (as planned), and the ministry started setting out five hundred lawn chairs and three hundred blankets for overflow seating on the lawn. Schuller reported that the facilities were "literally bursting at the seams."[4] But the good news of strong attendance quickly soured into an abiding concern. He stressed that the success of *Hour of Power* and its ability to lure tourists to worship "threaten[ed] the Garden Grove Community Church. Each week, some three to five hundred visitors arrived from all over the country, persons who watched the 'Hour of Power' on TV and wanted to worship in the church while in Southern California on vacation. The regular members of the church couldn't find a place to sit. It was a huge growth-restricting problem, the result of success."[5] Schuller consistently understood church growth as functionally related to the physical capacity of the building.

Everything seemed to be expanding quickly, and Schuller needed to catch up. With the steady development of amusement parks and shop-

---

3. Nason and Nason, *Robert Schuller*, 213.

4. Robert H. Schuller, *My Journey: From an Iowa Farm to a Cathedral of Dreams* (San Francisco: HarperOne, 2001), 338.

5. Nason and Nason, *Robert Schuller*, 213-14.

160   CHAPTER 7

ping malls all around him, he felt a compulsion to pursue a bigger, more robust built environment for congregational life. Nason reported that the minister "really believed that God wanted his church to grow. . . . [Schuller] understood the problem and knew the solution rested in the construction of a new sanctuary. Not to move ahead with it was selfish on his part and went against his concept of himself as a servant first."[6] With disquiet about stagnation plaguing his mind, Schuller by the mid-1970s had again grown restless. The minister needed a new project to solve the problem of growth. While the hybrid sanctuary had received welcome reviews, its size proved limiting to attendance. Even more, its sight lines offered only marginal production values for the broadcast of *Hour of Power*. Schuller got to work.

Building the hybrid sanctuary had been a bruising process for Schuller. Nason reported that the minister felt scarred by the experience—so much so that it chilled his tentative plans for an even larger edifice. The church consistory also noticed the strain on infrastructure. Resolving to address the issue, they voted to engage an architect to accommodate the growth, but their decision left Schuller "troubled" and internally "screaming to escape."[7] He claimed in his autobiography that he had grown "sick and tired of wearing the cap of architect/developer/fundraiser."[8] He asserted that he offered zero enthusiasm for the project, and it largely stalled for two years. In fact, Schuller revealed that a rainstorm that had chased congregants home during a worship service served as the catalyst that finally changed his mind on new construction. People needed to enjoy nature during worship—but they should also be comfortable.

Though unable to muster much, if any, possibility thinking, Schuller felt compelled under church law to follow the instructions of the GGCC consistory for a new, larger facility. As the ministry began to consider building a larger structure, both Schuller and Arvella set themselves to finding a suitable architect (Neutra had recently passed away, and Schuller had officiated at his funeral). On a long flight, Arvella stumbled across a magazine article about the Fort Worth Water Gardens and its

---

6. Nason and Nason, *Robert Schuller*, 213.
7. Schuller, *My Journey*, 338.
8. Schuller, *My Journey*, 338.

designer, Philip Johnson.[9] After Arvella shared the magazine, Schuller planned his pursuit.

Johnson's interest in landscape design offered an intriguing complement to Neutra's biorealism, and the minister perhaps saw another opportunity to design a building to create resonance. He secured a meeting with Johnson in the architect's New York office. Having never heard of the minister, Johnson thought Schuller had made the appointment to interview for a job and sent an assistant to receive him. The minister clarified that he wanted to hire Johnson to design an all-glass sanctuary that would seat three thousand people. The architect expressed concern, both about an all-glass structure at that scale in an earthquake-prone area and about the potential costs. In response, Schuller suggested that the architect (1) hire the best engineers and (2) draft a plan that would inspire financial donors.

Johnson's first set of drawings deeply disappointed the minister. Sure, the renderings included an all-glass ceiling, but they also indicated a flat block-like structure with solid, brick walls. Schuller wanted the entirety of the structure sheathed in glass. Johnson eventually caught Schuller's vision—with the help of a $200,000 retainer. In November 1975, Johnson walked into Schuller's office with a model that captured the minister's vision: a star-shaped, naturally cooled, all-glass structure that measured 414 feet in length and twelve stories at its highest point—the Crystal Cathedral in its earliest form. The architect elaborated: "The sanctuary will seat three thousand people. From the inside you'll look out to see sky and trees, but from the outside the windows will be black mirrors to deflect the hot sun, reflect the sky and trees, and give privacy to the worshipers from outside gawkers. It will be the largest space-frame structure in the world."[10]

With a revised and genuinely exciting architectural plan in hand, the minister expressed delight—until the next month when he heard the cost estimate: $7 million. GGCC's lender at the time, Farmers and Merchants Bank, had a loan limitation of $4 million. Schuller would again have to be GGCC's loan advancement officer.

9. Nason and Nason, *Robert Schuller*, 215–16.
10. Schuller, *My Journey*, 349.

162 CHAPTER 7

How Do You Pay for a Cathedral?

By this time the minister had already written out a well-developed "philosophy on capital." In a "special report" distributed to the consistory of the church, Schuller stated that as a "dynamic business for God," churches would always "require cash." Thus, an entrepreneurial minister risked too much if he waited for congregants to open their wallets beyond the 10 percent they should already be giving; the minister had to be willing to borrow funds to accommodate the inevitable new members who would eventually help to repay the loans. In other words, Schuller made clear to his leadership that his "philosophy of growth" necessarily included a "philosophy of capital debt." Borrowing as much as possible to expand the built environment of the ministry functioned as one of the minister's central strategies.[11]

Schuller clearly knew he needed a lot of positive attention to have any chance of raising the necessary financing. As he announced the plans for the new church construction in 1975, the minister sent personal letters to the editors of all the local newspapers—the *Orange County Register, Anaheim Bulletin, Daily Pilot, Daily News Tribune, Daily Star Progress, Long Beach Press-Telegram, Orange County Evening News*, and *Orange City News*—inviting them to the twentieth anniversary celebration of Garden Grove Community Church. The missive indicated that luminaries, including Art Linkletter and George Beverly Shea, would be in attendance and that the evening would conclude with "a grand array of aerial fireworks."[12]

While celebrating the plans, Schuller also knew the costs would likely strain the congregation. To prepare members, the anniversary celebration booklet also included a survey. Questions inquired about annual family income, what percent of family income was contributed to GGCC, willingness to consider tithing one's net worth rather than

11. A Special Report from Robert H. Schuller to the Consistory, September 23, 1975, Shepherd's Grove Church Archives, Irvine, CA (hereafter cited as SGCA).

12. Schuller to Bertha Barron, November 14, 1975, CC-Anniversary Celebration, Twentieth, 1975, Robert H. Schuller/Crystal Cathedral (hereafter cited as RHS/CC), box 5, Hope College Archives and Special Collections, Holland, MI (hereafter cited as HCASC).

income, and understandings of the definition of "tithe."[13] Schuller's financial reconnaissance would allow him to quantify both the capacity and the interest in giving toward the project, valuable information for obtaining additional bank credit and big donations.

In case the audience lacked the imagination to see how they could participate in financing the construction, Schuller made sure to include in a printed program for the evening anniversary event an opportunity for the audience to engage in a "trusting expectation"—a written statement of purpose, or pledge, ready for them to use to donate funds for the construction of the Cathedral. For clarification, the document noted that a "trusting expectation" did not constitute a legal pledge or debt, necessitate membership at the church, represent a "casual offering that can be easily afforded," or manifest as an "act of resented necessity." On the other hand, the trusting pledge did represent an "expression of worship" that would be "sacrificial," as it would be "the first expenditure" made "from the money God sends."

Clothing his pitch in recognizable symbolism, Schuller included in the printouts a striking facsimile of a stock or bond note that indicated a dubious "Guaranteed Return upon Investment" and featured a verse from Malachi: "'Bring the whole of the tithe into my house and test me now in this way,' says the Lord. . . . 'If I will not open the windows of the heavens, and pour out for you a blessing until there is no more need.'" Under the note, a reassurance that it was not a problem to make a trusting expectation as means to instigate more income and wealth from God: "Trying to get more income for family benefit is a pure motive . . . so even if your only motive would be more income . . . try it . . . prove Him."[14]

A fiscally concerned Schuller also knew that a significant construction campaign for the new building could divert from the general budget ($3 million annually in the mid-1970s). Yet the minister suggested that the congregation should, somehow, *double* their giving in 1976. He broke this down for his members, suggesting a plan to make that possible. First, the minister seemed to have some serious questions about how his congrega-

---

13. "Gross Income? Salary? Take-Home Pay? Any Level of Gift to the Church?" CC-Anniversary Celebration, Twentieth, 1975.

14. CC-Anniversary Celebration, Twentieth, 1975.

164   CHAPTER 7

tion spent their money: "All of us waste time, money, energy, clothes, and opportunities. It's incredible how much money is wasted on food! Most Americans are overweight. In addition, an incredible amount of money is wasted on alcohol, tobacco, and consumption that hurts more than it helps!" Second, Schuller suggested that congregants consider dipping into estates to give to the construction project. Finally, perhaps his congregation should be creative and work harder to increase their income: Schuller reported that a seventy-eight-year-old member had engaged in a direct sales program to earn more money to give to the ministry. If she could work harder, why not the rest of the congregation?[15]

Even with all that cajoling, Schuller worked the numbers and realized that members of his congregation alone could not muster the necessary funds to pay for the Crystal Cathedral.[16] Concerned about the viability of the project, the minister cold-called John Crean, a wealthy Orange County resident, in April 1976. He and his wife, Donna, had given $1 million to start construction on a YMCA in Anaheim, and the minister sensed a philanthropic opportunity.

Crean took the meeting with Schuller but demurred when the minister asked for $1 million to start the fund-raising for the new church structure. He had never attended GGCC, although he described himself as a "good Lutheran," and allowed Schuller to offer a prayer at the end of their meeting. Never missing an opening, Schuller used the opportunity for a rhetorical flourish: "O God, I'm so thankful that Mr. Crean would like to give a million dollars. Is it possible for You to figure out a way for him to do what he would like to do but can't?"[17] Perhaps moved by the audacity of Schuller's prayer, Crean called the next day with his mind changed—the minister could count on a $1 million lead-off gift from him.

The inaugural financial gift from Crean buoyed the minister. In addition, Schuller received free publicity when he booked an appearance

---

15. "Come Celebrate with Us!" Promotional flyer for Tenth Anniversary Celebration, 1980, Dennis Voskuil Papers, Holland, MI (hereafter cited as DVP). CC-Anniversary Celebration, Twentieth, 1975.

16. At that point, the price tag had doubled from the $5 million Schuller initially reported in 1975: Special Report from Robert H. Schuller to the Consistory, September 23, 1975.

17. Schuller, *My Journey*, 352.

ACCOMMODATING—AND INSTIGATING—GROWTH **165**

on *The Donahue Show.* Perhaps most significantly, host Phil Donahue himself fawned over a scale model of the Cathedral and exclaimed, "If the Lord ain't in there, he isn't in town!"[18]

But significant monetary challenges remained. The price tag for construction abruptly ballooned from $7,000,000 to $10,000,000 as the church's lay leadership decided to add a 45,000-square-foot basement. Schuller needed to get creative—he did not have many more "John Creans" in his Rolodex. He would have to devise a plan that drew in many, many smaller donations. Inspiration struck when Schuller remembered memorial plaques that he had often seen attached to traditional brick churches. What if each of the ten thousand glass panes on the church became, instead, a "memorial window" that could be purchased for $500? Simple, strategic, and supereasy to communicate, the plan worked. Within five months, every window had been purchased, raising $5 million.[19]

Despite notable milestones in raising necessary funds to keep construction on track, the building project could not move quickly enough. The inflation of the late 1970s increased the bids for construction even higher, topping $13 million. Within a couple of years, the overall cost of the Cathedral had almost doubled. At one point, the minister became so disillusioned with the continually mounting project costs that he decided to halt all efforts and stop construction.

In the summer of 1977, Schuller sat down at the family cabin in the mountains and wrote a news release: "The Crystal Cathedral project will be abandoned. As the bids came in, the cost rose from ten million dollars to nearly fifteen million dollars. This exceeds our church's capabilities."[20] Schuller acknowledged that writing the release proved cathartic—he felt an immediate relief.

Wanting to keep the momentum, the minister next dialed John Crean, the first major donor, to let him know that the church would be

---

18. "Dr. Robert Schuller Interviewed on the Donahue Show," 1976, transcript, folder "Crystal Cathedral Robert H. Schuller—Interviews, 1976," box 26, Robert H. Schuller Collection (HCASC), 37.

19. Schuller, *My Journey*, 354.

20. Schuller, *My Journey*, 359.

166 CHAPTER 7

returning his $1 million donation. Upon hearing Schuller's explanation, Crean resisted: "Schuller, dig a hole. Keep my donation and use it to dig a hole for the foundation. A hole shouldn't cost more than a million dollars. Will it?"

An off-balance Schuller responded, "Uh . . . no."

"Okay, then . . . dig a hole! Somehow, someway, the money will come."[21]

Crean had just given the minister a tour de force lesson in his own possibility thinking.

Building a Money-Generating Monument

As Schuller raised money for the Crystal Cathedral, he pressed potential benefactors aggressively. A May 1976 letter to Jay Van Andel, cofounder of the Amway Corporation headquartered near Grand Rapids, Michigan, demonstrated the minister's framing of the Cathedral as a monetizing facility. Schuller had earlier suggested a $1 million donation. Van Andel resisted. Undaunted, the minister asserted the necessity of the new structure: "The Crystal Cathedral, dedicated debt-free, will enable us to attack one of the major problems facing our world. For we will have 4,100 income producing seats. . . . The facility will, in effect, be a 'money-generating factory' to produce wealth that will sustain great international mission programs."[22] Van Andel, though, proved unpersuaded, and Schuller wrote later in 1976 with more fervor: "I need to meet with you, Jay, at a time and a place convenient with you. At that time I want to discuss with you the possibility of your participation. I would prefer to talk with you personally and privately about this and will be happy to fly anywhere, any time so that we can pray about it and finally determine what God wants you to do. Jay, I await your instructions."[23]

Schuller saw 1977 as a significant year for his ministry. In January, the *Hour of Power* headquarters opened. In March, the Chapman Avenue bridge opened—linking the *Hour of Power* headquarters to the rest

---

21. Schuller, *My Journey*, 360.

22. Schuller to Van Andel, May 27, 1976, CC-Correspondence, RHS/CC, box 40 (HCASC).

23. Schuller to Van Andel, December 7, 1976, CC-Correspondence, RHS/CC, box 40 (HCASC).

ACCOMMODATING—AND INSTIGATING—GROWTH **167**

of the campus.[24] Perhaps most importantly, Schuller's plans for an all-glass exterior could not have been approved any later—in February 1977 a California law went into effect that prohibited the construction of any building with exterior walls comprised of more than 50 percent glass. The renderings for the Cathedral had been submitted ten days prior to the law going into effect.[25] And in December 1977, GGCC held the ground-breaking ceremony for the Crystal Cathedral—digging the symbolic, no-going-back hole that Crean had suggested. Though he appeared delighted that day, internally Schuller reported that he carried acute anxiety about the fact that the congregation currently had only $2 million in hand for a project that would cost more than six times that amount.[26]

The minister's concern compounded as construction began and donations failed to arrive at the needed rate. Contractors threatened to not only stall the project but also padlock the fencing around the site. The ministry needed another $1 million by June 18, 1978. Schuller demonstrated his own commitment by selling his "study apartment" in Laguna for a little under $200,000 (in his autobiography he noted that it had been purchased for only $36,000 with a down payment provided by his inheritance from his father's estate). Beyond that, their daughter, Carol, sold her horse and donated the money to Cathedral construction.

Over and over, Schuller felt a consistent and pervasive fear about an uncompleted Cathedral. In the spring of 1978, the $1 million payment came due—and again the ministry simply did not have the funds. Nason recalled a despondent Schuller: "Out of ideas, out of energy, out of enthusiasm. He actually sat down and wrote the bulletin announcement for that Sunday, acknowledging total failure and inability to complete the Cathedral."[27] Illuminating the potential depths of Schuller's despondence, Nason worried about the toll the failure would take on the minister, expressing "doubt [Schuller] would be able to live with himself afterwards."[28]

24. Robert H. Schuller, *Your Church Has a Fantastic Future! A Possibility Thinker's Guide to a Successful Church* (Ventura, CA: Regal Books, 1986), 47.

25. Erica Robles-Anderson, "The Crystal Cathedral: Architecture for Mediated Congregation," *Public Culture* 24, no. 3 (2012): 593.

26. Schuller, *My Journey*, 362.

27. Nason and Nason, *Robert Schuller*, 227.

28. Nason and Nason, *Robert Schuller*, 227.

168   CHAPTER 7

Again, though, at the last moment, a dramatic gift appeared. The same day that Schuller wrote the failure announcement, he received a letter from a former congregant who now resided in Northern Ireland, offering encouragement. Schuller reconsidered publishing the bulletin announcement and, instead, decided to execute Million-Dollar Sunday—an extraordinary, one-day effort where the congregation gave everything they could to meet the million-dollar payment. Nason reckoned that many members had already been double-tithing, so this new effort would be a financial stretch for many.

The following Sunday, GGCC held their special million-dollar service to raise the remainder of the needed $1 million—including hard hats cleverly utilized as collection plates and wheelbarrows to deliver the cash and checks to the counting room. In yet another dramatic moment of fundraising, the congregation gave more than what was required: $1.4 million. The *Christian Herald* magazine wrote about the financial achievement and wondered whether the one-day haul for a church should become a category for *The Guinness Book of World Records*.[29] Within the next year, the project would receive two separate, unsolicited checks for $1 million each from Foster McGraw, CEO of America Hospital Supply, Inc.[30] Later, when Arvella made plans for an elaborate pipe organ, Schuller described his bitter disappointment when he realized that they had no funds for it. But then their friend from Chicago, Hazel Wright, offered yet another $1 million to pay for the Cathedral organ to fulfill Arvella's vision.

Despite the litany of *ex machina* gifts, after the hole had been dug for the Crystal Cathedral in late 1977, Nason reported that 1978 represented "the worst year in the history of the Schuller family and the Garden Grove Community Church."[31] As costs escalated by the millions of dollars for the new construction, the minister again worried that there existed no plausible method for financing the Cathedral to completion. He lamented that the "rotting skeleton on his church grounds" would forever serve as glaring evidence of the failure of possibility thinking and the theology of self-esteem. Schuller "felt his entire career was on

---

29. "New Category," *Christian Herald*, September 1978 (DVP).
30. Schuller, *My Journey*, 384 and 387.
31. Nason and Nason, *Robert Schuller*, 225.

the line."[32] Feeling acute pressure, the minister became "downright cantankerous a lot of the time."[33]

At this moment, like so many others, the possibility thinker succumbed to feelings of anguish. Nason witnessed the minister's moments of crises often and reported a typical episode: "When a crisis came up, we knew what to expect. [Schuller] would just throw his arms up in the air. 'I can't take anymore! I can't handle it!' And he would bury his face in his hands and start to cry."[34] And it seemed that the minister often liked to make his assistant the scapegoat—Nason estimated that Schuller had fired him "five or six times" over their years together.

Even as fiscal concerns mounted in 1978, the year proved to be an especially painful one for the Schuller family. While in South Korea for a church-growth conference in July, the minister and Arvella learned that their thirteen-year-old daughter, Carol, had been badly hurt in a motorcycle accident in Iowa.[35] A collision with a car had sent Carol flying ninety feet into a rural ditch. She lost over seventeen pints of blood, and the trauma to her left leg meant amputation. Carol also fought a severe infection from having landed in waste water that had drained into the ditch from a nearby hog yard—the bacteria from the slaughterhouse proved resistant to any known antibiotics. Michael Nason called the Schullers to deliver the news and booked a private Lear jet (paid for by a church benefactor) for the flight from Seoul to Sioux City, Iowa.[36]

Upon arrival at the hospital, Schuller reported in his autobiography that Carol spoke to the minister as soon as he entered her recovery room:

32. Nason and Nason, *Robert Schuller*, 226.

33. Nason and Nason, *Robert Schuller*, 242.

34. Nason and Nason, *Robert Schuller*, 242.

35. The Schuller children often spent a good portion of their summer vacations with family in Iowa. See "Orange City Oracle," *Alton (IA) Democrat*, July 20, 1961, https://tinyurl.com/mrxst4hc. See also Stan Folkema, "Correspondence," *Sioux County (IA) Capital*, June 24, 1965, https://tinyurl.com/59h4m34a, and Sheila Schuller Coleman, *Robert Schuller: My Father and My Friend* (Milwaukee: Ideals Publishing Corp., 1980), 83–93.

36. James Penner, *Goliath: The Life of Robert Schuller* (Anaheim, CA: New Hope Publishing, 1992), 251–56 and 289–304; Nason and Nason, *Robert Schuller*, 233 and 236; and "Girl Loses Leg in Crash," *Sioux County (IA) Index*, July 13, 1978, https://tinyurl.com/3nrzhspe.

170 CHAPTER 7

"Dad, I think I know why the accident happened. . . . God has a special ministry for me. He wants me to help people who have been hurt like I'm hurt."[37] Although still deeply concerned, Schuller recollected that the attitude and determination of his young daughter made him realize that "all [he had] sacrificed—reputation, social standing, the easy life—to bring [his] message of hope had been worth it, because [he was] looking at this little girl who has discovered that God never leaves where he finds you."[38] For Carol, the road to recovery remained long. The infection threatened her life and mandated multiple surgeries. However, by Christmas of 1978, she managed to briefly stand on her prosthetic leg. Schuller described it as the happiest Christmas of his whole life.[39]

The Last Push

As Carol mended from her injuries, Schuller remained haunted by his commitment to the Cathedral. Nothing would be easy in finishing the Crystal Cathedral. Though the crowning achievement of his ministry, Schuller found the years building the Crystal Cathedral to be "full of misery and pain." Nason, his assistant, echoed that sentiment when he reported that the minister "went through hell trying to build that building."[40] Nason described the minister as irritable and difficult to be around in 1979, and that "he cried easily over his own problems."[41] The dual crises of Carol's accident and the Cathedral's construction financing had taken a toll. Even though these concerns dampened Schuller's joy as he monitored the construction of his monumental church, he was delighted that six thousand people showed up on two separate November 1979 afternoons to witness the activation of the new fountains on the campus and the first opening of the enormous ninety-foot "Cape Canaveral" doors.[42]

By December 1979, the costs had increased again, now to $16 mil-

37. "Efforts to Help Schuller Girl Remain Uncertain," *Alton (IA) Democrat,* July 19, 1978, https://tinyurl.com/bdezw38c, and *Schuller, My Journey,* 374–75.

38. Schuller, *My Journey,* 375.

39. Nason and Nason, *Robert Schuller,* 241.

40. Nason and Nason, *Robert Schuller,* 219.

41. Nason and Nason, *Robert Schuller,* 242.

42. Schuller, *Your Church Has a Fantastic Future!,* 48. So named because of the

ACCOMMODATING—AND INSTIGATING—GROWTH **171**

lion—while the ministry had raised only $12 million. How many more unexpected $1 million gifts could Schuller expect? The minister doubted that many more such donors remained. So, he got entrepreneurial: the new building as an entertainment venue could become a source of revenue itself. In February 1980, Schuller invited opera singer Beverly Sills to present her final gala recital in and for the benefit of the unfinished Crystal Cathedral. They sold each of the seats at the concert for $1,000. It was an inspired decision.

Drawn by Sills's celebrity voice and the uniqueness of the new cathedral, people filled the seats, and the evening turned out to be a financial success. Sonically, though, the glass surfaces of the Cathedral proved to be disastrous. Schuller himself recalled: "Her soprano voice, usually rich and lovely, bounced from one glass wall to another. I was horrified. Shrill sounds filled the Cathedral."[43] He also defended the event: "The acoustical criticisms were very unfair. Miss Sills, when she was here, the windows were still uninstalled, the acoustical devices were unfinished."[44] One reporter described the Cathedral as a "reverberating airplane hangar."[45] Despite all that, Nason reinterpreted the potential calamity as one more clever move by Schuller:

> How do you deflect away from a negative and come up with a positive? That's PR 101. Okay? In the face of criticism of the building, they decided that they were going to have an opening of the Crystal Cathedral, but it had to be something bigger and splashier than anything that had ever been done. The decision was to have Beverly Sills sing at the Crystal Cathedral for an opening night. It turned out to be the final solo performance of her career, a perfect PR opportunity, and it was a huge media turn out.
>
> Beverly Sills appeared on Johnny Carson the next night, and he made a whole thing about her at the Crystal Cathedral, joking about

---

manner in which they replicated the doors used for NASA shuttle launches. See https://sah-archipedia.org/buildings/CA-01-059-0107.

43. Schuller, *My Journey*, 392.

44. Interview, Robert Schuller and Dennis Voskuil, March 3, 1983 (DVP).

45. Nason and Nason, *Robert Schuller*, 248.

172 CHAPTER 7

Windex, saying, "You sang last night at the Crystal Cathedral." Can you imagine? And they showed a clip of it, and she turned to Carson and said, "Yes, you can still hear me singing." She took [attention] away from the money and started to concentrate on the building itself. It became a media sensation for the next several weeks. That was a really big deal. Criticism on the cost of the church stayed within the church community, and the general public just shrugged their shoulders.

From then on, the building itself became a great vehicle for events like the Glory of Christmas, the Glory of Easter, all those kinds of things that Schuller did in the use of the building.[46]

Whether the Sills concert functioned as a public relations boon or disaster, construction plowed ahead afterward. In the months before the opening of the Crystal Cathedral, Schuller demanded that the rest of the campus also look presentable—although most visitors would be preoccupied with the main sanctuary, the minister knew that any shabbiness on the campus would be duly noted. Of course, addressing all the necessary maintenance of a growing campus continued to strain the budget. Larry Gates, the church's executive administrator at the time, described it as leading to a "cash crisis."[47] The ministry slashed budgets and incurred "severe personnel cuts."[48] An assistant pastor at the time reported that Schuller found himself "in a desperate struggle to keep the project afloat."[49]

The last Sunday service in the Neutra-designed hybrid sanctuary occurred on September 7, 1980. Just prior to the close of the service, the entire congregation of 1,500 followed Schuller and his son, Robert A. (now also ordained as a minister in the RCA), to the Cathedral for the benediction.[50] The Cathedral officially opened the following week, September 14, 1980. Schuller described the day as exhilarating. It marked the beginning of an era that he described in his autobiography as "the

---

46. Interview with Mulder, January 22, 2018.
47. Larry Gates, *Dwelling in Schullerland* (Nashville: Winston-Derek, 1985), 31.
48. Gates, *Dwelling in Schullerland*, 31.
49. Gates, *Dwelling in Schullerland*, 36.
50. Schuller, *My Journey*, 393–94.

Summit Years."[51] The minister welcomed the congregation (although Schuller labeled it an "audience"), saying, "Today we dedicate this cathedral to the glory of man for the greater glory of God." All then rose to sing a song written by Schuller. The last verse included these lyrics:

> People, people, trust God's dream
> That can feed your self-esteem
> Christ will build your life anew
> God loves you, and I do too.[52]

Keenly aware of the potential criticism of the cost of the structure, Schuller made great pains to communicate that the Cathedral would be dedicated free of debt. The minister reported that the board, at a meeting the previous day, had instructed him to report the solvency during the worship service. Perhaps more importantly, Schuller wanted to demonstrate the gravitas of the board members themselves. In a highly choreographed manner, the camera found each of the sharply dressed men as Schuller read their names—nearly all corporate executives from across the United States.[53] Schuller needed that moment of clear and resonant legitimacy. The freedom from debt and the tacit endorsement from the parade of successful businessmen offered clear evidence that his Orange County ministry demonstrated the most successful principles for church growth and management. The alignment of his market-oriented church to the broader logic of market society could not be more obvious.

Schuller reveled that first day in the new edifice. Johnson's creative design required no heating or cooling plant—louvers in the glass walls allowed cross-ventilation, and the reflective glass of the windows deflected the hottest sunrays. Critics did note miscalculations that resulted in poor sight lines and the unresolved "capricious acoustics throughout."[54] And

51. Schuller, *My Journey*, 395.

52. "Reformed Church in America Celebration of Dedication," September 14, 1980 (SGCA).

53. Mark T. Mulder and Gerado Martí, *The Glass Church: Robert H. Schuller, the Crystal Cathedral, and the Strain of Megachurch Ministry* (New Brunswick, NJ: Rutgers University Press, 2020), 2.

54. Franz Schulze, *Philip Johnson: Life and Work* (New York: Knopf, 1994), 341.

174   CHAPTER 7

yet, at least one critic admitted that the Cathedral represented a "showpiece worthy of the two talents of the two virtuosos, Philip [Johnson] and the preacher, most responsible for it."[55] The unlikely pairing had, at the very least, produced a church building that demanded attention, an architectural marvel that continues to be admired today.

Somehow, Schuller understood the atheistic Johnson to be a kindred spirit. Some have surmised that the architect did his best to "feign piety" when in the minister's presence—even allowing Schuller-led prayers with Johnson's design staff.[56] At the opening of the Cathedral, Johnson went even further, intimating that he had been singularly inspired by God. When Schuller pulled him up to the pulpit during the service, he asked Johnson, "Tell us, Philip, what went through your mind when you designed this beautiful building?" The architect solemnly responded: "I thought I knew history. I thought I knew what the Gothic spires of old stood for. The Romantic period and the thirteenth century period were the highest periods, perhaps, in spiritual Christianity. I thought I knew how to combine these things to create a great tower. I was wrong. I could not have done this—I have to say it humbly, and I don't ever feel humbly, but I do this morning—I got help, my friends. I think you all [voice breaks] know where that help came from."[57] Perhaps Johnson simply got caught up in the moment. When an interviewer later confronted the architect about his newfound spirituality, a sheepish Johnson "put his head in his hands in mock shame, then grinned" and wondered out loud: "Wasn't that *awful!*"[58]

The building was a spectacle that drew commentary both locally and abroad. Because of Johnson's association with the design, some local architecture critics lauded the Cathedral as the most significant opening in Orange County since Disneyland—and noted synergy in that both places "offered a temporary escape from reality within a sunny constructed environment."[59] One Italian design magazine, *Domus*, though, derided the

---

55. Schulze, *Philip Johnson*, 341.

56. Mark Lamster, *The Man in the Glass House: Philip Johnson, Architect of the Modern Century* (New York: Little, Brown, 2018), 373.

57. Schulze, *Philip Johnson*, 341–42.

58. Quoted by Schulze, *Philip Johnson*, 342.

59. Lamster, *The Man in the Glass House*, 374.

church as an "imaginary museum where all tragedy has been banned. The noise of the world does not penetrate [Johnson's] Crystal Cathedral."[60] Another suggested that the move from the hybrid church to the Cathedral represented a type of growth akin to that of "an upgrade from shopping center to full-scale mall."[61]

More than that, though, some scholars considered the opening of the Crystal Cathedral as nationally symbolic. Architecture critic Jane Holtz Kay argued the Crystal Cathedral epitomized the United States' abdication of the social and built environments to the automobile. She noted that a society revealed its true values in architecture—and the late twentieth-century US built environment bore witness to the "mastery of the automobile everywhere."[62] She alluded to the "glass complex" as a manifestation of an idolatry that sacrificed traditional religious symbols to the hegemony of car-based convenience. Kay derided the Cathedral: "a logo of God on the run, it was fronted by parking, its spiritual glitz a hymn to the asphalt Almighty."[63]

Another critic, Deyan Sudjic, compared Schuller's role in broadening the appeal of architecture to mass audiences as akin to what Oprah Winfrey's book clubs did for new writing. In other words, the minister invited an audience with limited occasions to consider building design an opportunity to appreciate it.[64] Sudjic assessed the building design on the campus as a form of "violent innovation" within religious architecture. Schuller, he insisted, implemented the architecture to demonstrate his continued "vigor and relevance."[65] Ultimately, he disparaged the architecture of the Garden Grove campus: "Schuller has built a church for the age of large-print books for the visually impaired. It leaves no room for doubt, personal interpretation, or subtlety."[66]

60. Quoted by Lamster, *The Man in the Glass House*, 374.

61. Lamster, *The Man in the Glass House*, 372.

62. Jane Holtz Kay, *Asphalt Nation: How the Automobile Took over America and How We Can Take It Back* (Berkeley: University of California Press, 1997), 273.

63. Kay, *Asphalt Nation*, 272.

64. Deyan Sudjic, *The Edifice Complex: How the Rich and Powerful Shape the World* (New York: Penguin Press, 2005), 296.

65. Sudjic, *The Edifice Complex*, 315–16.

66. Sudjic, *The Edifice Complex*, 304.

176 CHAPTER 7

Critiques aside, undoubtedly, the move to the Cathedral enhanced the aesthetics of *Hour of Power*. In fact, much of the sanctuary design reflected considerations for television production. Though the Cathedral was built with television audiences in mind, Schuller still hated the thought of television equipment cluttering its elegant beauty.[67] By 1981, *Hour of Power* had become a juggernaut. The show registered as the highest-rated religious broadcast in the United States, Canada, Australia, and on the Armed Forces Television Network.[68] Schuller also considered his broadcast to be singular: "The *Hour of Power* was the only televised weekly church service during which people of *all* races, ethnic origins, and political affiliations could look forward to hearing the weekly guests. There was no political bias to our program, just testimonials to the power of possibility thinking."[69] The impressive list of guests appearing every week ranged from film star Charlton Heston to Vice President Dan Quayle to General Norman Schwarzkopf.

The completion of the Cathedral marked yet another pivotal moment for the ministry. It served to distance Schuller from any would-be competitors in the world of religious broadcasters: "The low-rent preachers, the Swaggarts and the Bakkers, were in trouble already, but the Crystal Cathedral left them for dead, like greasy spoons trying to compete against the confidence of the McDonald's-style fast-faith corporate steamroller."[70] With the Cathedral, Schuller moved to a strata above local Orange County pastors and beyond the boundaries of his own denomination to become a large-footprint corporate entity with a grand profile and an international presence.

Living in (and with) the Cathedral

For better or worse, the Crystal Cathedral would become the most striking symbol of the Orange County ministry. It cost a lot and caught the

---

67. Nason and Nason, *Robert Schuller*, 249.

68. "'Hour of Power' Rated Number One," *Cathedral Chronicle*, September 1981, 2 (DVP).

69. Schuller, *My Journey*, 406.

70. Sudjic, *The Edifice Complex*, 310–11.

eye. Tired of criticisms regarding the financing of the Cathedral, Schuller claimed that the ministry had spent three years trying to raise funds for a "pedestrian black box" with "no basement" that would have still cost over $5,000,000 because of "union labor costs and material costs in Southern California." However, "because it was a boring structure," the campaign only raised $250,000.[71] Schuller remained adamant that he had no choice but to build the Cathedral as a grand structure.

Schuller's grandson, Bobby, who would eventually ascend to the church's pulpit and host of *Hour of Power*, stated that "the Crystal Cathedral itself is a theology, the building is built for unchurched people. It wasn't just designed because the weather in California is great. It was designed as a metaphor, that you can see into the church and we can see out to the world."[72] In other words, the design of the church allowed for more permeable boundaries between "the church" and "the world." The Cathedral would not merely look out at society but actively participate in it. Such a move made passing in and out of the church easier. What remained to be seen, though, was whether anything distinctively Christian had been lost in brokering the relationship between church and society.

Wesley Granberg-Michaelson, an executive officer of the RCA, surmised that Schuller had stumbled into "the right place and the right time." Focusing on his preaching skills, he believed that the minister's gift had been an innate ability to contextualize a theology for the American suburbs: "The way the Crystal Cathedral grew in the religious world was similar to the way Disneyland grew in the entertainment world. The same culture, the same time, and it became a resounding success. And that's not a critique. Whatever else you want to say about Bob's ministry, it was highly contextualized to the culture. You could say it was too contextualized, that it forgot some of the gospel, that's always a debate in issues of gospel and culture. But he was a genius at figuring out how to understand a particular culture and then relate religious life within it."[73]

71. Interview, Robert Schuller and Dennis Voskuil, March 3, 1983 (DVP).
72. Interview with Mulder, May 16, 2017.
73. Interview with Mulder, October 17, 2016.

178 CHAPTER 7

Richard Mouw, president of Fuller Theological Seminary in Pasadena, echoed that sentiment. Mouw recalled his discussions with Schuller:

> He always began conversations with me, just the two of us, telling me what an expert he was on John Calvin because he wrote some kind of compendium piece. I had a conversation with him once and said, "You know, you are one of the key contextualizers in theology in North America." He said, "What do you mean?" I said, "In missiology, we talk about contextualization. If I were going to be a missionary in some village in Africa that's animist, I'd have to study animism and see how I would bring the good news to an animist culture." I said, "You've done that with Southern California therapeutic self-actualization culture."[74]

For both men, Schuller had discovered a code for unlocking the felt needs of upwardly mobile suburbanites living in a market-driven society—and the wherewithal to attract loyal people to fund building a structure of the magnitude of the Crystal Cathedral represented that success.

Some, though, interpreted the crowning achievement, the opening of one of the country's most iconic religious buildings, as the beginning of the end for the ministry. Robert A. Schuller, the Schullers' son, suggested the building symbolized the moment when the ministry lost part of its identity: "When they opened the Crystal Cathedral, it changed everything. As far as the local [GGCC] church is concerned, there were decisions that my parents made that completely changed the local impact [that] was all a part of the demise of the Crystal Cathedral."[75] Robert A. continued, "I think the opening of the Cathedral was the death of [GGCC]." A married couple who had been members for decades similarly remarked that "the building of the [Crystal Cathedral] changed the whole dynamics of the Garden Grove Church. Building the glass church—it became world famous." The local church was swallowed up in a global ministry.

As the 1980s dawned, Schuller attained the position of arguably the nation's highest-profile church minister (assuming that Billy Graham

---

74. Interview with Mulder, February 22, 2017.
75. Interview with Mulder, May 17, 2017.

would be better understood as primarily an evangelist). In 1978 and again in 1982, the *Christian Century* ran a poll to determine the "most influential persons" in the field of religion. Schuller was one of only four religious leaders to be named both years. In describing the Orange County minister, the magazine editors said he had "popularized the teachings of church-growth theorists by putting them into practice in his ministry" and that "if his Nielsen ratings are correct, when Baptists stay at home to watch the electronic church, he's the one they watch the most."[76]

Though the long-lasting implications of the Crystal Cathedral could be argued, there remained no doubt that it allowed Schuller to establish a tangible marker of his success as a religious entrepreneur. The profile, though, continued to draw scrutiny. A young assistant professor at Schuller's alma mater, Hope College, wrote a manuscript that considered the theological implications of his fellow alumnus's Southern California megachurch. As Dennis Voskuil shopped his prospectus, he received a letter back from an editor, Marlin VanElderen, at Eerdmans Publishing (a Christian publisher in Grand Rapids, Michigan) that they had a "keen interest" in a book about Schuller's theology but also had reservations:

> Many evangelicals make an implicit distinction between criticizing a fellow-Christian in oral remarks and committing those remarks to the more permanent form which a book lends them. Were we to publish such a book, we would be immediately confronted by two troublesome responses—1) that of the large share of our usual audience who admire Schuller and want to hear nothing that tarnishes his image in their minds, and 2) that of an even larger group who are not personally taken by "the Hour of Power," but those whose attitude is that if he is such "a blessing" to some people it is best not to criticize him.

VanElderen also noted that "Schuller's own hypersensitivity to criticism" offered a variable to consideration of publication as well. In the end, though, the editor acknowledged that to allow these concerns to

---

76. "Naming the Influentials," *Christian Century*, January 6–13, 1982, 3–4 (DVP).

180   CHAPTER 7

prohibit the publication of a book would be nothing short of "craven." He encouraged Voskuil to send along the manuscript.[77]

Both wary and intrigued about being the subject of an entire book (which Eerdmans would indeed publish in 1983 as *Mountains into Goldmines: Robert Schuller and the Gospel of Success*), Schuller could not resist a conversation with Voskuil. The professor made a trip to Garden Grove for a face-to-face meeting. After navigating his way to Schuller's office on the twelfth floor of the Tower of Hope, Voskuil finally had his interview. He asked the megachurch minister whether he thought that the opening of the Crystal Cathedral represented the pinnacle of his career—and whether he could rest now and enjoy the legacy of his ministry. Schuller demurred and indicated he desired to expand his influence:

> I think the main goal now is to hopefully communicate the theology of self-esteem, this is like the most important thing, and I am outlining five different theologies. The first is the theology of self-esteem, which will produce a theology of communications, and that will produce a theology of evangelism, and that will produce a theology of social ethics, and that will produce a theology of economics and politics. But all is tied together by the ultimate human value, which is the need for dignity. Now to take that in stride, the other theologies of communications, ethics, evangelism, economics, I don't know if I'll have the ambition to do the work, no, I may be too lazy to do it, but I should do it. I want to do it. I ought to do it.[78]

After the publication of *Mountains into Goldmines*, Schuller asserted to *Publishers Weekly* that he had not read the book; he insisted, "I have nothing positive to say about that book. I have no respect for a man who calls himself a scholar and writes about a person and doesn't even ask for an interview."[79] Schuller's claim about Voskuil, though, proved du-

---

77. VanElderen to Voskuil, April 24, 1980 (DVP).

78. Schuller and Voskuil interview.

79. Lloyd Billingsley, "The Gospel according to Schuller," *Eternity*, November 1983, 26 (DVP). Indeed, in research for this volume, Voskuil generously shared with us the recordings and transcripts from both interviews of Schuller.

ACCOMMODATING—AND INSTIGATING—GROWTH **181**

bious, as the author thanked the minister in the preface for granting two interviews as he researched the book.[80] Indeed, it seems that Schuller's narratives about himself could, at times, forgo inconvenient or irritating facts. After an interview, one journalist described Schuller's annoyance with Voskuil's book as "keen" and that the minister described it as just another in a series of "cheap shots" and "hatchet jobs."[81] Living in a glass church proved to include significant liabilities.

The Cathedral raised Schuller's stature, and it also prompted discussion of his legacy. Was the Orange County minister now positioned to rest assured in a confident future? More than two decades of ministry yet remained. And as much as he had achieved, change was constant, and Schuller found that the actuality of stability remained elusive.

80. Voskuil, *Mountains into Goldmines*, xi.
81. Bruce Buursma, "Positive Preacher Has Problems," *Indianapolis Star*, September 3, 1983 (DVP).

8

TURBULENCE AND CONTROL IN THE 1980S

With the opening of the Crystal Cathedral, Schuller settled into routines, many of which centered on his own performance.[1] Every Sunday, the minister followed a familiar morning schedule. He arrived in his Cadillac and parked in a reserved spot on the lower level of the Cathedral. (He would eventually graduate to a Chrysler stretch limousine with a chauffeur. "The story" on the stretch limo was, according to the chauffeur, as follows: "The police chief in City of Orange where Dr. Schuller lived thought it might be a good idea if he would have someone drive for him because he would tend not to pay attention too much to his driving.")[2]

One of the first people at the church, the minister hustled into his study to make final adjustments to the sermon for the day. Next, a quick hair trim in the personal barbershop adjacent to the study. During the haircut, Schuller would receive guests and review last-minute instructions for the broadcast recording. From there, he headed down the hall-

---

1. Regarding the interconnection between preaching and performance, see Gerardo Martí, "'I Was a Muslim, but Now I Am a Christian': Preaching, Legitimation, and Identity Management in a Southern Evangelical Church," *Journal for the Scientific Study of Religion* 55, no. 2 (2016): 250–70; Aida I. Ramos, Gerardo Martí, and Mark T. Mulder, "The Strategic Practice of 'Fiesta' in a Latino Protestant Church: Religious Racialization and the Performance of Ethnic Identity," *Journal for the Scientific Study of Religion* 59, no. 1 (2020): 161–79.

2. Interview with Mulder, January 22, 2018.

way for makeup. Colors had to remain consistent from week to week—"And, most of all, the California tan must be evident."[3]

Shortly thereafter, the call to worship could be heard, and Schuller would ascend the side stairs from his lower-level study. The stage work helped to affirm the minister's legitimacy and gravitas. Fountains inside and out started to gurgle, and the "Cape Canaveral" doors began their ninety-second journey across the side of the Cathedral so those remaining in their cars in the parking lot could access the service. With the close of the call to worship, the cameras found the minister, and, employing a theatrical voice, he declared: "This is the day the Lord has made; let us rejoice and be glad in it!"[4] The staging and production values established the minister's charisma. One journalist remarked, "No television director could ask for a more inspirational opening." And then he emerged: "When the blue-robed, silver-haired Rev. Robert Schuller appears, there is no doubt about it: the star has arrived."[5]

Although Schuller was quite charming and seemingly mild-mannered in public and when broadcast on camera, a 1983 profile in the *Los Angeles Times* revealed a different persona: "The private Schuller—particularly among strangers but even around faithful staff, friends, and wife—is often surprisingly aloof, stiff, and uncomfortable, sullen and sour at times, defensive at others. In conversation, he is perpetually dominant, both condescending and pedantic. He displays not the slightest trace of spontaneous humor, rarely smiles, and never seems to laugh."[6] A close friend explained the contrast: "It became a little bit of Bob's Achilles heel in that he was not really an extrovert. He was an intense, Iowa farm boy who had been through tragedy, difficulties, and stresses, and a lot of personal and spiritual [troubles] as a young man. He developed the persona because he had the smart, eclectic personality to recognize that if he wanted to do something significant it had better

3. Larry Gates, *Dwelling in Schullerland* (Nashville: Winston-Derek, 1985), 75.

4. Gates, *Dwelling in Schullerland*, 75–76.

5. Richard Stengel, "Apostle of Sunny Thoughts," *Newsweek*, March 18, 1985, 30, in Dennis Voskuil Papers, Holland, MI (hereafter cited as DVP).

6. Bella Stumbo, "The Time Muhammad Ali Asked for Robert Schuller's Autograph," *Los Angeles Times*, May 29, 1983, https://tinyurl.com/29rprty5.

184   CHAPTER 8

involve a total package."[7] Schuller spoke to his audience about ways to manage their lives while, at the same time, he struggled to manage his own self. In contrast to his calm and cheerful demeanor on camera, those who knew Schuller on a personal level reported that he "had a temper when properly provoked."[8] And the 1980s would see frequent occasions for that provocation.

Schuller published multiple books during the decade, in which he detailed his theology for living as well as his method for church growth and management to serve those ends. His messages therefore touched both pulpit and pew, contributing to adjacent developments regarding evangelicalism's engagement with the therapeutic self in America. And the minister commanded enough stature that in 1983, he charged $10,000 for a forty-five-minute performance.[9] Not everyone approved. His pastoral performance, which featured messages centered on self-management, remained a significant target for critics.

Sociologist James Davison Hunter remarked that during the 1980s "fascination with the self and human subjectivity" became an established feature of evangelicalism—and that Schuller played a key role in that trend when he published *Self-Esteem: The New Reformation* in 1982.[10] Whereas Christians traditionally marked themselves with notions of restraint and asceticism, the revised version of the latter half of the twentieth century adopted patterns of self-expression and self-realization over and above self-sacrifice. The minister legitimized self-actualization by framing it within biblical and Christian symbolism. In fact, Hunter highlighted Schuller's "boldness" in shaping and reflecting evangelical assumptions "that the attention the self is receiving is legitimate and that the self, as the repository of human emotions and subjectivity, has intrinsic and ultimate worth and significance." Even though Schuller received widespread criticism, "most Evangelicals" came to "share the

---

7. This quote and those following were told to Mulder in interviews. For more on anonymous quotes, see "A Note on Sources."

8. Gates, *Dwelling in Schullerland*, 62.

9. Bruce Buursma, "Positive Preacher Has Problems," *Indianapolis Star*, September 3, 1983 (DVP).

10. James Davison Hunter, *Evangelicalism: The Coming Generation* (Chicago: University of Chicago Press, 1987), 69.

assumptions upon which [*Self Esteem* was] based." Moreover, according to Hunter, evangelicals in the late twentieth century embraced these theological alterations that fundamentally assaulted "traditional assumptions about the self."[11] Schuller's own message, then, became a catalyst in a core revision of historic Protestantism that Hunter claimed "undermined" the faith tradition's infrastructure.[12] He argued that it had become "clear, then, that Evangelicals generally and in the coming generation particularly have adopted patterns which even a generation ago (not to mention a century ago) would have been considered improper if not scandalous. What had been a cause for judgement is presently (for most Evangelicals) entirely uncontroversial or else celebrated as part of the Christian experience."[13]

In some ways, Schuller occupied a strange place within American religious culture. He seemed conservative—but always careful not to come off as overly judgmental. He appeared on television weekly. He officiated at funerals for such high-profile figures as Bob Hope, Hubert Humphrey, Evel Knievel, and Lucille Ball.[14] Although Schuller's messages could be seen as compromising the rigors of Christian devotion and humility in favor of stroking the egos of his listeners, a closer read of Schuller's messages suggests that he no longer held the same faith in abiding structures that his pastoral peers and other commentators did. Institutions were quickly shifting, with old arrangements falling away as others emerged. The demand that individuals continue to subsume themselves to previously established structures increasingly left them groping for guidance, unable to steady themselves amid constantly changing circumstances. Facing constant novelty, individuals were offered continuously new sources for self-formation and self-construction, leading to new religious sensibilities.[15] Already, those who had attempted to faithfully abide by conventional Christian standards found themselves

11. Hunter, *Evangelicalism*, 71.

12. Hunter, *Evangelicalism*, 73.

13. Hunter, *Evangelicalism*, 75.

14. Deepa Bharath, "Crystal Cathedral Founder to Officiate at Evel Knievel's Funeral," December 5, 2007, *Orange County Register*, https://tinyurl.com/yeuax3np.

15. Gerardo Martí, "Religious Reflexivity: The Effect of Continual Novelty and Diversity on Individual Religiosity," *Sociology of Religion* 76, no. 1 (2015): 1–13.

186 CHAPTER 8

needing to reconstruct their values and recalibrate their commitments, even reinventing traditions in unanticipated ways.

It is clear that Schuller developed his theology based on a pastoral vision of his suburban congregation. He believed that the pace of market society, with its rapid shifts and resulting uncertainties, left individuals unmoored. The sociologist Ulrich Beck described the condition of our modern age as a "risk society," one that is radically "individuated," because human beings are being steadily abandoned by holistic structures, leaving them to craft their own biography, manage their uncertainty, and fend for themselves.[16] At times, stability can be achieved, perhaps for a while, yet the developments of modernity more often than not result in unexpected crises for the great majority, with people facing personal and professional circumstances beyond their control.

Schuller's possibility thinking based itself on securing paths of action, and the theology of self-esteem sought to shore up a person's dignity as he or she does so. The minister concluded that it was incumbent upon moral leaders to offer vision to people finding their way through a maze of morphing structures, and, even more, to encourage them and strengthen their resolve to go beyond coping with change to taking advantage of emergent opportunities, using this historic era to exercise their budding autonomy and create unforeseen futures. So while Schuller did not stress self-sacrifice—after all, a rapidly changing culture and the unavoidable demands to make it in a market-driven society already required so much from everyone—he did insist that people dedicate themselves to participating in the market through lives of service, seeing needs and filling them, both personally and professionally.

Because the strains of modern life are frequently overwhelming, Schuller committed himself to preaching positively for his audience's sake, making his messages relevant to their everyday lives. Now, for

---

16. See Ulrich Beck, *Risk Society: Towards a New Modernity* (London: Sage, 1992); Ulrich Beck and Elisabeth Beck-Gernsheim, *Individualization: Institutionalized Individualism and Its Social and Political Consequences* (London: Sage, 2002); Ulrich Beck and Johannes Willms, *Conversations with Ulrich Beck* (Cambridge: Polity, 2004). For an ecclesial discussion using Beck's theorizing, see Gerardo Martí and Gladys Ganiel, *The Deconstructed Church: Understanding Emerging Christianity* (New York: Oxford University Press, 2014).

better or worse, the minister was seen as the face of a newly birthed therapeutic, church-growth Christianity—a novel faith tradition that stripped away obstacles and disciplines of the religion in exchange for happiness and self-actualization. Schuller concluded that the contours of Christianity were shifting, and he responded by offering the seemingly least-threatening version of that modification. And while many readily saw Schuller's warmhearted outreach to the public, fewer recognized that his messages were intimately tied to a methodology to renew the structure of the church that would be imitated by fellow pastors—a bold, long-term, and strategic project to remake the church in service to a changing culture.

The Microscope Intensifies

A former employee who had previously been in the banking industry remembered Schuller as "one of the most hardened businessmen" he had ever encountered.[17] He asserted that *intensity* offered the best insight into Schuller: "That intensity, combined with the energy of ten people and a striving for perfection, drives him onward and upward." But the same employee also acknowledged that the minister could be quite "complex" as well and that, because he functioned as such a visionary, Schuller spent "very little time on day-to-day mundane problems."[18] Although he attended a lot of committee meetings quite faithfully, he would frequently be described as getting bored and distracted—walking from the table in the Tower of Hope to look down at the Cathedral, drifting in and out of the conversation. In some instances, the minister simply excused himself from the meeting and advised the remaining committee to "carry on."[19]

Schuller became even more business-minded regarding opportunities presented by the Cathedral itself. The relative success of the Beverly Sills concert in raising $3 million in one night convinced the pastor that the Cathedral could host a range of performances—and continue to generate

17. Gates, *Dwelling in Schullerland*, 99.
18. Gates, *Dwelling in Schullerland*, 98.
19. Gates, *Dwelling in Schullerland*, 98.

188 CHAPTER 8

revenue on days other than Sunday. In 1980, seeking to meld spiritual uplift with possibilities for additional revenue, the ministry initiated a theatrical production, *The Glory of Christmas*, and, following its great success, *The Glory of Easter* in 1985. The *Glories* became synonymous with the Cathedral—to the point that the ministry reported 200,000 attendees for the two productions annually.[20] In 1982, *Christianity Today* underscored the scope of the "largest Christmas pageant in the country," *The Glory of Christmas*: $1 million in production costs, 400 cast members, 16 live animals, a 120-musician orchestra prerecorded in London for the sound track, and 40 performances.[21] Unique and impressive, every performance was a major event. The investment paid off, and the *Glories* continued to bring in millions in revenue for decades.

The stunning scale of *Christmas* instigated a new idea for Schuller: hosting events as much as possible, reframing the Cathedral as an Orange County cultural center: "Our church has never limited ourselves to only our congregation. We have always seen ourselves as a place to also serve the secular community; a place to enlighten, to inspire, entertain."[22] Soon enough, the Cathedral hosted famous acts that ranged from Lawrence Welk to Tony Bennett to Victor Borge to Robert Goulet to the Fifth Dimension. The facility grew so busy that the ministry installed its own Ticketron booth.

Successes lured cheering crowds but also drew less favorable scrutiny from state government officials. The concert series became too lucrative and attracted the attention of the California Board of Equalization. The assigned investigator, William Grommet, marveled, "This church is commercialized to a much greater extent than I've ever encountered in the state." After studying the details, the state board found "repeated use

20. Robert H. Schuller and James Coleman, *A Place of Beauty, a Joy Forever: The Glorious Gardens and Grounds of the Crystal Cathedral in Garden Grove, California* (Garden Grove, CA: Crystal Cathedral Creative Services, 2005), 48.

21. Lloyd Billingsley, "A Crystal Cathedral Spectacular: Christmas Pageant Is Reputed to Be the Country's Largest," *Christianity Today*, January 22, 1982, 34.

22. Herman Wong, "Arts Plans Reflected Schuller's Optimism," *Los Angeles Times*, May 4, 1983, CC-Tax Situation, 1983, 1984, Robert H. Schuller/Crystal Cathedral (hereafter cited as RHS/CC), box 29, Hope College Archives and Special Collections, Holland, MI (hereafter cited as HCASC).

TURBULENCE AND CONTROL IN THE 1980S **189**

of the property for profit organizations and by nonprofit organizations that do not qualify for the [tax] exemption."[23]

The California Board of Equalization noted in its report that Sunday breakfast and brunch cost $4.95 and $6.95, respectively—and that as many as 1,000 people could be served. Schuller attempted to maintain the tax-exempt status by preemptively canceling the 1982–1983 "Season of Spectaculars" concert series in the fall of 1982. In spite of that effort, Grommet remarked: "I am not aware of any operation in the state of California where there has been such an obvious abuse of the exemption of property for religious purposes."[24] Howard Whitcomb, Orange County's tax project manager, also quipped, "Certain types of classical or popular concerts don't become a religious endeavor just because they're held in a religious hall. That's common sense." He added, "it's something else to go all-out to sell tickets to the general public, to use Ticketron services and charge $14.00 a head and go beyond your own congregation and others who seek a religious experience."[25]

Schuller suddenly found his ministry's tax-exempt status threatened by the revenue-enhancing nature of the Cathedral as a performing arts center for Greater Orange County. He announced that the ministry would litigate against the state's attempt "to tax our pulpit, our choir loft, or our cross and church."[26] Not knowing how the ministry would pay its tax bill, Schuller went on the offensive. He called a press conference and suggested that the specter of harassment from the state against the Cathedral should be chilling for all other religious and charitable groups.[27] The minister also asserted to his council that the sum total value of the social

23. Wong, "Arts Plans Reflected Schuller's Optimism," and Herman Wong and Richard C. Paddock, "Schuller Church Stripped of Its Tax-Exempt Status," *Los Angeles Times*, May 4, 1983, CC-Tax Situation, 1983, 1984, RHS/CC, box 29 (HCASC).

24. "Crystal Cathedral Loses Tax Exemption," *Church Herald*, January 21, 1983, 25 (DVP).

25. Herman Wong, "The Tax Man Shatters the Dreams of Concerts in Crystal Cathedral," *Los Angeles Times*, December 15, 1982 (DVP).

26. Press Release, "Crystal Cathedral, under Protest, Borrows Money to Pay Taxes," August 31, 1983, CC-Tax Situation, 1983, 1984, RHS/CC, box 29 (HCASC).

27. Press Release, "Crystal Cathedral, under Protest, Borrows Money to Pay Taxes."

190   CHAPTER 8

services provided by faith-based organizations like the Crystal Cathedral outweighed the cost of their tax-exempt status: "There isn't a doubt in our mind that whatever tax advantages are extended to churches, synagogues, and temples in this country are far more than offset by untold savings in county, state, and social services."[28]

Unconvinced, in December 1982, the State of California revoked all property tax exemptions for the Crystal Cathedral. At a press conference called in response to the state's ruling, a magnanimous—perhaps chastened—Schuller argued for all the social good that the Crystal Cathedral provided Orange County and the nation, but also allowed: "All we are talking about in the final analysis is the flow of money to meet community needs. If a final, irreversible, and just conclusion is drawn that we owe taxes, that I do not see as a problem at all. It is simply another bill that will need to be paid. I will trust that we will have enough support from friends that our offerings will allow us to pay our bills. We always have. We always will. What is important to remember is that all gifts made to this ministry are tax deductible."[29] In May 1983 the board ruled that the ministry owed $400,000 in back taxes.[30] The ministry ultimately paid $473,000 in back taxes in 1983—with a note of protest that the state's position amounted to "religious harassment."[31]

The pressures for revenue only continued as the complexity in the operations of the ministry increased. Larry Gates, a church development officer at the Cathedral, often accompanied Schuller when he traveled in the early 1980s. His conversations with Schuller on flights and during meals led Gates to believe that the ministry found itself once again in a "time of real financial crisis."[32] At one point, the ministry seemed des-

---

28. Robert H. Schuller to members of the Crystal Cathedral Consistory, December 28, 1982, Shepherd's Grove Church Archives (hereafter cited as SGCA).

29. Robert H. Schuller to members of the Crystal Cathedral Consistory, December 28, 1982. Schuller included his December 21 printed remarks as an enclosure.

30. "Church on Coast Loses Tax Status," *New York Times*, May 5, 1983 (DVP).

31. "Crystal Cathedral to Pay Back Taxes on Concert Receipts," *New York Times*, August 31, 1983, https://tinyurl.com/yc7rtw73. See also Press Release, "Crystal Cathedral Borrows Money to Pay Taxes under Protest," August 30, 1983, CC-Tax Situation, 1983, 1984, RHS/CC, box 29 (HCASC).

32. Gates, *Dwelling in Schullerland*, 67.

TURBULENCE AND CONTROL IN THE 1980S **191**

perate to solicit donations across the entire country, identifying as many potential benefactors as possible.[33] The multiyear construction of the Cathedral had also worn on the congregation. Schuller's relationships "with his congregation had slowly deteriorated over the three years of construction." Between the pressures of fundraising and the criticism he had received, coupled with the trauma of Carol's accident, he had "gradually withdrawn from the mainstream of church life."[34] In fact, the Cathedral construction "had caused rifts, there was no doubt about it."[35]

Adapting to a Higher Profile

Certainly, the scrutiny of the ministry and the minister broadened and intensified after Schuller opened the Crystal Cathedral. Even an alumni publication from Hope College noted the minister's sensitivity to criticism: "The Rev. Robert H. Schuller '47 is of the opinion that people who live in glass churches shouldn't have stones thrown at them." Unable to ignore the critique from a fellow alumnus, Schuller responded with a tone of condescension in the same magazine: "The only people who criticize the Crystal Cathedral are people not committed to great art and architecture, but committed to—and deeply motivated by—mediocrity."[36]

He continued to preach warmth from the pulpit, laced with his possibility thinking, yet the consuming focus on organizational challenges and possibilities hindered direct pastoral touch with his own parishioners. Indeed, the move into the Cathedral left some members cold. One church administrator recalled that "many in the congregation were not taken with the new personnel and their policies, it seemed. It was clear that the next few months were going to be less than harmonious."[37] Schuller had been distracted by project management and became less available for his own church. The minister had to work to reconcile with

33. Gates, *Dwelling in Schullerland*, 66–67.
34. Michael Nason and Donna Nason, *Robert Schuller: The Inside Story* (Waco, TX: Word, 1983), 253.
35. Nason and Nason, *Robert Schuller*, 253.
36. Eileen Beyer, "Robert Schuller: Crystal Persuasion," *News from Hope College*, October 1980, 8 (DVP).
37. Gates, *Dwelling in Schullerland*, 31.

192 CHAPTER 8

his congregation. Nason described the next few months wherein the minister applied himself "to the cementing of the congregation, to meeting them at their level, where they are, and opening up to them on a more intimate plane." These efforts included Schuller making himself more accessible, including mingling with worshipers after services and shaking hands with people who had stayed in their cars for the drive-in.[38]

As greater public involvement removed him from immediate engagement with his church, the opportunities to experience direct criticism seem to have increased. The larger silhouette of the ministry made for an easy target. At one point, the minister wondered to an interviewer, "There isn't a building of this quality in any county, in any community, anywhere in America, including college campuses. . . . Why do they pick on me when colleges and universities do it?"[39]

Perhaps the most hurtful critique appeared in the pages of his own denomination's magazine, the *Church Herald*. Wendell Karsen, an RCA missionary in Hong Kong, eviscerated what he saw as the profligate financial waste of the Cathedral.[40] Karsen cast the Cathedral as unchecked extravagance in a world of poverty—an embarrassment to the denomination. Schuller would later describe it as "the most damning article ever written about our ministry, before or since."[41] The minister, though, again defended the financial investment of the Cathedral: "Didn't they realize that not one dollar went into the building? All the money went into checks that went into the pockets of laborers and truck drivers, and yes, even ore miners!" Moreover, "critics such as Reverend Karsen failed to see the role played by great monuments to faith throughout the history of the church. The cathedrals at Chartres and Notre Dame, along with Westminster Abbey and St. Peter's in Rome, continue to inspire us centuries after the last workers set the last stone in place and inlaid the last stained-glass window."[42] Schuller insisted the building was not a sign of

38. Nason and Nason, *Robert Schuller*, 254.

39. Interview, Robert Schuller and Dennis Voskuil, March 3, 1983 (DVP).

40. Wendell Karsen, "The Crystal Cathedral Distorts 'Success,'" *Church Herald*, January 23, 1981, 17.

41. Robert H. Schuller, *My Journey: From an Iowa Farm to a Cathedral of Dreams* (San Francisco: HarperOne, 2001), 406-7.

42. Robert H. Schuller, *My Journey*, 407.

opulence but an enduring testimony to their shared faith, one that would stand the test of time.

Though the Cathedral served as an easy mark, Schuller surely resented further attention that overflowed following the foibles of fellow televangelists during the 1980s. At one point, he intimated that Jim Bakker's and Jimmy Swaggart's respective scandals had had residual effects on his ministry. Schuller opined that their respective shenanigans over the past years created a climate of "anti-television ministries" to the point that the Crystal Cathedral Ministry had become "vulnerable to unreasonable, unfair, and damaging attacks."[43]

As suggested by James Davison Hunter, Schuller also became a symbol of the soft-sell form of Christianity that had taken root throughout much of the United States—especially in the postwar suburbs. In the pages of the *Christian Century*, Schuller became indicative of a lamentable development as the church growth movement received scrutiny as a contemporary heresy: "One of the worst distortions of the church that American ingenuity, born of an outworn capitalist mentality ('if it succeeds, it is right'), could possibly devise."[44] The author identified Schuller as a proponent of the movement, whose possibility thinking nurtured a context to develop a personality cult.[45]

Historians Jeffrey Hadden and Charles Swann described Schuller as "one of America's most flamboyant preachers" and the Crystal Cathedral as "a soaring, stunning monument in glass."[46] Perhaps because of his "flamboyance," the RCA—his own denomination—refrained from ever sponsoring broadcasts of *Hour of Power*. Indeed, Schuller's mainline Protestant background and training made him an outlier on Sunday morning religious programming. He himself took great pains to distance *Hour of Power* from the competitors, some of whom he considered "charlatans."[47] Perhaps owing to his RCA roots, Schuller's television audience

43. Year End Report of the Crystal Cathedral Ministries, December 31, 1988 (SGCA).

44. Ralph Elliot, "Dangers of the Church Growth Movement," *Christian Century*, August 12–19, 1981, 799 (DVP).

45. Elliot, "Dangers of the Church Growth Movement," 799–801.

46. Jeffrey K. Hadden and Charles E. Swann, *Prime Time Preachers: The Rising Power of Televangelism* (Reading, MA: Addison-Wesley, 1981), 10.

47. Hadden and Swann, *Prime Time Preachers*, 31.

194   CHAPTER 8

drew from atypical geographies. While Oral Roberts, Rex Humbard, Jimmy Swaggart, and Jerry Falwell relied on decidedly Southern US audiences (all drew at least 44 percent of their audiences from the South), Schuller relied on the Midwest (33.2 percent) and East (24.0 percent) for the majority of his viewers. Despite his Orange County location, Schuller drew only 12.7 percent of his audience from the West—worse than all competitors other than Roberts.[48]

Schuller took confidence in the popularity of the broadcast, growing more comfortable with standing apart from other ministries. Celebrities like Frank Sinatra watched *Hour of Power*. He told Schuller that he watched the program every Sunday before he went to Mass (and, of course, *almost* sang a solo on the broadcast, according to Schuller).[49] Indeed, in the early days of the Cathedral, Schuller garnered enough stature that he eschewed membership in the National Religious Broadcasters. Explaining why he didn't belong to the organization, Schuller explained to a journalist: "There are certainly some fine people in that group, and it's not the dues—what is it, $200 a year? And I don't want to seem snobbish or stand-offish. It's just that. . . . It's just that—who *needs* them?"[50]

The minister's profile expanded as he continued to appear on *Hour of Power*, traveled around the country as a speaker, and published books where he offered both his theology and advice for better living and life management. And as Schuller wrote and published in the 1970s and 1980s, critics noted the stream of thought where the minister had located himself. Indeed, when Schuller published *Self-Esteem* in 1982, he assumed it would be an unprecedented disruption of traditional Christianity. Though it failed to have the scope of influence the minister anticipated, the book did become a cultural touchstone because of the intervention of Chicago insurance magnate W. Clement Stone. Stone himself practiced mentalism and New Thought and estimated that Schuller's synthesis with Christianity had created something every pastor in the country should know. Schuller's assistant Michael Nason recalled the scenario:

48. Hadden and Swann, *Prime Time Preachers*, 60–61.
49. Nason and Nason, *Robert Schuller*, 200.
50. Stumbo, "The Time Muhammad Ali Asked for Robert Schuller's Autograph."

TURBULENCE AND CONTROL IN THE 1980S   **195**

Clement Stone bought the book direct from the publisher, and they mailed it to every pastor in America that year. That was like a bombshell going off because it became very controversial. Both positive and negative, the detractors were all over Schuller's case and in the media, and pastors were in their pulpit speaking against it. At the same time, there were pastors speaking in favor of his position and what he was saying. That was one of the big, big moments in his ministry that caused other pastors to sit up and take notice of this guy out in California, people who really didn't know who he was, and that is when he became the magnet for pastors to pay attention to his message, not only in books but also on television. So the attention was positive and negative.[51]

The book, the broadcast, and the Cathedral reverberated with each other to broaden Schuller's platform—alongside the criticism that came with it.

Mentalism and Self-Help

With cumulative stresses amid his many successes, the minister was not always content throughout the 1980s. For a person associated with self-esteem and possibility, Schuller was periodically consumed by his own fear of failure. The degree of competition he felt, and the struggle for the survival of his ministry, seemed never ending. A sense of security was fleeting. At one point in his early days in Garden Grove, he awakened from a nightmare in tears and prayed, "Oh, God, please take me. Just a fatal heart attack would solve all my problems. Give me a way out gracefully."[52] Such a dramatic statement illustrated the severe levels of panic that would rise in Schuller when confronted by problems beyond his control—wishing for death as a solution. When he discussed possibility thinking and self-esteem, it almost certainly functioned as a form of self-talk, an internal therapy or reminder of personal value and worth.

Certainly, Schuller cultivated a theology rooted in a depth of Reformed theological tradition, yet it was specifically suited to the com-

---

51. Interview with Mulder, January 22, 2018.
52. Stumbo, "The Time Muhammad Ali Asked for Robert Schuller's Autograph."

196 CHAPTER 8

bination of busyness and uncertainty in the lives of his market-imbued members. Even more, his theology spoke to himself, his own restless and ambitious self. He found no need to wallow in sinfulness or to seek sanctuary in a transcendent, otherworldly hope. Instead, Schuller shaped a theology that would be *useful*, enhancing a person's ability to take action. Possibility thinking oriented entirely around the instrumental, bolstering the capacity of individuals to act, to embody their faith with confidence, overcoming inevitable failures, and reaching for the dreams that inspire them, even when they seem out of reach.

Schuller's form of Christianity leaned heavily into the American lineage of mentalism or New Thought—what Norman Vincent Peale crafted into "positive thinking." In a 1990 editorial, the RCA's very own *Church Herald* acknowledged that no one should be surprised that both Peale and Schuller frequently found themselves cited as part of the New Age movement.[53] In fact, already in the 1970s, critics used the label "Schullerism" to describe the brand of Christianity that espoused an accommodating New Age-y message that affirmed the pursuit of wealth.[54] Of course, Schuller would argue that he remained as orthodox as ever; his theology simply prioritized the pursuit of the "unchurched."

It remains difficult to overestimate Schuller's devotion to positive—or possibility—thinking. (Remember the letter to Jesse Jackson in which the minister described his subscription to positive thinking as "almost [as] important as the resurrection of Jesus Christ.")[55] That sentiment, of course, would likely have proved quite troublesome for Schuller if it were more widely known. The minister, though, offered little evidence that he worried much about whether he had strayed outside the bounds of orthodox Christianity—his theology, after all, necessarily pressed the edges of accepted dogma as the "New Reformation." The *appearance* of orthodoxy always, however, remained a concern at the ministry. Nason once commented about his boss's theology: "Although Dr. Schuller

---

53. John Stapert, "A New Age Challenge," *Church Herald*, March 1990, 6 (HCASC).

54. See especially Martin D. Geleynse, "Review of *You Can Become the Person You Want to Be* by Robert H. Schuller," *Calvin Theological Journal*, November 1974, 252.

55. Nason and Nason, *Robert Schuller*, 152, and Schuller to Jackson, June 13, 1975, CC-Correspondence, 1975, RHS/CC, box 4 (HCASC).

TURBULENCE AND CONTROL IN THE 1980S **197**

takes a roundabout way of getting there, a way that many fundamentalists wouldn't approve, he eventually arrives at the same destination as they."[56]

Schuller personally never claimed to be anything other than a Calvinist—even if he found some of the doctrine distasteful. For instance, he expressed a great deal of disregard for total depravity: "If you say a person is totally depraved, totally decadent, totally sinful and there is no value at all within him, that's not scriptural."[57] Moreover, he indicated that he would never deign to preach a sermon regarding election or predestination while on *Hour of Power*. In practice, though, Schuller's reconceptualization of original sin led him away from his Reformed and Calvinist roots. While the traditional doctrine cited rebellion and pride as the impetus for sin and brokenness in human societies, Schuller insisted, instead, that negative self-image remained most fundamental. That is, because of a lack of self-esteem, humans refrain from trusting others, "so they wear masks; at their deepest levels they find it impossible to be totally honest, even with those they love."[58]

In practice, then, the minister's theology offered a repudiation of aspects of Calvinism. In fact, within Schuller's theological imagination, Jonathan Edwards likely represented only the worst aspects of Calvinism. Edwards's depictions of God's wrath and hellfire functioned as a rhetorical tool to exhort mass audiences to "turn from sin and await the conversion that depends on God's grace."[59] Schuller discarded any discourse related to human depravity in favor of his theology of self-esteem. The minister assumed he had to in order to appeal to any significant swath of the American public given the issues they face in contemporary society. While many in the United States might have still considered themselves Calvinist, "the doctrine of predestination had been rejected by most segments of American Protestantism, and the doctrine of human depravity

56. Nason and Nason, *Robert Schuller*, 158.

57. Robert H. Schuller, *Your Church Has a Fantastic Future! A Possibility Thinker's Guide to a Successful Church* (Ventura, CA: Regal Books, 1986), 118.

58. Nason and Nason, *Robert Schuller*, 154.

59. Marsha Witten, *All Is Forgiven: The Secular Message in American Protestantism* (Princeton: Princeton University Press, 1993), 79.

198 CHAPTER 8

was on the wane" already by the end of the nineteenth century.[60] Because of that, a little over half of a century later, Schuller had to puzzle together a coherent, appealing message of Christianity that sidestepped the condemnation of sin and provided people a sense of self-control.

As a pastoral imperative, Schuller explicitly offered a nontraditional understanding of sin and hell that he calculated would resonate with his audience due to the practicalities of their social existence. To be sure, both of his definitions struck traditional Christians and critics as highly problematic. At one point, Schuller indicated that Augustine's claim that human frailty owed mostly to pride and too much liking of the self was simply wrong.[61] The minister described sin as "any act or thought that robs [oneself] or another human being of his or her self-esteem." And Schuller defined hell as "the loss of pride that naturally follows separation from God—the ultimate and unfailing source of our soul's sense of self-respect."[62] Thus people found themselves in hell when they lost their self-esteem.

Moreover, individuals without self-esteem would find it impossible to be possibility thinkers. As evidence, Schuller claimed that "the priceless value of every person" undergirded the Lord's Prayer as its most basic theme. The minister even posited the therapeutic nature of the prayer: "Jesus begins the prayer by giving us an in-depth therapy for our inferiority complex."[63] In this vein, Schuller critiqued his own denomination's doctrine: "Classical Reformed Theology declares that we are born rebellious sinners. But that answer is too shallow. It ignores the tough question: Why would love-needing persons resist, rebel against, and reject beautiful love? The answer? We are born nontrusting. Deep down we feel we are not good enough to approach a holy God. It is a perverted perfectionism that keeps us from [drawing] close enough to God to believe in him."[64]

60. Witten, *All Is Forgiven*, 80.
61. Joel A. MacCollum, "Self-Love: How Far? How Biblical? How Healthy?" *Eternity*, February 1979, 23–24.
62. Robert H. Schuller, *Self-Esteem: The New Reformation* (Waco, TX: Word, 1982), 14.
63. Robert H. Schuller, *Self-Esteem*, 58.
64. Robert H. Schuller, *Self-Esteem*, 64.

Quoting Scripture was never enough to articulate his messages. Schuller said he felt called to a more "systematic approach to theology" rather than a more "traditional Biblical approach." Based on his aversion to implementing Scripture in his sermons, it seems clear that Schuller gauged his audience as post-Christian. Nason described the rationale of his boss: "[Schuller] contends this because the people he is trying to reach don't accept the Bible. If he starts out by quoting heavily from a source that most of them don't consider reliable, he's not going to get to first base."[65] Spiritual formation would need to look different from mere review of scriptural readings. By interpreting principles and applying them to their lives directly, Schuller assumed that biblical truth was already embedded in his messages.

Schuller's emphasis on self-esteem and possibility thinking over and against sin and condemnation flowed well within a stream of self-actualization in America in the latter half of the twentieth century. Sociologist Micki McGee traced the pervasiveness of self-discipline and self-help throughout American culture and described four of Schuller's books published in the 1980s—*Tough Times Never Last, But Tough People Do!* (1983); *Tough-Minded Faith for Tender-Hearted People* (1985); *The Be (Happy) Attitudes* (1985); and *Be Happy You Are Loved* (1986)—as the minister's "buck-up" series. That is, readers just need to adjust their attitudes and try harder. McGee also identified Schuler as a primary practitioner of the "maudlin exemplar"—using stories of folks haunted by the specter of physical impairment who find ways to triumph over their adversity. Such stories proved useful to Schuller because of the implicit (sometimes explicit) framing: "Oh, you think you have problems? I will tell you about someone with *real* problems. Now that you have heard about that, what do you really have to complain about?" Schuller also tended to utilize his family's tornado experience to similar ends.

According to McGee, the maudlin exemplar would then be utilized to assure the audience that no matter their terrible circumstances, they remained "individually still in charge of their own lives, demonstrating self-mastery in the face of unexpected events." The pivot to a "doctrine of self-mastery" functioned as the moment of realization: "The fact that

---

65. Nason and Nason, *Robert Schuller*, 152.

200   CHAPTER 8

there are forces beyond one's control is acknowledged and then dismissed with the message that it's not what life hands you, it's how you handle it."[66] The maudlin exemplar functioned as a maneuver to communicate through a story that misfortune could in fact be managed and that future success depended on self-mastery.

Possibility thinking, at its core, resided in the notion of mastery. The individual has a degree of influence over every aspect of one's life—if only the person rigidly maintains the right mental posture. As evidence, Schuller trotted out celebrities who used positive thinking to overcome obstacles. For example, President Gerald R. Ford discussed his wife's substance-abuse battle. In another instance, Los Angeles mayor Tom Bradley reported that positive thinking had been crucial in helping him to overcome racism.[67] And yet Schuller himself wrestled with an inability to master his own doubts.

The failure to live up to his theology haunted the minister. Arvella described Schuller as suffering from an acute lack of self-esteem: "I can feel his insecurity many times, especially when we're in a roomful of strangers."[68] Perhaps revealing the depths of his fragility, Schuller disputed his wife's assessment: "Even if my wife said that, I would not agree that I am insecure. I would say that I am merely cautious. Yes, cautious. I don't want to be hurt, and I don't want to hurt others. So, I need (before relaxing) to figure out where a person is coming from, you know?"[69]

For Arvella, positive thinking became a force of determination and merit—it seemed that an individual's free will and hard work would unfailingly lead to good results: "When individuals clear their minds of the cancerous disease of self-pity, anger, and resentment, they begin to heal and learn how to grasp hold of new ways, new ideas."[70] In their own family, the trauma of Carol losing her leg to amputation offered an example of facing unexpected and uncontrollable crisis. Yet, her re-

66. Micki McGee, *Self-Help, Inc.: Makeover Culture in American Life* (New York: Oxford University Press, 2005), 151.

67. Stumbo, "The Time Muhammad Ali Asked for Robert Schuller's Autograph."

68. Stumbo, "The Time Muhammad Ali Asked for Robert Schuller's Autograph."

69. Stumbo, "The Time Muhammad Ali Asked for Robert Schuller's Autograph."

70. Arvella Schuller, *The Positive Family: Possibility Thinking in the Christian Home* (Garden City, NY: Doubleday, 1982), 112.

TURBULENCE AND CONTROL IN THE 1980S **201**

sponse and their working through the convalescence from the injury offered the most robust affirmation of "immersing their children—from day one—in positive thinking, positive talking, and positive actions."[71] Arvella described how it worked: "Brainwashed with positive thinking, Carol's mental attitude holds the key to her determination not to feel handicapped."[72] The Schuller family believed in willpower and grit: "Those families that refuse to feed their mental appetites on negatives will become *better* instead of *bitter* individuals."[73]

To reinforce their commitments to possibility thinking, the Schullers often looked to similar others who could confirm their methodology—the minister, in fact, once suggested that not everything could be learned from books, that parents must also rely on common sense more than "intellectuals" who could be "moral and spiritual fools."[74] For instance, Arvella once related the story of sitting on a flight next to a successful gentleman—as evidence of his success, he had a doctoral degree and homes in New York, Colorado, California, and Venezuela. Seeing an opportunity, Arvella asked him how he wanted to be remembered. He responded: "For never quitting!" Arvella then revealed in her book on positive parenting, that she followed up with another question about what might be wrong with American families. Compelled by his answer, Arvella passed it along for her readers: "He was emphatic in stressing that 'lack of motivation is the major cause of problems in American homes.'"[75] In short, families just need to be positive and try harder—to change their attitude and effort.

To their credit, the Schullers as parents also attempted to be consistent in that they claimed to raise their family with the same principles they advocated for church management. They saw themselves as representing "a culture and heritage" to their five children.[76] Arvella and Schuller suggested that the "happy family" began with the parents and that they

71. Arvella Schuller, *The Positive Family*, 111.

72. Arvella Schuller, *The Positive Family*, 110.

73. Arvella Schuller, *The Positive Family*, 112.

74. Robert H. Schuller, *God's Way to the Good Life* (Grand Rapids: Eerdmans, 1963), 56–57.

75. Arvella Schuller, *The Positive Family*, 131.

76. Robert H. Schuller, *God's Way to the Good Life*, 55.

202   CHAPTER 8

needed to "make decisions" to start building positive home lives.[77] Such an assumption, though, left little room for disruptions that could be outside of the parents' control. Strong enough belief and commitment, it would seem, could overcome any and all obstacles.

Softening the Contours of Christianity

In the introduction to *Self-Esteem*, Schuller expressed a concern that the church's "power, membership, and influence" were in decline in Europe and the United States. The minister estimated that "theocentric communication" at the expense of meeting human needs had mitigated the church's role in contemporary society. Beyond that, the Reformers had the benefit of working and preaching within overwhelmingly Christian societies—they didn't have to "impress the unchurched."[78] Although most surveys in the early 1980s would have reported[79] that the vast majority—almost 90 percent—of the US population identified as Christian, Schuller framed his "missional" work as that of the underdog: "Today the sincere, Christian believer is a minority."[80] As such, contemporary pastors should position themselves as missionaries. After all, missionaries had recently been employing techniques where, instead of ineffectively spouting off about theological concerns, they focused on medicine, language, and agriculture in order to foster a "humane approach."[81] For Schuller, that particular strategy necessarily fixated on the "deep needs" of the unchurched. In a pluralistic world, ministers also had to take care not to offend potential congregants. That translated into stressing tolerance.[82]

Though his exposure to Norman Vincent Peale left him open to and curious about the use of psychology, Schuller became even more convinced that theology should become more therapeutic after attending the World Psychiatric Congress in Madrid, Spain, in 1967. That same year he published *Move Ahead with Possibility Thinking: A Practical and Spiritual*

77. Arvella Schuller, *The Positive Family*, 125.
78. Robert H. Schuller, *Self-Esteem*, 12.
79. See, for instance, this Gallup poll: https://tinyurl.com/3d456ewh.
80. Robert H. Schuller, *Self-Esteem*, 13.
81. Robert H. Schuller, *Self-Esteem*, 13.
82. Witten, *All Is Forgiven*, 23.

Challenge to Change Your Thinking and Your Life—the public unveiling of "possibility thinking." The book jacket of this unapologetic and obvious derivative of Peale's "positive thinking" promised to reveal the "powerful formula" that would allow readers to "build a great new life." The book's release initiated a steady stream of messages and publications.

Though he published numerous other books, Schuller declared that *Self-Esteem* represented his magnum opus. As the subtitle suggested, Schuller estimated that the volume's synthesis of theology and psychology would catalyze a second Protestant Reformation. In the introduction, Schuller provocatively claimed that "a person is in hell when he has lost his self-esteem."[83] Although many would be scandalized by Schuller's amalgamation of theology and psychology, in truth, the minister operated within the truly American lineage of New Thought or mentalism that could be traced to a disparate family tree that included a wide array of forms and practitioners ranging from Ralph Waldo Emerson to Christian Science to Dale Carnegie.[84] One critic summed up Schuller's possibility thinking as "a form of mental reprogramming based on visualization, affirmation, and repetition."[85] The minister himself became the prototype of the trend wherein churches "increasingly sacrificed doctrinal tradition to embrace growth for its own sake, and positive thinking turns out to be a crucial catalyst for growth."[86]

Critics understood Schuller as accommodating secularism, but the minister countered that, actually, positive Christianity would overwhelm all other competing concepts because it worked as a "bigger, better, and more beautiful idea."[87] As Schuller surveyed the state of Christianity in the late twentieth century, he assessed that the faith tradition would soon be leaving the "Reactionary Age"—an era that began with the Protestant Reformation and by Schuller's reckoning would end in 1999—and soon enter the "Age of Mission."[38] The latter would be marked

83. Robert H. Schuller, *Self-Esteem*, 15–16.
84. Barbara Ehrenreich, *Bright-Sided: How Positive Thinking Is Undermining America* (New York: Picador, 2009), 52–53 and 86–90.
85. Ehrenreich, *Bright-Sided*, 134.
86. Ehrenreich, *Bright-Sided*, 136.
87. Robert H. Schuller, *Self-Esteem*, 173.
88. Robert H. Schuller, *Self-Esteem*, 174.

204 CHAPTER 8

by a "theology for church growth" and "a theology for success."[89] In a word, it would be a Christianity suited to the contours of the market.

While Schuller proved charismatic on Sunday mornings as he exhorted from the pulpit, commentators at the time noted that the minister demonstrated a true gift for charm at more secular venues: "Unfettered by any need to even obliquely refer to Jesus Christ, liberated from the need to be a polished TV performer, he turns into a swooping, exuberant, first-rate stand-up comic."[90] And as Schuller attempted to make Christianity more relatable, he strategically avoided negative associations with organized religion. Religion and faith, by definition, appeal to things that remain superempirical, beyond evidence. In his attempt to reach the rational unchurched, Schuller jettisoned mystery in favor of an almost scientific appeal. Thus, the minister no longer delivered sermons. Instead, he offered "inspirational messages." Not content with "minister," Schuller cast himself as a "therapist, a mass psychologist." He suggested that *Hour of Power* avoid the label of "religious broadcast" in favor of a "therapeutic injection of spiritual vitamins."[91]

Schuller enjoyed great fame yet remained subject to great scrutiny from other Christian leaders. On November 1, 1992, the minister appeared live on air as a guest on *The White Horse Inn*, a Christian talk show that broadcast widely in Southern California on radio station KKLA (99.5 FM) Sunday nights at 9 p.m. The host, Michael Horton, was known to proudly carry the banner of theological orthodoxy in the Reformed tradition. It was clear from the first question of the program, described as "A Debate with Robert Schuller," that Horton targeted Schuller as a potential heretic.[92] Calling for "a second reformation based on God-esteem and Christ-esteem" rather than Schuller's proposed reformation based on self-esteem, Horton hounded the minister on his understanding of salvation. Schuller agreed that sin was real ("we are sinners by nature") and that Jesus was the only hope for salvation ("a redemptive relation-

---

89. Robert H. Schuller, *Self-Esteem*, 175.

90. Stumbo, "The Time Muhammad Ali Asked for Robert Schuller's Autograph."

91. Stumbo, "The Time Muhammad Ali Asked for Robert Schuller's Autograph."

92. See "A Debate with Robert Schuller," White Horse Inn, November 1, 1992, https://tinyurl.com/2s4478e7.

TURBULENCE AND CONTROL IN THE 1980S 205

ship"), but the terms and meanings of human depravity, God's wrath, and Christian responsibility to convey the gospel were among the many things that required "interpretation." Even the Heidelberg Catechism, which Schuller said he had "memorized," remained subject to dispute.

Horton insisted that the Bible approached various issues in quite specific ways, while a seasoned Schuller, having to represent himself repeatedly over the years, spoke in his rich baritone voice that "the Bible is addressed to believers," and that it requires "theological interpretation" to be applied to today's listeners: "Just because it's in the Bible, doesn't mean we should preach it." The minister elaborated: "I'm interested in attracting people, not driving them farther away," and "I preach the way Jesus did, but I don't preach, probably, the way Paul did." He emphasized compassion and humility, attentiveness to listeners who experienced difficult life circumstances, and sensitivity to those who may not have the background to understand challenging and off-putting scriptural texts. Schuller explained, "People are not going to be attracted to Jesus Christ unless we hit them at a point of need. The point of need is a problem in their life."

A dissatisfied Horton continued what he described as a "charitable but direct conversation." With a rhetorical persistence that asserted his more correct doctrinal views (peppering questions, asking for scriptural text proofs, restating Schuller's words, pushing back on the minister's responses), Horton irritated his guest. As Horton pressed for biblical fidelity, Schuller in turn argued for the need to be discerning in our communication, insisting, "if we're wise, there's language we will not use." For evidence, Schuller noted that Jesus "didn't humiliate people like preachers do." Following up, Horton wondered, "Are you not obligated to tell people the truth?" Twenty minutes into the hour, the conversation became heated, with Schuller at times raising his voice and sharply cutting Horton off, then, catching himself, immediately calming down to explain, once again, his own views.

At about thirty minutes, Schuller asked to leave, seeming to end the interaction. Yet a few minutes after the break, a door is heard to open, and the minister returned. "I'm back," he announced into the microphone. "This is Robert Schuller." (Later, after a phone-in caller thanked "Dr. Schuller for having the integrity to come back to the show," Schuller

206 CHAPTER 8

quipped that "he had to go to the bathroom.") Schuller continued to articulate his views, while a skeptical Horton returned to drilling the minister. Schuller explained he had been willing to talk about "Reformation theology in relation to modern evangelicalism," what his written invitation indicated as the theme, but charged Horton with writing out questions without alerting him in advance and pulling quotes out of context. "That was not hospitable, I don't treat people that way, and I hope you convert and change." He disparaged the program: "You folks have your own agenda." Taking advantage of Schuller in midargument, Horton announced a live caller with "a question for Dr. Schuller." Between Horton and a steady stream of comments from call-in listeners, Schuller frequently countered by saying, "I never said *that*," framing and reframing his theological convictions in his usual, straightforward manner—while refusing the stark doctrinal terms that would appease his more strictly conservative audience.

Still, the minister described himself during the program as a Calvinist, defined the gospel as summarized in John 3:16, and spoke of the need for repentance. "You can't win an argument with me, I'll tell you why: You haven't been criticized as much as I have. [Raising his voice] I have been criticized so much by so many people so many times for 20 years," and admitted to being upset because he believed he was being misquoted. Schuller expressed his understanding of his own call to ministry, recalling, "I came to California not to be a pastor of a church but to be a foreign missionary to a pagan country called 'intelligent, educated, nonbelieving people.'" At several points after that moment, a dispirited minister refused to comment much further, sensing futility against a set paradigm both Horton and his listeners shared but did not conform to Schuller's own views: "You've been educated, but you've also been indoctrinated." The minister summarized the differences for Horton: "You and I aren't going to ride on the same bus. I don't want to ride on a bus where the guy keeps laying the wrath of God on people, and you do."

Critics like Horton refused nuance and repeatedly insisted that Schuller's preaching sought solely to comfort listeners. In *All Is Forgiven: The Secular Message in American Protestantism*, Marsha Witten argued that religious discourse could be classified as either resistance or accommodation. Witten explained that accommodation referred "to the

TURBULENCE AND CONTROL IN THE 1980S   **207**

adjustments that religion makes in its practices, pronouncements, and creeds to bring them in conformity with the values and behaviors of secularity."[93] Resistance, on the other hand, reacted against secular culture and enacted buffers within the religion to shield it from the pressures of modernity.[94] Schuller, quite obviously in her assessment, chose the accommodation route. The minister sought to reassure attenders and affirm their economically striving lifestyles. In fact, fundamentalists represented to Schuller those who had embraced the resistance strategy—and he betrayed his disregard for that movement by understanding "fundamentalist" as an epithet. Moreover, Witten noted that shrewd ministers like Schuller realized that their competitors included not just other churches in the region or on a different channel but worldviews such as "Marxism, humanism, scientism, and even, most recently, the cult of physical perfectionism."[95]

When Witten introduced the concept of "God as Daddy, Sufferer, Lover, and Judge," she quoted Schuller as epitomizing the trend toward a therapeutic notion of God and religion: "Affirm OUT LOUD: 'I am God's friend. God loves me. If God has chosen me for His friend, I must be a marvelous person.'"[96] The therapeutic God "relieves negative feelings, especially anxiety and doubt."[97] And that version of God, Schuller assumed, presented the most attractive deity to the "unchurched" that the minister most desired to reach.

As a thought commodity, then, this kind of analysis asserts that ministers like Schuller sold a message that needed to be ever more attractive to the fickle, wandering eyes of the potential audience. In that scenario, a condemning, doom-and-gloom message would be avoided. Witten elaborated: "The moral and spiritual demands that religion places on adherents tend to be underplayed or explicitly denied." Punishment and retribution would then be ignored or dismissed in favor of an empha-

93. Witten, *All Is Forgiven*, 18.
94. Witten, *All Is Forgiven*, 24.
95. Witten, *All Is Forgiven*, 22.
96. Robert H. Schuller, *Believe in the God Who Believes in You: The Ten Commandments; A Divine Design for Dignity* (Nashville: Nelson, 1989), quoted by Witten, *All Is Forgiven*, 31 (capitalization in original).
97. Witten, *All Is Forgiven*, 35.

208 CHAPTER 8

sis on "emotional and material pleasures" that naturally followed from Christian practice and belief.[98] She even specifically cited Schuller's reinterpretation of the Ten Commandments (they were "meant—not to take the fun out of life—but turn on the sun in our life")[99] as an exemplar of this practice. Witten also noted that pastors who utilized psychology—or synthesized it with their religious tradition—were trying to excise the supernatural or mysterious elements. A demythologized religion allowed for greater acceptances among the rational "consumers" of religion pursued by seeker churches.[100]

Food, Fitness, and Fidelity—but No Politics

Politically, Schuller attempted to remain above the fray.[101] Because he saw himself delivering a form of therapy, the minister felt a necessity to remain an assumed ally of his audience members. To defend his attempt at being apolitical, he reminded any interlocuters that he saw himself as a mass therapist—and if patients knew that they held a political view in opposition to that of their counselor, they would remain more guarded and intimidated. When once confronted with the fact that Cathedral press packets identified him as a registered Republican, the minister exclaimed, "That's not possible!" and phoned an administrative assistant to immediately create new documents without the political party registration. Turning back to the reporter who had informed of the political affiliation, an "openly belligerent" Schuller explained, "I may be a registered Republican, but as you *know*, you've got to register one way or the *other* in California! It doesn't mean I'm a Republican! Don't *call*

98. Witten, *All Is Forgiven*, 22.

99. Robert H. Schuller, *Believe in the God Who Believes in You*, quoted by Witten, *All Is Forgiven*, 22.

100. Witten, *All Is Forgiven*, 23.

101. The avoidance of politics was in sharp contrast to other religious groups that sought to distinguish themselves by their political stances. For a prominent example, see Andrew Gardner and Gerardo Martí, "From Ordaining Women to Combating White Supremacy: Oppositional Shifts in Social Attitudes between the Southern Baptist Convention and the Alliance of Baptists," *Religion and American Culture: A Journal of Interpretation* 33, no. 2 (Summer 2022): 202–35.

me a Republican! I cross over all the time! I voted for Tom Bradley, for instance!" In a sign of his commitment to nonpartisanship, the minister quickly regretted his undisciplined attempt to distance himself from the Republican Party. He wearily sighed and acquiesced, "I voted for Tom Bradley because I think he has tremendous character, he has integrity, he's a good administrator—and he's a *very* positive person. He's a possibility thinker, *absolutely*."[102]

And though his ministry grew through decades of racial tumult, the minister mostly resisted entering a potentially divisive conversation. Living in a highly segregated region, Schuller rarely encountered racial diversity throughout most of his ministry, and he demonstrated a limited understanding of racism in its institutional or policy forms. Having moved from a rural white community to a suburban one, he lacked both the experience and the motivation to pursue a deeper understanding of racial injustice. While the minister said the Christian church had a "pitiful record" of addressing the social injustices of society, he also offered meager solutions in terms of systems and structures. As might be expected, he assessed that racism stemmed from the "defensive reaction of a fearful, non-self-esteeming person."[103] With that in mind, the church should be in the business not of condemning racists but, rather, of "disarming" them "until they no longer feel threatened, and victimized."[104]

Though Schuller hesitated to discuss politics or structural racism, certain social issues seemed to trouble the minister. In a conversation with a journalist, Schuller reported his concern about herpes: "'It's worse than it's ever been!' Schuller exclaimed, looking horrified. 'Do you know that we have over 20 million people who have herpes? It's America's number one social disease! It's terrible! Incredible!' Thumping his desk repeatedly for emphasis, he seemed genuinely aghast. 'It's the closest thing, I think, that our country has ever been to a national disaster, and we don't even realize how serious it is!'"[105]

---

102. Stumbo, "The Time Muhammad Ali Asked for Robert Schuller's Autograph."
103. Robert H. Schuller, *Self-Esteem*, 162.
104. Robert H. Schuller, *Self-Esteem*, 163.
105. Stumbo, "The Time Muhammad Ali Asked for Robert Schuller's Autograph."

210   CHAPTER 8

The minister's preoccupation with a sexually transmitted disease may have been a strategy for distancing himself from the peccadilloes of 1980s televangelists. When he explained his Christian faith, he reported that it functionally made him a better person—someone who never "committed fornication or adultery. . . . I mean, whatever else, my wife doesn't have to worry about who I'm going to, eh, sleep with." The emphasis on sexual purity may also have contributed to his connection with a more conservative Christian orthodoxy, signaling his sympathy with culture warriors in a manner that otherwise might have signaled polarization from the pulpit. Such sympathies were selectively revealed, as when he dismissed President Richard Nixon's indiscretions in the Watergate scandal: "I've never heard of Richard Nixon being accused of embezzlement of funds . . . or fornication or adultery"—indicating that money mismanagement or sexual impropriety struck the minister as some of the worst sins.[106]

Though he avoided explicit political stances, that did not mean that Schuller failed to have personal opinions—he could become quite passionate over issues that others might consider banal. For instance, the minister had once suggested to California governor Edmund G. "Jerry" Brown Jr. that restaurants no longer offer complimentary bread and butter: "The biggest waste in America today is in the restaurants. When you order food, they immediately put the bread and butter in front of you, whether you want it or not! This is billions, *tons* of bread and butter going down the tubes in a hungry world!"[107] Intimates of the minister indicated that he struggled with his weight, and easy temptations like complimentary bread and butter frustrated him.

In fact, while Schuller offered proud pronouncements regarding his sexual fidelity, he loathed his relationship to food. As suggested earlier, the minister wrestled with his weight. In person, people who had only glimpsed Schuller on television expressed surprise at the minister's size—one interviewer described him as "more massive than you would expect" and being "large-boned, not slim or svelte."[108] His relationship with food

106. Stumbo, "The Time Muhammad Ali Asked for Robert Schuller's Autograph."
107. Stumbo, "The Time Muhammad Ali Asked for Robert Schuller's Autograph."
108. Dennis Voskuil, "Reflections on Interview: Robert H. Schuller," June 4, 1980 (DVP).

seemed to be a fixation. In fact, his daughter reported that on summer vacations in Iowa, she would catch the minister eating apple pie before breakfast—and that "he looked up with the same guilty look of a young boy with his hand caught in the cookie jar."[109]

Schuller himself once recounted a trip to Florida where he succumbed to temptation. After feeling that he had been overweight for a number of years, he had committed to a diet plan. Going to dinner one evening while on the trip, he vowed to restrain himself. Once at the table, though: "I ate *everything*! I ate butter. I ate rich sauces. I ate the breads. To top it all off, I even ate the *pie*! I was so stuffed that I woke up only a few hours later. And I have never, *never* in my life been with a woman sexually other than my wife. I have never been with a prostitute. But, ah, I felt just as, as, ah *unclean*, yes, as *dirty* as if I had committed adultery or fornication. I suddenly realized that I was incurably addicted to food like, like, an alcoholic is addicted to alcohol!"[110]

Wrestling with the new realization of his food addiction, Schuller prayed for deliverance (in a fairly doubt-filled, nonevangelical manner): "And so I prayed. I said, 'Jesus Christ, I don't know if you are dead or alive, if you are real or only a myth—but can you help me?'" The minister recounted having a vision in the wake of his prayer. He saw a flooded river with an uprooted tree floating down the waters. He continued: "I *knew* that the tree floating by was my *body*! And I *knew* that the gentle water that looked so safe was bread! Butter! Ice cream! Cookies! I knew it all!" Schuller then intuited a message that told him that he had been snatched from destruction: "I knew at that second that I was snatched. Snatched from the permanent destruction of breads, of butters, of pies, potatoes, and ice creams and cakes. And so I see that as my personal experience with Jesus Christ." Despite that triumphant episode, Schuller had failed to harness his relationship with food. After regaling the journalist with the dramatic details, the minister acknowledged that he remained overweight as he "[stared] morosely at his midriff."[111]

---

109. Sheila Schuller Coleman, *Robert Schuller: My Father and My Friend* (Milwaukee: Ideals Publishing Corp., 1980), 89.

110. Stumbo, "The Time Muhammad Ali Asked for Robert Schuller's Autograph."

111. Stumbo, "The Time Muhammad Ali Asked for Robert Schuller's Autograph."

212   CHAPTER 8

Attempts to manage his own weight affected his approach to meals. Nason confirmed Schuller's troubled relationship with food. Over their many hours together, he noticed that the minister devised a number of interesting strategies to avoid consuming too much food. For instance, Schuller would destroy food on flights to eliminate the temptation: "First, he mixes the salad, entree, and dessert together. Then he empties all the salt and pepper all over it. Then he pours the cream and sugar on it and stirs it all up together, even emptying any leftover salad dressing on top." Nason could not hide his revulsion. "The results are disgusting."[112]

Schuller's concern for his own physical appearance extended to those around him. One employee described attempting to meet the minister's "standards of personal appearance" as a "challenge."[113] Having difficulty managing his weight through diet, Schuller began most mornings, even as he aged, with a 5:00 a.m. three-mile run with Arvella.[114] The Crystal Cathedral also included a gym and workout facility so that congregants could better manage their own health. The jogging and health-food craze characteristic of sunny Southern California surely contributed to a concern for one's body image and the importance of seeming fit.

The Master and the Method

Four years after the publication of *Self-Esteem*, Schuller published a volume in which he offered his principles for church growth. In the opening pages of *Your Church Has a Fantastic Future!*, Schuller recounted being inspired by George Truett, the Dallas pastor he had studied in seminary and who had built "the largest" Baptist church in the world.[115] Written in 1986, the volume contains the minister's clearest and most digestible vision of church growth—the back cover includes a quote from Schuller: "I am absolutely convinced that if you follow the prescriptions laid down in this book, your church will grow."

None other than C. Peter Wagner, professor of church growth at Fuller Theological Seminary in Pasadena, wrote the foreword to the

---

112. Nason and Nason, *Robert Schuller*, 181.
113. Gates, *Dwelling in Schullerland*, 89.
114. Stumbo, "The Time Muhammad Ali Asked for Robert Schuller's Autograph."
115. Robert H. Schuller, *Your Church Has a Fantastic Future!*, 26.

TURBULENCE AND CONTROL IN THE 1980S   **213**

book. Wagner lauded Schuller while also hinting that readers probably wondered how the minister arrived at such effective results without having first created a social scientific methodology: "Not only does he operate on the sound intuitions which eventuate in dramatic church growth, but he has an unusual ability to help others do the same." Wagner found Schuller so impressive that he assigned the minister's books in his doctor of ministry classes and that "few books have been so helpful in enabling pastors and other church leaders to understand the reasons for growth or nongrowth and to make the necessary adjustments to lead their churches into a better future." Finally, Wagner was "personally indebted to Robert Schuller" for what he knew and taught about church growth.[116]

Schuller confidently predicted that church-growth Christianity very soon would become an irresistible force of religious revival in the United States. Quite vividly, the minister suggested that he would be standing before leaders in the year 2000 to celebrate the victory of the "Church in America" over the naysayers who had predicted its demise. Schuller described the scene: "It will be a thrill to look across America in the year 2000 and see tremendous institutions in every significant city carrying out fantastic programs to heal human hearts, to fill human needs; enormous centers of human inspiration where people rally by the thousands and tens of thousands on Sundays and gather seven days a week for spiritual and personal growth. These tremendous spiritual-growth centers, these dynamic inspiration-generating centers, these great family-development centers will be proof positive of a renewed, revitalized, and resurrected Church."[117]

Most importantly, the minister assumed that it would be *his* method that catalyzed much of the church growth. Schuller believed in the power of a sound technique and strongly asserted the benefits of management and methods to address any problems. Schuller assumed he understood the ministerial fear of failure. In a country where secularism seemed to be on the rise, these concerns expanded from professional to existential. Schuller claimed that he had developed the method for the era. In his mind, churches did not grow by accident. If ministers followed his guidance, they would find themselves as leaders of great new "inspiration centers."

116. Robert H. Schuller, *Your Church Has a Fantastic Future!*, 15–16.
117. Robert H. Schuller, *Your Church Has a Fantastic Future!*, 55–56.

214 CHAPTER 8

Quite obviously, Schuller possessed enormous confidence in his methods of church growth—and he advocated that they would work anywhere. To illustrate his point, the minister employed an example from the South Bronx, a locale about as far away from Garden Grove as possible. Schuller reported that a pastor from the South Bronx had attended a session of his Institute and became convinced that the methods could even translate to his parish, in a neighborhood full of abandoned buildings and "junkies." Schuller exclaimed: "Imagine having to seek bank financing in that community! But he did it, and he and his church built a new $700,000 building."[118] His method had a geographic transferability.

Even into the 1980s Schuller really desired to franchise the concept of walk-in, drive-in churches. The minister saw himself as the architect of the development and set about raising $800,000 from RCA congregations for a "national chain of Walk In–Drive In Churches." In fact, Schuller claimed that "God has called on the oldest Protestant denomination in America to carry out the newest and most exciting approach to national evangelism."[119] Though the plan never came to full fruition, Schuller continued to discuss a $1,000,000 donation from his ministry to the RCA for this endeavor three decades after its initial implementation.[120]

When Schuller imagined the multiplication of churches, he saw corporate templates. At one point, Schuller articulated the synergy he saw between his ministry and the Amway corporation—a multilevel marketing business. The minister described Amway as the world's largest organization of positive-thinking people and that the Crystal Cathedral, "to a great degree," could be considered "*a ministry of Amway*, unofficially, totally."[121]

Beyond physical disruptions to traditional congregational life—and perhaps most counterintuitively—Schuller advocated that churches be-

118. Robert H. Schuller, *Your Church Has a Fantastic Future!*, 57.

119. "Walk In, Drive In Church News," Garden Grove Community Church, June 1969 (SGCA).

120. Robert H. Schuller to members of the Crystal Cathedral Consistory, December 28, 1982. See also draft mailer from GGCC to Note Holders, November 1974, GGCC Stewardship Materials, RHS/CC, box 6 (HCASC).

121. Transcript, Robert H. Schuller, "Message for Possibility Thinkers at the Meadow Spring Extravaganza '93," March 6, 1993, RHS/CC, box 30 (HCASC) (emphasis added).

come *more secular* to combat growing secularism. That is, if a congregation asserted that all its music on Sunday mornings remain "religious" or "contain references to God or Jesus or the Holy Spirit, or to sin and salvation, we are going to reduce our effectiveness as a mission." The minister continued by musing that a secular song might be more appropriate at times than anything in the hymnbook. For Schuller, the church becoming more secular meant becoming more familiar, more relatable (and we see echoes of that sentiment at sites like Saddleback, also located in Orange County, where the range of ministry and worship venues allows participants to enter into a church that mimics the spaces in which they spend their time during the week).[122]

Even as he promoted the volatile idea of becoming more secular, Schuller also demonstrated his insights on smaller details and logistics. For example, the minister possessed an uncanny understanding of the centrality of the automobile as the linchpin of American suburban life— it functioned to tie together the disparate networks of the middle-class families abiding there. Because of that, Schuller valued easy parking almost as much as architectural design. Though he never studied urban planning, he intuited that the suburban malls owed a modicum of their success to easy, free parking: "Look at the old downtown sections of cities in this country. The original merchants were so swamped with new customers when the first suburbs were built that they were confident of their continued success. They were not, however, sustained by growth for long. Soon they found that they were incapable of handling the crowds. Parking became impossible. So, enterprising merchants began building great new shopping centers on the outskirts of the old towns. The result? With the new shopping centers in business, the old downtown merchants died—strangled by growth."[123]

Indeed, Schuller's interpretation of church-growth Christianity resonated with the parking lot–saturated suburbs of 1980s America. He had mainstreamed a version of mentalism that synthesized the most palatable aspects of Christianity and made them market-ready for sig-

---

122. Justin Wilford, *Sacred Subdivisions: The Postsuburban Transformation of American Evangelicalism* (New York: New York University Press, 2012).
123. Robert H. Schuller, *Your Church Has a Fantastic Future!*, 79.

216   CHAPTER 8

nificant swaths of the country. In fact, in his landmark book *Bowling Alone*, tracing the decline of social capital in the United States, political scientist Robert Putnam identified faith communities as "arguably the single most important repository of social capital in America" and as incubators for "civic skills, civic norms, community interests, and civic recruitment."[124] Moreover, Putnam highlighted the Crystal Cathedral as an exemplar of how religious institutions directly support a vast array of social activities beyond worship: "In January 1991 the weekly calendar of the Crystal Cathedral, an evangelical church in Garden Grove, California, included sessions devoted to Women in the Marketplace, Conquering Compulsive Behaviors, Career Builders' Workshop, Stretch and Walk Time for Women, Cancer Conquerors, Positive Christian Singles, Gamblers Anonymous, Women Who Love Too Much, Overeaters Anonymous, and Friday Night Live (for junior high schoolers). The Garden Grove Crystal Cathedral also includes restaurants and a Family Life Center with a swimming pool, weight room, saunas, and steamrooms."[125]

Schuller understood his advocacy for a secularized Christianity as an attempt to craft a pastoral paradigm suited to the circumstances of people who inevitably must live in and respond to the market. His convictions regarding the pervasiveness and unavoidability of the market influenced both his message and his method. The successful church would be competitive and crafty, attuned to currents of culture as it participates in that same culture, not as an outsider but as an integral player in the shaping of the future. Schuller said to pastors not only that their "church has a fantastic future" but also that, in order to have a future at all, they must deliberately adopt nonchurch forms and styles, redefining Christian involvement in the contemporary world, even when it seems as if the church is not acting in a Christian manner at all.

To be sure, his messages specifically aimed at pastors received both wide embrace and broad condemnation. Despite an array of buildings and best sellers, a string of impressive financial achievements and a global television audience, many writers and thinkers persisted in seeing

---

124. Robert Putnam, *Bowling Alone: The Collapse and Revival of American Community* (New York: Simon & Schuster, 2000), 66.

125. Putnam, *Bowling Alone*, 66.

Schuller as a hollow figure. His upbeat media presence proved an easy target for more orthodox Christian pastors concerned about "rightly dividing the Word" of the Bible; they industriously parsed and reproached his ambiguity. Even so, in mocking the minister, critics gave evidence of Schuller's stature across American life. His celebrity status and ubiquitous platform became fodder for comedians and cultural critics alike.

In *Roger and Me*, a searing 1989 documentary critique of the patent selfishness of capitalist lords of industry, director Michael Moore lampooned Schuller for the manner in which his church-growth philosophy rested on the assumption of the unassailability of free-market principles. Moore's cameras followed Schuller (who had been generously paid $20,000 by the mayor of Flint, Michigan) as he traveled to the Rust Belt to soothe recently unemployed General Motors employees—devastated by the movement of auto-manufacturing jobs from their city to Mexico. During his Flint talk, the minister offered his beleaguered audience well-worn platitudes like "Tough times don't last, tough people do" and "Just because you've got problems is no reason to be unhappy."[126] Moore and his audience chuckled at the absurdity of "possibility-thinking" your way out of becoming the collateral damage of the global economy. For them, Schuller epitomized an out-of-touch huckster, simply content to continue sanctifying the capitalist status quo.

Yes, Schuller had detractors, and their critiques surely bothered him. However, the minister had methods suited to the contemporary market. And, more importantly, the evidence that his method worked. The Crystal Cathedral Ministry by the end of the decade functioned as arguably the best-known religious "business" in the country. The big question, now, was: What next? Staying still in a moving culture was never an option. A static ministry was a dying ministry. The religious-industrial complex that Schuller had created demanded unremitting growth simply because ongoing expansion was required just to keep pace with social change. Where would the minister take his ministry in the next decade?

126. See https://aadl.org/node/246644.

9

GOOD IMAGE AND GLOBAL INFLUENCE
IN THE GLORY DAYS

Always concerned about his own image and that of the ministry, Schuller proved especially protective during the 1980s as a cohort of television evangelists found themselves mired in scandal. In one instance, Schuller had to make a trip to Las Vegas, a city he avoided at all costs because of its association with debauchery and sin. If he had to travel there, Schuller desperately wanted to remain incognito.

While waiting in a hotel lobby as his traveling companion, Michael Nason, checked them into their rooms, Schuller turned bright red as he heard over the intercom: "Paging Dr. Schuller, Dr. Robert Schuller. Would Dr. Schuller please come to the white paging phone?"[1] As he approached the desk, the minister found Nason laughing—he had played a joke on Schuller, letting everyone in the hotel and casino know that the television pastor deigned to visit sinful Las Vegas.

Unamused, Schuller rectified the situation: he immediately went to the front desk to make his own paging request. Soon the lobby speakers rang out: "Paging Jerry Falwell, Pastor Jerry Falwell. Paging Mr. Roberts, Mr. Oral Roberts. Paging Dr. Graham, Dr. Billy Graham." Schuller explained to Nason: "Now they'll think there's a religious convention in town!"[2]

1. James Penner, *Goliath: The Life of Robert Schuller* (Anaheim, CA: New Hope Publishing, 1992), 344.
2. Penner, *Goliath*, 345.

Cathedral as Circus

Fred Swann, the longtime organist Schuller lured away from Riverside Church in Manhattan to the Crystal Cathedral, remembered his time with the ministry fondly. During the 1980s, the Cathedral became a Southern California destination, a religious attraction a mere ten-minute drive from Disneyland, where Schuller himself featured as a celebrity. Massive crowds gathered just about any time they opened the doors. Swann described the bustle of the campus at its peak: "I was there in the glory days. Practically all the time I was there, the Cathedral filled in twice on Sunday mornings, big crowds on Sunday night. Of course, at Christmas and Easter, we had to have 6, 7, 8, or 9 services. Christmas Eve services, we had to start at 2 in the afternoon, and we had them every 45 minutes, and, somehow or other, all the people who were handling everything got the building empty, the parking lot empty, then the parking lot filled again, and the Cathedral filled again in about 20 minutes."[3]

Despite the predictable, massive flow of people, the machinery of the ministry remained dependent on the conscious coordination of its founders. A copastor with the ministry noted that when things hummed at the Cathedral, it hinged on the synergy between the married couple at the center: "From day one, Bob and Arvella became one in their thoughts, in their directions, in their planning. They were a team, without question they were a team." Knowing the many pieces that had to fit together every Sunday, the copastor marveled at the design of the services, claiming that "the Cathedral was built as kind of a three-ring circus—you have the pulpit area, you have the organ and choir, and you had the communion table over here." Arvella was crucial to operations. "And she came out with an awful lot of great ideas. The whole thing of the *Hour of Power* was very much her idea. It was Arvella that took it and began to learn where cameras should be, what they should be looking at, how do you maneuver all this stuff."[4] The design and particularity of the sanctuary—

3. Interview with Mulder, May 16, 2017.
4. As told to Mulder in an interview. For more on anonymous quotes, see "A Note on Sources."

along with Arvella's attention to detail—allowed the Cathedral to stand out within its own niche of televangelism.

Schuller's preaching operated as the central event. Martha Solomon, a professor of speech, assessed Schuller as "the most successful" and "most palatable" of the 1980s televangelist cohort because of his unique set of rhetorical skills. In fact, Solomon estimated that the minister's visibility and success stemmed directly from his "amalgamation of secular and spiritual values" that produced "a rhetorically powerful version of American Civil Religion."[5] In Solomon's estimation, Schuller's appeal rested on his sly ability to synthesize spiritual virtue and occupational success—the minister offered an appealing "religious rationalization and sanction for individualism."[6] In his messages, Schuller sanctified self-interest and allowed his audience a strategy for reconciling the apparent tensions between Christian notions of self-sacrifice and the capitalist pursuit of wealth and comfort. That is, the minister offered the most appealing message of accommodation to the circumstances his people faced in market society.

In a sense, according to Solomon, the minister sacralized the American Dream: "In Schuller's reinterpretation, one is encouraged to turn from abnegation and self-accusal to self-affirmation. The penitential turning *from* the world to concentrate on spiritual matters becomes a celebratory *seeking out* of worldly possibilities. This pursuit of secular opportunities is, of course, one avenue for achieving the American Dream."[7] More than that, Solomon also detected some classism within the minister's rhetoric, in that he had designed "a theology for the middle class and then asserted its generalizability to all."[8] The minister's appealing message rested on the hope that everyone could navigate the labor market in such a way that social mobility existed for all who had enough talent and gumption to both see their potential and act upon it.

---

5. Martha Solomon, "Robert Schuller: The American Dream in a Crystal Cathedral," *Central States Speech Journal* 34 (Fall 1983): 172–86, 173.

6. Solomon, "Robert Schuller," 176.

7. Solomon, "Robert Schuller," 178.

8. Solomon, "Robert Schuller," 185.

GOOD IMAGE AND GLOBAL INFLUENCE IN THE GLORY DAYS · 221

Navigating the Scandals of 1980s Televangelism

With the conviction that they had a message that everyone needed to hear, Christian preachers had long been using any technology available to broadcast their convictions. George Whitefield used tents to deliver his dramatic sermons to tens of thousands outdoors—becoming "colonial America's first celebrity."[9] And on Christmas Eve in 1906, a scientist in Massachusetts broadcast the twentieth century's first wireless voice in a Christian program to ships at sea. By the mid-1920s, over six hundred stations sent out programming—and almost every one included some form of religious content. In their book *Prime Time Preachers: The Rising Power of Televangelism*, Jeffrey Hadden and Charles Swann described the advent of television as ushering in the second generation of electronic communication in the late 1940s. In less than fifteen years, 90 percent of households in the United States owned a television. Almost from the beginning, religious leaders understood its broadcasting significance.[10]

Schuller admired Catholic bishop Fulton Sheen, one of the first religious broadcasters to emerge as a star (a statue of him was featured on church grounds)—and the early days saw cooperation between mainline Protestants, Catholics, Jews, and Southern Baptists to share the mandated free network time. Evangelicals, though, uniquely understood the massive potential. Women like Aimee Semple McPherson and Kathryn Kuhlman were counted among the first innovators.[11] And men like Rex Humbard, Jerry Falwell, and Pat Robertson dove into television without a lot of resources—"At the time they began, each of the television ministers seemed to have a good bit more faith and courage than wisdom or cash."[12] However, by the 1980s, these televangelists had honed their craft to the

9. John Wigger, *PTL: The Rise and Fall of Jim and Tammy Faye Bakker's Evangelical Empire* (New York: Oxford University Press, 2017), 3.

10. Jeffrey K. Hadden and Charles E. Swann, *Prime Time Preachers: The Rising Power of Televangelism* (Reading, MA: Addison-Wesley, 1981), 8–10.

11. See Edith L. Blumhofer, *Aimee Semple McPherson: Everybody's Sister*, Library of Religious Biography (Grand Rapids: Eerdmans, 1993), and Amy Collier Artman, *The Miracle Lady: Kathryn Kuhlman and the Transformation of Charismatic Christianity*, Library of Religious Biography (Grand Rapids: Eerdmans, 2019).

12. Hadden and Swann, *Prime Time Preachers*, 10.

222   CHAPTER 9

point that social theorist Jeremy Rifkin asserted that because of their electronic communications networks, "the evangelical community is amassing a base of potential power that dwarfs every other competing interest in American society."[13] Indeed, televangelists like Falwell and Robertson would eventually flex their influence into the political arena as well, helping to create the Moral Majority and the more informal New Christian Right—both very much aligned with conservative political causes.

With all that sway, though, many of the televangelists found themselves mired in scandals in the 1980s. Schuller had already mostly condescended to his televangelist competition. In fact, with his mainline Protestant credentials, Schuller represented an aberration in religious broadcasting—a world that tended to be dominated by evangelical and fundamentalist Christians.[14] Indeed, he framed himself as offering something quite different from their less dignified broadcasts. Nevertheless, as Jim Bakker and Jimmy Swaggart became embroiled in separate scandals, Schuller's anxiety grew. Would his ministry be tainted via guilt by association?

The minister watched for evidence that his own broadcast was being affected, and he attributed a drop in viewership from two million in 1986 to one and a half million in 1987 to canceled contracts by television stations who wanted nothing to do with the fouled reputation of Christian celebrity preachers.[15] Amid the scandals that abruptly shook American Christianity, Schuller and his ministry managed to successfully distance themselves from the maelstrom. He documented the apparent strength of his own *Hour of Power*. The minister once reported that "the total number of Americans watching all religious television ministries on Sunday mornings dropped from the pre-scandal high of six million viewers to four million. But our share of the market would climb to forty percent of all viewers—far and away the biggest share of the religious market."[16] Though many found aspects of the ministry questionable, the

---

13. Quoted by Hadden and Swann, *Prime Time Preachers*, 7–8.

14. Hadden and Swann, *Prime Time Preachers*, 7.

15. Robert H. Schuller, *My Journey: From an Iowa Farm to a Cathedral of Dreams* (San Francisco: HarperOne, 2001), 418.

16. Schuller, *My Journey*, 421.

GOOD IMAGE AND GLOBAL INFLUENCE IN THE GLORY DAYS   **223**

Crystal Cathedral managed to maintain distance from any association with the catastrophic atmosphere of moral scandal. However, Schuller found it difficult to avoid all threats to his image.

Though Schuller cast himself as above the fray when it came to his television minister competitors, by 1987 their myriad sexual and financial scandals began to wear on the Orange County ministry. Polls indicated that "Jim and Tammy Bakker's sex-and-money troubles in the PTL ministry and Oral Roberts' controversial claims have cast a shadow."[17] In the wake of scandals, donations declined for *Hour of Power* by $4.6 million between 1986 and 1987. The Crystal Cathedral congregation's dependence on the television donations made the situation even more perilous: "The church, which nourished the TV ministry at its birth 17 years ago, is now its ward."[18]

It did not help to dissipate the musk of financial scandal when the ministry in early 1987 presented "an inaccurate and incomplete financial summary." The leadership framed the issue as "math mistakes"—the one-page statement wrongly projected a $1 million deficit; however, they later reported to the Orange County assessor a $5 million surplus.[19] In fact, after the opening of the Cathedral, both expenses and income rose dramatically. In 1980, *Hour of Power* took in $16.1 million while spending $17.0 million. Five years later, those numbers floated upward to $39.7 million and $37.0 million, respectively.[20]

In 1987, as televangelists seemed bent on outdoing each other in sordid sexual and financial scandals, the CNN news program *Crossfire* broadcast an episode considering the state of television ministries. *Newsweek*'s religion editor, Kenneth Woodward, offered an assessment of the Garden Grove minister: "Schuller doesn't preach the gospel, he just preaches positive thinking." Beyond that, Woodward dismissed the entire cohort as

17. Scott Fagerstrom, "Trying Times: TV Preachers' Problems Cloud Schuller Ministry," *Orange County Register*, August 9, 1987, Dennis Voskuil Papers, Holland, MI (hereafter cited as DVP).

18. Ronald Campbell, "Empire Shows Signs of Financial Strain," *Orange County Register*, August 9, 1987 (DVP).

19. Ronald Campbell, "Candor: Schuller More Open about Finances in Wake of PTL's Woes," *Orange County Register*, August 9, 1987 (DVP).

20. Campbell, "Empire Shows Signs of Financial Strain."

224 CHAPTER 9

lacking in theological education. Schuller refused to allow these aspersions to stand. In a sharply worded letter to Woodward, the minister insisted that if Woodward observed him for fifty-two weeks a year, he would note that the "central subjects" of creation, incarnation, crucifixion, and resurrection remained consistent in his preaching. Schuller also reviewed his curriculum vitae for the journalist: "I may indeed be the *only* one that has an earned undergraduate degree from an accredited college and university: Hope College. Accredited by the North American Association of Colleges and Universities. And then I went on to complete my 3 years of post-graduate studies in theology at Western Theological Seminary in Holland, Michigan. In seminary, for my thesis, I compiled the first Topical and Scriptural Index to The Christian Religion by John Calvin—a feat never before performed. And this was done under faculty supervision." Schuller then requested that Woodward reconsider his "reckless" and "irresponsible" insinuations since they seemed liked a contemporary form of McCarthyism.[21] In a further bid for legitimacy, the minister discussed at length how the Crystal Cathedral's affiliation with the RCA afforded the ministry a higher level of accountability than any other comparable religious broadcaster.

The correspondence between the journalist and the minister resumed some years later after Woodward wrote negatively about the Cathedral. Schuller again felt it necessary to respond to criticism, including the assertion that Ruth Peale, Norman Vincent's wife, told Woodward that she had suggested that Schuller repackage "positive thinking" as "possibility thinking." The minister disputed Peale's contention: "It is not correct that Ruth Peale suggested the label, 'Possibility Thinking.'" In addition, Schuller expressed his wish that Woodward take time to fully understand his theological arguments, reminding the journalist, "I have a hard and heavy theology which my public platforms do not appropriately allow opportunity to express."[22] (Although such a claim of a lack of opportunity to adequately articulate his belief system seems dubious for someone who published over two dozen books, Schuller always insisted that the depth of his theology was rarely, if ever, understood by others.)

21. Schuller to Woodward, June 16, 1987, Kenneth L. Woodward Papers, University of Notre Dame Archives.
22. Schuller to Woodward, February 26, 1997, Kenneth L. Woodward Papers.

GOOD IMAGE AND GLOBAL INFLUENCE IN THE GLORY DAYS   **225**

Given the vivid defense offered in Schuller's letter, Woodward could not resist a riposte. The journalist sent an unsparing missive a few months later. Woodward was no stranger to Schuller's messages, and he had wrestled with Schuller's claims written in *Self Esteem*, published fifteen years earlier. Revisiting the minister's writings, Woodward wondered how "the Scriptures in any way" supported pages 151–156 in Schuller's book *Self-Esteem*. He went on, "I most certainly do not regard salvation as a 'rescue from shame to glory.' I find a little insecurity does a lot of good, and too much security a major obstacle to salvation." The journalist then pivoted to critique Schuller's historical knowledge and limited library: "Regarding your history timeline on page 174, only someone who does not know church history would regard the period from 1000 to 1516 as darkly as you do. But then I suspect you have never read Aquinas, Dominic, Bonaventura or any of the great spiritual and learned figures of that great age. Nor would any church historian see the Reformation as anything less than an age of great schism. Your view shows you haven't forgotten all you learned in Calvinist seminary, just the important parts." Then Woodward moved to the crux of his concern: "My problem, you see, is this: if folks are given a bastardized, self-congratulatory form of religion and then are told that that is Christianity, they will never recognize the authentic article."[23] A seemingly chastened Schuller responded a week later in an extremely brief letter: "Thank you for your thoughtful letter. Our minds must meet again—somehow. I know I can learn from you."[24] The minister could not muster a follow-up defense and acquiesced to Woodward.

Fortunately, his fellow California Reformed churches expressed no interest in squabbling with their most high-profile congregation. Schuller's clout in the RCA became readily apparent again in 1987. In an effort to distance his ministry from other televangelists embroiled in financial scandals, Schuller appeared on ABC's *Nightline* to claim that he remained fiscally accountable to the denomination: "I happen to belong to the oldest Protestant denomination with an unbroken ministry in the United States of America, the Reformed Church in America. And I have to present a full financial report to the denomination and we've

---

23. Woodward to Schuller, April 25, 1997, Kenneth L. Woodward Papers.
24. Schuller to Woodward, May 1, 1997, Kenneth L. Woodward Papers.

226 CHAPTER 9

been in business a long time. . . . If I fall in error, I can be defrocked."[25] Two members of the RCA's Classis California, though, registered their concern that Schuller had overstated his level of accountability to the point of being "misleading"—indeed, while the *congregation* had a financial accountability through the denomination, the *corporation*, Robert Schuller Ministries, received no oversight from the RCA. Moreover, the congregation planned to sell the entirety of its property to the corporation—and then rent it back (a plan that could be interpreted as wresting control of the church property away from the denomination, since in RCA church polity, the classis actually controlled the property rather than the congregation).

Not wanting to antagonize their highest-profile minister, the rest of the delegates to Classis California scrambled to reassure Schuller that they had no qualms with his plan to sell the church property and no concerns about the financials of the Cathedral. The president of Classis California, Mark Rozelle, wrote Schuller within two weeks of the classis meeting. Rozelle acknowledged that the classis discussed the transfer of the Cathedral from the congregation to the corporation, especially since it seemed that criticisms had been voiced at the RCA's denominational headquarters about the atypical arrangement. However, Rozelle assured Schuller that for Classis California:

> —we have absolutely no suspicion of any wrong doing on your part,
> —we have absolutely no desire to assert ourselves over the Robert Schuller Ministries,
> —we believe the news articles have picked at insignificant matters in a feeble attempt to expose problems in your ministry,
> —we did not hear what you said on Nightline and thus have no opinion on whether you overstated your (that is Robert Schuller Ministry's) accountability to us and in fact have no suspicion that you did overstate the matter,

---

25. Scott Fagerstrom, "Schuller Remarks Upset Reformed Church Officials," *Orange County Register*, April 30, 1987, CC-Correspondence, Robert H. Schuller/Crystal Cathedral (hereafter cited as RHS/CC), box 38, Hope College Archives and Special Collections, Holland, MI (hereafter cited as HCASC).

—we feel that our role is to support you always and to confront you and any other pastor as a loving brother in the event any major wrong doing could be proved.[26]

The obsequiousness from local denominational figures demonstrated that, though he might have been tarnished by the televangelism scandals, Schuller would manage to retain enough luster to continue exerting his considerable pastoral authority. Indeed, the minister reported to his board in 1988 that he had maintained a rare level of esteem in the eyes of the public, according to *Time* magazine: "Left personally unscathed in all the turmoil were more churchly TV preachers such as Billy Graham and Robert Schuller."[27]

Overcoming Critique and Bolstering an International Influence

In spite of the local denominational support, Schuller surely recognized the orthodoxy of Woodward's incisive response. In many ways, the critiques were posed from a conventional theological paradigm. At the same time, it is clear that the minister did not agree. His frustration stemmed from his inability to articulate his theology in a manner that would satisfy the journalist. Having spent years honing a message that would appeal to his church members and broadcast audience, he frankly lacked the time—and perhaps the interest—needed to fully reframe his theological convictions in a more academically rigorous manner. Note Schuller's frequent reference to his careful indexing of the writings of John Calvin. Having accomplished this work to the satisfaction of his esteemed professors assured him that he not only understood dense theological writings but also had the intellectual capacity to work through them. All he needed was the time required to do such work. Practically speaking, his pastoral responsibilities never allowed him to return to the intensity of such scholarship.

26. Rozelle to Schuller, May 13, 1987, CC-Correspondence, RHS/CC, box 38 (HCASC).

27. Year End Report of the Crystal Cathedral Ministries, December 31, 1988, Shepherd's Grove Church Archive, Irvine, CA (hereafter cited as SGCA).

228   CHAPTER 9

Schuller felt he had to defend himself from a high-profile journalist like Woodward, because he believed that he had concocted a modern and more relevant form of Christianity—a new reformation, in fact, that should not be threatened by potshots in the pages of weekly magazines. Ideally, it seemed the minister desired to assemble a pseudodenomination in his image. Schuller would claim that "many ministers in America were looking for a new network of positive-thinking churches."[28] His ambition for a new style of church apart from the RCA grew in light of his single-handedly nurturing the largest congregation in the country's oldest denomination. Richard DeVos, cofounder of Amway and an *Hour of Power* board member, recommended that the minister begin establishing that network. Schuller, though, astutely expressed concern that he would face accusations of trying to start a new denomination. These cross-tensions caused him to consider leaving the full-time pastorate behind to live life as an author and consultant.

In the end, many like Woodward scorned his efforts because Schuller attempted to craft a new paradigm for ministry, metaphorically building a plane as he was flying it, yet he did not often succeed in convincing those unwilling to move away from what appeared to be a more "true" and more "sacred" sense of what the church should be. With a steady sequence of congregational challenges, the near constant strategic problem solving and management of his churches, in addition to his marriage and family life, Schuller had spent virtually all of his intellectual energy on memos and messages, matching vision to viable and actionable options, maneuvering resources and mobilizing staff, lay leaders, and volunteers in the service of creating the structures that had the best chance of taking a freshly incarnated church into the next century. And with every step he felt he had mastered, he would turn to his pastoral peers—whoever would listen—sharing his own learning, providing a model and template of ministry for others to follow.

Even while doing the consuming work of leading his church, the minister retained plans to publish a multivolume systematic theology that synthesized "the positive insights of twentieth-century psychology with biblical and historical theology going back through Wesley, Calvin, and

---

28. Schuller, *My Journey*, 355.

Saint Augustine." The writing would distill a new synthesis of Christianity and New Thought (though Schuller never used that framing). The potential significance of the projected volumes allowed the minister to express confidence that he could support his family on royalties and lecture fees. After all, at that moment, he had "finished the job," and what more could he do in Orange County?[29] He also redefined his "congregation" to include "hundreds of thousands every Sunday from New York to California."[30] And a recent trip to the USSR had offered Schuller a tantalizing vision of the global possibilities of his mission: "I was coming home with a fresh world perspective, and all I could see were faces of spiritually hungry humans." The minister desperately desired to cast a larger shadow. But how?

Enter Rupert Murdoch. The manner in which Schuller forged his ministry throughout the mid-1980s' religious broadcasting tumult brought him to the attention of the media magnate. The grandson of a Presbyterian minister, Murdoch had quietly attended services at the Cathedral and found Schuller's message attractive. He invited the minister to a meeting in Beverly Hills. After pleasantries, Murdoch revealed his purposes: he planned to start Sky Channel, a satellite television provider that would be the first to cover the entirety of Europe. He wanted one hour of religious programming every week, and he wanted that to be the *Hour of Power*. Even better, Murdoch offered Schuller the programming slot free of charge. How could the minister say no?

In early February 1989, Sky Channel started broadcasting *Hour of Power* all over Europe, which further attracted attention of other powerful men. The breakthrough across the Atlantic Ocean caught the attention of Armand Hammer, head of Occidental Petroleum. Hammer had significant ties in the USSR and had spent time with the nation's new head of state, Mikhael Gorbachev. He considered the Soviet president amenable to a more peaceful coexistence with the United States and saw Schuller as an avatar of America's positive intentions—after Schuller had reached out with a short letter.[31] Hammer thought *Hour of Power* should also cross the Pacific Ocean, and so he called Schuller between services on a Sunday morning:

29. Schuller, *My Journey*, 336.
30. Schuller, *My Journey*, 337.
31. Penner, *Goliath*, 351.

230 CHAPTER 9

"I've been one of your television parishioners for over ten years now, Bob. It's time for Russia to get the rich and rare religion you preach."[32]

Hammer explained his enthusiasm for moving Schuller's broadcast into Soviet Russia: "You've changed my life. If Murdoch can get you on television in Europe, I can get you on in the USSR!"[33] He went on to tell the minister, "Your message could help set the stage for ending the Cold War. We've got to get your positive message of peace-generating religion on television!"[34] Hammer, Arvella, and Schuller started making plans to travel to Moscow.

The trio arrived in Moscow in December 1989 via a flight on Hammer's private jet, OXY One.[35] Hammer negotiated for Schuller to sit for a recorded interview that would air on a national television broadcast on December 25, Christmas Day. The minister described the moment as "the most important speaking assignment in my earthly life."[36] For Schuller, it represented an opportunity to change the course of geopolitical history. As he prepared to enter the studio, he saw the stakes clearly:

> Hopes for a peaceful resolution to this Cold War topped the concerns and prayers of all our leaders. Gorbachev would certainly be listening. All of the members of the Politburo would be tuned in. No American had ever been given such a platform from which to speak to all of the people in the entire USSR, along with all of the Eastern bloc nations! One TV network, with its one and only channel—"Channel One"—was piped into every TV-equipped in every one of the seventeen republics that made up this Union of Soviet Socialist Republics. It was the largest mind-control television network. My audience would be in the hundreds of millions![37]

The interviewer asked Schuller for an example of a typical sermon from him. The minister immediately told the story of his daughter

32. Schuller, *My Journey*, 424, and Penner, *Goliath*, 388.
33. Schuller, *My Journey*, 424.
34. Schuller, *My Journey*, 428.
35. Penner, *Goliath*, 387.
36. Schuller, *My Journey*, 437.
37. Schuller, *My Journey*, 438.

GOOD IMAGE AND GLOBAL INFLUENCE IN THE GLORY DAYS **231**

Carol's accident and her successful resolve to overcome adversity through the faith that gave her hope. He then concluded with a call for peace between the United States and the USSR.

According to Schuller, the Soviet authorities reported that the broadcast yielded its largest audience in history—two hundred million viewers across the USSR and Eastern bloc countries. Roughly four months later, when visiting the United States for a summit with President George Bush, Gorbachev himself requested that Schuller join a luncheon at the Russian Embassy in Washington, DC.[38] Thrilled for the opportunity, the minister agreed. Even better, Gorbachev singled out Schuller during his remarks as the "man who had calmed our nation."[39] At the same meeting, the minister learned that a condensed version of *Hour of Power* would begin airing in the USSR in the near future (called *From Spirit to Spirit*), a fortuitous development that fell in line with Gorbachev's initiatives to return religion to Soviet public life.[40]

Part of *Hour of Power*'s appeal in the Soviet Union, and then Russia, was due to the fact that Schuller appeared more ecumenical than other US televangelists. In other words, his more open form of Christianity did not explicitly or implicitly critique Russian Orthodox Christianity.[41] In fact, at one point, Schuller expressly indicated that he understood and supported the history and "unique position of the Russian Orthodox Church."[42]

By the late 1980s, enthusiasts hailed Schuller as an exemplar of modern Christian ministry, while critics scorned his popularity. Despite a steady stream of religious and pop culture critiques, the minister remained a force in American Christianity. Schuller himself noted his singular status: "We are the only church and I'm the only minister of any religion that speaks

---

38. For a glimpse of the emotional connection between Schuller and Soviet president Mikhail Gorbachev, see *Hour of Power* episode 1603: https://www.youtube.com/watch?v=y3G5JOCokGU.

39. Schuller, *My Journey*, 443.

40. Victoria Smolkin, *A Sacred Space Is Never Empty: A History of Soviet Atheism* (Princeton: Princeton University Press, 2018), and "Schuller to Air Spiritual Programs in Soviet Union," *Los Angeles Times*, November 24, 1990, https://www.latimes.com/archives/la-xpm-1990-11-24-ca-4588-story.html.

41. Wesley Granberg-Michaelson to Schuller, September 26, 1995 (SGCA).

42. Wesley Granberg-Michaelson to Metropolitan Kirill, September 26, 1994 (SGCA).

232 CHAPTER 9

every Sunday morning on Channel One out of Moscow." At one point, all fifteen Soviet republics could watch *Hour of Power*. Beyond that, the minister claimed "over ten million people will be listening out of the 300 hundred million who can tune it in—and they will be tuning in in Iraq, Iran, and Israel, over Sputnik. This is the only television thing of its kind."[43]

The Near Fatal Injury

As the ministry entered the 1990s and celebrated the tenth anniversary of the Cathedral, Schuller's stature in the world remained high. He had been elevated to the international stage with his forays into Europe and the Soviet Union. The Cathedral itself seemed to be capped with the addition of a fifty-two-bell carillon and the Crean Spire (so named because benefactor John Crean donated another $2 million).[44] As construction appeared settled for the moment on the campus, the minister increased his travel. His expanding his global influence motivated greater connections with people overseas. In September 1990 Schuller arrived in the Netherlands with his assistant and friend, Michael Nason, and son-in-law, Paul Dunn. The trip included European stops, including a meeting with Pope John Paul II in Rome, and then concluded in the USSR.

Upon departure from the Amsterdam airport to drive to the hotel, Schuller bumped his head getting into the car. Although the incident hurt badly and left the minister with a throbbing headache, he pressed on with the day's itinerary. It seemed an innocuous bump. The seemingly insignificant incident with the car roof, though, eventually catalyzed an immediate emergency and, for some confidants, represented a pivotal moment for the ministry when Schuller lost at least a measure of his prowess and stamina.

Upon returning to the hotel, Schuller begged off dinner with his companions, hoping a night of rest would deliver relief from the headache. Drawing water for a bath after receiving four aspirin from the concierge was the last event the minister would remember for weeks. The next

43. Transcript, Robert H. Schuller, "Message for Possibility Thinkers at the Meadow Spring Extravaganza '93," March 6, 1993, RHS/CC, box 30 (HCASC).

44. Robert H. Schuller and James Coleman, *A Place of Beauty, a Joy Forever: The Glorious Gardens and Grounds of the Crystal Cathedral in Garden Grove, California* (Garden Grove, CA: Crystal Cathedral Creative Services, 2005), 120-27.

morning, when Schuller failed to arrive for breakfast, Nason and Dunn became worried. The minister had collapsed on his balcony—his body blocking the outward-swinging French doors. A hotel employee managed to get to Schuller and open the door only by scaling a ladder placed horizontally from a neighboring balcony.

Schuller had suffered a severe hemorrhage in his brain requiring eight hours of surgery. The doctors estimated that twenty more minutes unattended on the balcony likely would have ended the minister's life. After surgery, he remained in Amsterdam in critical care for two weeks before finally being flown back to Los Angeles on September 16. Emergency surgeries left the minister temporarily bald and permanently carrying a ten-inch scar. While he was lying in the hospital, Arvella turned to her son-in-law, James Penner, and said, "He's afraid no one wants him anymore."[45]

Soon after Schuller's injury, the ministry sent almost 400,000 letters to supporters in order to clarify the situation. After explaining that the minister had sustained a subdural hematoma, the telegram reported that Schuller "seems to have complete motor skills." Moreover, "in the meantime, be assured that you will receive the same powerful and positive inspiration here at the Crystal Cathedral and from your television screen every Sunday during the Hour of Power time slot. There will be no compromise in the power of the music. There will be no compromise in the delivery of every spoken word."[46]

Schuller recovered slowly. Later, he noted in his autobiography that after returning home Arvella scolded him for trying to change a lightbulb from a stool. The minister recalled his response and seemed to suggest a newfound emotionalism: "I begin to cry again. I cry a lot these days."[47]

Nurturing Protestant Christianity in Soviet Russia

Even a near fatal brain injury did not keep Schuller from thinking about the scope of his influence. As Schuller recuperated, he also ruminated

45. Penner, *Goliath*, 23.

46. Memorandum, Jim Coleman to Hour of Power Managers and Supervisors, Crystal Cathedral Ministers and Department Heads, September 10, 1991, CC-Correspondence, RHS/CC, box 38 (HCASC). The memorandum included a sample of the telegram that had been sent.

47. Schuller, *My Journey*, 457.

234 CHAPTER 9

on his disrupted trip to the USSR. The minister preferred that the Soviet people had the opportunity to watch *Hour of Power* in its entirety—rather than the abbreviated thirty-minute version, *From Spirit to Spirit*. In June 1992, he flew to Moscow to negotiate a new contract that would allow for the full-hour version. Although he had to wait until forty-five minutes before his flight back to the States departed, Schuller eventually received the necessary signatures. The first full *Hour of Power* aired on June 7, 1992.[48]

A year later, though, the minister yearned to see tangible results. For Schuller, broadcasting into the former Soviet Union represented more than mere religious revivalism. The minister harbored distinctively political intentions. His church had provided a platform, and now his messages held the potential for transforming an entire nation. The *Hour of Power* broadcast offered the means for exporting a philosophy that would elevate the individual over the collective, break the ideological mold of communism, and initiate a new era of peace and prosperity. In light of this grand project, he wondered: "Was it really making a difference? Our message of possibility thinking was and is so strongly focused on the power of individualism. Without being confrontational, how could it penetrate a society steeped in collectivism, a people indoctrinated to believe in the wisdom of surrendering decision-making to authority figures?"[49] Schuller decided that he needed to return to the former Soviet Union to assess his influence.

The new Russian government continued to be in flux. Gorbachev had recently been ousted from the presidency and replaced by Boris Yeltsin. Realizing the shifting access to power, the minister immediately brokered a meeting with Vyacheslav Voklov, Yeltsin's deputy chief, in 1993. Schuller claimed that Voklov offered effusive praise for the minister's role in attempting to establish democracy in Russia: "I knew then that seeing you and hearing you would, more than anything else, inspire people to believe in themselves enough to go to polls and vote for democracy! And your sermon—I swear—was as if planned just for Russia on this historic

---

48. Schuller, *My Journey*, 465–66, and "Former Soviets Getting Taste of Schuller's 'Hour of Power,'" *Deseret News*, April 6, 1992, https://tinyurl.com/srpuj66t.

49. Schuller, *My Journey*, 466.

GOOD IMAGE AND GLOBAL INFLUENCE IN THE GLORY DAYS **235**

Sunday. . . . I knew that God had sent you here to inspire the people to believe in themselves and vote for a new country with freedom in the hands of the people."[50] Even with such glowing praise, Schuller sought assurances regarding the continued impact of *Hour of Power*.

The country now allowed more freedom to practice religion, but they favored the Russian Orthodox version of Christianity. For example, the Russian parliament passed limitations on proselytizing, creating a certificate program for approval from the government and the Orthodox Church to allow "full freedom to minister." For US ministries, the certificate program to mitigate conversion efforts precluded evangelism programs by Roman Catholics, Seventh-day Adventists, the Salvation Army, Baptists, Billy Graham, Pentecostals, and Methodists. In a complexly regulated atmosphere, the minister proudly noted that "they made one exception for their first American preacher in Russia: in 1999 they issued certificate number 001 to the Crystal Cathedral Ministries and to me, Robert Schuller."[51] Although the minister acknowledged that others certainly played significant roles in also influencing a new openness toward religion in what had been the USSR, he took a great deal of pride in his part.

Indeed, Schuller enjoyed high status in the late 1990s. In a 1997 profile, *Christianity Today's Leadership Journal* asserted that "It would not be overreaching to say that without Schuller and the Crystal Cathedral, there would likely be no Willow Creek Community Church, no Saddleback Community Church, or the thousands of other seeker-oriented churches around the country."[52] In addition, megachurch expert Warren Bird credited Schuller with pioneering several trends, including naming a denominational church a "community church," preaching a "message" rather than a sermon, using a nontraditional setting for worship services (a drive-in theater), conducting door-to-door market research, training pastors in *leadership*, and televising a weekly church service.[53] His suc-

---

50. Schuller, *My Journey*, 467.

51. Schuller, *My Journey*, 468.

52. "How Schuller Shaped Your Ministry," *Leadership Journal*, Spring 1997, http://www.christianitytoday.com/le/1997/spring/7L2114.html?paging=off.

53. Warren Bird, "How Robert H. Schuller Shaped Your Ministry," *Leadership Network*, April 2, 2015, https://churchleaderinsights.com/how-robert-schuller-shaped-your-ministry/.

236 CHAPTER 9

cesses were obvious—Schuller made sure to promote every high point of his ministry—and church leaders from across America sought out his guidance for growing their own churches.

While these accolades accumulated during the 1990s, as Schuller began to be more reflective as he aged and pondered his close scrape with death, he wondered, "What power do I have in the position I occupy today?" The question betrayed his preoccupation with control: "Overestimating my power—surrendering to ego, letting praise inflate my self-regard—would lead to irresponsible goal-setting. The fallout from such excess would be dangerous to my emotional well-being, my ministry, my staff, and my supporters."[54] He began to list his accomplishments: thirty books published (indeed, the minister used his vacations to write books),[55] the Leadership Institute, motivational lecturer commanding $15,000 per booking (a fee, Schuller noted, triple that of Peale), a list of disciples that included Rick Warren at Saddleback Church and Bill Hybels at Willow Creek, and the development of the Crystal Cathedral campus. With this impressive list, the minister wondered whether he should be thinking about "hanging it up."[56] Schuller found himself in his midsixties, knowing that the RCA typically assumed sixty-eight as the age for retirement. He decided, no.

Even as he expanded his global influence, Schuller could not help but continue to look to traditional markers of church growth and vitality: new construction. His first contract with the RCA had called him to "build a church," and since that time he had reveled in his role as a property developer. His identity demanded that he continue building—a tangible artifact to further assure the perpetuity of the church—at least one more architectural wonder to cap the campus. Landlocked, the church could only expand by purchasing surrounding houses as they became available. Yet, Schuller realized that ten more acres would allow the Cathedral to expand to forty acres and allow more parking and a visitor's center. Having secured the services of Richard Neutra and Philip John-

---

54. Schuller, *My Journey*, 469.

55. Penner, *Goliath*, 409.

56. Schuller, *My Journey*, 470-72. Hereafter, page references to this work will be placed in parentheses in the text.

son in the past, the minister would not settle for a middling architect for what could be his final building. Schuller entered into negotiations with Richard Meier, designer of the Getty Museum in Los Angeles. The process would prove expensive. In the end, this last building would contribute significantly to the fate of the ministry in the first decade of the new century.

One More Dalliance with Politics

Schuller's move across nation-states and into higher realms of political power raised his perspective above the long-term critiques from pastors and other commentators. Now, the minister was immersed in world-historic interactions. And Schuller's connections to power expanded with the size of his church.

In January 1997, Schuller received an invitation to attend the inauguration of President Bill Clinton. Though the minister had been friendly with politicians from all ideologies, his commitment to not offending had entrenched a safe-distancing posture. The decision to attend the inauguration did not signal that Schuller necessarily endorsed Clinton or his administration's policies. Rather, for the minister, it affirmed his ascension as more than a local church pastor. With his work in the Soviet Union, he now saw himself as an international influencer. When meeting Clinton just before the ceremony in the Oval Office, Schuller blessed the president with Isaiah 58:12—"You shall be the repairer of the breach and the restorer of the paths to dwell in." Schuller described Clinton as visibly moved: "He blinked once or twice, obviously taken aback. Then he fumbled in his pocket, drew out a piece of paper, and asked me to write it down" (479).

Seemingly so struck by the verse the minister had shared with him, Clinton invited Schuller to sit next to his wife, Hillary Rodham Clinton, at the State of the Union address just a few weeks later. Clinton even mentioned the minister by name during the address as among "those whose lives reflect our shared values and the best of what we can become when we are one America" and then read Isaiah 58:12. Though Schuller clearly reveled in the moment, a vivid indication of his stature, he also reported receiving blowback from more conservative elements of his audience and congregation—including facetious letters wondering whether

238 CHAPTER 9

the cozying up to the president meant that there would now also be a "Hillary Clinton abortion clinic next to the Crystal Cathedral" (481).

Schuller, though, liked the proximity to power. Later that same month, he and Arvella accepted the Clintons' invitation to stay a night at the White House in the Lincoln Bedroom. That night Clinton borrowed a copy of Schuller's coauthored book, *The Power of Being Debt Free*. Two years later, Schuller would receive a letter from the president indicating that his newest Social Security plan would allow the country to become debt-free by 2018. He accorded gratitude to the minister for inspiring him with the book and indicated that he became a "possibility thinker" on the issue because of it (491).

Schuller's warmth toward Clinton, though, cooled when it became clear that the president had engaged in sexual activity with an intern in the Oval Office. The minister recoiled at the idea that he could be tainted by his friendship with Clinton. Schuller was reluctant to comment publicly on the scandal—even while being queried by many for his opinion. In his autobiography, the minister claimed that he relented only when the editor of the *New York Times*, somewhat dubiously, wanted an op-ed piece from a "positive national and world religious leader." Schuller obliged and wrote an essay that implied that Clinton should resign in the best interests of the nation—in order to save it from the divisiveness of an impeachment. The president, of course, did not heed Schuller's advice. The minister only risked wading into national politics because he interpreted the situation as nonpartisan; Clinton had engaged in "immoral conduct" (486–90).

In an interview, Schuller expressed dismay, in retrospect, regarding a meeting the two men had had earlier in the year in the Oval Office: "[The president] did it with such passion and with his eyes locked on me. He lied. Blatantly. He's the third public man to do that to me—Nixon and Agnew lied to me, bluntly, boldly. And now Clinton."[57] The minister eventually also penned a more aggressive op-ed in the *Wall Street Journal*, directly addressing the president: "I ask that you look within your conscience and summon the will and strength to end this agony. By step-

---

57. John M. Broder, "Clinton Turns to Pastors for Solace," *New York Times*, September 11, 1998, https://tinyurl.com/4vbc5dev.

ping aside, you can spare our nation weeks, perhaps months, of divisive debate and repulsive testimony."[58] After the trial, Clinton seemed to hold no grudges toward Schuller—even writing letters to the minister.[59]

In fact, later in 1997, Clinton invited Schuller to join the US delegation to the funeral for Mother Teresa. In a fortuitous turn, Schuller found himself seated next to Doug Coe on the long flight home. Coe had for almost three decades organized the President's Prayer Breakfast in Washington, DC, and possessed an almost shadow influence in US politics.[60] *Time* magazine once described Coe as a "stealth Billy Graham."[61] The *New York Times* described him as "an evangelical leader who gained influence with powerful figures around the world as head of a prominent but secretive faith-based organization."[62] Schuller viewed the long conversation as a watershed event where he learned from Coe how to witness to "the non-Christian world."[63]

Schuller yearned for even greater influence beyond the church world and into more secular arenas. Coe advised the minister to consider dropping the moniker "Christian." It carried too much negative weight in much of the world where Christianity had been associated with conquerors and colonizers. Instead, Coe suggested, whenever possible, to use "follower of Jesus Christ" because "our mission is not to convert people to a new religion, but rather to inspire them to be followers of Jesus Christ."[64] The minister found himself convinced. He recalled: "As our plane prepared to land in Washington, I was prepared to lift my ministry to a higher level of holy mission. My ministry of evangelism had

---

58. Robert H. Schuller, "Spare Us a Trial, Mr. President," *Wall Street Journal*, December 21, 1998, https://www.wsj.com/articles/SB914190242498781500.

59. Schuller, *My Journey*, 491.

60. For more on Coe, see Jeff Sharlet's *The Family: The Secret Fundamentalism at the Heart of American Power* (New York: Harper, 2008). Sharlet describes an invisible network of Christian evangelical men who see themselves as compelled to change the world.

61. Zach Montague, "Doug Coe, Influential Evangelical Leader, Dies at 88," *New York Times*, February 22, 2017, https://tinyurl.com/2wp8z7mf.

62. Montague, "Doug Coe, Influential Evangelical Leader, Dies at 88."

63. Schuller, *My Journey*, 484.

64. Schuller, *My Journey*, 484.

240   CHAPTER 9

been redesigned! My forces would shift from a mission of conversion to a mission of mercy."[65]

What that adjustment in pastoral mission actually meant remains somewhat elusive. Some critics would likely accuse Schuller of shading toward universalism. However it is assessed, Schuller had long stepped outside of conventional Christian circles, attempting to integrate his church into the broader structures of society. Some read this as moving away from Christianity, but, in actuality, his ministry consisted of frequent and varied attempts to move away from the strict boundaries that had long defined the Christian church. Was it time to more boldly consider other options?

Thinking about Legacy

As the minister aged, he continued to deal with health issues. In December 1997, Schuller suffered a minor heart attack. While the *New York Times* simply indicated that the minister drove himself to the hospital after experiencing chest pains, Schuller himself reported that a longtime congregant—with whom he had scheduled a meeting that had seemed regrettable on a particularly busy day—suggested that he looked wan and worried aloud that he might be experiencing early symptoms of a heart attack. She made the minister promise to see his doctor that day. Though he doubted the "diagnosis," Schuller obliged and later had an emergency angioplasty surgery.[66] By all accounts, he made a full recovery.

Returning to better health, Schuller enjoyed a high-profile opportunity in 1999 to employ Coe's advice for expanding his reach beyond conventional Christian circles. The minister received an invitation to address the congregation of Shaykh Ahmad Kuftaro, the grand mufti of Syria. The minister later reported that he understood this opportunity to be in parallel to that of President Clinton, who concurrently hosted peace talks in Washington between Israel's prime minister, Ehud Barak, and Syria's president, Bashar al-Assad. Indeed, Schuller framed the signifi-

---

65. Schuller, *My Journey*, 485.

66. "Robert H. Schuller Has Minor Heart Attack," *New York Times*, December 14, 1997, https://tinyurl.com/3upxfz5u. Also see Schuller, *My Journey*, 477–78.

cance of the invitation: "I would be the first Christian minister to preach a full-length sermon in one of the world's most influential mosques."[67]

When Schuller met the grand mufti in Syria before his appearance, he recalled feeling the presence of God and indicated the sensation felt similar to those he had experienced upon meeting Mother Teresa and Billy Graham. The minister also retraced a conversation he had with the grand mufti:

Schuller: "How many Christians are there in Syria?"

Grand Mufti: "I would say that there are about 17 million!"

Schuller: "How could that be?"

Grand Mufti: "Muhammad wrote a book called the Koran in which he shared the faith that Jesus was born of the Virgin Mary and performed miracles and will someday come again to judge all people. He taught that peace was the great message of Jesus. 'Islam' means 'peace.' So in that sense we cannot be good and true Muslims if we are not also Christians."[68]

Schuller did not comment on the grand mufti's assessment and expressed that he felt a kinship while in Syria—especially the morning call to prayer, "a public voice that calls out over the city to remind everyone that there's a Supreme Being superior to and more important than day-to-day drudgery."[69]

Later that day, the minister spoke in the mosque to a reported crowd of fifteen thousand and recounted that as he stood before the crowd of devout Muslims, he felt convicted that both he and the grand mufti labored "doing God's work together."[70] In fact, Schuller invited the grand mufti

67. Schuller, *My Journey*, 493.
68. Schuller, *My Journey*, 497–98.
69. Schuller, *My Journey*, 498.
70. For more on Schuller's reflection on the meeting, see Julia Lieblich, "Audience of Many Faiths Joins Schuller in Mosque for an 'Evening of Hope,'" *Chicago Tribune*, November 2, 2001, https://tinyurl.com/bdeebx2s.

242   CHAPTER 9

to be a worship guest at the Crystal Cathedral (a heart issue precluded the trip). The minister finally assessed the grand mufti to be "truly one of the great Christ-honoring leaders of faith."[71]

His international travel and exposure to other religious traditions had left Schuller with an even broader vision as he entered the twenty-first century: "I'm dreaming a bold impossible dream: that positive-thinking believers in God will rise above the illusions that our sectarian religions have imposed on the world, and that leaders of the major faiths will rise above doctrinal idiosyncrasies, choosing not to focus on disagreements, but rather to transcend divisive dogmas to work together to bring peace and prosperity and hope to the world."[72] The minister's emphasis on "positive thinking" over and above idiosyncratic doctrine likely would strike critics as another drift toward universalism. Schuller, though, ever cagey, aware of the potential of religious debate quagmires, and struggling to find new language to accommodate his seemingly less orthodox convictions, remained somewhat elusive on the topic.

In July 2000, Schuller received an honorary doctorate in psychology and theology from the Orthodox University of Moscow. The minister assessed the degree to be the capstone of his career—especially since no other American before had been so honored.[73] With that kind of framing—thinking about "capping off" his ministry—Schuller began to consider succession at the Crystal Cathedral and on *Hour of Power*.

71. Schuller, *My Journey*, 501–2.
72. Schuller, *My Journey*, 502.
73. Schuller, *My Journey*, 504.

10

THE MINISTRY COLLAPSES

Schuller delighted in walking his church grounds. The array of buildings with specific purposes reminded the minister of the family barnyard in Iowa. Even as he fondly recalled his childhood, he consistently referred to it taking place "nowhere"—in other words, an out-of-the-way place that accorded no stature or profile. For Schuller, success in California represented evidence that he had become "someone" of significance in a "somewhere" locale.[1] With his massive campus in the entertainment hub of Southern California, Schuller had clearly established the premier ministry in the United States.

The honors accumulated. Noting the scope of Schuller's ministry, Loretta Sanchez, his representative from the US Congress, in February 2000 commemorated the thirtieth anniversary of *Hour of Power* with a speech on the House floor. Sanchez lauded Schuller for his consistent "message of hope and positive thinking."[2] Moreover, she noted that over 30 million people in more than two hundred countries watched the program. A few years later, Sanchez nominated Schuller for a Congregational Gold Medal.[3] In March 2004, no less than President George W. Bush visited the Los Angeles Convention Center to promote his Faith-Based and Com-

1. Robert Schuller, *My Journey: From an Iowa Farm to a Cathedral of Dreams* (New York: HarperCollins, 2001), 509.

2. Congressional Record (Bound Edition), Volume 146 (2000), Part 1, https://tinyurl.com/4bsj6c8u.

3. H.R. 3600—Dr. Robert Schuller Gold Medal Act, 109th Congress (2005–2006), https://tinyurl.com/yc5ubu75.

244 CHAPTER 10

munity Initiatives. While there, the president paid homage to Schuller: "I appreciate Robert Schuller coming—I'm honored you're here—from the Crystal Cathedral. They even beamed his program into Midland, Texas. [Laughter] Thanks for coming, sir. You made a huge difference."[4]

With government officials commemorating his influence, Schuller had also been considering how to cap his career. He saw his honorary doctorate from Moscow Orthodox University as affirmation of his synthesis of psychology and theology. He saw the distinguished alumni award from WTS as denominational acceptance of his theology of self-esteem. And the minister saw the Lifetime Achievement in Excellence Award from the American Institute of Architects as "crowning" his "addiction" to excellent building design.[5]

What had seemed to be an unassailable megachurch empire late in the 1990s and early in the new century, though, would be in disarray less than a decade later. At the very end, Schuller ended up suing his own bankrupt ministry. Why? Numerous reasons, of course. The significance resided, however, in the precariousness of the unrelenting nature of a continually growth-pursuing Christianity.

One More Building . . .

In those early years of the twenty-first century, Schuller knew that he would eventually have to turn over his pulpit and recede from the spotlight. Yet he itched to build. At the same time, the achingly slow process of purchasing neighboring homes as they became available frustrated the minister. One disinterested owner proved a tough negotiator—and he owned the last lot needed before construction on a new visitor's center could begin. The asking price: $1 million for a 1,200-square-foot house that sat on an eighth of an acre. Schuller grew impatient, though, and claimed that God had told the minister to quit being "materialistic" and "hung up on money." To that end, according to Schuller, God told him to

---

4. Weekly Compilation of Presidential Documents Volume 40, Number 10 (Monday, March 8, 2004), https://tinyurl.com/yc6t7k4c.

5. Schuller, *My Journey*, 512-13. Hereafter, page references to this work will be placed in parentheses in the text.

"offer the seller of that home what he wants, and the money will come. Trust me!" (506–7). The minister did as told, and he closed the deal. True to form, Schuller reported that the ministry, shortly thereafter, received yet another check for $1 million from a total stranger.

The latest windfall, however, would only cover the last needed lot. To finance actual construction, the ministry obtained a loan for $20 million (507). Part of the spectacular cost would go to another accomplished architect: Richard Meier, fresh off designing the Getty Center in Los Angeles (opened in 1997). Schuller and Meier began to plan in earnest. The minister betrayed little concern about the financing. He had done this many times before. The template he had established had always worked—if only barely. Little did he know, though, that this last building gamble would prove too tenuous. As the financial environment again shifted, the debt would stretch, become a millstone, and contribute to the shattering of the Crystal Cathedral Ministry.

As Schuller built his capstone project for the campus, he seemed to anticipate that he likely had entered the waning days of his life and ministry. With that in mind, in 2001 he published his autobiography (daughter Carol helped ghostwrite it). The concluding pages hinted at the end of his career. Construction had begun on what would be his last building. And he reflected upon the key role the Schuller children—and their spouses—played in the ministry. The passage, in fact, reads as publicly advocating for his family to remain in control of the ministry (even though RCA church polity included no protocols for handing down a church within a family): "With this talented, dedicated, generous, trustworthy, trained family team woven into the fabric of our ministry, I can rest assured that the Crystal Cathedral will continue its influence well beyond my own lifetime" (514). The desire to pass the ministry down to the Schuller children forced the minister into contortions and implausible arguments.

Before any transition occurred, the construction project needed to be financed and completed. In typical fashion, Schuller went ahead with the construction plans with only vague financing. He hoped that a dynamic marketing scheme would provide the necessary subsidies and scheduled the groundbreaking ceremony. Despite the impending bad weather that rushed the groundbreaking ceremony for the new building (initially named the International Center for Possibility Thinking,

246   CHAPTER 10

eventually changed to the Welcoming Center), Schuller felt optimistic. He remembered his head spinning with "the pleasure of the moment" (513). On site, the United States Naval Academy glee club sang, for some reason, "Anchors Aweigh" and "America the Beautiful."

Beyond the loan for $20 million, the minister went to a familiar tactic to instigate smaller gifts. For this iteration, though, instead of selling panels of glass, he sold individual bricks of optical glass for walls within the interior of the structure. It would not be enough.

The Welcoming Center ended up costing approximately $47 million (over $80 million in inflation-adjusted dollars in 2024). The five-level modernist structure included multiple cafés, a gift shop and bookstore, a three-hundred-seat performing arts theater, a chapel, a museum, and a spacious lobby for receiving visitors.[6] Architecture critic Deyan Sudjic described the Welcoming Center as having the "shade of BMW dealership silver"—entirely tracking with the "best-seats-in-the-house view of an Orange County freeway."[7] Indeed, the building design manifested as so futuristic that it served as the headquarters for Starfleet in the 2013 film *Star Trek: Into Darkness*.[8] Some saw the new structure as an unseemly facility designed to invent new ways to harvest money from visitors to the campus: "And now Richard Meier has added his steel drum to offer visitors something to do when services are over."[9]

When Sudjic visited the Welcoming Center shortly after it had opened, the architect insightfully deduced a ministry in financial trouble. Sudjic noted the Schuller quip that "There is never a money problem, only an idea problem" had been inscribed on a stainless steel plaque on a wall on the interior; nevertheless, he speculated that the building did, indeed, have funding issues: "But to judge by the exposed roof trusses,

6. Raymond J. Elson, Casey Kennedy, and Mark Wills, "The Crystal Cathedral and Its Demise," *Journal of Business Cases and Applications* 18 (September 2017): 1-13, https://www.aabri.com/manuscripts/172634.pdf.

7. Deyan Sudjic, *The Edifice Complex: How the Rich and Powerful Shape the World* (New York: Penguin Press, 2005), 295.

8. Kevin Sablan, "Action Picks Up for Filming in O.C.," *Orange County Register*, April 29, 2013, https://www.ocregister.com/2013/04/29/action-picks-up-for-filming -in-oc/.

9. Sudjic, *The Edifice Complex*, 299.

and the air-conditioning ducts visible in the exhibition space, there is still room for a few more donations to finish off the museum that motivates."[10] Assessing the building in relation to its primary promoter, Sudjic jested that the minister "could teach Donald Trump a thing or two about self-promotion"—an apt comparison since both men counted Norman Vincent Peale as a mentor.[11]

Other ministry decisions beyond the newest building contributed to financial strain. In terms of further promotion and revenue, the ministry had found *The Glory of Christmas* and *The Glory of Easter* so successful over so many years that they decided to add a third event: *The Glory of Creation*. In 2005, the ministry spent between $13 million and $15 million to underwrite the grand production. The show featured massive digital screens and elaborate sets and included a red-carpet premier. Without the celebratory gravitas and rituals associated with a Christian holiday, though, *Creation* never gained a robust audience, and the ministry never restaged the production after losing an estimated $5 million.[12]

Creditors later alleged that the ministry became so strained that it drew more than $10 million around that time from a maintenance endowment established to meet other church expenses and salaries.[13] Combined with the massive mortgage for the Welcoming Center, the losses incurred by *Creation* left the ministry financially overextended by the middle of the 2000–2009 decade. A Cathedral ministry board member later rued to *Christianity Today* that "It wasn't the bad times that got us; it was the good. We overbuilt."[14]

Succession and Passing On the "Family Farm"

Even while he continued to build, expand, and strain the ministry, Schuller planned for his succession. Already in 1985, one associate regis-

10. Sudjic, *The Edifice Complex*, 304.

11. Sudjic, *The Edifice Complex*, 306.

12. Elson, Kennedy, and Wills, "The Crystal Cathedral and Its Demise."

13. William Vanderbloemen and Warren Bird, *Next: Pastoral Succession That Works* (Grand Rapids: Baker Books, 2014), 102.

14. Ken Walker, "Church Drops Mortgage for Expansion," *Christianity Today*, September 27, 2011, quoted by Vanderbloemen and Bird, *Next*, 103.

248   CHAPTER 10

tered concerns about how the minister more and more surrounded himself with "relatives" who also received "more and more responsibility and became more and more vocal regarding operation and direction of the ministry."[15] A copastor at the Cathedral confided his concern in an email to Ronald Keener, longtime editor of *Church Executive* magazine: "There is the question of salaries for the Schuller family members. Officially, they will tell you a low figure but that does not include things like cars, perks, housing allowances, and a multitude of goodies that nobody really knows about. They are masters at hiding stuff."[16]

The specter of nepotism began to shadow Schuller. In a May 1987 congregational meeting, the minister lamented the "evil, demonic forces" that sought to destroy his ministry and followed with a letter to the church that he suspected "enemies" within his own organization. It seemed the impetus for the discord originated from congregants who resented what they perceived as kin favoritism in the fact that eight Schuller family members drew salaries from the ministry.[17]

Beyond that, longtime members became "disenchanted" with Schuller's newfound aloofness after the opening of the Cathedral. The minister began to be perceived as "untouchable."[18] Schuller would often leave immediately after services through a door in the basement: "People at the church got the impression that Schuller intentionally was avoiding the sort of personal contact he had as a young minister."[19]

The minister began to close ranks, orienting discussions toward entrusting all operations and the future direction of the church to his immediate family. In 2001, Schuller distributed among the board and ministry leaders a written rationale, "The Schuller Family in Ministry: Portfolio," to explain why the ministry should be handed down to the Schuller children. This bold

15. Larry Gates, *Dwelling in Schullerland* (Nashville: Winston-Derek, 1985), 102.

16. Email, anonymous pastor to Keener, March 30, 2010, Ronald Keener Papers, Chambersburg, PA.

17. Ronald Campbell, "Family Affair: Eight Members of Schuller Clan Have Ministry Jobs," *Orange County Register*, August 9, 1987, Dennis Voskuil Papers, Holland, MI (hereafter cited as DVP).

18. Scott Fagerstrom, "Trying Times: TV Preachers' Problems Cloud Schuller Ministry," *Orange County Register*, August 9, 1987 (DVP).

19. Fagerstrom, "Trying Times."

document from the elder Schuller insinuated a foregone conclusion that, of course, the Schuller children would inherit the work of his church. The minister indicated that the ministry had long "regarded the idea of families working together in ministries as fundamental to our value system and faith."[20] Schuller recounted that he had found "tremendous joy" in "*employing* families." He also claimed that "Family Policies and Procedures" had been practiced since the beginning of the ministry. These included:

> No family member is placed into an autonomous position within the management of accounting and finances—all are answerable to higher financial personnel;
> No two family members work together in areas of finance and fund-raising;
> No family member may decide salary amount, benefits packages, or raise earnings of another family member. All compensatory decisions regarding family members must be approved by the Finance Committee of the Board while other family members abstain from voting power in relation to such a decision;
> Family members may report to other family members in areas of creativity, programming, production, public relations, writing, research, etc. However, the budget of these areas must be under the guidelines and control of the C.F.O. who is to remain a non-family executive.

Schuller also reported that he and Arvella understood their children as the "strong foundation for the entire Crystal Cathedral Ministries."[21] The Schuller children, then, "inherited, not a corporate dynasty, but a spiritual obligation and calling to carry that distinctive message to their own generations. Such sacred charges were given to families again and again in Holy Scripture."[22] Schuller obviously felt defensive about his children and their spouses all being employed within the ministry.

20. Robert H. Schuller, "The Schuller Family in Ministry: Portfolio," October 2001, updated October 2007, p. 1, Ronald Keener Papers, Chambersburg, PA.
21. Schuller, "Portfolio," 2.
22. Schuller, "Portfolio," 2.

250 CHAPTER 10

Schuller expended considerable energy in an attempt to keep the leadership of the ministry to his immediate family. His arguments appealed to the politically conservative ethos of his church members. As described in an analysis of several televangelist ministries, including Schuller's, who also touted a family business model, "the family business is part of the moral-political message of the New Christian Right. It represents family traditionalism and individual economic libertarianism."[23] For example, Schuller claimed that negative attitudes about "rich families staying in power" had crept into society only recently because of "left wing liberals and socialists expounding a Marxist philosophy." He drew on anticommunist roots to persuade his critics. With another tack in argument, Schuller also urged that "nepotism" should be redefined as a positive word. After all, the Bible offered numerous examples of "family ministry." The minister offered what he saw as scriptural examples:

> The book of Numbers is, in its entirety, a book of genealogy.
> The apostles baptized not only individuals, but entire households.
> Mary, the mother of Jesus, and Elizabeth, the mother of John the Baptist, were cousins.
> The 12 disciples of Jesus included Peter and Andrew (two brothers), James and John, cousins of Jesus. (Matthew 4:18)
> At the crucifixion, Jesus' mother, her sisters, and Jesus' cousin, John, ministered to Him. (Mark 15:40, 16:1)
> The feeding of the five thousand—Jesus' family also benefitted from the miracle.
> Jesus depended upon the support of family as He served on earth. Support came in the forms of emotional, relational, and financial [backing].[24]

With this biblical evidence presented, Schuller betrayed a sense that some staff had begun to resent the favors afforded the Schuller family. The minister lamented that his family had been perceived "only as dollar signs" and that "practical steps" had to be taken "to embrace this family

---

23. Razelle Frankl, "Teleministries as Family Businesses," *Marriage & Family Review* 15, no. 3–4 (1990), 195–205, here 199.

24. Schuller, "Portfolio," 3–5.

who have not shunned but eagerly embraced the calling of God on their lives." To that end, the minister encouraged the board of trustees to draft a resolution that affirmed "the philosophy of families in ministry."

In 2004 Schuller began introducing his son, Robert A. Schuller, as the next head of the Cathedral ministry. A well-crafted launch for the succession included numerous lunches and dinners with benefactors around the country so that they could be convinced of the soundness of the plan and Robert A.'s abilities to lead the ministry—after all, the younger Schuller had been pastoring his own congregation in San Juan Capistrano since 1981. In the moment, the ministry seemed healthy. In 2005, the congregation reported to the RCA that they included 1,000 confessing members, 4,320 inactive members, and 4,374 baptized members—for a total of 9,694 members. The leadership also claimed an average worship attendance of 4,402. The church spent $8,578,015 on "congregational ministry and mission." At the same time, the congregation reported only $199,902 of debt.[25] And in 2006, Robert A. ascended to the pulpit at the Cathedral.[26]

Materials included in the "Portfolio" further revealed how concerned Schuller had become regarding the criticism of nepotism within the ministry. In 2007 he attached an addendum to the document wherein Arvella, each of the Schuller children, and their respective spouses submitted a rationale for their role in the ministry. In fact, the sense that the Schullers would hand the ministry over to their children and their respective spouses had become an open secret within the congregation. A longtime member remarked, "Arvella at least, if not both she and Bob, proclaimed that this was a family affair. And the [Schuller] kids were raised with that attitude."[27]

Passing along the ministry—which encompassed both the income and the influence generated by keeping control of the congregation—as an inheritance to his children became a persistent assumption, present in di-

25. RCA's Annual Consistorial Report for the Crystal Cathedral, December 31, 2005, Shepherd's Grove Church Archives, Irvine, CA.

26. Laurie Goodstein, "Dispute over Succession Clouds Megachurch," *New York Times*, October 23, 2010, https://www.nytimes.com/2010/10/24/us/24cathedral.html.

27. This quote and those following told to Mulder in interviews. For more on anonymous quotes, see "A Note on Sources."

alogues and planning about the future, even though it fostered tensions. A close friend of the Schullers shared how insiders assessed the situation similarly: "The whole entitlement thing was a big, big, big issue." From the standpoint as a close observer of the ministry, this former member stated, "The real Achilles heel, really a big one, was that ugly word 'nepotism.' And Arvella was the one most to blame for this. If you were a family member and you wanted a job, you got one. And before the fall [i.e., bankruptcy of the church] there were an awful lot of black S class Mercedes-Benzes on lease [through the church]. And some other pretty comfortable lifestyle stuff from too many other people. The younger generation thought this was the way it ought to be."

The push to keep the ministry within the family became divisive. In a different interview, another family friend of the Schullers used the same term, "Achilles heel," in echoing a similar sentiment: "I think Bob and Arvella's Achilles heel was the family, wanting them involved. And I know where they came from, they were betrayed before, and they felt their family would carry on their dream. But they didn't take into account their family's dynamics." A representative of the RCA who sat on the Cathedral ministry board recalled, "I remember saying to board members at one point, 'What we really need to do is have a nationwide search for the very best preacher who could fill Bob's shoes.' That could have been the way to go, but Bob was not going to hear of it. It was going to be [Robert A]. And if you tried to counter that or fight that or move in a different direction, you just had chaos." Within the congregation, there seemed to be an unrest percolating around the Schuller family as they assumed positions and lived lifestyles that increased the strain on a ministry that, from all appearances, had begun to ebb.

Even the Schullers' son, Robert A., acknowledged that Arvella instigated the desire to keep the ministry in the family—and that it likely contributed to its demise: "[My mother] wanted to maintain control. My father didn't care. He wasn't mentally there enough to care; my mother did, and she wanted to. And she wanted to maintain control in order to protect all her children—make sure they would all have worthwhile, well-paying jobs with the Cathedral." Robert A. attributed the expectation that the ministry would be inherited by the children as residue from the Schullers' Iowa farm background. In that agricultural community, "the farm came first. Because the farm meant life or death, if they don't have a farm, they don't have a livelihood, they're homeless, they're without food and they don't have anything."

Indeed, throughout the Midwest, when farmers retired, they would move into town and the children would assume responsibility for the day-to-day operations. However, the parents maintained partial ownership of the operation and drew rental income. Robert remarked that the "farm then takes care of [the parents]. That's the way it works. They rent it out until they die, and then it's sold, and it's given to the family members in equal portions."[28] In this way, the elder mom and dad Schuller understood the ministry to be their Southern California farm. The farm metaphor was real, and they passed it along to their children.

However, the metaphor of farm inheritance failed to translate into the practicality of church succession. Robert A. explained further: "Obviously, [my parents] couldn't sell the church and divvy it up among the family members. What they could do is they could give responsibility to all the family members—which would basically do the same thing: Give them all jobs, give them something significant, and then the church could take care of our kids until they die. And then they've done their responsibility as far as parents are considered, the farm's done what it's supposed to do."

A copastor from the Cathedral corroborated Robert A.'s interpretation of events from his own observations. He occupied the only staff office on the fourth floor in the Family Life Center, a restricted space, which was often used for meetings between the Schullers since they could be assured of privacy. He frequently overheard conversations between the pastor and his wife, and one incident stood out:

> I came out of the restroom when I heard them talking. I stopped because I just didn't want to be in their presence at that point. Having just had a meeting, I knew that they would be hot and bothered, but I heard them.
>
> He said, "Arvella, the kids need to earn their own way in this world and in this life. We should not be just handing them everything on a platter."

28. Interview with Mulder, May 17, 2017.

And she said, "No, Bob, this is the family business. This is what it's all for. When we leave, they have this whole thing—a piece of the pie."

It was such that all of them [the immediate family] had a different division, so that was her idea.

The divvying up of the ministry proved much more difficult than any of the Schullers had supposed—especially as the ministry began to buckle under the weight of financial problems, incurred first by the costs of the Welcoming Center and *The Glory of Creation*, and then exacerbated by the nationwide financial crisis of 2007 and 2008. The parents had determined that the Schuller children would take over—they failed, though, to consider the roles to be filled by the siblings and in-laws and the overall fragility of the ministry. Indeed, according to the former copastor, the spread of the ministry among family members failed to strengthen the ministry; instead, it further weakened it. As he summed it up: "And so it collapsed."

The scope and profile of the Cathedral ministries had masked its weaknesses. A board member had wondered for years in advance how the succession would proceed: "We'd sit in board meetings and sometimes privately and sometimes more in public, we'd tend to raise this issue: How do we think about a transition?" Concern about the future of the ministry after the elder Schuller retired was persistent. "This is what any thoughtful board member would do if you're stewarding an organization." The magnitude of the financial obligations added to the concern. "You have a $50 million budget, plus everything [staffing, building and land management, broadcast ministry, etc.]." The patterns of financial risk were fraught: "He [Schuller] always ran everything right to the wire. The ministry was always right on the brink of financial liability because of the way he just always pushed things. [As a board member] you knew there was so much dependent upon him. It also meant that there was an organizational fragility there."

As the ministry began to flounder because of its overreliance on family and insiders, the same member of the board found the structure of leadership wanting. "The board of the Crystal Cathedral Ministries was a good example of poor governance. It was filled with conflicts of interest. It had family members who were board members who were getting a salary

THE MINISTRY COLLAPSES   **255**

from the organization. This wouldn't pass the 101 on how you put together a board." A smaller church may have been able to maneuver obligations or manage a smaller debt. Perhaps a fresh entrepreneurialism may have considered alternative options for managing a way out of the current crisis. But at this point, the elder Schuller turned surprisingly conservative.

The largeness of operations had become unwieldy, and the additional considerations inherent to the mammoth size of the debt and the overlapping program and staffing commitments that needed to be met just to sustain the status quo were overwhelming. An increased bureaucracy assumed predictability. But the broader environment of financing and donation was not the same. Attempts to abstract from the playbook of maneuvers from the past and apply them to present circumstances proved insufficient to the substantial challenges at hand. The elder Schuller no longer possessed the agility to replicate the fixes from before. Instead, he hoped to continue the momentum of the church until the next Schuller generation could reinvigorate the velocity of the church for its next iteration of growth.

As debts accrued and donations faltered, the Crystal Cathedral Ministry failed to have sound structures in place to respond. From fiscal year 2008 to fiscal year 2009, revenues from the ministry dropped from $26,686,756 to $18,896,238—a nearly $8 million loss.[29] The national housing mortgage crisis that occurred that year had taken its toll on viewers of *Hour of Power* and rippled into the budget of the broader ministries. The entirety of the Cathedral ministry had become dependent on the broadcast. An administrator at the church described the situation: "First of all, the *Hour of Power* donations drop off—that was the first indication." Much of the ministry could not exist "without the *Hour of Power* [because] all these programs were funded by that—that's where the extra money came from."

In response to the abrupt shortfall, Robert A. attempted to trim the budget by "trying to get rid of all the family members that were on the payroll." Removing family members from employment was not only against established custom, but also it represented a personal offense to his siblings. Unsurprisingly, the church administrator reported, "that didn't sit well with the sisters and the brothers-in-law." The morphing succession plan—haphazard at the start and always uncertain in the

29. Elson, Kennedy, and Wills, "The Crystal Cathedral and Its Demise."

256 CHAPTER 10

details of expected execution—was plagued by the radical financial crises, which instigated a profound estrangement among members of the Schuller family. Although Robert A. had been nurtured to succeed his father in the pulpit, he now found himself on the outside of the ministry. Robert A. had attempted to address the entanglements of family and governance, but it cost him dearly.

In an effort to guarantee strides toward accountability and transparency, Robert A. instigated his plan to restructure the board, and then he found himself on the wrong side of his parents, Schuller and Arvella. After all, Robert A.'s plan to remove conflicts of interest necessarily meant that his parents, sisters, and brothers-in-law would all lose their seats on the board. Schuller rebuffed his son's plan. Instead, he advocated for his daughters' alternate proposal in July 2008 to create a three-person "Office of the President." Two of the three members of this copresidency turned out to be Robert A.'s brothers-in-law.

The fallout from Robert A.'s attempt to shore up church governance apart from family ties continued to impact the young leader's own ministry. It was at this point that the elder Schuller indicated to Robert A. that he would no longer preach on *Hour of Power*. From then, Robert A. would simply be the pastor of the local—and by this time greatly diminished—congregation. Robert A. described this in his own book as a "demotion," a brusque shift in status catalyzed by members of his "own immediate and extended family."[30] Feeling that all the power in the ministry truly rested with the revenue-producing broadcast rather than the congregation itself, Robert A. resigned from his position in October 2008, after a short stint of only two years.[31]

At a January 2009 meeting, Sheila Schuller Coleman responded to Robert A.'s leaving the ministry by suggesting that the problem was personal, not structural, and ultimately resided between the father and son: "We had two pastors in the family who couldn't even talk to each other."[32]

---

30. Robert A. Schuller, *When You Are Down to Nothing, God Is Up to Something: Discovering Divine Purpose and Provision When Life Hurts* (New York: Faith Works, 2011), 119–20.

31. Elson, Kennedy, and Wills, "The Crystal Cathedral and Its Demise."

32. Deepa Bharath, "Rifts, Debt Tear at Crystal Cathedral," *Orange County Reg-*

Robert A. assessed that his sisters felt compelled to side with their father: "They had to pick someone, and I don't blame them for choosing their father."[33] Amid the turmoil, Arvella remained adamant that the Schuller children would always have roles within the ministry. In her mind, they had earned it: "Our children, since they were little, have been involved. There is no job on the campus that they have not done. They've cleaned toilets, they've sorted the mail, and they've answered phones."[34] Deep immersion in the ministry translated for her into ultimate ownership.

Later in 2009, Schuller appointed his daughter, Sheila Schuller Coleman, to the head of the ministry—just months after having declared that, after Robert A.'s exit, the next senior pastor would *not* be a Schuller. Ministry leaders and congregants, while respecting Coleman's experience and expertise as an educational professional, wondered about her bona fides as a minister. Resistance to the appointment affected the staff. Most notably, Coleman's appointment caused disillusioned worship musicians Roger Williams and Don Neuen to resign. Neuen described himself as "heartbroken" by the direction of the ministry.[35] In the interim, Schuller, his daughter, and guests all preached on *Hour of Power*. The board hoped that the ministry would soon regain its strength. In July 2010 Schuller retired, although retaining his position on the board.

Declining Health

As the financial books and organizational structures of the Cathedral ministries spiraled, concerns over Schuller's health created another stress point. Though he maintained his position for the entirety of the first decade of the 2000s, some insiders felt that the minister had never been the same since the brain hemorrhage in the Netherlands. A copastor confided that by the earlier 2000s the staff "noticed that he was declining, because [Schuller would] be talking and he'd reach over to Arvella

---

ister, October 24, 2010, https://www.ocregister.com/2010/10/24/rifts-debt-tear-at-crystal-cathedral/.

33. May 2017 interview.
34. Bharath, "Rifts, Debt Tear at Crystal Cathedral."
35. Bharath, "Rifts, Debt Tear at Crystal Cathedral."

and say, 'uh, what'd they say, what's happening?' And we could tell that his dementia was starting, and it just got worse."

Schuller's grandson Bobby agreed with concerns over his grandfather's health and its effect on the broader ministry: "I watched the whole [collapse of the ministry] unfold. The main reason, I mean if you're going to peg it to one reason, the reason [the ministry] fell apart was because my grandpa got Alzheimer's."[36] Although the elder Schuller had strained the ministry from its beginning, continuing to pursue more building projects and keeping finances of the church at the edge of sustainability, it appeared to everyone that he was also the key person who kept the ministry going. His ambitions pushed the ministry, yet his capacity for leadership to mobilize people and resources also sustained it over time. Any diminishment of the ministry was quickly attributed to the debility of its founder and longtime leader.

Bobby and others became convinced that it was the onset of dementia that crippled the capacity of the ministry: "That's the reason, if you had to put it in one sentence, and that was the beginning of a domino effect. He had Alzheimer's and was still trying to lead, and so it was causing all sorts of confusion between him and my dad [Robert A.] because one day he would say one thing and the next another. Technically, it wasn't Alzheimer's, it was dementia." For Bobby and others, "dementia" was a term that represented a perceived loss of mental functioning. Yet it wasn't a medical diagnosis regarding the onset of symptoms; rather, it was traced back to when he struck his head in 1991 in Amsterdam, which required hours-long brain surgery. As Bobby summarized, "You know, hindsight is 20/20, but, looking back, I think that he never quite recovered from his head injury."

Bobby also reported that the head injury caused a change in the elder Schuller's personality. When Bobby was younger, the grandson knew Schuller had a "temper" and an "edge." He also described his grandfather as possessing "a ruthless drive to thrive and succeed, and a total passion for doing nothing less than absolute excellence to be the very best at everything." But by the early 2000s, this aggressive determination "went away, and he got really weepy, he cried a lot, he was very emotional, and forgetful."

36. Interview with Mulder, May 16, 2017.

The diagnosis of dementia was shared by other family members, especially Robert A., who echoed the sentiment of his son regarding the aging minister: "My father by 2000 had really, really [declined]—his dementia was at the point where he was not able to follow a program and know when it was time for him to step up to the podium. I'm sitting on the podium, and he's saying, 'Do I go up now?' 'No, after this song.' And we've got everything printed out, and everything highlighted [showing] when he goes up, every word and every song. I mean, anyone with any cognitive skill should be able to know when it's time for them to go up."

Robert A. spent much time thinking about his father's decline and its effect on the ministry. According to him,

> By 2000, my dad's out of the picture. You put him in front of a camera with a script? He's great. You'd never in a million years realize there was anything wrong. But if you asked him to get in the car and find his way to a hotel in Los Angeles? There's no way he could ever do that. By 2000, he could not do that, no matter what. He couldn't figure out how to use a cellphone in 2000. He couldn't make a phone call. I mean, the list goes on and on. And my mother protected him to the nth degree, keeping it a secret, because if the word got out that that's how bad it was, she loses all control.

Repeatedly, Robert A. stated that he believed his father's head injury had permanently and profoundly impacted his ability to lead the congregation:

> When he came back from the Netherlands, he never was completely the same again. That happened in 1991, and I'd say two, three years later, he seemed to be normal to some degree—except for the fact that he would cry almost every time he would talk with somebody.
>
> My mother started writing his sermons after that accident, and they clearly weren't as good as his [own writing]. He never [fully recovered], he didn't have the [same feel]. I don't think his sermons had the same impact after that. He used notes a lot more than he did prior to [the accident]. His delivery and his sermons were just not the [same] quality.

CHAPTER 10

> I would say the number one reason the Cathedral completely failed by 2010 was my father's mental capacities. His dementia. That's the number one cost. Based upon his inability to make decisions, to remember circumstances, his inability to stay the course, his inability to withstand persuasion. Anyone he trusts [could] persuade him to do anything they wanted him to do. He just didn't have the mental capacity to do what he knew [was best], what he had always wanted to do, and had done. He lost that ability.

Though the family and the Cathedral ministry largely shielded Schuller's health from public scrutiny, it became apparent to many around him that the minister, at the very least, showed signs of serious decline. His charismatic dynamism receded. As the ministry careened through financial and transitional crises, Schuller no longer possessed the verve to save the church by casting vision for another bold project that would capture the imagination of benefactors and the public. Growth had stopped. And without growth, the whole project slid backward into an existential crisis.

Consistent with Schuller's own ecclesial philosophy, without growth, the church was perishing.

A Slow-Motion Collapse

The manner in which the Cathedral ministry crumbled late in the first decade of the twenty-first century has been described as a "squandered legacy." At one point, the Crystal Cathedral drew billing as one of Orange County's top tourist attractions—families visiting Disneyland just down the road would fill out their vacation by attending Sunday worship at the Cathedral. The scope of ministry dwarfed most competitors: in 2005, the congregation managed a budget of $80 million. For comparison, that same year, the city of Garden Grove had a budget of about $90 million.[37]

By the end of the decade, though, unignorable evidence of financial concern emerged. A May 2009 report titled "Crystal Cathedral: The State

---

37. Bharath, "Rifts, Debt Tear at Crystal Cathedral."

of Our Church and Global Ministry" indicated to congregants that debt would force the sale of the ministry's Rancho Capistrano campus—a 170-acre retreat center donated by John Crean in 1982 located in nearby San Juan Capistrano. The site hosted conferences, retreats, Christian schools, and a satellite church where Robert A. had been lead pastor. Counter to Schuller's mode of operation, the ministry would be using the $35 million from the sale to retire long-term debt that had been accrued during recent construction (the document specifically identified the Memorial Gardens, the Family Life Center, and the Welcoming Center as financial stressors). In pinpointing the source of the unresolved financial burden, the authors of the report noted "a significant portion of this debt occurred in 2002 when well-meaning individuals could not deliver $25 million in pledges due to the '.com bubble burst.'"[38]

The windfall from the sale of Rancho Capistrano proved inadequate. In October 2010, after Schuller's retirement, the Cathedral filed for Chapter 11 bankruptcy. The extent of the fiscal strain became more fully realized. At the time of the filing, the ministry claimed a $36 million mortgage and overall debt of about $48 million to 550 different creditors. In the effort to stay afloat, the church sold assets and laid off about 150 staff members. Donations in 2009 fell by 24 percent compared to 2008. According to Schuller's son-in-law, Jim Penner, the majority of the ministry's finances were tied up in assets, leading to insufficient liquidity for paying vendors. Some in the ministry insisted that the Cathedral's economic misfortunes could be traced to the national economic crisis. Others, though (including Robert A.), suggested that the *Creation* production catalyzed the collapse when it lost $5 million in 2005.[39] Staff salaries and benefits had added to the burden. The bankruptcy filings indicated that twenty family members alone received compensation from the ministry exceeding $1.9 million.[40]

From a cursory glance, it would seem safe to assert that the Cathedral simply suffered from a bungled transition plan. Robert A., though,

---

38. "Crystal Cathedral: The State of Our Church and Global Ministry," May 2009, 11, Ronald Keener Papers.

39. Bharath, "Rifts, Debt Tear at Crystal Cathedral."

40. Vanderbloemen and Bird, *Next*, 103.

argued that the ministry actually had instigated a well-designed succession plan. He argued that his father simply could not let go of "his baby." Robert A. elaborated that "energetic, successful, bright individuals have a hard time relinquishing power. Such individuals did not succeed in life by letting go"—and that, simply put, explained his father's inability to walk away from the ministry. Robert A. also felt he had been undermined by his sisters when he attempted to clear the board of any family members or individuals who had contracts with the church so that it could be "completely autonomous."[41]

Reporting from the *Orange County Register* at the time of the bankruptcy filing indicated that all of the Schuller children still received a salary from the ministry, and the total reached almost $1 million—without factoring in housing, car, or other discretionary spending allowances. In 2010, shortly after the ministry filed for bankruptcy, Schuller's son-in-law, Jim Penner, maintained his possibility thinking, predicting to the local newspaper that the ministry was "going to come out of this." Ignoring glaring concerns, Penner expressed optimism in a purported stalwart character of the ministry: "When all this is done, the story that will be written is how the Crystal Cathedral walked the path of faith and serves as a shining example. Our doors are still open, and it's business as usual."[42] But optimism regarding the future of the ministry proved to be unfounded.

Once the bankruptcy was announced, the shock reverberated widely, and rampant speculation followed. An early analysis from Douglas J. Swanson surmised, "The ministry's failure is unprecedented among televangelists and will undoubtedly be the focus of much scholarly inquiry."[43] No less than *Christianity Today* declared that the bankruptcy of the Crystal Cathedral represented "a poignant moment in the history of modern evangelicalism" that should have caused the entire religious

41. Bharath, "Rifts, Debt Tear at Crystal Cathedral."
42. Bharath, "Rifts, Debt Tear at Crystal Cathedral."
43. Douglas J. Swanson, "The Beginning of the End of Robert H. Schuller's Crystal Cathedral Ministry: A Towering Failure in Crisis Management as Reflected through Media Narratives of Financial Crisis, Family Conflict, and Follower Dissent," *Social Science Journal* 49 (2012): 485–93, here 486.

tradition to reconsider its emphasis on making the gospel culturally relevant.[44] An editorial in *Church Executive*—a bible for megachurch administrators—described the Crystal Cathedral collapse as a "Christian tragedy." Moreover, the editor lamented that, more than anything else, "the Crystal Cathedral self-destructed, ending a marvelous ministry."[45]

Financially, the bankruptcy effects rippled beyond the local Garden Grove ministry. At one point, the *Orange County Register* profiled Christina Oliver, a farmer whose family had supplied livestock for the Cathedral's *Glories* productions for almost three decades. When the ministry failed to pay the roughly $56,000 owed to Oliver, her family found itself unable to pay their own bills and subsequently lost their property to foreclosure.[46]

True to tenets of possibility thinking to the end, the ministry initially attempted a bold campaign to fund-raise itself out of bankruptcy. On July 31, 2011, daughter Sheila Schuller Coleman declared that the board would not consider selling its facilities to appease creditors. Instead, she announced a "Miracle-Faith" campaign that targeted raising $50 million by Thanksgiving. It was an ambitious goal motivated solely by outstanding balances. The endeavor, though, fizzled by late summer. It had garnered a scant $172,775.50 in its first two months before its ultimate, quiet suspension.[47]

The eventual bankruptcy proceedings prompted a "fire sale" of all assets for "a fraction of their value."[48] To appease the creditors, the ministry was forced to sell its most valuable asset—the famous campus itself. The Catholic Diocese of Orange saw an opportunity. For the diocese, the Cathedral had

---

44. "Cracks in the Cathedral: Why We Are Better Off Letting God Make the Gospel Relevant," *Christianity Today*, January 10, 2011.

45. Ron Keener, "Christian Tragedy," *Church Executive*, February 2012, 5, Ronald Keener Papers.

46. Bharath, "Rifts, Debt Tear at Crystal Cathedral."

47. Deepa Bharath, "Crystal Cathedral Board OKs Chapman University Purchase Offer," *Orange County Register*, October 27, 2011, https://tinyurl.com/2jnys9us.

48. Douglas J. Swanson and Terri Manley, "Squandering a Legacy, and Building One: How Robert H. Schuller Lost the Crystal Cathedral, and How the Catholic Church Captured It" (manuscript presented at the Western Social Sciences Association, Annual Conference, Albuquerque, NM, April 2014), 4.

264 CHAPTER 10

stunning appeal—they rightly saw the Cathedral as an "iconic property."[49] For over a decade, leaders had been pursuing a property that would accommodate a 2,500-person sanctuary. To find adequate space in a crowded Orange County, the diocese anticipated spending $100 million for the land and another $100 million for the construction.[50] In anticipation of a move, they were financially poised to seize an opportunity when it arose.

A bidding war erupted between Chapman University and the Catholic Diocese of Orange. Complicating matters further, a bid of $46 million from Chapman reportedly "touched off a battle between church insiders, the Schuller family members who are running the ministry, and the creditors committee."[51] The appeal of the Chapman bid rested on the opportunity for the Cathedral ministry to rent and possibly even repurchase some of the buildings on the campus. However, the Diocese of Orange eventually responded with a bid of $53.6 million in cash.[52] The bidding continued, and the diocese eventually agreed to a purchase price of $57.5 million in early 2012.[53]

The bankruptcy proceedings happened quickly, disrupting the lives of many, most especially the retirement plans for the founders, Schuller and Arvella. The couple had assumed that the ministry would compensate them indefinitely for his role as "roving ambassador" and through intellectual property rights—in short, they anticipated retirement pay from the ministry for the rest of their lives. With bankruptcy, those payments ceased. In turn, Schuller and Arvella resigned from the board—citing "an adversarial and negative atmosphere"—and sued the ministry.[54]

---

49. Robert W. Artigo, *Neither Crystal nor Gold: The Transformation of the Crystal Cathedral into Christ Cathedral* (Lubbock, TX: Lighthouse Catholic Publishing, 2021), 75.

50. Swanson and Manley, "Squandering a Legacy, and Building One," 8.

51. Deepa Bharath and Ronald Campbell, "Chapman's Offer Heats Up Crystal Cathedral Bankruptcy," *Orange County Register*, July 6, 2011, https://tinyurl.com/yt7ebwju.

52. Bharath, "Rifts, Debt Tear at Crystal Cathedral."

53. Ian Lovett, "Founding Family Decides to Leave Crystal Cathedral," *New York Times*, March 11, 2012, https://tinyurl.com/55782bcy.

54. Stuart Lavietes, "Rev. Robert Schuller, 88, Dies; Built an Empire Preaching Self-Belief," *New York Times*, April 2, 2015, https://tinyurl.com/yphp4y4r.

In 2012, the bankruptcy court ruled against Schuller on grounds that his lawyers failed to produce proper legal documentation to account for his and Arvella's understanding of the ministry's commitments to them since most of the agreements had been verbal.[55] Their daughter, Carol Schuller Milner, later revealed that her parents had been "left financially crippled by the loss of their retirement income previously promised by the organization" and ended up "living on social security" alone.[56]

Many critics felt vindicated as they saw the rapid decline of Schuller's ministry. The master of the church market could not avoid the unintended consequences of his own principles. Over a little more than half a century, Schuller's ministry in Orange County would move from unhoused (borrowed theater parking lot) to incomparable Cathedral (an architectural marvel) to rental space (a Catholic parish just down the street). Along the way, conflicts and near failures remained largely hidden. Succession to both the pulpit and the broadcast proved fraught, campus expansion overextended the ministry, and the financial flows dwindled, ultimately leading to the bankruptcy of the ministry. His touted "possibility thinking" as a form of faith served to fuel overconfident projections of continued development. Compounded by abrupt shifts in demographic patterns of migrating churchgoers and sharp constriction in the availability of credit, Schuller's last vision project for yet another beautiful building proved fatal to the entire enterprise.[57]

The End

More bad news would come in 2013: Schuller learned in August that he had esophageal cancer. At that point, the minister's overall health began a precipitous decline. In those years, friends and copastors confided that they had trouble locating either Schuller or Arvella. One

---

55. Vanderbloemen and Bird, *Next*, 104.

56. Kimberly Winston, "Crystal Cathedral Founder's Memorial Covered by Crowdfunding Campaign," *Washington Post*, April 21, 2015, https://tinyurl.com/mphfxt6e.

57. For a more complete narrative on the eventual collapse of Schuller's ministry, see Mark T. Mulder and Gerardo Martí, *The Glass Church: Robert H. Schuller, the Crystal Cathedral, and the Strain of Megachurch Ministry* (New Brunswick, NJ: Rutgers University Press, 2020).

decades-long copastor reported: "I was not allowed to visit [Schuller]. We used the same barber, Schuller and I, and the barber would call me and say, 'Schuller's coming in Tuesday or Thursday' or whatever, so we would meet there." Another described the many steps he took to find the minister, eventually discovering he resided in a local nursing home: "Finally, through the underground, we found out where he was in Newport, and they said, 'Now, when you go there, don't stop at the desk because they will not let you in if you say 'Bob Schuller.' [All of the Schuller family] just had him totally confined." This same copastor lamented that in the nursing home he found Schuller largely incommunicative: "That poor guy, he's sitting in a wheelchair, all crumpled up. [He] really didn't communicate with [anyone] at all." Finally, a former congregant lamented: "From a lot of church members' perspective, the last year or two of his life, we were out of it. We were out of the loop, and there's been no closure."

Six months after Schuller's cancer diagnosis, in February 2014, Arvella passed away at University of California, Irvine Medical Center from natural causes after a brief illness at age eighty-four.[58] A friend of the Schullers assessed that "when Arvella died, [her husband] died along with her. He just went downhill." Another elaborated how crucial Arvella had been for the minister, as she had been in all aspects of their life together, recalling, "Arvella was his ultimate protector and ultimate radar sensor." In describing her role in relation to her husband, this friend explained: "She could pick up trouble on the horizon a lot faster than he could because Bob was essentially a promoter and salesman at heart. As the old proverb goes, 'You can also sell a salesman.' Arvella, on the other hand, was a whole lot more cautious, and she did not mind breaking laws and crunching toes to protect Bob and the ministry, and she did so frequently."

With Arvella gone, Schuller's decline intensified, and he passed away at Artesia Christian Home in Artesia, California, in April 2015 at

---

58. Nicole Santa Cruz, "Arvella Schuller Dies at 84; Wife of Crystal Cathedral Founder Robert Schuller," *Los Angeles Times*, February 11, 2014, https://tinyurl.com/4pe434vr.

eighty-eight years of age. His obituary in the *New York Times* quipped that he had "built an empire preaching self-belief."[59] The minister would be remembered in the paper of record for representing "a new wave in mainstream American Protestantism, one that held out hope not just for achieving personal salvation, its traditional concern, but also for solving personal problems."

On April 20, the Schuller family laid their father to rest on the grounds of the church he so proudly built—although the ministry he founded no longer owned or controlled the campus. The Diocese of Orange, the new owners of the rechristened Christ Cathedral, in partnership with an anonymous benefactor, covered the costs of his burial after a "GoFundMe" campaign instigated by daughter Carol Schuller Milner only raised about $6,000 of its $30,000 goal.[60] Adding insult to injury, several individuals left hurtful comments on the site without offering a donation. In their remarks, bitterness was clearly evident: "Some of the [Schuller] children seem to try to siphon every last drop before the spigot is shut forever. So sad and embarrassing that this mercenary mentality is how many people will ultimately remember Robert and Arvella, two legendary leaders." Indeed, to be forced to *borrow* the place that Schuller had nurtured for his megachurch to hold his funeral represented an ignominious capstone to the minister's legacy.

Today, Schuller rests in a prominent burial plot on church grounds, next to his dear wife, Arvella, as part of a small cemetery just a few hundred feet from the pulpit where he had preached for over thirty years. Perhaps the proudest photograph ever taken of Robert H. Schuller, wearing a burgundy suit, arms outstretched, was staged at the corner of the new Cathedral. It marked a moment of triumph, a fulfillment of a dream, and a seeming guarantee of the future. Although the glass exterior of the Cathedral continues to shine, the reputation of the pastor has dulled, his audacious efforts to reshape the future of Christianity moving toward obscurity. As he witnessed the negotiations for the Ca-

59. Lavietes, "Rev. Robert Schuller, 88, Dies."
60. Winston, "Crystal Cathedral Founder's Memorial Covered by Crowdfunding Campaign."

268 CHAPTER 10

thedral property during bankruptcy proceedings, Schuller remarked that he hoped it would continue as a church.[61] And his desire was fulfilled. In the end, Schuller appeared to be much less concerned about the persistence of his own reputation and much more about the persistence of his church, in the hope that the church he cherished would continue to live on in perpetuity.

61. Nicole Santa Cruz, Ruben Vives, and Mitchell Landsber, "Orange County Diocese to Buy Bankrupt Crystal Cathedral," *Los Angeles Times*, November 18, 2011, https://tinyurl.com/2ktp32tw.

EPILOGUE

THE IMPERATIVE OF CHURCH GROWTH

In his first, explicit advice manual, Robert H. Schuller stated his ecclesial philosophy in its most succinct form: "Your church must either grow or perish."[1] For him, the church faced an existential polarity: either upward or downward, expanding in influence and size or descending into irrelevance and oblivion. The minister understood the imperative of church growth not as motivated by ego or desire for status but, fundamentally, as a blunt calculation regarding the existence of Christianity in the modern world. And he insisted that the binary, either-alive-or-dead prognosis for the church functioned as a matter of choice, the outcome resting in the hands of its most dedicated leaders.

Choice remained axiomatic to Schuller's entire orientation to the world. He postured himself toward action, and he sought in his ministry to convey an alignment for his audience that empowered them to act. In perhaps his most famous volume, *Tough Times Never Last, but Tough People Do!*, Schuller insisted, "this book will inspire you to take action to make a bold and daring move." Schuller assumed people would experience failure, perhaps repeatedly. And yet—"This book will get you started on the path to success once again."[2] Schuller embedded in his argument a sense that the necessity for action should be attributed not

---

1. Robert H. Schuller, *Your Church Has Real Possibilities!* (Glendale, CA: G/L Publications, 1974), 30.

2. Robert H. Schuller, *Tough Times Never Last, but Tough People Do!* (New York: Bantam Books, 1984), 9–10.

270 EPILOGUE

to the failure of the individual but to the inevitability of social change. People required inspiration, not because they had failed as individuals due to lack of effort but because fundamental shifts in society had created new anxieties and stressors.

Indeed, Schuller attributed the need to make bold actions for a specific reason: "an era has come to an end." In *Tough Times*, he described the broader context faced by his readers: "This book will inspire you to take action to make a bold and daring move; to make a creative transition, recognizing an era has come to an end. The factory will never reopen. The steam engines are never going to be manufactured again. Sometimes the cup has fallen. It is broken. 'All the king's horses and all the king's men couldn't put Humpty Dumpty together again.' Now you may need to absorb the spills and develop new skills. This book will get you started on the path to success once again."[3]

Schuller believed that broad societal changes were disrupting industries, displacing workers, and leaving them with nothing to depend on but themselves alone for survival—as seen in his speech to unemployed auto workers in Flint, Michigan. He sought to reach people he perceived as vulnerable to these newly changed circumstances, appealing to their initiative and inventiveness to forge for themselves a new future. Schuller, of course, harbored his own constant fear of failure—knowing that, the minister surely wrote these words as much for himself as the audience.

For Schuller, the Christian church remained similarly vulnerable to changed circumstances. The church, as a sort of industry itself, had been radically disrupted. Congregations closed, and pastors found themselves displaced. The typical "factory" of the American church would never reopen. The usual "steam engines" of spiritual formation would not be reignited again. New mechanisms for spiritual development would need to be fabricated. Schuller repeatedly told his fellow clergy that rather than lament their own disruption, pastors needed to reinvent themselves, learning new skills, crafting a new church with novel approaches capable of ministering in this transforming society. In an altered environment, pastors had the obligation to reach out to the people they sought to serve with different strategies. After all, people increasingly harbored a skep-

---

3. Schuller, *Tough Times Never Last*, 9–10.

THE IMPERATIVE OF CHURCH GROWTH   **271**

ticism that the church could speak to their circumstances. Pastors should recognize that they had experienced disruptions and, in turn, boost them with a God-inspired confidence to keep them moving forward.

Schuller consistently emphasized forward movement. For example, in *The Pastor's Church Growth Handbook*, the minister contributed the chapter "Three Characteristics of a Successful Pastor." First, he defined the pastor's role, which "very simply, is to lead—to think ahead, to plan for the future, to search for possibilities, to envision problems and dream up solutions, and then to communicate these possibilities and problem-solving ideas to the church decision-makers." Second, the "successful" pastor set "specific measurable goals." Once the pastor found assurance that a goal could be deemed "inspired by God," especially that the goal is "pacesetting" (meaning no other pastor is already meeting the needs established by this goal and that the objective will "bring glory to God"), then the next step was just "to get the job done." Ambition and risk—and the possibility of failure—for the pastors who followed Schuller's advice remained implicit. Nevertheless, he encouraged pastors, "you can be assured of exciting new challenges," and "the people whose problems will be solved by our goal will know that you are in God's business."[4]

By connecting pastors with the word "business"—which he did frequently—Schuller signaled his conviction that contemporary clergy needed to attune their leadership to the mechanisms of the market. As he stated explicitly, "Much as it may offend many leaders in the Christian church, the truth remains that the parish church is in the business of 'retailing religion.'"[5] Speaking of the day-to-day life of working congregants, Schuller over and over again urged pastors to orient their churches to be in sync with the broader culture. In any message or publication directed to church pastors, he stressed the need for continually reinventing aspects of ministry. If its leaders failed to engage in revised practices, drawing on the strategies of the most successful business enterprises of the day, then the church would evaporate into obsolescence.

4. Robert H. Schuller, "Three Characteristics of a Successful Pastor," in *The Pastor's Church Growth Handbook: America's Leading Authorities on Church Growth Share the Keys to Building a Dynamic Church*, ed. Win Arn (Pasadena, CA: Institute for American Church Growth, Church Growth Press, 1979), 92–94.

5. Schuller, *Your Church Has Real Possibilities!*, 18.

The Farm and the Church

Schuller's experience of being raised on the family farm in Iowa—the family business—had given him a sense of the planning and financing required for such an endeavor. Despite bearing the brunt of uncertain weather and pricing, Schuller came away grasping the depth of responsibility his father felt for taking care of his family and his need to be savvy in thinking toward the future. Indeed, successful farming demanded careful planning and crafty strategy in the face of uncertainty—be it catastrophic weather events or market volatility.

Yet the church did not immediately seem to be subject to market forces in the same way as did the family farm. For Schuller, the dynamics and insularity of growing up within a Dutch Reformed enclave insulated the church against most threats. The immigrant Dutch community of northwest Iowa sustained a strong church due to their deep ethnic commitments. They shared an intense loyalty to their congregations rooted in long-term tradition and a common religio-ethnic identity.[6] In that context of a powerful social cohesion that binds communities of overwhelmingly similar values and experiences (what sociologist Emile Durkheim termed "mechanical solidarity"),[7] strategic planning did not seem to apply to the local church. They could not fathom a future where their church would not exist. As long as their community persisted, so would their church. The church would surely endure because it functioned as the hub of the community.[8]

After encountering more cosmopolitan circumstances, Schuller adopted a more market-oriented perspective toward Christianity. He first

---

6. It should be noted that in 2017 the northwest corner of Iowa, with its numerous Dutch Reformed communities, received attention because of its outlier status as a "thriving" rural community in the United States. See Larissa MacFarquhar, "Where the Small-Town American Dream Lives On: As America's Rural Communities Stagnate, What Can We Learn from One That Hasn't?" *New Yorker*, November 6, 2017, https://tinyurl.com/4ny6fn45.

7. Emile Durkheim, *Division of Labor in Society* (New York: Free Press, 2014).

8. For more on the insular nature of Dutch Reformed social circles, see Mark T. Mulder, *Shades of White Flight: Evangelical Congregations and Urban Departure* (New Brunswick, NJ: Rutgers University Press, 2015).

realized the scope of the market when glimpsing non-Reformed congregations along the road as he passed through Iowa and Illinois on his way to Hope College. After seminary, moving to pastor a church outside of Chicago, and then on to Southern California, Schuller found himself removed from a richly traditioned church culture rooted in ethnic commitments. He began asking new questions. What happens when migrants like he and his wife move away from their ethnic enclaves? How do pastors create strong churches away from singular ethnic or historical ties? These questions prompted Schuller to reconsider every aspect of his church ministry.

At best, denominational monikers served as an initial step toward commitment. But even in his early ministry, Schuller could see that his Reformed church siblings, along with the Baptists, Methodists, Presbyterians, and others, possessed an openness to moving into different religious traditions. With the growth of the Sunbelt economy, rapid metropolitan expansion, and the ease of transportation allowing people to relocate into expanding suburbs for new job opportunities, new communities developed that did not depend on ethnic or even religious ties. Schuller recognized that the mass movements of a mass society initiated a new challenge for fostering meaningful church connections.

The notion of a church market is an abstraction. Yet, for Schuller it was not. When Schuller arrived in Orange County, he encountered a congested crossroads of religion. Lagging behind the enterprising work of other denominations, with few Reformed members to draw on, and no space available to rent, a persistent Schuller believed he could still work his way into a vital ministry. The minister surely navigated a cognitive dissonance wherein he maintained market convictions amid a profound belief that the church was a spiritual entity, a God-initiated and God-breathed endeavor, one fueled by the Holy Spirit but also able to unleash its power. Nevertheless, in his belief in leadership as a tangible activity that guided the building of churches, Schuller saw congregations as tied to undeniable sociological dynamics. Churches, like business and other human entities, required intentionality to persist. Doing so, the minister actively co-opted the workings of social structures and human behavior, like purchasing advertisements, coaxing guest choirs and speakers, dressing in a suit in the hot California sun, and consciously enacting profit-oriented business strategies of finance, building, and property development to draw in strangers—even if they chose to stay in the family car.

The "mission church" he felt called to establish in Garden Grove, California, would need to transcend ethnic and denominational loyalties. Despite occasional nods toward the RCA, Schuller did not constrain himself to denominational particularism and instead positioned his ministry as a player that could draw anyone from anywhere. In doing so, he assumed a mass of people who could potentially be attracted. He would place confidence not in the growth of families within his church but rather in the intentional attraction of migrants. He believed his church uniquely positioned itself to benefit from the expectation of a flow of people, a process in the twentieth century that included engaging advertising and marketing agencies as well as harnessing the ubiquity of highways and accessibility of private transportation. As Schuller noted, "I have a vast market of unchurched people to reach."[9] Effectively attracting the expanding population of the "unchurched" became the strategic pathway to the continued growth—and therefore survival—of his congregation.

A Market-Oriented Christianity

Schuller believed that American churches required new and extraordinary efforts to sustain their existence—just as his father saved the farm by harvesting corn during a drought just to plant it as seed the next season. He assessed his social environment and perceived that the monopoly of the sacred by Christian churches had begun to collapse. Schuller spent his life attempting to protect the sanctity of his church, and if it was to endure for posterity, radical measures needed to be implemented. In considering how to accomplish his pastoral ministry—from the goals he employed to the strategies he pursued—the minister drew from the cultural options he saw as available at the time.

His approach to church growth evidenced the market-oriented Christianity he embodied, a new kind of knowledge of changing cir-

9. Schuller, *Your Church Has Real Possibilities!*, 114.

THE IMPERATIVE OF CHURCH GROWTH **275**

cumstances that the minister applied to pastoral sensibilities. Schuller seemed to intuit that social change did not just disorient, it could also destroy, and that certain social structures—like the Christian church—required intervention if they were to persist: "Times change. You may have to change your whole corporate structure."[10] To accomplish that change, the minister borrowed heavily from the successful business strategies he witnessed in Southern California and beyond.

Indeed, rather than relying on ethnic or denominational ties, Schuller shifted in his pastoral ministry to appealing to the contemporary felt needs of suburban, newly arrived, economically-aspirational, and middle-class white families, creating charismatic connections based on their struggle to adapt to new circumstances in Southern California. The minister described the "unchurched" demographic that he anticipated: "These people are primarily business and professional people, a unique target market."[11] He came to believe that as cities and suburbs became migrant destinations, pastors needed to be more attentive to creating new bonds.

The expanding suburban landscape already featured churches of various sizes and styles. Church competition was rampant. With a mass market relocating across regions, making for an increasingly portable population, there came a new congregational challenge of appealing to increasingly fickle and highly mobile spiritual consumers. Schuller explained how he responded: "We directed our efforts toward them, assuming that they have needs in their lives that they would like the church to meet" (208).

By avoiding the particularism of a denomination, the minister augmented his church's competitive stance, which he deemed necessary to resist pressures that would prohibit it from growing—or even existing. His mission church would position itself to compete in a proliferating Christian marketplace of churches. As Schuller summarized, "we found

10. Schuller, *Tough Times*, 218.

11. Schuller, *Your Church Has a Fantastic Future! A Possibility Thinker's Guide to a Successful Church* (Ventura, CA: Regal Books, 1986), 208. Hereafter, page references from this work will be given in parentheses in the text.

that our target market of business and professional people wanted the church to blend traditional values and experiences with a contemporary attitude of openness and warmth" (210). In the enactment of his ecclesial strategy, Schuller's ministry accentuated both tangible and measurable aspects. He knew that in order to secure donors and giving members, the church needed to be perceived as enduring and stable: "We found that they [our target market] value land and building because of the stability and longevity they represented" (210). Therefore, buying land became necessary to establish the overall capacity for enacting the ministry in the contemporary world. The financing of such a ministry required a measurable quantification that could be demonstrated to lenders.

The capacity to measure attendance, giving, and land was vital to securing the capital necessary to expand the ministry further. Quantifying aspects of the church allowed for the creation of tangible goals with which to approach donors. Schuller once claimed: "All I have to do now is make a big, beautiful, successful and inspiring impression on all of these unchurched people in the county, and we'll build a great church for our Lord" (287). Those who recognized and valued the logic of the market perceived in these upwardly moving measures an assurance of progress that promised continual gain.

More fundamentally, the embrace of free-market capitalism as a spiritual virtue and the focus on the perceived therapeutic needs of members and potential attenders motivated the minister's priority to rebuild the church. The life and ministry of Robert Schuller in the latter half of the twentieth century was caught up in what economic historian Karl Polanyi described as "the Great Transformation," specifically, "the utopian endeavor of economic liberalism to set up a self-regulating market system."[12] Polanyi's notion of "great transformation" summarized a profound pattern of historical shifts from the later 1800s into the 1930s that moved human society from being able to control the market through customs and state authority to "the market" *itself* dictating the activity and structure of the rest of society—a sweeping reversal in power. Polanyi

---

12. Karl Polanyi, *The Great Transformation: The Political and Economic Origins of Our Time* (Boston: Beacon, 1957 [1944]), 29.

traced the reversal: "Instead of economy being embedded in social relations, social relations are embedded in the economic system."[13] The market became a force unto itself—and to be reckoned with. As a powerful social force, "the drive for a competitive market acquired the irresistible impetus of a process of Nature. For the self-regulating market was now believed to follow from the inexorable laws of Nature, and the unshackling of the market to be an ineluctable necessity."[14] The market system had become disembodied from society in the latter nineteenth century, forcing all human structures and relations to bend to its dictates.

The minister recognized intuitively that the American church found itself subject to the market system, and therefore that dynamic necessitated that church leaders participate in market processes. Schuller's underlying ministry philosophy rooted itself in conceiving of the church as participating in a market. And to do so successfully, churches would need to adopt market mechanisms to achieve the market goal of gain, that is, expansion, increase, and growth. In a sense, Schuller spent considerable energy detailing transferable, competitive market strategies that would apply to any context—since he assumed the emerging ubiquity of the market for churches in a suburbanizing United States.

In short, Robert H. Schuller redefined religious assumptions and practices and crafted a market-oriented Christianity. The minister believed that church leaders had no choice but to reckon with market dynamics. Yet, rather than be dismayed by such a realization, Schuller's participation in the church market carried an assumption that he could compete successfully. In encouraging other ministers, Schuller consistently conveyed an optimism (possibility thinking, a theology of self-esteem) that they could simultaneously control their operations while successfully participating in this rapidly shifting market. As organizations, churches did not simply float through culture, unmoored by material conditions. They participated in culture, and church leaders could make bold decisions to vary and adapt their approach to ministry and structure their actions with intention to affect the outcomes.

13. Polanyi, *The Great Transformation*, 57.
14. Polanyi, *The Great Transformation*, 57.

278   EPILOGUE

An Ecclesial Response to Rapid Social Change

Ultimately, Schuller's response in crafting a market-centered Christianity represented an ecclesial response to rapid social change. The minister rejected the assumption that churches possessed an immunity to social change and urged church leaders to adopt the mind-set of first accepting change and then planning to manage it.[15] The accelerated pace of social change demanded a new breed of pastors who would embrace new administrative systems and structures.

For Schuller, pastors should press their churches to move as fast as or faster than the culture, deploying resources to outpace their potential obsolescence. This represented the minister's metaphorical tornado. Encountering this whirlwind of societal change, Schuller concerned him-

---

15. Interestingly, Hartmut Rosa (*Resonance: A Sociology of Our Relationship to the World* [New York: Polity, 2019], 413) himself believed that the Christian Scriptures and church calendar have "all proved to be largely resistant to imperatives of innovation, acceleration, or escalation," adding that religious belief and practice were "precisely not dynamic, indeed possibly not even capable of dynamization." Thus, "traditional religions, at least in their Judeo-Christian and Islamic forms, thus appear to at least also—if not primarily—function as a potentially indispensable *antithesis* of the escalatory and dynamizing logic of modernity." Rosa specifically speaks of the Catholic Church as "precisely not dynamically stabilized . . . if not downright static." He believed "that innovation, acceleration, and growth are not inherent structural requirements and thus are not absolutely necessary to reproduce and stabilize the church as an institution." However, if his example of Christian religion essentially relies on examples of the Roman Catholic Church or fundamentalist strains of Islam, he radically oversimplifies in order to forward his argument. Of course, Rosa never met Robert Schuller, and he obviously missed out on contemporary understandings of the sociology of religion, especially those reflecting the "new paradigm" as documented by R. Stephen Warner ("Work in Progress toward a New Paradigm for the Sociological Study of Religion in the United States," *American Journal of Sociology* 98, no. 5 [1993]: 1044–93). See also Courtney Bender, *The New Metaphysicals: Spirituality and the American Religious Imagination* (Chicago: University of Chicago Press, 2010); Gerardo Martí, *A Mosaic of Believers: Diversity and Innovation in a Multiethnic Church* (Bloomington: Indiana University Press, 2005); Gerardo Martí and Gladys Ganiel, *The Deconstructed Church: Understanding Emerging Christianity* (New York: Oxford University Press, 2014).

self with designing a new approach to ministry that would at least allow American Christianity a chance to withstand the gale.

Sociologist Hartmut Rosa theoretically explained the social change the minister detected and sought to manage when he argued that "the experience of modernization is an experience of acceleration."[16] Schuller instinctively grasped Rosa's analysis of modernity in guiding his ministry by taking seriously that there is a temporal structure to society—and made more acute by the fact that he ministered in an era where religion as a traditional mooring found itself undermined, viscerally upending received forms of traditional and religiously sanctioned forms of life.[17] In this new societal environment, the challenge of sustaining the church's institutional importance proved formidable.

In order to maintain a prospect of surviving, let alone thriving, churches and pastors needed to practice active management, an ongoing exercise of intentional organizational leadership, since "growth, acceleration, and innovation are not self-executing or self-guiding processes."[18] Contemporary clergy, then, must embrace "flexibility, agility, multitasking, life-long education, and the continual need for improvement"—all the virtues promoted for achieving success in a market society.[19] The drive for growth and the demand for innovation manifested as a distinctive religious consequence of modernity.

The Crystal Cathedral and its attendant ministries actualized Schuller's convictions about how churches should respond to the tides of social change. The minister followed his own advice, as he wrote in *Your Church Has Real Possibilities!*, "Learn to accommodate. Prepare to compromise. Plan to adjust. A different style, a new policy, a change in tradition—all are opportunities to grow."[20] According to Schuller, clergy could no longer rest on the assumption of orthodox theological knowledge. Instead, they needed to enact a new type of understanding embedded in a new

16. Hartmut Rosa, *Social Acceleration: A New Theory of Modernity* (New York: Columbia University Press, 2013), 21.

17. Rosa, *Resonance*, 408.

18. Rosa, *Resonance*, 426.

19. Filip Vostal, "Towards a Social Theory of Acceleration: Time, Modernity, Critique," *Revue Européenne des Sciences Sociales* 2 (2014): 235-49, here 239.

20. Schuller, *Tough Times*, 122.

organizational style that they would need to "constantly update."[21] The minister understood intuitively that ensuring a future for the church necessitated "growth, acceleration, an increasing innovation in order to maintain and reproduce its structure."[22]

The principles that drove Schuller were the same as those that drove societal structures as a whole, described by Rosa as "the triad of growth, acceleration, and innovation, i.e., by the pressure to grow, to become faster, and to be capable of changing."[23] With the accelerated pace of change being unavoidable, the temporal perspective hovered as the only filter of evaluation, a sense that an expiration date looms for even the most cherished beliefs and practices. Rosa described the felt desperation instigated by leaders like Schuller experiencing acceleration: "*we must run ever faster in order to maintain our place in the world.*"[24] In the end, the minister not only participated in shaping his church to dynamically adjust to an accelerated pace of change but also enabled pastors and churches to learn his techniques to mimic the market, fostering and institutionalizing an ecclesiology he believed to be best suited to an accelerating—and simultaneously secularizing—society.

A focus on the pace of change translated into an ecclesiology of working quickly and decisively—ministerial response times needed to be nimble since situations change fast and the amount of time to act becomes ever shorter.[25] Indeed, according to Rosa's chronology, the contemporary surge of acceleration started in the 1970s coincided with the priority brought to Schuller's own expansion of the ministry: building projects, creating the Leadership Institute, and broadcasting *Hour of Power*. In fact, the larger the congregation, the more intense the demand to relate to broader dynamics of the social structure, making megachurches particularly vulnerable to larger socio-structural developments.

With the need to be actively responsive, the minister believed that denominations had become albatrosses—too slow and too deliberative.

21. Rosa, *Resonance*, 415.
22. Rosa, *Resonance*, 402.
23. Rosa, *Resonance*, 407.
24. Rosa, *Resonance*, 415.
25. Rosa, *Social Acceleration*, 71.

"They dictate policy," Schuller complained. "Directives are sent down to the churches and all are expected to carry out the orders. A pastor or a church that resists is seen as noncooperative."[26] Better to become "community churches," as explicitly suggested by Schuller. The pace of change exceeded the capacity for denominational leaders to pursue consensus through lengthy dialogue—and required decisive action now. The back-and-forth deliberation, calibrating experience with theology and assessing orthodoxy and preferences, proved to be ill-suited in Schuller's estimation to the new atmosphere of acceleration and hindered processes leading to growth.

The times demanded authoritative, guiding head pastors. With no time for deliberation, executive action proved indispensable, modeled on the nimble ability seen among successful business entrepreneurs. He constantly prodded pastors to act decisively: "I must often advise pastors. 'You take command. You have the freedom to sell that property! Release yourselves from bondage! Break loose from the chains that bind you. Break forth into the freedom of dynamic leadership!'"[27]

For the church to survive, in Schuller's mind, it must relentlessly expand in order just to maintain pace with other escalations characteristic of the time.[28] To alleviate ubiquitous anxiety about the future, pastors needed to take the initiative to lead, acting to make change more manageable, installing deliberate measurement and rational calculations to allow operations to be more predictable.[29] In Rosa's words, church leaders must "develop resources, open markets, activate social and psychological potentials, enhance technological capabilities, deepen knowledge bases, improve possibilities of control, and so on."[30] Indeed, making the world controllable is a major driving force of modernity.[31] New performance criteria are cultivated, like sales figures and numbers of publications, which in church life translate into attendance, audience share, buildings, and budget.

26. Schuller, *Your Church Has a Fantastic Future!*, 342–43.
27. Schuller, *Your Church Has Real Possibilities!*, 58.
28. Hartmut Rosa, *The Uncontrollability of the World* (New York: Polity, 2020), 8.
29. Rosa, *Uncontrollability of the World*, 15, 39.
30. Rosa, *Uncontrollability of the World*, 10.
31. Rosa, *Uncontrollability of the World*, 3, 4.

282 EPILOGUE

Considered as a whole, the minister's religious project of congregational growth involved a hastening in response to the accelerating velocity of social change and constant innovation. Pastors could no longer rely on generations of preserved theological knowledge that have been handed down but must now by guided by a new "logic of novelty."[32] Leaders like Schuller who demonstrate agility, quickness, and media competence become the authorities on how to manage institutions by moving ahead of the speed curve. They win legitimacy by being viewed as leaders who capture and tame change in service of their churches, becoming exemplars for others.[33]

Rapid Change and the Need for Human Connection

Schuller's diagnosis of the modern world also led to his pastoral approach to addressing the needs of people, as found in his possibility thinking and theology of self-esteem. For him, church growth depended on effective outreach based on meeting felt human needs. Indeed, he emphatically stated, "The most important question facing the church is: 'What are the deepest needs felt by human beings?'"[34] He styled himself as a mass psychologist, so his understanding of those needs emerged from distinctly contemporary ills—what Rosa described as "crises of resonance."[35]

For Rosa, people today yearn for and pursue "resonance," meaning an experiential connection with others interpersonally, people as a whole community, nature as part of the world, and even a spiritual connection to God—all of which have been deeply challenged by the dissonances that manifest from societal acceleration. Similarly, Schuller intuited that the rapid social change resulted in profound alienation, which could only be resolved, however temporarily, with experiences of embodied connections—social, experiential, spiritual—that produced a satisfying

32. Klaus Dörre, Stephan Lessenich, and Hartmut Rosa, *Sociology, Capitalism, Critique* (London: Verso, 2015), 284.

33. For instance, see the ministry of pastor Erwin McManus as described in Martí, *A Mosaic of Believers*.

34. Robert H. Schuller, *Self-Esteem: The New Reformation* (Waco, TX: Word, 1982), 13.

35. Rosa, *Resonance*, 430.

resonance. Resonance, though essential, tended to prove elusive. In his pastoral ministry, Schuller strove to craft messages and create environments that would dependably stimulate a connection to God as well as to family, friends, community—even the impressive church campus and its multipurpose buildings served these ends.

For Schuller, his church effectively solved the modern crises of resonance. While Rosa believed resonance could be accomplished through reading, playing sports, listening to concert music, or walking in the outdoors, Schuller clearly believed the experience of church—liturgy, community, and preaching—offered the richest route to resonance.[36] The minister assumed that the church building and the grounds of the campus allowed for a person to have reliable encounters and generate repeatable experiences. Impressive church architecture and grounds aligned with on-campus sponsorship of the arts and musical events (often celebrity-driven). Deeper connections with other people would be fulfilled not only through family and fellowship via affinity groups but also through productive and purposeful employment, for example, of Christian ethics and meaningful meeting of needs exercised in an assumed cooperative market of business activity: "Would this be a great thing for God? Would it be a great thing for Jesus Christ? Would it be a great thing for our community? Would it help a lot of human beings? Would it solve a lot of human problems? Is anybody else doing the job right?"[37]

Schuller consistently filtered "the good life" through his ecclesiology. For the minister, the buildings themselves created ongoing opportunities for resonance with nature and art, drawing more people and more giving, which necessitated even more space and more buildings. Schuller's impetus to design a "glass church"—what became the Crystal Cathedral—did not simply harken back to the years spent worshiping at

---

36. On the emotionality of church experience, see Gerardo Martí, *Hollywood Faith: Holiness, Prosperity, and Ambition in a Los Angeles Church* (New Brunswick, NJ: Rutgers University Press, 2008); Gerardo Martí, "Maranatha (O LORD, Come): The Power-Surrender Dynamic of Pentecostal Worship," *Liturgy* 33, no. 3 (2018): 20–28; James K. Wellman, Katie Elaine Corcoran, and Kate J. Stockly, *High on God: How the Megachurch Won the Heart of America* (New York: Oxford University Press, 2020).

37. Schuller, *Your Church Has Real Possibilities!*, 75.

a drive-in theater, but represented an architectural choice to embrace *biorealism*, prompting a connection to the cosmos as a whole and achieving a more direct access to God's goodness and presence in the world. Schuller developed the church campus around the celebration of sculptures and pleasures of water features. The style of the buildings themselves would replicate a magnificence similar to the cathedrals of Europe. The glass church as a physical space, open to the sky, connected with the natural elements in an attempt to produce resonance in the ministry every week.

Most importantly, the most central essential experience of resonance for the minister—connecting to the ultimate reality of God—would be achieved in worship: inspiration from preaching, congregational singing, and spiritual encouragement through Bible reflection and affirming prayer. In services, bringing in celebrity guests, who tingled with the charisma of having overcome spectacular personal circumstances or achieved great successes, was an attempt to predictably produce resonance in the ministry every week. Doing so in a predictable manner would draw more people. The success of bringing Norman Vincent Peale to his pulpit became the prime example. Broadening the experience via televised services, the church could meet the needs of millions around the world.

By integrating these varied initiatives, Schuller created a template for pastors to meet the challenge of acceleration through the ongoing exercise of provoking resonance. Schuller and other church-growth pastors acknowledged that their largely suburban members were subject to the disorienting pace of social change and the many ills associated with it, especially the difficulty of mastering one's own fate.[38] For Schuller, the shifting foundations merited pastoral response since it was literally impossible for people to stand aside and not be affected by these changes.[39] He modeled for other church-growth pastors how to lead their churches to be consonant with the rapid pace of social change and how to preach

---

38. See Isaac Ariail Reed, "Hartmut Rosa's Project for Critical Theory," *Thesis Eleven* 13, no. 1 (2016): 122–29, doi: 10.1177/0725513616638464.

39. See Vostal, "Towards a Social Theory of Acceleration: Time, Modernity, Critique."

THE IMPERATIVE OF CHURCH GROWTH **285**

messages that addressed the consequences of vicissitudes endured by their members. He believed that anxiety, stress, and personal discontent had increased—remember his 1987 book *The Be (Happy) Attitudes*—because he surmised these as central symptoms of modernity.[40] Through his theology of self-esteem and focus on possibility thinking, Schuller prioritized a concern for individual threat to self-esteem and the incapacity to see possibilities amid a shifting social landscape. With possibility thinking in particular, the minister sought to resource his audiences to confront the challenge to keep open promising futures.

More specifically, Schuller's possibility thinking spoke to the manner in which people sought to find ways to direct their own selves. His grasp of pastoring individuals accepted that the modern self could be made accessible as a manageable entity. Characterizing effective self-management as "leadership," Schuller wrote, "Leadership is willing to face the awareness that I can—and probably must—make personal decisions, and making a decision is choosing the possibility, selecting an option! What it all amounts to is: Leadership is the determination that I am going to be an individual, not just a drop in the bucket. Not just a part of a collection, but a person! Not just a puppet, but a person."[41]

Freedom resided at the root of his possibility thinking, offering assurance that every person could achieve and act willfully to succeed at home, work, and marketplace with the right attitude: "You can accomplish anything you imagine."[42] Schuller seemed willing to acknowledge that "autonomy, then, comes to mean the *power, the freedom and the security to shape and build one's life*."[43] As Rosa suggested, "we experience self-efficacy not as dialogic attainment, but primarily as a control and management technique."[44]

Most crucially, in a boost to self-esteem, Schuller advocated that the self can be managed to fit the needs of the market. Through myriad stories and exemplars, the minister repeatedly advised that by attuning one-

40. Robert H. Schuller, *The Be (Happy) Attitudes: 8 Positive Attitudes That Can Transform Your Life* (New York: Bantam Books, 1987).

41. Schuller, *Your Church Has a Fantastic Future!*, 339.

42. Schuller, *Your Church Has a Fantastic Future!*, 342.

43. Dörre, Lessenich, and Rosa, *Sociology, Capitalism, Critique*, 87.

44. Rosa, *Resonance*, 430.

self to the market, it became possible "to create employment opportunities" for oneself.[45] Timing remained important: "Pace yourself. Now you wait. Now you move. Now you race! Now you rest. Now you leap! Now you walk slowly. Possibility thinkers don't quit—they change their pace to win the race."[46] And willingness to change offered a key: "Repentance means to change directions—set new goals and establish new standards. Pick up on God's dream for your life!"[47] As Schuller counseled, "Decisions must never be based on ego needs. They must be based on human needs and market pressures that transcend your own desires. Ask the *market* what needs are undeveloped."[48]

Even with this advice, Schuller seemed to understand the illusory nature of complete satisfaction. Both he and Arvella advocated for a strong family life as a counterpoint to the unrelenting pace of competition, given that the pressures of accelerating social change wreaked havoc on family relationships. As Rosa described, "the imperatives of escalation, which constantly demand more efficient development of potential, higher productivity, comprehensive quality control, and speedier fulfillment of promises of residence, ceaselessly collide with the temporal and dispositional demands of resident relationships."[49]

The task of self-mastery brought its own consequences. Although "autonomy and authenticity represent the cornerstones of the modern conception of a successful life,"[50] the self-mastery required to do so inhibited our capacity for relationships. The cultivation of the self became a "game" that revolved around "competition and recognition," which evolved into "an endless performative struggle."[51] The demands of the market catalyzed a "compulsion to prove oneself over and over," since "there is no certainty that status, once achieved, will be maintained."[52]

45. Schuller, *Tough Times*, 40.
46. Robert H. Schuller, *Tough-Minded Faith for Tender-Hearted People* (Nashville: Nelson, 1983), 139.
47. Schuller, *Tough-Minded Faith*, 251.
48. Schuller, *Tough Times*, 118, 193.
49. Rosa, *Resonance*, 431.
50. Dörre, Lessenich, and Rosa, *Sociology, Capitalism, Critique*, 74.
51. Dörre, Lessenich, and Rosa, *Sociology, Capitalism, Critique*, 85.
52. Dörre, Lessenich, and Rosa, *Sociology, Capitalism, Critique*, 87.

Indeed, Schuller never explicitly promised people that any achieved status would be permanent or that happiness would remain constant. The minister only persistently advocated for one control in what he viewed as permanently unsettled times: one's own attitude. Even so, whether in sermons or writings, the end point always rested in a total trust in God. In *The Be (Happy) Attitudes*, after exhorting for pages and pages a fundamental change in mind-set, Schuller recognized that disastrous consequences still loomed, and that tragedy could still strike. On the final page, the minister advocated for a simple, evangelistic faith, achieved through a simple prayer: "Jesus, I need a friend as I journey through life. Right now I'm asking You to be my best friend and to keep the Be-Happy Attitudes flowing through my mind. Amen."[53]

The Sustainability of Ecclesial Escalation

To cope with acceleration, Schuller seemed to conclude that the stabilization of any church required it to be "dynamic, that is, it needs progressive growth, acceleration, and innovation just to reproduce its social structure and to maintain its status quo."[54] At the same time, he found that acceleration had become almost tyrannical as the rate of cultural obsolescence increased. Church leaders like Schuller pursued church growth out of a desire for greater stability, to overcome the inertia of death and decline. But in his pursuit of growth, Schuller encountered the limit of continual escalation, finding (in Rosa's words) that "the more innovative we are and the faster we get, the more difficult it will be next year to exceed this year's achievements and maintain these rates of escalation."[55] The rapid pace in pursuit of stability accentuated a new kind of precariousness in just "keeping up."

53. Schuller, *The Be (Happy) Attitudes*, 231.
54. Bjørn Schiermer, "Acceleration and Resonance: An Interview with Hartmut Rosa," *Acta Sociologica* 25, no. 3 (2020), https://tinyurl.com/2esawaat; see also Rosa, *Resonance*, 406; Dörre, Lessenich, and Rosa, *Sociology, Capitalism, Critique*, 283, 304; Rosa, *Uncontrollability of the World*, 8.
On "dynamic stabilization," see Dörre, Lessenich, and Rosa, *Sociology, Capitalism, Critique*, 282–83.
55. Rosa, *Resonance*, 407.

Moreover, churches perceived as successful saw their problems compounded—their relative ascendancy invited competition. Indeed, Schuller's ministry revealed how a market-oriented Christianity in pursuit of growth made competition normative for clergy. As seen throughout his ministry, Schuller did not operate only in a marketplace for potential individual members. He also participated in a broader ecosystem of other churches and pastors observing his movements. It may be surprising to see how growing churches necessitates competition as an organizing principle. In fact, Rosa clarified that competition itself is based "on the idea of *outperforming* one's competitors and thus on the idea of *escalation*."[56] The ecclesial equivalent of "keeping up with the Joneses" made further quickening a requirement of matching—if not exceeding—the ministry now perceived to be necessitated by the surrounding culture. Ironically, despite the aim to achieve control over the fate of the church, the resulting competition generated "constant turmoil and insecurity."[57]

Competition among growth-oriented pastors offered little to encourage camaraderie or collective efforts, thus adding to a sense of independence and isolation. The desire for autonomy among church-growth practitioners like Schuller drew from a commitment to ensuring their churches not depend on other bodies, existed on their own, and retained an ability to consummate their own decisions. Certainly, Schuller believed that as a pastor he had freedom to guide the operations of his own congregation. The concern of Schuller and his wife, Arvella, for their children to succeed them in the family ministry evidenced their desire for freedom and the certainty of their own autonomy. Schuller asserted his freedom so regularly that his denomination frequently questioned his commitment. He also moved away from accountability structures like the National Religious Broadcasters. He exercised his own freedom even over his own board, strategizing to secure greater leverage for his own sense of what the future demanded.

The ultimate foundering of the Crystal Cathedral can be traced to the constant effort to maintain pace with an ever-accelerating culture. A dynamically stabilized congregation—one that continually accommodates

56. Rosa, *Resonance*, 418.
57. Rosa, *Resonance*, 418.

THE IMPERATIVE OF CHURCH GROWTH   **289**

strategic changes while both absorbing growth and creating capacity for even more growth—required more and more effort to operate, with tangible strains increasing every year.[58] As Rosa noted, "the faster, the more innovative, and the more dynamic we already are, the more energy, power, and effort it takes to grow, accelerate, and increase innovation rates."[59] Schuller himself reported, "The more successful we became, the more problems I had."[60] Even maintenance of the status quo required intensification such that the practices of acceleration became increasingly difficult to sustain. Seen via Schuller's own experience, these intensified efforts become untenable. Once adopted, the imperative of acceleration becomes tyrannical—the velocity of change intensifies, eventually outstripping the possibility to sustain.[61]

The pressures of growth in an atmosphere of acceleration intensified Schuller's innovation and competition; moreover, these same pressures also "induced compulsions accompanying them."[62] Schuller fell victim to these compulsions, which appeared unavoidable given that escalation is required just to keep an institution's status quo viable.[63] The minister fell into a restless cycle, summarized by Rosa in the sentiment that "next year we will have to be a little faster, more efficient, more innovative, better, if we want to maintain our place in the world—and the year after that, the bar will be set a little bit higher still."[64] Schuller's never-ending search for growth and expansion vividly manifested this inclination. Rosa himself did not believe that ongoing innovation and acceleration were sustainable, and that control was elusive, assuming that such action would inevitably exhaust all energy and possibility under constraints of material resources of time and physical energy. Success did not allow

---

58. Rosa, *Resonance*, 425. See also Mark T. Mulder and Gerardo Martí, *The Glass Church: Robert H. Schuller, the Crystal Cathedral, and the Strain of Megachurch Ministry* (New Brunswick, NJ: Rutgers University Press, 2020).

59. Dörre, Lessenich, and Rosa, *Sociology, Capitalism, Critique*, 286.

60. Schuller, *Tough Times*, 61.

61. Dörre, Lessenich, and Rosa, *Sociology, Capitalism, Critique*, 287.

62. Dörre, Lessenich, and Rosa, *Sociology, Capitalism, Critique*, 90.

63. Rosa, *Resonance*, 407. Two pages later, Rosa described this scenario: "A compulsion to escalate is necessary to maintain the systemic status quo."

64. Rosa, *Resonance*, 407.

290 EPILOGUE

for a resting point. Nevertheless, Schuller persisted—until the enterprise could no longer sustain itself.

The Church Must Grow or Perish

Raised in the vicissitudes of agricultural Iowa, Schuller understood what lacking control meant. One dry season or one stormy evening changed the fortunes of family farms. As a minister he would create bulwarks to protect his ministry from the maelstrom of social change that threatened to leave the church behind. Utilizing the tools of organizations successful in market competition, Schuller attempted to provoke connection to others and to God in order to stimulate the church growth that would draw people, meet their psychological needs, and sustain Christianity in the United States for the decades to come.

As a religious leader, Schuller perceived the storm clouds of growing secularity. As the cultural dominance of Christianity waned in an accelerating society, the minister instinctively sought to maintain resonance through a business model of growth. After revealing a scale model of the anticipated Crystal Cathedral on *The Phil Donahue Show*, Schuller described to the audience his strategy for relevance: "The only way to handle competition is to compete against yourself. I tell people, 'do a little better job next year than what you did this year. And keep that going and in 20 years, you'll be some place.'"[65] For Schuller, Christianity should not recede into a refuge; it should anticipate fierce winds and constantly build symbols, signs, and structures that attested to a faith that remained relevant even as society changed.

Adapting to the logic of the unrelenting market, though, proved too exhausting. In a demoralizing conclusion, the ministry folded in on itself, unable to maintain the pace, collapsing in the face of overextension, unstable economic markets, and a fickle audience. Schuller left little to chance and orchestrated every possible detail of ministry—never allow-

---

65. "Dr. Robert Schuller Interviewed on the Donahue Show," 1976, transcript, folder "Crystal Cathedral Robert H. Schuller—Interviews, 1976," box 26, Robert H. Schuller Collection (HCASC), 37.

ing for a moment of stasis for his church. At the end, the delicate balance proved too precarious. The minister found that the constant effort to stabilize his market-oriented Christianity lost its ability to maintain any sustainable equilibrium. In seeking growth, his immediate ministry ultimately perished—although the final fate of the Christian church at large remains to be seen.

A NOTE ON SOURCES

Robert H. Schuller realized during a high school play performance that he actually loved drama and the attention it garnered. Thereafter, he lived a great deal of his adult ministry life in the public eye, constantly producing different forms of content. For us as researchers, that meant a lot of source material: dozens of books, recordings from the Leadership Institute, VHS tapes of four decades of *Hour of Power* episodes (some of which can be viewed on YouTube), op-eds, and a range of documents created during fifty-five years of professional ministry. In short, a lot of words. But he also left behind artifacts that ranged from architectural edifices to sculptures to fund-raising tchotchkes and trinkets. In addition, Schuller, when he passed away in 2015, left behind a lot of individuals whom he had impacted—and who expressed enthusiasm for discussing the minister. In our effort to better understand how Robert Schuller exemplified his era of American Christianity, we attempted to plumb every possible depth—recorded words, meaningful objects, and the people who knew him.

Beyond examining the forty linear feet of material on Schuller and the Crystal Cathedral at the Hope College Archives and Special Collections, we spent time in the Garden Grove Public Library and the Shepherd's Grove Church archives in Newport Beach, California, and managed to access the papers of scholars and journalists who had followed the minister closely for years—those of Dennis Voskuil (author of the first significant study of Schuller's theology) and Ronald Keener (longtime editor of *Church Executive* magazine). Both of these men demonstrated signifi-

294   A NOTE ON SOURCES

cant generosity opening to us their personal papers. Voskuil even shared a three-hour recording of Schuller working with him meticulously through his galleys for what would become *Mountains into Goldmines: Robert Schuller and the Gospel of Success* (also, coincidentally, published by Eerdmans). Schuller initially disliked what Voskuil had written, assuming that he had been misunderstood yet again. We also gained access to the galleys themselves and saw Schuller's personal edits. Keener, for his part, had a longtime interest in the Cathedral and Schuller because of its stature within American Christianity. By the time of the collapse of the ministry, Keener had developed discreet correspondence with co-pastors at the Cathedral—he shared many emails with us in which they conveyed their insiders' knowledge.

We also secured archival papers from both New Brunswick Theological Seminary (a Reformed Church in America seminary) and the University of Notre Dame (for the Kenneth Woodward correspondence with Schuller). The array of archives to which we gained entrée included personal correspondence (ranging from Johnny Carson to Norman Vincent Peale to Jesse Jackson), internal memoranda, and meeting minutes. In addition to these archival papers, we also utilized books and articles written about Schuller in particular, the church growth movement, and the social and demographic changes that catalyzed so much religious energy and inventiveness in Southern California in the latter half of the twentieth century. Schuller's own biography, of course, offered us a map onto which we could plot our own analysis and assessment of the minister's life. Three biographies—written by Schuller's own daughter, son-in-law, and longtime loyal assistant (and his assistant's wife)—helped flesh out narrative and further establish reliability.

In addition to written words, we benefited from so many who knew Schuller and wanted to have conversations with us (totaling almost forty semistructured interviews). We conducted interviews in person from the Midwest to California (and in the latter, as far north as Pasadena and as far south as Laguna Beach). In rare instances, on-site interviews proved unfeasible and we had conversations via the telephone or Zoom. These rich conversations form the backbone of the book—though most acknowledged that Schuller left behind a somewhat mixed legacy, the warmth and fondness for the minister—and Arvella—remained consistent. Our interviewees expressed delight in discussing the heyday of the ministry, but also willingly shared insights and anecdotes as the ministry struggled in the decade 2000–2009. We have identified the public figures we interviewed. However, for friends, parishioners, and fellow ministry leaders, we followed our disciplinary practice of confidentiality—protecting the identity of interviewees to allow for more fulsome conversations.

In terms of artifacts, we made use of digital recordings of *Hour of Power* and A&E's episode of *Biography* on Schuller. We also had the opportunity to visit Orange County numerous times, spending time on the church grounds—touring the facilities, viewing the statuary, hearing the fountains, paying respects in the cemetery. In fact, Kymmberly Binnquist, senior property manager for the campus, guided Mulder on an insightful tour where she explained the transformation of the Crystal Cathedral into Christ Cathedral. Martí had personally experienced different iterations of the campus, having grown up in Garden Grove, with continued occasions with family still living there to see and learn about recent developments. Of course, much of the time, we found ourselves simply strolling the sprawling campus of the now–Christ Cathedral. In one instance, worshipers at a Spanish-language Sunday afternoon Mass spilled out of the Neutra-designed hybrid sanctuary in early January while, at the same time, a Vietnamese American group of Youth for Christ gathered on the lawn. In another case, we were afforded a guided tour of the entire campus as the diocese made a years-long remodel—including trips up the Tower of Hope to view Schuller's former office and the Chapel in the Sky. These visits also included worship services with the remnant Crystal Cathedral congregation after they had moved down the road to the former St. Callistus's after selling their facility to the Diocese of Orange. Mulder had the opportunity to join the congregation for the momentous 2,000th recording of the *Hour of Power*. That same day, Mulder presented early findings for what would become *The Glass Church* to an adult Sunday school group who had been longtime members of the Cathedral. Mulder also had the opportunity to visit Schuller's home area of northwest Iowa and his first church in Riverdale, Illinois (no longer an RCA congregation, it has become Ivanhoe Iglesia Renovacion Cristiana).

Finally, we found our theoretical filters significantly resourced by the thinking of Hartmut Rosa and Karl Polanyi. Their contributions regarding social acceleration and market society, respectively, helped us to interpret how Schuller functioned as an avatar of dominant religious orientation that has emerged over the last half of a century: a market-centered Christianity.

BIBLIOGRAPHY

Abrams, William. "'Possibility Thinking' and Shrewd Marketing Pay Off for a Preacher." *Wall Street Journal*, August 26, 1976.

Adams, Courtenay. "The Peak of Possibility Thinking: Robert H. Schuller's Crystal Cathedral in Orange County, California during the 1980s." Master's thesis, University of Calgary, 2012.

Ahlersmeyer, Thomas Robert. "The Rhetoric of Reformation—a Fantasy Theme Analysis of the Rhetorical Vision of Robert Harold Schuller." PhD diss., Bowling Green State University, 1989.

Ammerman, Nancy Tatom. *Congregation and Community*. New Brunswick, NJ: Rutgers University Press, 1996.

Andersen, Kurt. *Fantasyland: How America Went Haywire; A 500-Year History*. New York: Random House, 2017.

Anker, Roy. *Self-Help and Popular Religion in Modern American Culture: An Interpretive Guide*. Westport, CT: Greenwood, 1999.

Archer, John. *Architecture and Suburbia: From English Villa to American Dream House, 1690-2000*. Minneapolis: University of Minnesota Press, 2005.

Artigo, Robert W. *Neither Crystal nor Gold: The Transformation of the Crystal Cathedral into Christ Cathedral*. Lubbock, TX: Lighthouse Catholic Publishing, 2021.

Artman, Amy Collier. *The Miracle Lady: Kathryn Kuhlman and the Transformation of Charismatic Christianity*. Library of Religious Biography. Grand Rapids: Eerdmans, 2019.

298 BIBLIOGRAPHY

Associated Press. "Robert H. Schuller Has Minor Heart Attack." *New York Times*, December 14, 1997. https://tinyurl.com/3upxfz5u.

———. "Robertson: Sharon's Stroke Is Divine Punishment." *USA Today*, January 5, 2006. https://tinyurl.com/5j22yzsd.

Atwood, Donner. "The Local Church's Edge." *Church Herald*, March 7, 1980.

Balmer, Randall. *Evangelicalism in America*. Waco, TX: Baylor University Press, 2016.

———. "The Genius of Robert Schuller." *Valley News*, April 12, 2015. https://tinyurl.com/3ry8t4uc.

Barron, Jessica M., and Rhys H. Williams. *The Urban Church Imagined: Religion, Race, and Authenticity in the City*. New York: New York University Press, 2017.

Bean, Lydia. *The Politics of Evangelical Identity: Local Churches and Partisan Divides in the United States and Canada*. Princeton: Princeton University Press, 2014.

Beardslee, John, III. "Who's against Communism?" *Church Herald*, April 20, 1962.

Beaty, Katelyn. *Celebrities for Jesus: How Personas, Platforms, and Profits Are Hurting the Church*. Grand Rapids: Brazos, 2022.

Benes, Louis H. "Community or Reformed Churches." *Church Herald*, November 10, 1950.

———. "New Hope for the Church." *Church Herald*, April 16, 1971, 6–8, 22.

Bharath, Deepa. "Chapman Increases Offer to Buy Crystal Cathedral." *Orange County Register*, November 2, 2011. https://tinyurl.com/26sexfhd.

———. "Crystal Cathedral Asks Vendors for Forgiveness." *Orange County Register*, April 10, 2010. https://tinyurl.com/nxh4kh6j.

———. "Crystal Cathedral Cancels 'Glory of Easter.'" *Orange County Register*, January 29, 2010. https://tinyurl.com/3enbwhau.

———. "Crystal Cathedral Choir Asked to Sign Anti-Gay Covenant." *Orange County Register*, March 16, 2011. https://tinyurl.com/3wu6t5ps.

———. "Crystal Cathedral Members Launch Petition Drive." *Orange County Register*, July 18, 2011. https://tinyurl.com/wy9yvfkp.

———. "Crystal Cathedral to Be Sold to Pay Millions in Debt." *Orange County Register*, May 27, 2011. https://tinyurl.com/f2629zzh.

———. "Crystal Cathedral Was an Icon of Tradition." *Orange County Register*, October 24, 2011. https://tinyurl.com/3h4taahn.

———. "Diocese Increases Offer for Crystal Cathedral to $55.4 Million." *Orange County Register*, November 10, 2011. https://tinyurl.com/mm9ju58s.

———. "Family Dynamics at Heart of Schuller Resignation." *Orange County Register*, December 16, 2008. https://tinyurl.com/38ydmvpt.

———. "Food Request for Rev. Schuller's Wife Sparks Outrage." *Orange County Register*, November 4, 2011. https://tinyurl.com/t5m6svvu.

———. "Former Crystal Cathedral Leader Robert H. Schuller in Critical Condition, His Family Says." *Orange County Register*, April 1, 2015. https://tinyurl.com/ycxv5pyx.

———. "Future of Crystal Cathedral Uncertain." *Orange County Register*, November 18, 2011. https://tinyurl.com/3m6mxx92.

———. "It's a New Time." *Orange County Register*, October 10, 2014. https://www.ocregister.com/2014/10/10/its-a-new-time/.

———. "Lawsuit: Schullers Gained as Crystal Cathedral Lost." *Orange County Register*, October 6, 2011. https://tinyurl.com/mhuc62b6.

———. "Pianist Williams: Schuller Kids Spoiled Crystal Cathedral." *Orange County Register*, June, 17, 2010. https://tinyurl.com/mufhb4zy.

———. "Rifts, Debt Tear at Crystal Cathedral." *Orange County Register*, October 24, 2010. https://tinyurl.com/mrx5j4dx.

———. "Schuller Sr. Speaks Out against Crystal Cathedral Anti-Gay Covenant." *Orange County Register*, March 17, 2011. https://tinyurl.com/5n6nn9sb.

———. "Vietnamese Shrine in Cathedral Plans." *Orange County Register*, December 8, 2016. https://tinyurl.com/3h2u3pab.

Bharath, Deepa, and Ronald Campbell. "Chapman's Offer Heats Up Crystal Cathedral Bankruptcy." *Orange County Register*, July 6, 2011. https://tinyurl.com/yt7ebwju.

———. "Crystal Cathedral Plan: Lease Its Way Out of Debt." *Orange County Register*, May 27, 2011. https://tinyurl.com/3cfaaxdw.

Bharath, Deepa, and Erika I. Ritchie. "Saddleback Takes Control of Crystal Cathedral Retreat." *Orange County Register*, May 12, 2010. https://tinyurl.com/2p9ysrz3.

Billingsley, Lloyd. "A Crystal Cathedral Spectacular: Christmas Pageant Is Reputed to Be the Country's Largest." *Christianity Today*, January 22, 1982.

———. "The Gospel according to Robert Schuller." *Eternity*, March 1983.

BIBLIOGRAPHY

Biography: Robert Schuller. A&E, 1998. https://www.youtube.com/watch ?v=U4nYEf8F-9g.

Bird, Warren. "How Robert H. Schuller Shaped Your Ministry." *Leadership Network*, April 2, 2015.

Blumhofer, Edith L. *Aimee Semple McPherson: Everybody's Sister*. Library of Religious Biography. Grand Rapids: Eerdmans, 1993.

Bottles, Scott L. *Los Angeles and the Automobile: The Making of the Modern City*. Berkeley: University of California Press, 1987.

Bowler, Kate. *Blessed: A History of the American Prosperity Gospel*. New York: Oxford University Press, 2013.

———. *The Preacher's Wife: The Precarious Power of Evangelical Women Celebrities*. Princeton: Princeton University Press, 2019.

———. "Why Are There So Few Mainline Celebrities?" *Faith and Leadership*, May 30, 2017. https://tinyurl.com/mr4dsxwu.

Bowler, Kate, and Wen Reagan. "Bigger, Better, Louder: The Prosperity Gospel's Impact on Contemporary Christian Worship." *Religion and American Culture: A Journal of Interpretation* 24, no. 2 (2014): 186–230.

Bratton, Susan Power. *ChurchScape: Megachurches and the Iconography of Environment*. Waco, TX: Baylor University Press, 2016.

Brechner, Elinor J. "Inspired or Pirated? Two Question Peale's Works." *Miami Herald*, July 28, 1995, sec. 1F.

Brenneman, Todd M. *Homespun Gospel: The Triumph of Sentimentality in Contemporary American Evangelicalism*. New York: Oxford University Press, 2013.

Broder, John M. "Clinton Turns to Pastors for Solace." *New York Times*, September 11, 1998. https://tinyurl.com/4vbc5dev.

Bruins, Elton J. "My Town Alto: The First Dutch Immigrant Community in Wisconsin." In *Diverse Destinies: Dutch Kolonies in Wisconsin and the East*, edited by Nella Kennedy, Mary Risseeuw, and Robert P. Swierenga, 83. Holland, MI: Van Raalte, 2012.

Butterfield, Stephen. *Amway: The Cult of Free Enterprise*. Boston: South End, 1985.

Campbell, Ronald. "Judge: Crystal Cathedral Sale Will Go Through." *Orange County Register*, January 31, 2012. https://tinyurl.com/34k4mn4r.

———. "Salaries of Principal Crystal Cathedral Employees." *Orange County Register*, November 17, 2010. https://tinyurl.com/mtv92pnw.

———. "TV Superstar: 'Hour of Power' Is No. 1 or 2 Religious Show." *Orange County Register*, August 9, 1987, M3. Dennis Voskuil Papers, Holland, MI.

"Cathedral Denies Board Fired Schuller." United Press International, July 4, 2011. https://tinyurl.com/3ev6btef.

Chandler, Russell. *Understanding the New Age*. Dallas: Word, 1988.

Chazanov, Mathis. "The Rev. Billy Graham Said Today He Experienced 'Total Liberty.'" United Press International, May 12, 1982. https://tinyurl.com/58zddbhz.

Christerson, Brad, and Richard Flory. *The Rise of Network Christianity: How Independent Leaders Are Changing the Religious Landscape*. New York: Oxford University Press, 2017.

Clary, David. *Soul Winners: The Ascent of America's Evangelical Entrepreneurs*. Guilford, CT: Prometheus Books, 2022.

Coleman, Sheila Schuller. *Robert Schuller: My Father and My Friend*. Milwaukee: Ideals Publishing Corp., 1980.

Congressional Record (Bound Edition). Volume 146 (2000), Part 1. https://tinyurl.com/4bsj6c8u.

Cooley, Charles Horton. "The Looking-Glass Self." In *Human Nature and the Social Order*, by Charles Horton Cooley, 179–85. New York: Scribner's Sons, 1902.

Copland, Christina. "The Demise of the Crystal Cathedral." PBS SoCal, December 20, 2017. https://tinyurl.com/d76jy3ac.

Corcoran, Katie E., and James K. Wellman Jr. "'People Forget He's Human': Charismatic Leadership in Institutionalized Religion." *Sociology of Religion* 77, no. 4 (2016): 309–33.

Cox, Claire. *The New-Time Religion: What Is Really Happening in Our Churches and among Churchgoers in America Today*. Englewood Cliffs, NJ: Prentice-Hall, 1961.

"Cracks in the Crystal Cathedral: Why We Are Better Off Letting God Make the Gospel Relevant." *Christianity Today*, January 10, 2011. https://tinyurl.com/bdh4hacr.

"Crystal Cathedral: The State of Our Church and Global Ministry." May 2009. Ronald Keener Papers.

"Crystal Cathedral to Pay Back Taxes on Concert Receipts." *New York Times*, August 31, 1983. https://tinyurl.com/yc7rtw73.

Cuniff, Meghann M. "Age, Income, Ethnicity: Latest Census Data Reveals

302 BIBLIOGRAPHY

All Facets of O.C." *Orange County Register*, December 29, 2014. https://tinyurl.com/56er6szc.

Curtis, Jesse. *The Myth of Colorblind Christians: Evangelicals and White Supremacy in the Civil Rights Era*. New York: New York University Press, 2021.

———. "White Evangelicals as a 'People': The Church Growth Movement from India to the United States." *Journal of Religion and American Culture* 30, no. 1 (March 20, 2020): 108–46.

Curwen, Thomas. "Robert Schuller's California Brand of Christianity." *Los Angeles Times*, April 2, 2015. https://tinyurl.com/yvn3tyc4.

Dart, John. "Schuller's New Center Faulted for Its Secular Look." *Los Angeles Times*, November 25, 1989. https://tinyurl.com/ms74dct5.

"Divine Property?" *Newsweek*, July 5, 1971.

Do, Anh. "Crystal Cathedral Enters a New Era as It Transforms into Christ Cathedral." *Los Angeles Times*, September 17, 2016. https://tinyurl.com/hz48uj2k.

Dochuk, Darren. *From Bible Belt to Sunbelt: Plain-Folk Religion, Grassroots Politics, and the Rise of Evangelical Conservatism*. New York: Norton, 2011.

Droog, Chester. "The RCA: Growing in the Southwest." *Church Herald*, June 7, 1985.

Durkheim, Emile. *Division of Labor in Society*. New York: Free Press, 2014.

Ehrenreich, Barbara. *Bright-Sided: How Positive Thinking Is Undermining America*. New York: Picador, 2009.

Ellingson, Stephen. *The Megachurch and the Mainline: Remaking Religious Tradition in the Twenty-First Century*. Chicago: University of Chicago Press, 2007.

Elliot, Ralph. "Dangers of the Church Growth Movement." *Christian Century*, August 12–19, 1981.

Elson, Raymond J., Casey Kennedy, and Mark Wills. "The Crystal Cathedral and Its Demise." *Journal of Business Cases and Applications* 18 (September 2017): 1–13. http://www.aabri.com/manuscripts/172634.pdf.

Emerson, Michael, and Christian Smith. *Divided by Faith: Evangelical Religion and the Problem of Race in America*. New York: Oxford University Press, 2000.

Enroth, Ronald. "A Self-Styled Evangelist Stretches God's Truth: Terry Cole-Whittaker Uses Television to Advance Her Own Version of the Gospel." *Christianity Today*, September 21, 1984, 73–75.

Eskridge, Larry. *God's Forever Family: The Jesus People Movement in America.* New York: Oxford University Press, 2013.

Exoo, George D., and George Tweed. "Peale's Secret Source." *Lutheran Quarterly* 9, Summer 1995.

Fagerstrom, Scott. "Schuller Remarks Upset Reformed Church Officials: Minister's Claim of Accountability Called Misleading." *Orange County Register*, April 30, 1987, sec. A1–A2.

Ferré, John P. "Searching for the Great Commission." In *American Evangelicals and the Mass Media: Perspectives on the Relationship between American Evangelicals and the Mass Media*, edited by Quentin J. Schultze, 99–117. Grand Rapids: Zondervan, 1990.

Finke, Roger, and Rodney Stark. *The Churching of America, 1776–1990: Winners and Losers in Our Religious Economy.* New Brunswick, NJ: Rutgers University Press, 1997.

Fishman, Robert. *Bourgeois Utopias: The Rise and Fall of Suburbia.* New York: Basic Books, 1989.

FitzGerald, Frances. *The Evangelicals: The Struggle to Shape America.* New York: Simon & Schuster, 2017.

Frankl, Razelle. "Teleministries as Family Businesses." *Marriage & Family Review* 15, no. 3–4 (1990): 195–205.

———. *Televangelism: The Marketing of Popular Religion.* Carbondale: Southern Illinois University Press, 1987.

Gardner, Andrew, and Gerardo Martí. "From Ordaining Women to Combating White Supremacy: Oppositional Shifts in Social Attitudes between the Southern Baptist Convention and the Alliance of Baptists." *Religion and American Culture: A Journal of Interpretation* 33, no. 2 (Summer 2022): 202–35.

Gates, L. *Dwelling in Schullerland.* Nashville: Winston-Derek, 1985.

Geismer, Lily. *Don't Blame Us: Suburban Liberals and the Transformation of the Democratic Party.* Princeton: Princeton University Press, 2015.

Gloege, Timothy E. W. *Guaranteed Pure: The Moody Bible Institute, Business, and the Making of Modern Evangelicalism.* Chapel Hill: University of North Carolina Press, 2015.

Goffman, Erving. *The Presentation of Self in Everyday Life.* Garden City, NJ: Doubleday, 1959.

Goldman, Marion, and Steven Pfaff. "Reconsidering Virtuosity: Religious

Innovation and Spiritual Privilege." *Sociology Theory* 32, no. 2 (n.d.): 128–46.

Goodstein, Laurie. "Dispute over Succession Clouds Megachurch." *New York Times*, October 23, 2010. https://www.nytimes.com/2010/10/24/us/24 cathedral.html.

Gorski, Philip. *American Covenant: A History of Civil Religion from the Puritans to the Present.* Princeton: Princeton University Press, 2017.

Graham, Ruth. "Church of the Donald: Never Mind Fox. Trump's Most Reliable Media Mouthpiece Is Now Christian TV." *Politico Magazine*, May/June 2018. https://tinyurl.com/ywjzz5wr.

Grem, Darren E. *The Blessings of Business: How Corporations Shaped Conservative Christianity.* New York: Oxford University Press, 2016.

Gribben, Crawford. "Holy Nation: America, Born Again." *American Interest* 11, no. 4 (November 22, 2015). https://tinyurl.com/2w3w39k4.

Hadden, Jeffrey K. "The Rise and Fall of American Televangelism." *Annals of the American Academy of Political and Social Science* 527, no. 1 (May 1993).

Hadden, Jeffrey K., and Charles E. Swann. *Prime Time Preachers: The Rising Power of Televangelism.* Reading, MA: Addison-Wesley, 1981.

Haddigan, Lee. "The Importance of Christian Thought for the American Libertarian Movement: Christian Libertarianism, 1950–71." *Libertarian Papers* 2, no. 14 (2010): 1–31. https://tinyurl.com/3jbs7cxw.

Hagerty, Barbara Bradley. "Catholic Church to Buy Famed Crystal Cathedral." NPR, November 18, 2011. https://tinyurl.com/4desjn2b.

Hardin, John Curran. "Retailing Religion: Business Promotionalism in American Christian Churches in the Twentieth Century." PhD diss., University of Maryland, 2011.

Heer, Jeet. "The Power of Negative Thinking." *New Republic*, October 16, 2017. https://newrepublic.com/article/145311/power-negative-thinking -trump-lessons-democrats.

Hinch, Jim. "Where Are the People? Evangelical Christianity in America Is Losing Its Power—What Happened to Orange County's Crystal Cathedral Shows Why." *American Scholar*, Winter 2014. https://the americanscholar.org/where-are-the-people/.

Hines, Thomas S. *Richard Neutra and the Search for Modern Architecture.* Berkeley and Los Angeles: University of California Press, 1982.

Hoogendoorn, Maurice. "A Thousand Times 'You Are Loved.'" *Dutch Newspaper*, April 6, 2018.

Horton, Michael. *Christless Christianity*. Grand Rapids: Baker Books, 2008.

"How Schuller Shaped Your Ministry: A Conversation with Robert Schuller." *Leadership Journal*. Accessed March 16, 2016. https://tinyurl.com/2s3w3kxs.

Hudnut-Beumler, James. *In Pursuit of the Almighty's Dollar: A History of Money and American Capitalism*. Chapel Hill: University of North Carolina Press, 2007.

———. *Looking for God in the Suburbs: The Religion of the American Dream and Its Critics, 1945–1965*. New Brunswick, NJ: Rutgers University Press, 1994.

Hunter, James Davison. *Evangelicalism: The Coming Generation*. Chicago: University of Chicago Press, 1987.

Hutchison, William R., ed. *Between the Times: The Travail of the Protestant Establishment in America, 1900–1960*. Cambridge: Cambridge University Press, 1989.

Jackson, Kenneth T. *Crabgrass Frontier: The Suburbanization of the United States*. New York: Oxford University Press, 1985.

Japinga, Lynn. *Loyalty and Loss: The Reformed Church in America, 1945–1994*. Grand Rapids: Eerdmans, 2013.

Joice, Lois M. "The Glass Cathedral That Grew in an Orange Grove." *Church Herald*, April 16, 1971.

Jones, Robert P. *The End of White Christian America*. New York: Simon & Schuster, 2016.

Kantzer, Kenneth S., and Paul W. Fromer. "A Theologian Looks at Schuller." *Christianity Today*, August 10, 1984.

Kay, Jane Holtz. *Asphalt Nation: How the Automobile Took over America and How We Can Take It Back*. Berkeley: University of California Press, 1997.

Keener, Ron. "Christian Tragedy." *Church Executive*, February 2012. Ronald Keener Papers.

Kerstetter, Todd M. *Inspiration and Innovation: Religion in the American West*. Oxford: Wiley Blackwell, 2015.

Kilder, Jeanne Halgren. *Sacred Power, Sacred Space: An Introduction to Christian Architecture and Worship*. New York: Oxford University Press, 2008.

———. *When Church Became Theatre.* New York: Oxford University Press, 2002.

Kirkpatrick, Ron. "Pastor Parlays Drive-In Sermon into National Fame." *Orange County Register*, March 5, 1978.

Kopetman, Roxana. "Crystal Cathedral: Schullers Lose in Court." *Orange County Register*, November 28, 2012. https://tinyurl.com/mpu3vvbm.

———. "Schuller Coleman Leaving: Crystal Cathedral Congregation Faces Split." *Orange County Register*, March 12, 2012. https://tinyurl.com/mra82k43.

———. "3 Schuller Family Members Fired from Crystal Cathedral." *Orange County Register*, March 7, 2012. https://tinyurl.com/bdbcd2nx.

Kopetman, Roxana, and Deepa Bharath. "'It Was a Life Well-Lived': Rev. Robert Schuller Leader of Crystal Cathedral and 'Hour of Power,' Dies at 88." *Orange County Register*, April 3, 2015. https://tinyurl.com/2s3exdbb.

Kotkin, Joel, and Marshall Toplansky. "OC Model: A Vision for Orange County's Future." Chapman University Center for Demographics and Policy, October 1, 2016.

Kruse, Kevin. *One Nation under God: How Corporate America Invented Christian America.* New York: Basic Books, 2015.

Kumar, Anugrah. "Bobby Schuller Encourages Crystal Cathedral to Press On." *Christian Post*, June 11, 2012. https://tinyurl.com/3w2am9vn.

Kvesic, Ivana. "Bobby Schuller Talks Starting Over, Returning to Crystal Cathedral." *Christian Post*, May 17, 2012. https://tinyurl.com/mv97szkd.

Lamster, Mark. *The Man in the Glass House: Philip Johnson, Architect of the Modern Century.* New York: Little, Brown, 2018.

Lane, Christopher. *Surge of Piety: Norman Vincent Peale and the Remaking of American Religious Life.* New Haven: Yale University Press, 2016.

"Larry King Live." January 23, 2006. Transcript accessed August 31, 2017. http://transcripts.cnn.com/TRANSCRIPTS/0601/23/lkl.01.html.

Lasch, Christopher. *The Culture of Narcissism: American Life in an Age of Diminishing Expectations.* New York: Norton, 1979.

Lassiter, Matthew D. *The Silent Majority: Suburban Politics in the Sunbelt South.* Princeton: Princeton University Press, 2006.

Lavietes, Stuart. "Rev. Robert Schuller, 88, Dies; Built an Empire Preaching Self-Belief." *New York Times*, April 2, 2015. https://tinyurl.com/yphp4y4r.

Lavin, Sylvia. *Form Follows Libido: Architecture and Richard Neutra in a Psychoanalytic Culture*. Cambridge, MA: MIT Press, 2004.

Lee, Shayne, and Phillip Luke Sinitiere. *Holy Mavericks: Evangelical Innovators and the Spiritual Marketplace*. New York: New York University Press, 2009.

Lindbeck, George A. "The Church's Mission to a Postmodern Culture." In *Postmodern Theology: Christian Faith in a Pluralist World*, edited by Frederic B. Burnham, 35–55. New York: Harper & Row, 1989.

Linton, Michael. "Smoke and Mirrors at the Crystal Cathedral." *First Things*, June 1997. https://tinyurl.com/3chkt5rw.

Lippy, Charles H., ed. *Twentieth-Century Shapers of American Popular Religion*. New York: Greenwood, 1989.

Lobdell, William, and Mitchell Landsberg. "Rev. Robert H. Schuller, Who Built Crystal Cathedral, Dies at 88." *Los Angeles Times*, April 2, 2015. https://tinyurl.com/4zz29u8v.

Lovett, Ian. "Founding Family Decides to Leave Crystal Cathedral." *New York Times*, March 11, 2012. https://tinyurl.com/55782bcy.

———. "Lasting Tributes Meet Early End in Bankruptcy." *New York Times*, September 5, 2013. https://tinyurl.com/e4pwseau.

Luhr, Eileen. *Witnessing in Suburbia: Conservatives and Christian Youth Culture*. Berkeley and Los Angeles: University of California Press, 2009.

Lynerd, Benjamin T. *Republican Theology: The Civil Religion of American Evangelicals*. New York: Oxford University Press, 2014.

Mariani, John. "Television Evangelism: Milking the Flock." *Saturday Review*, February 3, 1979.

Martí, Gerardo. "Ethnographic Theology: Integrating the Social Sciences and Theological Reflection." *Cuestiones Teológicas* 49, no. 111 (2022): 1–18.

———. "Ethnography as a Tool for Genuine Surprise: Found Theologies versus Imposed Theologies." In *The Wiley Blackwell Companion to Theology and Qualitative Research*, edited by Pete Ward and Knut Tveitereid, 471–82. Hoboken, NJ: Wiley Blackwell, 2023.

———. "Found Theologies versus Imposed Theologies: Remarks on Theology and Ethnography from a Sociological Perspective." *Ecclesial Practices* 3, no. 2 (2016): 157–72.

———. *Hollywood Faith: Holiness, Prosperity, and Ambition in a Los Angeles Church*. New Brunswick, NJ: Rutgers University Press, 2008.

——. "'I Was a Muslim, but Now I Am a Christian': Preaching, Legitimation, and Identity Management in a Southern Evangelical Church." *Journal for the Scientific Study of Religion* 55, no. 2 (2016): 250–70.

——. *A Mosaic of Believers: Diversity and Innovation in a Multiethnic Church.* Bloomington: Indiana University Press, 2005.

——. "New Concepts for New Dynamics: Generating Theory for the Study of Religious Innovation and Social Change." *Journal for the Scientific Study of Religion* 56, no. 1 (2017): 6–18.

Martí, Gerardo, and Gladys Ganiel. *The Deconstructed Church: Understanding Emerging Christianity.* New York: Oxford University Press, 2014.

Martí, Gerardo, and Mark T. Mulder. "Capital and the Cathedral: Robert H. Schuller's Continual Fundraising for Church Growth." *Religion and American Culture: A Journal of Interpretation* 30, no. 1 (Winter 2020): 63–107.

Martin, William. *With God on Our Side: The Rise of the Religious Right in America.* New York: Broadway Books, 1996.

Marty, Martin E. "Feeling Saved and Feeling Good." *New York University Educational Quarterly* 9, no. 3 (Spring 1978): 2–8.

McCoy, Esther. *Richard Neutra: Masters of World Architecture Series.* New York: George Braziller, 1960.

McGee, Micki. *Self-Help, Inc.: Makeover Culture in American Life.* New York: Oxford University Press, 2005.

McGirr, Lisa. *Suburban Warriors: The Origins of the New American Right.* Princeton: Princeton University Press, 2001.

Mead, George Herbert. *Mind, Self, and Society.* Chicago: University of Chicago Press, 1934.

Mehta, Seema, Christopher Goffard, and Anh Do. "Hillary Clinton Turned Orange County Blue: Minorities and College-Educated Women Helped Her." *Los Angeles Times*, November 9, 2016. http://www.la times.com/politics/la-me-oc-clinton-20161109-story.html.

Meyer, Donald. *The Positive Thinkers: Popular Religious Psychology from Mary Baker Eddy to Norman Vincent Peale and Ronald Reagan.* Middletown, CT: Wesleyan University Press, 1988.

Miller, Donald E. *Reinventing American Protestantism: Christianity in the New Millennium.* Berkeley: University of California Press, 1999.

Miller, Holly. "Living on the Edge." *Saturday Evening Post* 273, no. 2 (April 2001): 36–39, 78.

Monsma, Stephen V. "What Is an Evangelical? And Does It Matter?" *Christian Scholars Review* 46, no. 4 (Spring 2017).

Montague, Zach. "Doug Coe, Influential Evangelical Leader, Dies at 88." *New York Times*, February 22, 2017. https://tinyurl.com/2wp8z7mf.

Mooney, Michael. "Why Joel Osteen Is the Most Popular Preacher on the Planet." *Success*, January 11, 2016. https://tinyurl.com/bdemrze3.

Mulder, John M. "The Possibility Preacher." *Theology Today* 31 (July 1974): 157–60.

Mulder, Mark T. *Shades of White Flight: Evangelical Congregations and Urban Departure*. New Brunswick, NJ: Rutgers University Press, 2015.

Mulder, Mark T., and Gerardo Martí. *The Glass Church: Robert H. Schuller, the Crystal Cathedral, and the Strain of Megachurch Ministry*. New Brunswick, NJ: Rutgers University Press, 2020.

———. "The President, the Pandemic, and the Limits of Positive Thinking." Religion News Service, March 30, 2020. https://tinyurl.com/342ac2uy.

Mulder, Mark T., Aida I. Ramos, and Gerardo Martí. *Latino Protestants in America: Growing and Diverse*. Lanham, MD: Rowman & Littlefield, 2017.

Nason, Michael, and Donna Nason. *Robert Schuller: The Inside Story*. Waco, TX: Word, 1983.

Neutra, Richard. *Survival through Design*. New York: Oxford University Press, 1954.

Oleszczuk, Luiza. "Crystal Cathedral's New CEO: Congregation, Donations Doubled after Schuller's Departure." *Christian Post*, March 31, 2012. https://tinyurl.com/yz5rkwfu.

———. "Dante Gebel's Hispanic Ministry to Leave Crystal Cathedral Campus." *Christian Post*, March 6, 2012. https://tinyurl.com/54r829fw.

Olmstead, Kathryn S. *Right Out of California: The 1930s and the Big Business Roots of Modern Conservatism*. New York: New Press, 2016.

Ortiz, Juan Carlos, and Martha Palau. *From the Jungles to the Cathedral: The Captivating Story of Juan Carlos Ortiz*. Miami: Vida, 2011.

Peale, Norman Vincent. *Enthusiasm Makes the Difference*. Englewood Cliffs, NJ: Prentice-Hall, 1967.

———. *The Power of Positive Thinking*. New York: Prentice-Hall, 1952.

BIBLIOGRAPHY

———. *Stay Alive All Your Life*. Englewood Cliffs, NJ: Prentice-Hall, 1957.

Penner, James. *Goliath: The Life of Robert Schuller*. Anaheim, CA: New Hope Publishing, 1992.

Phillips-Fein, Kim. *Invisible Hands: The Businessmen's Crusade against the New Deal*. New York: Norton, 2009.

Plantinga, Neal. "Schullerism and Church Growth." *Banner*, March 19, 1976.

Polanyi, Karl. *The Great Transformation: The Political and Economic Origins of Our Time*. New York: Farrar & Rinehart, 1944.

Pritchard, Gregory A. "The Strategy of Willow Creek Community Church: A Study in the Sociology of Religion." PhD diss., Northwestern University, 1994.

———. *Willow Creek Seeker Services: Evaluating a New Way of Doing Church*. Grand Rapids: Baker Books, 1996.

Putnam, Robert. *Bowling Alone: The Collapse and Revival of American Community*. New York: Simon & Schuster, 2000.

Putnam, Robert D., Lewis M. Feldstein, and Don Cohen. *Better Together: Restoring the American Community*. New York: Simon & Schuster, 2003.

Ramos, Aida I., Gerardo Martí, and Mark T. Mulder. "The Strategic Practice of 'Fiesta' in a Latino Protestant Church: Religious Racialization and the Performance of Ethnic Identity." *Journal for the Scientific Study of Religion* 59, no. 1 (2020): 161-79.

Religion News Service. "Schuller's Tree of Life Community Church to Merge into Shepherd's Grove." Press release, February 16, 2015. https://tiny url.com/yvjkjef2.

"Retail Religion: Robert Schuller, an Entrepreneur of Televangelism and Megachurches, Died on April 2nd." *Economist*, April 11, 2015. https://tinyurl.com/3rv9w85s.

Richardson, Kip. "Gospels of Growth: The American Megachurch at Home and Abroad." In *Secularization and Innovation in the North Atlantic World*, edited by David Hempton and Hugh McLeod. New York: Oxford University Press, 2017. doi: 10.1093/oso/9780198798071.001.0001.

———. "The Spatial Strategies of American Megachurches." *Oxford Research Encyclopedia of Religion*, May 2017. https://tinyurl.com/yeyjvkkk.

Ridder, Herman J. "How We Did It: The Schuller Film Workshop." *Church Herald*, January 23, 1981, 14-15.

Robles-Anderson, Erica. "The Crystal Cathedral: Architecture for Mediated Congregation." *Public Culture* 24, no. 3 (2012).

Roorda, Jan. "A Call to Live Joyously: Dr. Robert H. Schuller, TV's Powerhouse of Spirituality Inspires Legions of Possibility Thinkers with His Vision of God's Belief in Man." *Saturday Evening Post* 250, no. 3 (April 1978): 54–57, 120.

Rosa, Hartmut. *Resonance: A Sociology of Our Relationship to the World*. New York: Polity, 2019.

——. *Social Acceleration: A Theory of Modernity*. New York: Columbia University Press, 2013.

Ruotsila, Markku. *Fighting Fundamentalist: Carl McIntire and the Politicization of American Fundamentalism*. New York: Oxford University Press, 2016.

Rybczynski, Witold. "An Anatomy of Megachurches: The New Look for Places of Worship." *Slate*, October 10, 2005. https://tinyurl.com/5ea9kyx.

Sablan, Kevin. "Action Picks Up for Filming in O.C." *Orange County Register*, April 29, 2013. https://www.ocregister.com/2013/04/29/action-picks-up-for-filming-in-oc/.

Santa Cruz, Nicole. "Arvella Schuller Dies at 84; Wife of Crystal Cathedral Founder Robert Schuller." *Los Angeles Times*, February 11, 2014. https://tinyurl.com/4pe434vr.

——. "Church Family Loses Court Ruling." *Los Angeles Times*, November 27, 2012. https://tinyurl.com/4w3fz7ez.

——. "Crystal Cathedral May Lose Spanish-Language Ministry." *Los Angeles Times*, November 19, 2011. https://tinyurl.com/2zv29a3r.

——. "Crystal Cathedral's Senior Pastor Says She's Leaving to Start a New Church." *Los Angeles Times*, March 12, 2012. https://tinyurl.com/9fjh2bhk.

——. "Crystal Cathedral's Tale of Two Ministers." *Los Angeles Times*, June 19, 2011. https://tinyurl.com/yumsubyv.

Santa Cruz, Nicole, Ruben Vives, and Mitchell Landsber. "Orange County Diocese to Buy Bankrupt Crystal Cathedral." *Los Angeles Times*, November 18, 2011. https://tinyurl.com/2ktp32tw.

Sargeant, Kimon Howland. *Seeker Churches: Promoting Traditional Religion*

BIBLIOGRAPHY

in a Nontraditional Way. New Brunswick, NJ: Rutgers University Press, 2000.

Schuller, Arvella. *The Positive Family: Possibility Thinking in the Christian Home*. Garden City, NY: Doubleday, 1982.

Schuller, Robert H. "The Drive-In Church—a Modern Technique of Outreach." *Reformed Review* 23, no. 22 (1969).

——. "Dr. Schuller Comments." *Christianity Today*, October 5, 1984, 12-13.

——. *God's Way to a Good Life*. New Canaan, CT: Keats, 1974.

——. *The Inspirational Writings of Robert H. Schuller*. New York: Inspirational Press, 1986.

——. *Life's Not Fair but God Is Good*. Nashville: Nelson, 1991.

——. "Make Them Want to Give." *Church Herald*, November 22, 1968. In Dennis Voskuil Papers, Holland, MI.

——. *Move Ahead with Possibility Thinking: A Practical and Spiritual Challenge to Change Your Thinking and Your Life*. Old Tappan, NJ: Spire Books, 1967.

——. *My Journey: From an Iowa Farm to a Cathedral of Dreams*. San Francisco: HarperOne, 2001.

——. *The Peak to Peek Principle: How Possibility Thinkers Succeed*. Garden City, NY: Doubleday, 1980.

——. "Profitable Living." Dennis Voskuil Papers, Holland, MI, 1955.

——. *Reach Out for New Life*. New York: Bantam Books, 1977.

——. "The Schuller Family in Ministry: Portfolio." October 2001, updated October 2007, p. 1. Ronald Keener Papers.

——. *Self Esteem: The New Reformation*. Waco, TX: Word, 1982.

——. *Self-Love: The Dynamic Forces of Success*. New York: Jove Books, 1969.

——. "Spare Us a Trial, Mr. President." *Wall Street Journal*, December 21, 1998. https://www.wsj.com/articles/SB914190242498781500.

——. "Tax Church Properties?!" *Church Herald*, March 13, 1964.

——. "Three Characteristics of a Successful Pastor." In *The Pastor's Church Growth Handbook: America's Leading Authorities on Church Growth Share the Keys to Building a Dynamic Church*, edited by Win Arn, 92-94. Pasadena, CA: Institute for American Church Growth, Church Growth Press, 1979.

——. *Tough-Minded Faith for Tender-Hearted People*. Nashville: Nelson, 1983.

——. *Tough Times Never Last, but Tough People Do!* New York: Bantam Books, 1984.

——. "Turn Your Scars into Stars." *Saturday Evening Post* 250, no. 3 (April 1978): 58-59, 98.

——. "We Can Be Strong." *Church Herald*, June 6, 1969.

——. "What's Wrong with the World?" *Church Herald*, February 11, 1995.

——. *When You Are Down to Nothing, God Is Up to Something: Finding Divine Purpose and Provision When Life Hurts.* New York: Faith Words, 2011.

——. *You Can Become the Person You Want to Be.* Old Tappan, NJ: Spire Books, 1973.

——. *Your Church Has a Fantastic Future! A Possibility Thinker's Guide to a Successful Church.* Ventura, CA: Regal Books, 1986.

——. *Your Church Has Real Possibilities!* Glendale, CA: G/L Publications, 1974.

Schuller, Robert H., for the Consistory of Garden Grove Community Church. Letter to the editor, *Church Herald*, August 26, 1966, 20-22.

Schuller, Robert H., and James Coleman. *A Place of Beauty, a Joy Forever: The Glorious Gardens and Grounds of the Crystal Cathedral in Garden Grove, California.* Garden Grove, CA: Crystal Cathedral Creative Services, 2005.

Schuller, Robert H., Kenneth S. Kantzer, David F. Wells, and V. Gilbert Beers. "Hard Questions for Robert Schuller about Sin & Self-Esteem." *Christianity Today*, August 10, 1984.

Schuller, Robert H., and H. Smart. "The Crystal Cathedral Hymn." *Crystal Cathedral News*, September 6, 1992.

Schultze, Quentin J., ed. *American Evangelicals and the Mass Media: Perspectives on the Relationship between American Evangelicals and the Mass Media.* Grand Rapids: Zondervan, 1990.

Schulze, Franz. *Philip Johnson: Life and Work.* New York: Knopf, 1994.

Schwaiger, Manfred. "Components and Parameters of Corporate Reputation—an Empirical Study." *Schmalenbach Business Review* 56 (January 2004): 46-71.

Sewell, Abby, and Nicole Santa Cruz. "Bankruptcy Filings Show Generous Pay for Relatives of Crystal Cathedral Founder." *Los Angeles Times*, December 3, 2010. https://tinyurl.com/25ymh3h6.

Sinitiere, Phillip Luke. "Salvation with a Smile: Joel Osteen, Lakewood Church, and American Christianity." In *Salvation with a Smile: Joel*

Osteen, Lakewood Church, and American Christianity. New York: New York University Press, 2015.

Slater, Don, and Fran Tonkiss. *Market Society: Markets and Modern Social Theory*. Cambridge: Polity Press/Blackwell, 2001.

Slaughter, Joseph P. *Faith in Markets: Christian Capitalism in the Early American Republic*. New York: Columbia University Press, 2023.

Smith, Sheila Strobel. "Complexities of Pastoral Change and Transition in the Megachurches of the Baptist General Conference, Evangelical Lutheran Church in America, and Presbyterian Church (USA)." PhD diss., Luther Seminary, 2010.

Smith, Warren Cole. "Bobby Schuller on the Crystal Cathedral Exodus." *World*, March 25, 2015. https://tinyurl.com/redv2k64.

Solomon, Martha. "Robert Schuller: The American Dream in a Crystal Cathedral." *Central States Speech Journal* 34 (Fall 1983): 172–86.

Spies-Butcher, Benjamin, Damien Cahill, and Joy Paton. *Market Society: History, Theory, Practice*. Cambridge: Cambridge University Press, 2012.

Stadtlander, John H. "Schuller Shows the Way." *LCA Partners*, April 1983, 11–14.

Stapert, John. "Lessons from RCA Church Growth: An Interview with Chester Droog." *Church Herald*, May 1, 1987.

———. "A New Age Challenge." *Church Herald*, March 1990.

———. "Robert Schuller Is from La Mancha." *Church Herald*, October 17, 1980, 8–9.

———. "Whose Cathedral?" *Church Herald*, June 19, 1987.

Stark, Rodney, and Roger Finke. *Acts of Faith: Explaining the Human Side of Religion*. Berkeley: University of California Press, 2000.

Stephens, Randall J. "Culture, Entertainment, and Religion in America." *Oxford Research Encyclopedia of Religion*, October 2017. https://tinyurl.com/272c4s4a.

Stout, Harry S. *The Divine Dramatist: George Whitefield and the Rise of Modern Evangelicalism*. Grand Rapids: Eerdmans, 1991.

Stumbo, Bella. "The Time Muhammad Ali Asked for Robert Schuller's Autograph." *Los Angeles Times*, May 29, 1983. https://tinyurl.com/29rprty5.

Sudjic, Deyan. *The Edifice Complex: How the Rich and Powerful Shape the World*. New York: Penguin Press, 2005.

Sutton, Matthew Avery. *American Apocalypse: A History of Modern Evan-

gelicalism. Cambridge, MA: Belknap Press of Harvard University Press, 2014.

Swanson, Douglas J. "The Beginning of the End of Robert H. Schuller's Crystal Cathedral Ministry: A Towering Failure in Crisis Management as Reflected through Media Narratives of Financial Crisis, Family Conflict, and Follower Dissent." *Social Science Journal* 49 (2012): 485–93.

Swanson, Douglas J., and Terri Manley. "Squandering a Legacy, and Building One: How Robert H. Schuller Lost the Crystal Cathedral, and How the Catholic Church Captured It." Manuscript presented at the Western Social Sciences Association, Annual Conference, Albuquerque, NM, April 2014.

Swedberg, Richard. "Markets as Social Structures." In *Handbook of Economic Sociology*, edited by Neil Smelser and Richard Swedberg. New York and Princeton: Russell Sage Foundation and Princeton University Press, 1994.

Thompson, Grahame, Jennifer Frances, Rosalind Levačić, and Jeremy C. Mitchell, eds. *Markets, Hierarchies, and Networks: The Coordination of Social Life*. London: Sage, 1991.

Thumma, Scott, and David Travis. *Beyond Megachurch Myths: What We Can Learn from America's Largest Churches*. San Francisco: Jossey-Bass, 2007.

Trounstine, Jessica. *Segregated by Design: Local Politics and Inequality in American Cities*. New York: Cambridge University Press, 2018.

Tweed, Thomas. *America's Church: The National Shrine and Catholic Presence in the Nation's Capital*. New York: Oxford University Press, 2011.

Vanderbloemen, William, and Warren Bird. *Next: Pastoral Succession That Works*. Grand Rapids: Baker Books, 2014.

Voskuil, Dennis. *Mountains into Goldmines: Robert Schuller and the Gospel of Success*. Grand Rapids: Eerdmans, 1983.

Walker, Ken. "Church Drops Mortgage for Expansion." *Christianity Today*, September 27, 2011.

Warner, Sam Bass, Jr. *The Urban Wilderness: A History of the American City*. Classics in Urban History 5. Berkeley: University of California Press, 1995.

Warner, R. Stephen. "Work in Progress toward a New Paradigm for the So-

BIBLIOGRAPHY

ciological Study of Religion in the United States." *American Journal of Sociology* 98, no. 5 (1993): 1044–93.

Weber, Max. *Economy and Society: An Outline of Interpretive Sociology*. Berkeley: University of California Press, 1978.

Wellman, James K., Jr. *The Gold Coast Church and the Ghetto: Christ and Culture in Mainline Protestantism*. Urbana: University of Illinois Press, 1999.

———. *Rob Bell and a New American Christianity*. Nashville: Abingdon, 2012.

Wellman, James K., Jr., and Katie E. Corcoran. "'People Forget He's Human': Charismatic Leadership in Institutionalized Religion." *Sociology of Religion: A Quarterly Review* 77, no. 4 (2016): 309–32.

Wellman, James K., Jr., Katie E. Corcoran, and Kate Stockly-Meyerdirk. "'God Is like a Drug . . .': Explaining Interaction Ritual Chains in American Megachurches." *Sociological Forum* 29, no. 3 (September 2014): 650–72.

Whitman, Ardis. "Four Remarkable Churches." *Reader's Digest* 117 (October 1980): 45–50.

Whyte, William H. *The Organization Man*. New York: Simon & Schuster, 1956.

Wigger, John. *PTL: The Rise and Fall of Jim and Tammy Faye Bakker's Evangelical Empire*. New York: Oxford University Press, 2017.

Wilford, Justin G. *Sacred Subdivisions: The Postsuburban Transformation of American Evangelicalism*. New York: New York University Press, 2012.

Williams, Daniel K. *God's Own Party: The Making of the Christian Right*. New York: Oxford University Press, 2010.

Winston, Kimberly. "Crystal Cathedral Founder's Memorial Covered by Crowdfunding Campaign." *Washington Post*, April 21, 2015. https://tinyurl.com/yzt8bnwy.

Witten, Marsha. *All Is Forgiven: The Secular Message in American Protestantism*. Princeton: Princeton University Press, 1993.

Wolterstorff, Nicholas. "The Grace That Shaped My Life." In *Finding God at Harvard*, edited by Kelly K. Monroe, 150–51. Grand Rapids: Zondervan, 1996.

Wong, Herman. "Arts Plans Reflected Schuller's Optimism." *Los Angeles Times*, May 4, 1983. CC–Tax Situation, 1983, 1984, Robert H. Schuller/

Crystal Cathedral, box 29, Hope College Archives and Special Collections, Holland, MI.

Wong, Herman, and Richard C. Paddock. "Schuller Church Stripped of Its Tax-Exempt Status." *Los Angeles Times*, May 4, 1983. Robert H. Schuller/Crystal Cathedral, box 29, Hope College Archives and Special Collections, Holland, MI.

Worthen, Molly. *Apostles of Reason: The Crisis of Authority in American Evangelicalism*. New York: Oxford University Press, 2014.

Wuthnow, Robert. *The Restructuring of American Religion: Society and Faith Since World War II*. Princeton: Princeton University Press, 1988.

Yardley, Jonathon. "Blessed Are the Self-Actualized." *Washington Post*, February 17, 1997. https://tinyurl.com/df5wyujw.

Zeiger, Mimi. "Johnson Fain's Church Swap." *Architect: The Journal of the American Institute of Architecture*, October 31, 2016. https://tinyurl.com/45a94tpe.

Zoellner, Tom, and Elaine Lewinnek. "Seeing Orange County." *Boom California*, February 13, 2018, 43. https://boomcalifornia.com/2018/02/13/seeing-orange-county/.

INDEX

acceleration, 67, 93, 280, 287, 289
accommodation, 206-7, 220
action, 269-70
advertising, 59, 60, 140
Alger, Horatio, 27
Ali, Muhammad, 13
All Is Forgiven (Witten), 206-7
American Convocation for Church
  Growth, 131
American Dream, 220
Amway, 56, 124, 127, 214
Anaheim Vineyard Christian Fellow-
  ship, 149
Arcadian Four, 41-42
Arn, Win, 131
automobile. *See* car culture

Bakker, Jim, 193, 222
Ball, Lucille, 152
Beck, Ulrich, 186
Beltman, Henry, 25
Beltman, Jennie. *See* Schuller, Jennie
  (née Beltman; mother)
biorealism, 92, 284
Bird, Warren, 235
board, church, 102, 173, 252, 256,
  264-65

Board of Domestic Missions (RCA), 82
Bowler, Kate, 57, 148
Bowling Alone (Putnam), 216
Bradley, Tom, 200, 209
Bredeson, Harold, 149
Brown, Edmund G. "Jerry," Jr., 210
Bryant, Bear, 13
"buck-up" series, 199
Bush, George H. W., 231
Bush, George W., 243-44
business. *See* capitalism; free enter-
  prise/market; marketplace

California, 80, 129, 190
California Board of Equalization,
  188-89
Calvary Chapel Costa Mesa, 149
Calvin, John, 40, 42, 227
Calvinism. *See* Reformed tradition
capitalism, 120, 133-38, 193, 276
car culture, 77-78, 109, 175, 215
Carnegie, Dale, 55, 67
chapel, Garden Grove, 82-83, 87, 88,
  90-91
Chapman University, 264
Christerson, Brad, 20-21
Christian Century, 179, 193

Christianity Today, 262–63
Christian Reformed Church in North America (CRC), 127–28
church: administration, 126; building, 22; and competition, 275, 286, 288; congregational culture, 75–76; and corporations, 16, 134; decline, 7, 12, 13, 128–29, 144, 202, 269; and ethnicity, 272–73; and farm, 272–74; integration, racial, 130–31; managerial techniques, 16, 68, 94, 130; and market, 7–9, 13–20, 81–82, 133–34, 144, 272–74; rebuilding, 3; and resonance, 283; seeker-sensitive, 99–100; and social change, 270–71, 278–82, 284–85; worship, 37, 183, 284. *See also* church growth
church-building boom, 1950s, 51–52
Church Executive, 263
church growth: and capacity, 159; escalation, 287–90; and future, 66–67; human need, 282; and leadership, 67–69; and marketplace, 7–9, 13–20, 81–82, 274–75; methodology, 4, 5, 213–14; philosophy, 269; and reshuffling, 72; and social change, 15, 281; stability, 287; techniques, 14–16
church growth movement (CGM), 8, 14–15, 18–20, 128–34
Church Herald, 68, 111, 118, 168, 192, 196
Church Management, 126
Church of the Air, 63
civil rights movement, 121–22
Classis California, 64, 81, 88, 133, 226–27
Clinton, Bill, 237–39, 240
Clinton, Hillary Rodham, 237–38
coal, 140
Coe, Doug, 239, 240
Coleman, Sheila Schuller (daughter), 26, 60–62, 256–57, 263

comfort, congregant, 112
communism, 118–20, 122, 135, 137
conservatism, 98–99, 185, 250
contextualization, 177–78
copastor, GGCC, 88
corporate evangelicalism, 135
Crean, Donna, 164
Crean, John, 164, 165–66, 232
Criswell, W. A., 131
criticism of Schuller, 6, 13, 19, 23, 74–75, 120–21, 129, 132, 146, 153, 173, 175, 177, 179, 184, 191, 192, 206, 216–17
Crossfire, 223
Crowell, Henry Parsons, 135–36
Crystal Cathedral. *See under* Garden Grove Community Church (GGCC)
"Crystal Cathedral: The State of Our Church and Global Ministry," 260–61
Curtis, Jesse, 19, 130, 132–33

Day, Doris, 152
debt, 140–41, 162, 173, 238, 255, 261
decorum, congregational, 125–26
DeHaan, Arvella. *See* Schuller, Arvella (neé DeHaan; wife)
Demand, H. P., 59, 67
denominations, 17–18, 20–21, 101, 102–3, 273, 275, 280–81
DeVos, Richard, 124, 228
dignity, 125
Diocese of Orange, 263–64
discipleship, 154
Dochuk, Darren, 71, 129, 136, 137
dominee, 25, 32, 36, 53
Domus, 174–75
Donahue, Phil, 19, 165
Driscoll, Mark, 6
drive-in church, 59, 73–81, 83–85
Dunn, Paul, 232–33
Durkheim, Emile, 272
Dutch Reformed. *See* Reformed tradition

economics, 276-77
Eddy, Mary Baker, 56
Edwards, Jonathan, 197
Eichenberger, Wilbert, 126
Elliot, Ralph, 132
Eternity, 20
evangelicalism, 20, 22, 99-100, 130, 135-37, 184-85, 221

faith, 10, 123-24
Falwell, Jerry, 221-22
Federal Housing Administration, 80
Film Workshop, 128
FitzGerald, Frances, 52, 99-100
Flint (MI), 217, 270
Flory, Richard, 20-21
Ford, Gerald R., 200
Ford, Glenn, 152
franchising, walk-in, drive-in churches, 214
freedom, 285, 288
free enterprise/market, 119, 130, 134-38, 217, 276. *See also* capitalism
Fuller Theological Seminary, 130

Garden Grove (CA), 65, 72-73. *See also* Orange County
Garden Grove Community Church (GGCC): acoustics, 171; architecture, 81, 91, 92-93, 94-95, 112, 173-75, 237, 246-47; attendance, 77-78, 84, 94, 138-39; bankruptcy, 261-64; campus, 90-91, 103-4, 160, 130, 172, 243, 263, 284; capacity, 146, 159; "Cape Canaveral" doors, 170, 183; Church of the Year, 112; as circus, 219-20; collapse of ministry, 254, 260-65, 288-89, 290-91; construction, 81-82, 103-5, 159-65, 167, 172, 191, 236, 244-46; copastor trouble, 88-89; cost, 161, 166-68, 170-71, 177, 244-46; criticism of Cathedral, 175, 188-90,

192-93; Crystal Cathedral, 10, 11, 15, 18, 110, 166-81, 187-92, 216, 219, 282-83; cypress trees, 96-97; drive-in, 74, 78, 83-84; facility, 160; financial loss, 255, 260-61; fund-raising, 82-83, 91-92, 108, 138-39, 162-68, 245-46; glass design, 161, 167; the *Glories*, 188; growth, 143-44, 159; and *Hour of Power*, 145-46, 166-67, 176; hybrid, 90, 92, 94, 103-4, 160, 172; mission, 274; name, 94; Peale visit, 84-85; performances, 171-72, 187-89; property, 91-93, 106, 110; sale of assets, 263-64; tax-exempt status, 118, 188-90; Tower of Hope, 106-9, 129; twentieth anniversary, 162-63; Welcoming Center, 244-46
Gates, Larry, 172, 190
George Nathan Makely prize, 44
Gloebe, Timothy, 135-36
Glory of Creation, The, 247, 261
God, 207
Goliath (Penner), 50
Gorbachev, Mikhael, 229, 231, 234
gospel of wealth, 129-30, 134-38
Graham, Billy, 127, 145, 178-79
Granberg-Michaelson, Wesley, 155-56, 177
grand mufti. *See* Kuftaro, Ahmad
Great Transformation, The, 276
Grommet, William, 188

Hadden, Jeffrey, 193, 221
Hamilton, J. Wallace, 59
Hammer, Armand, 229-30
hell, 198
heresy, 193, 204
herpes, 209-10
Holland (MI), 37-38
Hollywood Presbyterian Church, 75
Holy Spirit, 149

322 INDEX

Home Owners Loan Corporation, 79–80
Hoover, J. Edgar, 119
Hope College, 38–42
Horton, Michael, 204–6
Hour of Power: accomplishment of Schuller, 6; Arvella's influence on, 147–48; celebrity interest in, 152, 194; and church growth movement, 19–20; and Coleman, 257; criticisms of, 19, 127, 129; finances, 146–47, 148, 255; and GGCC, 145–46, 154, 166–67, 176; international broadcast, 229–32, 264; and Reformed Church in America, 193; Robert A., removal from, 256; success of, 148, 150, 152, 154–56, 176, 243–44
Hudnut-Beumler, James, 55, 137
Humbard, Rex, 221
Hunter, James Davison, 184–85, 193
Hybels, Bill, 4, 16–17

impossibility thinkers, 144
independent apostles, 20
Independent Network Charismatic (INC) Christianity, 20–21
Institute, the. *See* Robert H. Schuller Institute for Church Leadership
Institute for Church Growth (Fuller), 131
Institutes of the Christian Religion (Calvin), 42, 56–57
Interstate Highway Act, 79
Iowa, 28
Ivanhoe RCA, 50–53, 58, 59–60, 63–64, 65, 69

Jackson, Jesse, 149–50
Jackson, Kenneth, 79
Jesus Christ, 85–86, 204–5
Jesus Movement, 125–26, 149
Johnson, Philip, 110, 161, 173–74
Jones, Robert P., 8

Kaiser, Edgar, 151
Karsen, Wendell, 192
Kay, Jane Holtz, 175
Keener, Ronald, 248
Kennedy, D. James, 131
Kerstetter, Todd, 99
KTLA-TV, 146
Kuftaro, Ahmad, 240–42
Kuhlman, Kathryn, 221

laity, 68–69
Lasch, Christopher, 57
leadership, 16, 21, 67–69, 97, 102, 110–11, 254–55, 279, 285
Leadership Institute. *See* Robert H. Schuller Institute for Church Leadership
Leadership Journal, 235
Leestma, Harold, 107
LeTournea, Robert, 136
LeTournea Technical Institute, 136
Lindquist, Raymond, 75
Linkletter, Art, 162

mainline Protestantism, 4–5
malls. *See* shopping centers
management/managerial technique, 16, 68, 94, 116–17, 130, 279
Marble Collegiate Church, 45, 103
marketplace: and Christianity, 274–77; and church growth, 7–20, 81–82, 133–34, 144, 272–74; and faith, 10, 123–24; and family, 116–17; and farm, 272–74; free market, 118–23; Great Transformation, 276–77; and individuals, 186; logic, 9–13; and ministry, 8–11; parishioners, 9; pastors, 271; seeker-sensitive churches, 100; and self-esteem, 285–86
Martin, Albert C., 106
McGavran, Donald, 15, 127, 131
McGee, Micki, 199
McGirr, Lisa, 71, 74

INDEX **323**

McGraw, Foster, 168
McPherson, Aimee Semple, 221
megachurches, 4, 5, 6, 16, 111–12, 235
Meier, Richard, 237, 245, 246
mentalism, 55, 57, 194, 195–202. *See also* New Thought
Million-Dollar Sunday, 168
Milner, Carol Schuller (daughter), 169–70, 200–201, 231, 245, 265, 267
Minder, Norman, 74
Miracle-Faith campaign, 263
missions, 202, 203–4, 274
modernity, 16, 67, 186, 207, 279, 281, 285
Moody, Dwight, 135
Moody Bible Institute (MBI), 135
Moore, Michael, 217
Mother Teresa, 239
Mountains into Goldmines (Voskuil), 180
Mouw, Richard, 178
Murdoch, Rupert, 229

Nason, Michael, 30, 50, 89, 107, 109, 113, 149, 158, 159, 167, 169, 192, 199, 212, 218, 232–33
National Council of Churches, 133
Neuen, Don, 257
Neutra, Richard, 92–93, 103, 106
New Deal, 136–37
Newkirk High School, 35
Newkirk Reformed Church, 32, 47
Newsweek, 129
New Thought, 55–56, 57, 196
New York, 150–51
Nixon, Richard, 210
Nykamp, Robert, 132

Oliver, Christina, 263
Olmstead, Kathryn, 98–99
Olson, Benjamin Franklin, 59
op-eds, Clinton scandal, 238–39
Orange County, 11, 12, 70–71, 78, 80, 97, 129–30, 174, 176, 188–89, 273

Orange County Register, 262, 263
Orthodox University of Moscow, 242
Osteen, Joel, 6

Pacific Drive-In Theatres, 83
parking, 20, 109–10, 139, 215
Peale, Norman Vincent, 45–46, 53–54, 55, 56, 57, 67, 83–87, 95, 109, 114, 118, 132. 150–52, 196, 202–3, 247, 284
Peale, Ruth, 114–15, 224
Penner, James, 30, 233, 261, 262
Phil Donahue Show, The, 165, 290
Plantinga, Neal, 153–54
Polanyi, Karl, 276–77
Poppen, Henry, 107
possibility thinking: Arvella, 115, 200–202; and bankruptcy, 262–63; Crean, 166; family, 115, 200–202; fund-raising, 166; and New Thought, 56; and Peale, 203, 224; Penner, 262; theology of Schuller, 4–6, 50, 55, 122–23, 186, 196–200, 202–3, 234, 242, 285; Tony Schuller, 30
poverty, 30–31
Power of Positive Thinking, The (Peale), 54
preaching. *See under* Schuller, Robert H., ministry
President's Prayer Breakfast, 239
Prime Time Preachers (Hadden and Swann), 221
Protestant Church Buildings, 93
Psalms, 118
psychology, 39–40, 54–55, 202–3, 282
Putnam, Robert, 216

race/racism, 130–31, 209–10
Rancho Capistrano campus, 251, 261
rebuilding, 2–3, 23–24
Reformed Church in America (RCA), 11, 19, 29, 33, 42, 72–73, 99, 101, 111, 118–19, 192–93, 225–26

324 INDEX

Reformed tradition, 18, 25, 36–37, 40, 43, 56, 65, 101, 153, 197, 206, 225
Republican Party, 208–9
resonance, 282–84
Rifkin, Jeremy, 221
Riverdale (IL), 50
Robert H. Schuller Institute for Church Leadership, 6, 17, 110, 113, 126–28, 131, 152–53
Robertson, Pat, 221–22
Robles-Anderson, Erica, 77
Roger and Me, 217
Roosevelt, Franklin, 136–37
Rosa, Hartmut, 67, 92–93, 279, 282–83, 285, 286, 288, 289
Rozelle, Mark, 226–27
Russia. *See* USSR

Sanchez, Loretta, 243
Sargeant, Kimon Howland, 17, 18, 99, 100–101
scandals, televangelists, 222–23
Schuller, Anthony (Tony; father), 1–2, 26–27, 29–32, 34, 104
Schuller, Arvella (née DeHaan; wife), 9, 47–50, 53, 61, 65, 72, 73, 75, 76–77, 96, 113–16, 120, 147–48, 160–61, 200–202, 219–20, 249, 251, 252, 253–54, 256–57, 264–65, 266, 288
Schuller, Bobby (grandson), 155, 177, 258
Schuller, Carol. *See* Milner, Carol Schuller (daughter)
Schuller, Henry (brother), 2, 39
Schuller, Jennie (née Beltman; mother), 26, 31–32, 34–35
Schuller, Margaret (sister), 1, 38
Schuller, Robert A., Jr. (son), 60, 172, 178, 251, 252–53, 255–57, 259–60, 261–62
Schuller, Robert H., early life and education: Arcadian Four, 41; call

to ministry, 25–26, 33, 42; church, 36–37; competition, seminarian, 44; cows, preaching to, 25–26; honorary doctorate, 242; Hope College, 38–42; Iowa, 5–6, 28, 37; military deferment, 39; Peale, influence of, 45–46; performer, 35–37; poverty, 27, 30–31; Truett, 43–44; Western Theological Seminary, 42–49
Schuller, Robert H., family: administration, 116; Arvella, marriage with, 47–50, 60–62, 113–17, 201–2, 266–67, 286; Bobby Schuller (grandson), relationship with, 155, 177, 258; daughter Carol's accident, 169–70, 200–201; Dutch ancestry, 28–29; "Family Policies and Procedures," 249; farm, Schuller, 1–3, 5–6, 27–30, 33–34, 40–41, 62, 121, 146, 252–53, 272–74; as father, 60–61; goals, 115–17; Henry Beltman (uncle), relationship with, 25–26, 36; Jennie Schuller (mother), relationship with, 35–36, 38–39; market logic, 116–17; ministry, involvement in, 249–56; nepotism, 248, 250–52; 1978, 168–69; parenting, 60–61, 115–17, 201–2; possibility thinking, 115, 200–202; Reformed tradition/RCA, 31–33; Robert A. (son), relationship with, 251–57, 259–62; salaries from ministry, 248, 254–56, 262; Sheila Schuller Coleman (daughter), relationship with, 256–57; succession, ministry, 247–57, 261–62; Tony Schuller (father), relationship with, 26–27, 34–35, 104; tornado, 1–3, 41–42
Schuller, Robert H., health and end of life: burial, 267; death, 4, 266–67; decline, 257–60; dementia, 258–60; esophageal cancer, 265, 266; exercise, 115; food, relationship with, 210–12;

INDEX **325**

head injury, 232–33, 257–60; heart attack, 240; nursing home, 266; rhinophyma, 89; smoking, 32, 40; weight, 21, 115, 210

Schuller, Robert H., ministry: accommodation, 206–7; "anti" preaching, 144; Arvella's role, 49–50, 53, 73–74, 147–48, 160–61, 219–20, 252–53; audience, 12–13, 19–20, 154–55; awards, 112, 242, 243–44; California, move to, 64–65, 70, 98–99; capitalism, attitude toward, 102, 134; celebrity status, 152, 154, 178–79, 194, 204, 235, 239–40; and church growth/CGM, 8, 14–16, 18–20, 67–68, 129, 131–34, 193, 212–15, 270–71, 274–75; communism, attitude toward and relationship with, 118–20, 122; condemnation in preaching, 43; cows, preaching to, 25–26; criticism, 6, 12–13, 19, 127, 129, 153–54, 175–76, 179–80, 191–92, 206, 216–17; dress, 21, 115; entrepreneurship, 6, 14, 19, 162, 171, 179; evangelicalism, 99–100; free enterprise/market, attitude toward, 119, 134, 217, 276; fund-raising, 63, 82–83, 91–92, 105, 107, 108, 127, 137–45, 146, 147, 148, 158–59, 162–68, 245–46, 263, 276; Hammer, 229–30; international reputation, 156, 242; Ivanhoe RCA, 50–53, 58, 59–60, 63–64, 65, 69; lawsuit of ministry, Robert and Arvella, 264–65; leadership, 67–69, 97, 101–2, 110–11, 113, 285; managerial technique/management, 68, 94, 116–17; the market, 7–8, 9–11, 58–59, 271, 272–77; maudlin exemplar, 199–200; and megachurches, 4, 6, 16, 111–12, 235; Murdoch, 229; nepotism, 248, 250–52; as pastor, 6, 102, 184, 191, 198, 271, 275, 280–81; and Peale, 45, 54–57, 83–87, 103, 109;

politics, 208–10, 237–40; preaching style, 82, 86–87, 120, 154, 220; psychology, 55, 202–3; publicity, 58; and RCA/Reformed tradition, 11, 36–37, 65, 92–93, 99–101, 118–19, 192–93, 225–26; rebuilding church, 2–3, 23–24; recruitment, 52–53, 58; relations with congregation, 191–92; rhetorical skills, 220; Robert A. (son) as head, 251–57; salaries, family, 248, 254–56, 262; salary, Schuller, 63–64, 248; Scripture, use of, 18, 76, 82, 143, 199, 205; and secularization, 11–12, 24; seeker-sensitive churches, 17–18, 99–100; Sheila Schuller Coleman (daughter) as head, 257, 263; social change, 7, 15, 61, 67, 185–87, 270, 275, 278–82, 284–85, 290; soft-selling, 193; succession, family, 247–57, 261–62; and televangelists, 218, 221–27; television ministry, 145–57, 193–94, 219–27; therapy, ministry and preaching as, 8, 13–14, 54–55, 76, 142–43, 184, 187, 202–7; tithing, 139, 142, 147, 162–63; tradition, 11, 21–22, 150; wonder years, 52. *See also* Garden Grove Community Church (GGCC); *Hour of Power*

Schuller, Robert H., personal life: anxiety, 21, 89–90, 158, 168–69, 285; Clintons, relationship with, 237–39; dress, 115; exercise, 115; fear of failure, 8, 30, 53–60, 89, 147, 167–69, 195; food, relationship with, 210–12; intensity, 187; Peale, relationship with, 54, 150–52; persona, 149, 183–84, 258; personal narrative, 25–28; race, 209; retirement, 236, 257, 264–65; routine, daily, 182–83; sexuality, 113–14, 209–11; and televangelists, 218

Schuller, Robert H., theology and

326 INDEX

thought: church growth, 204; debt and lending, 140–41; depravity, total, 40, 43, 197–98; God, 207; the good life, 283–84; heresy, 193, 204; hope, 43; Horton debate, 204–6; *Institutes* index, 56–57; New Thought, 55–57, 196; orthodoxy, 11, 120–21, 149–50, 196–97; Peale, 54–57, 83–87; possibility/positive thinking, 4–6, 50, 55, 122–23, 186, 196–200, 234, 242, 285; predestination, 197–98; and psychology, 39–40, 124; Reformed (Calvinist) tradition, 18, 25, 40, 42–43, 56, 101, 195, 197–98, 206, 225; salvation, 204, 225; Scripture, 199; self-actualization, 199; self-esteem, 8, 55, 57, 151, 180, 184–86, 197–200, 203, 285–86; self-mastery, 199–200, 285–86; sin, 32, 43, 128, 197–98, 204–5; universalism, 240, 242; Woodward, correspondence with, 223–25

Schuller, Robert H., writings: autobiography, 3, 26, 28, 63, 245; *Move Ahead with Possibility Thinking*, 112, 202–3; *Self-Esteem*, 194–95, 203, 225; *The Be (Happy) Attitudes*, 285, 287; *The Pastor's Church Growth Handbook*, 271; *The Power of Being Debt Free* (coauthored), 238; *Tough-Minded Faith for Tender-Hearted People*, 9–10, 123; *Tough Times Never Last, but Tough People Do!*, 269–70; *Your Church Has a Fantastic Future!*, 14, 212; *Your Church Has Real Possibilities*, 153, 279; *Your Future Is Your Friend*, 121

Schuller, Sheila. *See* Coleman, Sheila Schuller (daughter)

Schuller, Violet (sister), 34

"Schuller Family in Ministry, The: Portfolio," 248–49, 251

Schwarz, Fred, 119

Scripture. *See under* Schuller, Robert H., ministry

secularism, 24, 203–4, 214–16, 290

seeker churches, 18, 99–100

self-actualization, 24, 184, 187, 199

self-esteem, 8, 55, 57, 151, 180, 184–86, 197–200, 202–3, 285–86

self-help, 199

self-mastery, 199–200, 285–86

sexist language, 147

Shea, George Beverly, 162

Sheen, Fulton, 221

shopping centers, 139–40, 216

Sills, Beverly, 171–72, 188

Simmons, Paul D., 19

Sinatra, Frank, 152, 194

60 Minutes, 148

Sky Channel, 229

Snyder, Tom, 134

soft sell, 100–101, 193

Solomon, Martha, 220

Star Trek: Into Darkness, 246

Stone, W. Clement, 194–95

Stumbo, Bella, 151

suburbs, 16–17, 79–80, 275

Sudjic, Deyan, 109–10, 112, 175, 246–47

Swaggart, Jimmy, 193, 222

Swann, Charles, 193, 221

Swann, Fred, 219

Swanson, Douglas J., 262

Syria, 241

taxation, 118, 188–90

televangelism, 193, 210, 218, 219–27

Temple Time, 54

theater, 35–36

theology. *See* Reformed tradition; Schuller, Robert H., theology and thought

therapeutic approach, 8, 13–14, 54–55, 76, 142–43, 184, 187, 202–7

INDEX

tornadoes, 1–3, 58
Truett, George, 43–44, 49, 212
Trump, Donald, 247

unchurched, 99, 103, 145, 202, 274, 275
USSR, 156–57, 229–37

Van Andel, Jay, 124, 127, 166
VanElderen, Marlin, 179–80
Van Wyk, Kenneth, 107
Voklov, Vyacheslav, 234
Voskuil, Dennis, 27, 179, 180–81

Wagner, C. Peter, 14, 131, 212–13
Wall Street Journal, 144–45
Walter J. Bennet Company, 145
Warren, Rick, 4, 16, 17
Wayne, John, 152
Welcome Travelers, 58–59

Western Theological Seminary (WTS), 42–46, 132
Whitcomb, Howard, 189
Whitefield, George, 100, 221
White Horse Inn, The, 204–6
Wichers, Willard, 39
Williams, Roger, 257
Willow Creek, 17
Willow Creek Association, 17
Winr., Wyatt T., 20
Witten, Marsha, 206–8
Wolterstorff, Nicholas, 36–37
Woodward, Kenneth, 223–25, 227
World War II, 35, 39
Worthen, Molly, 16
Wright, Hazel, 168

Yeltsin, Boris, 234

Titles published in the

LIBRARY OF RELIGIOUS BIOGRAPHY SERIES

Orestes A. Brownson: *American Religious Weathervane*
by Patrick W. Carey

The Puritan as Yankee: A Life of **Horace Bushnell**
by Robert Bruce Mullin

A Life of **Alexander Campbell**
by Douglas A. Foster

Duty and Destiny: The Life and Faith of **Winston Churchill**
by Gary Scott Smith

Emblem of Faith Untouched: A Short Life of **Thomas Cranmer**
by Leslie Williams

Her Heart Can See: The Life and Hymns of **Fanny J. Crosby**
by Edith L. Blumhofer

Emily Dickinson *and the Art of Belief*
by Roger Lundin

God's Cold Warrior: The Life and Faith of **John Foster Dulles**
by John D. Wilsey

A Short Life of **Jonathan Edwards**
by George M. Marsden

The Religious Journey of **Dwight D. Eisenhower**: *Duty, God, and Country*
by Jack M. Holl

Charles G. Finney *and the Spirit of American Evangelicalism*
by Charles E. Hambrick-Stowe

William Ewart Gladstone: *Faith and Politics in Victorian Britain*
by David Bebbington

One Soul at a Time: The Story of **Billy Graham**
by Grant Wacker

An Odd Cross to Bear: A Biography of **Ruth Bell Graham**
by Anne Blue Wills

A Heart Lost in Wonder: The Life and Faith of **Gerard Manley Hopkins**
by Catharine Randall

Sworn on the Altar of God: A Religious Biography of **Thomas Jefferson**
by Edwin S. Gaustad

The Miracle Lady: **Katherine Kuhlman**
and the Transformation of Charismatic Christianity
by Amy Collier Artman

Abraham Kuyper: *Modern Calvinist, Christian Democrat*
by James D. Bratt

The Religious Life of **Robert E. Lee**
by R. David Cox

Abraham Lincoln: *Redeemer President*
by Allen C. Guelzo

Charles Lindbergh: *A Religious Biography of America's Most Infamous Pilot*
by Christopher Gehrz

The First American Evangelical: A Short Life of **Cotton Mather**
by Rick Kennedy

Aimee Semple McPherson: *Everybody's Sister*
by Edith L. Blumhofer

Mother of Modern Evangelicalism: The Life and Legacy of **Henrietta Mears**
by Arlin Migliazzo

Damning Words: The Life and Religious Times of **H. L. Mencken**
by D. G. Hart

Thomas Merton *and the Monastic Vision*
by Lawrence S. Cunningham

God's Strange Work: **William Miller** *and the End of the World*
by David L. Rowe

One Lost Soul: **Richard Nixon**'s *Search for Salvation*
by Daniel Silliman

Blaise Pascal: *Reasons of the Heart*
by Marvin R. O'Connell

Occupy Until I Come: **A. T. Pierson** *and the Evangelization of the World*
by Dana L. Robert

The Kingdom Is Always but Coming: A Life of **Walter Rauschenbusch**
by Christopher H. Evans

Oral Roberts *and the Rise of the Prosperity Gospel*
by Jonathan Root

*Strength for the Fight: The Life and Faith of **Jackie Robinson***
by Gary Scott Smith

*A Christian and a Democrat: A Religious Life of **Franklin D. Roosevelt***
by John F. Woolverton with James D. Bratt

***Francis Schaeffer** and the Shaping of Evangelical America*
by Barry Hankins

*The Church Must Grow or Perish: **Robert H. Schuller** and
the Business of American Christianity*
by Mark T. Mulder and Gerardo Martí

***Harriet Beecher Stowe**: A Spiritual Life*
by Nancy Koester

***Billy Sunday** and the Redemption of Urban America*
by Lyle W. Dorsett

***Howard Thurman** and the Disinherited: A Religious Biography*
by Paul Harvey

*We Will Be Free: The Life and Faith of **Sojourner Truth***
by Nancy Koester

*Dancing in My Dreams: A Spiritual Biography of **Tina Turner***
by Ralph H. Craig III

*Assist Me to Proclaim: The Life and Hymns of **Charles Wesley***
by John R. Tyson

*Prophetess of Health: A Study of **Ellen G. White***
by Ronald L. Numbers

***George Whitefield**: Evangelist for God and Empire*
by Peter Y. Choi

*The Divine Dramatist: **George Whitefield** and the Rise of Modern Evangelicalism*
by Harry S. Stout

*A Prairie Faith: The Religious Life of **Laura Ingalls Wilder***
by John J. Fry

*Liberty of Conscience: **Roger Williams** in America*
by Edwin S. Gaustad